WAR TOURISM

WAR TOURISM

SECOND WORLD WAR FRANCE FROM DEFEAT AND OCCUPATION TO THE CREATION OF HERITAGE

BERTRAM M. GORDON

CORNELL UNIVERSITY PRESS
Ithaca and London

First published 2018 by Cornell University Press

Printed in the United States of America

Library of Congress Cataloging-in-Publication Data

Names: Gordon, Bertram M., 1945– author.
Title: War tourism : Second World War France from defeat and occupation to the creation of heritage / Bertram M. Gordon.
Description: Ithaca : Cornell University Press, 2018. | Includes bibliographical references and index.
Identifiers: LCCN 2018017119 (print) | LCCN 2018018664 (ebook) | ISBN 9781501715884 (epub/mobi) | ISBN 9781501715891 (pdf) | ISBN 9781501715877 | ISBN 9781501715877 (cloth ; alk. paper)
Subjects: LCSH: Tourism—France—History—20th century. | Germans—Travel—France—History—20th century. | Dark tourism—France—History—20th century. | Heritage tourism—France—History—20th century. | World War, 1939–1945—France. | War and society—France—History—20th century. | Collective memory—France—History—20th century.
Classification: LCC G155.F8 (ebook) | LCC G155.F8 G67 2018 (print) | DDC 338.4/79144—dc23
LC record available at https://lccn.loc.gov/2018017119

To Suzanne, my wife, without whom I would never have been able to write this book

Contents

Preface   ix

Introduction: Tourism, Aesthetics,
and War   1

1. The Emergence of France as a Tourist
   Icon in the Belle Époque   20

2. Two 1940 Sites as Symbols: The
   Maginot Line and the Compiègne
   Railway Car   53

3. The French as Tourists in Their
   Occupied Country   64

4. German Tourism in Occupied France,
   1940–1944   99

5. The Liberation, 1944: Normandy
   and Paris   146

6. Sites of Memory and the Tourist
   Imaginary   163

7. Tourism, War, and Memory in Postwar
   France   193

   Conclusion: Tourism and Appropriate
   Remembrance   213

Appendix: References and Sites   227
Notes   229
Index   299

PREFACE

Studying the linkages between the Second World War and tourism in France brings together two widely researched fields that have until now been approached separately. After having written *Collaborationism in France during the Second World War*,[1] followed by subsequent articles on this subject, however, I discovered the extensive tourism that had occurred in occupied France during the war and the wartime memory tourism (*tourisme de mémoire*) thereafter. Connecting the events of the war to issues of tourism in France opened a whole new dimension for me. By the mid-1990s, the Second World War era had attracted enough study to become the second-most popular area for doctoral dissertations on France, behind only the 1789 Revolution.[2] The academic study of tourism, reflecting the exponential growth of the industry, has also taken off in the late twentieth and early twenty-first centuries, a phenomenon I traced in an article published in the *Journal of Tourism History*, itself created only in 2009.[3]

In the writing of this book, there are many people and organizations to thank, and they are mentioned in the relevant notes. A book such as this could not have been written without the help of many in the French National Archives (Archives nationales) in Paris, the Bibliothèque nationale française, the Archives de la Préfecture de police in Le Pré-Saint-Gervais, and the Bibliothèque de l'histoire de la ville de Paris. The Bibliothèque du tourisme et des voyages—Germaine Tillion, also in Paris, with its rich collection of literature on tourism and its history was also an important aide in my research.

I am also indebted to the National Endowment for the Humanities Research Grant for College Teachers and Independent Scholars for supporting my research in France, as well as the Institut d'histoire du temps présent, where, with its director Henry Rousso and other colleagues there, I was able to deepen my understanding of Second World War France as a research associate in 2001–2. Mills College research grants have also generously assisted my research and writing of this book.

My study of the culture of tourism has been aided immensely by my participation in the meetings with the many excellent scholars from various disciplines organized by the Tourism Studies Working Group (TSWG) at the University of California at Berkeley, with special thanks to U. C. Berkeley professor emeritus of anthropology Nelson Graburn for his work with the TSWG and his personal advice and encouragement. My colleagues in the meetings of the International Commission for the History of Travel and Tourism (ICHTT) have also been helpful in my exploration of tourism studies and I thank the International Committee of Historical Sciences, the ICHTT's parent organization, for helping fund my travel to organize and participate in several tourism history sessions at its 2015 conference in Jinan, China. I am indebted as well to Daniel Letouzey, who guided me through many of the *sites de mémoire* in Normandy, and to local historian Rémy Desquesnnes of the Conseil régional de Basse-Normandie, who introduced me to several archives and archivists there. Alain Carteret, historian of the city of Vichy, generously shared his knowledge of its history with me as we explored its sites together and the late Maryvonne Mardaci introduced me to war sites in Brittany.

I also offer special thanks to Emily Andrew, senior editor at Cornell University Press, and Bethany Wasik, assistant editor, for their good work and counsel in guiding this book through the publication process. With their excellent editorial work and counsel Susan Specter and Amanda Heller helped polish the final text. My thanks also go to David Prout for his careful and first-rate work preparing the index for this book. The anonymous readers of my original manuscript made invaluable suggestions that definitely strengthened this work. Ian C. Dengler has been a steady friend and source of ideas throughout. With her own abiding interest in France, Suzanne Perkins-Gordon has been a wonderful companion and has learned more about tourism and Second World War France than she ever expected to know. Finally, my deepest thanks go to Sydney, Kevin, and Zachary, who brought a different kind of joy into my life while I was working on this book.

WAR TOURISM

Introduction

Tourism, Aesthetics, and War

Accompanying the victorious German army into Paris in June 1940, the American correspondent William L. Shirer observed:

> Most of the German troops act like naïve tourists, and this has proved a pleasant surprise to the Parisians. It seems funny, but every German soldier carries a camera. I saw them by the thousands today, photographing Notre-Dame, the Arc de Triomphe, the Invalides. Thousands of German soldiers congregate all day long at the Tomb of the Unknown Soldier, where the flame still burns under the Arc. They bare their blond heads and stand there gazing.[1]

Tourism during the Second World War in France was not limited to victorious soldiers, whether German from 1940 through 1944 or Allied afterward. With three-fifths of France occupied after June 1940, hotels requisitioned for military use by the Germans, and gasoline and food in short supply, conditions hardly seemed propitious for tourism, but it did not cease. The Michelin guidebook for the Auvergne region in 1942 advised its readers to visit the area by train, bus, bicycle, or even on foot.[2] A spirit of "life goes on," or quest for normalcy, typified the 400,000 French pensioners with paid vacations who found lodgings in some of the two thousand hotels recommended by a hotel service in August 1942.[3] Postwar heritage tourism, or *tourisme de mémoire* (memory tourism), later transformed places such as the village of

Arromanches-les-Bains, a spa prior to the Second World War, into a site of memory along the Normandy landing beaches in the years since.[4]

This book is set in the context of my continuing interest in the history of the French collaboration with Nazi Germany during the Occupation, which dates back to the political rhetoric of the late 1960s, when, to paraphrase the words of Jean Plumyène and Raymond Lasierra, everyone was someone else's "fascist."[5] During the 1970s, I interviewed some thirty to forty former French supporters of Nazi Germany for *Collaborationism in France during the Second World War,* which was published in 1980.[6] These interviews included two meetings with Marc Augier, who wrote about travel in the French periodicals *Sciences et voyages, Paris Soir,* the *Revue camping,* and the *Revue du ski* during the 1930s.[7] Augier's romanticized vision of touring led him to skiing trips to Scandinavia in the late 1930s and the "adventure" of participating with the German forces in the war against Soviet Russia during the early 1940s. During the Occupation years, he helped create the pro-German Jeunesses de l'Europe nouvelle, which by late 1941 was organizing camping expeditions to Germany. Augier described its first open-air Franco-German camping expedition, to last throughout the next winter, in the pro-German language of the day. "Whether it rains or snows," he wrote, "our leisure activities will be the leisure activities of conquest as we wish to train tough and joyous men."[8] He cited the painter Marcel Gromaire's comment in 1937 to the effect that "the leisure of the future will be that of conquest or decadence."[9]

My focus on tourism as related to the war, however, resulted from a chance discovery in the Bibliothèque nationale (National Library, now the Bibliothèque nationale de France, or BNF) in France in 1996. While working on an unrelated research project in the annex of the old library in Versailles, I came across a collection of *Der deutsche Wegleiter* (The German Guide), also known as *Wohin in Paris?* (Where in Paris?), a bi-weekly German-language tourist guide to France published during the Occupation. Produced by local people in France, the *Wegleiter* opened another vista into the dimensions of wartime collaboration. It was described in a 2013 French translation of some of its articles as a combination of *Pariscope* and the *Guides bleus,* combining humorous anecdotal stories, similar to those in the *Saturday Evening Post* of the era, together with the tourist information that might be found in today's *Where* magazines.[10] Perhaps because the *Wegleiter* was published in German—or, more likely, that tourism as a subject was considered unworthy of academic research—there was virtually no literature about it. It became the beginning of my exploration of, first, German tourism in occupied France, followed by the French tourism industry during the war, and subsequently by wartime memory tourism since.[11] As the history of wartime France was debated during the last decade of the twentieth century and into the twenty-first, it became clear that the dimension of tourism was missing and that its study could help elucidate the cultural values behind victors and vanquished both before and after 1945.

Too often the history of tourism in the twentieth century is depicted as stopping in 1939 only to resume again after 1945.[12] There was, of course, an attenuation of tourism and its related industries during the war, but they persisted, even if altered and restricted, and planning for postwar tourism continued as well. Sites and circuits linked to the memory of the battles, the concentration camps, the Resistance, and the collaboration became pillars of postwar tourism in France. Postwar memory tourism became highly commercialized, and many in the tourism industry recognized it, contributing to making France one of the largest receivers of international tourists in the world.

France during the Second World War

The history of France during the Second World War, with its dramatic moments of Adolf Hitler touring Paris in June 1940, D-Day and the liberation of France beginning in Normandy in June 1944, and the failure of the Germans to destroy Paris in August 1944, has been told and retold many times. With Germany defeated in 1918, Alsace-Lorraine returned, and an even more extensive empire than before, France had become the dominant power on the European continent. By 1940, this had all changed. Political discord at home, restlessness in the empire, and a resurgent Germany posed challenges that led to renewed war in 1939. The outbreak of the Second World War that year was followed by the German conquest of Poland and then a protracted period of relative inaction, known in France as the *drôle de guerre*, or "phony war," on the western front as the French remained behind their defensive fortifications along the Maginot Line and the Germans waited for an opportune moment to attack. In May 1940 German forces crossed into the Netherlands and Belgium and, using coordinated air and tank attacks to pierce the French lines, broke through, leading to what became a series of defeats of the French. One and a half million French soldiers were taken prisoner by the Germans.[13] Paris was declared an open city, meaning that it would not be defended, on 10 June, the day when Italy also declared war against France. Four days later, German forces entered an undefended Paris.

As the government headed south to avoid contact with the victorious German forces, Premier Paul Reynaud resigned on 16 June and was succeeded by Marshal Philippe Pétain, remembered for having led the successful defense of Verdun against a German onslaught during the First World War in 1916. Portrayed popularly as a humane military leader who, with concessions to the soldiers, had successfully suppressed military mutinies among the French ranks in the following year, Pétain had become an immensely popular figure in interwar France. While some in the government urged a flight to French North Africa and continuation of the war from there, and General Charles de Gaulle fled to continue the war in London, Pétain, to whom many looked as a savior in a time of crisis, insisted on remaining in France. On 22 June, his government signed an armistice with the Germans, which at Hitler's insistence took place in Marshal Ferdinand Foch's railway car in a clearing near the town of Compiègne in the forest in Rethondes in northeastern France, the site of the 1918 armistice that ended World War I. Two days later, the new French government signed an armistice with the Italians.

The June armistice divided France into a German occupied zone in the north and west and an unoccupied or "free" zone in the center and southeast. In addition, a smaller area around Lille in the far north was administered by the German military command in Belgium, and Germany ultimately annexed Alsace and Lorraine. An Italian occupied zone was established along the French-Italian border in the southeast. The divisions intensified the difficulties of travel at a time of growing material shortages. Roughly two-fifths of France remained unoccupied after June 1940, but conditions there seemed hardly more propitious for tourism than in the occupied zone. Having fled Paris, the government moved to the spa resort town of Vichy, where Pétain transformed the parliamentary French Republic into the French State (État français), an authoritarian government committed to accommodation with what many anticipated would be a permanent European "New Order" under Nazi leadership.[14] In addition to lining up with Axis Europe, the new government at Vichy had a domestic agenda focused on an authoritarian state and what were perceived as traditional values, encapsulated in the formula "Labor, Family, Fatherland," replacing "Liberty, Equality, Fraternity."[15] Its National Revolution promoted a return to the soil and a promotion of the peasants and their lifestyles, which would have its own tourism implications for rural France. As Julian Jackson wrote, quoting Marc Bloch, "Vichy was turning France into a 'vast antiquarian museum.'"[16]

The shortages that followed the 1940 defeat grew worse as the war went on and German exactions increased. The June 1940 armistice required the French government to pay Occupation costs of 20 million Reichsmarks per day. As Shannon L. Fogg notes, some 2.4 metric tons of wheat, 891,000 metric tons of meat, and 1.4 million hectoliters of milk were transferred from France to Germany.[17] A rationing system, introduced by the Vichy government in September 1940, dropped as low as nine hundred calories per day for some categories of adults by the latter stages of the Occupation. The result was barter and a black market as many struggled to secure enough to eat.[18] Rationing of gasoline was severe. As of 1 May 1941, the monthly allowance was half of what it had been the previous March and one-fourth that of June 1940, when France was already at war.[19]

By early October a law authorized the internment of foreign Jews, and police raids began in May 1941. The German invasion of the Soviet Union in June 1941 brought the communists into the Resistance, creating a tension that would later be perceptible in postwar monuments and memory. Vichy's anti-Jewish policies culminated on 16–17 July 1942, when some 13,152 foreign-born Jews or Jews of foreign origin were herded into a bicycle-racing stadium, the Vélodrôme d'Hiver (Vel d'hiv) including 4,115 children, and kept in miserable conditions. Most were deported and never returned. This and similar events described by the historian Rosemary Wakeman as "scenes of hideous repression" during the German occupation were, in her words, the "real public spectacles."[20]

Late 1942 through early 1943 marked a turning point in the war as the British stopped a German advance at El Alamein in Egypt, the Americans thwarted a Japanese raid and destroyed much of the Imperial Air Force at Midway, and the Soviets stopped the Germans at Stalingrad. On 8 November 1942, Anglo-American forces landed in French Algeria and began a military campaign that by spring 1943 resulted in the liberation of all North Africa from Axis rule. German forces responded by occupying the southern two-fifths of France which had been the "free zone," and on 1 March 1943, the demarcation line separating the two zones was removed. French authorities took over the monitoring of people transiting between the two zones, and more normal postal service was resumed. Following the Italian capitulation to the Allies in September 1943, the Germans occupied the Italian zone in France, giving them effective control over the Côte d'Azur. There, as three years earlier in Paris, the Germans commandeered hotels, including those in Nice previously used by the Italians to shelter Jews from France and elsewhere in Europe. Corsica, occupied by the Italians in November 1942, was liberated in October 1943.[21]

By early 1944, the Vichy government had become virtually a fascist state with its paramilitary organizations waging open warfare in collaboration with the Germans against the increasingly well-organized Resistance. Vichy forces fought the Resistance and hunted Jews, communists, and Freemasons in a French civil war, while Resistance activists assassinated those accused of collaboration with Vichy and the Germans. Marshal Pétain's visit to Paris following an Allied bombing raid in April, the invasion of Normandy in June, and the liberation of Paris in August were all significant events witnessed by many who were conscious that they were present at a moment of notable historical change. Even if many of these observers did not travel very far and did not travel in organized groups, they were the curious or, in the words of the nineteenth-century writer Hippolyte Taine, "sedentary tourists [who] look at the mountains from their windows."[22] They viewed the spectacles with a curiosity similar to the imaginary that is at the heart of tourism. In this sense, the success of the Normandy invasion made Vichyites and collaborators the objects of tourist curiosity, evident, for example, in the crowds that watched shorn women, denigrated as *"collabos,"* paraded through the streets after the Liberation.

Tourism and Its Continuities in Wartime France

Organized tourism and personal vacation travel continued as well despite the very substantial privations of war and occupation during the early 1940s as some of the French continued to take holidays and go on tour while others planned for a postwar reprise. French tourism planners worked assiduously during the war to prepare for what they hoped would be a better future, no matter who the victor. The occupying German forces organized tens of thousands of tours in Paris and elsewhere in France for their personnel, building on an already established tourist imaginary of France, or in Noel Salazar's description of the tourist imaginary, a set of "ideological, political, and socio-cultural stereotypes and clichés," as a primary destination to be seen and, in some ways, admired.[23] Although French tourism history has been written about at length, less well studied in its history is the place that it holds in the Second World War, possibly having spared Paris and the rest of the country extensive destruction both in 1940, when the Germans marched through following their victory, and again when they were expelled in 1944.

Accordingly, this book takes a look into a different, and seldom addressed, aspect of war in general, and the Second World War in particular, specifically its interactions with the world of tourism in France both during and since the war.[24] France, a country with a long history of attraction for tourism and currently the world's leader in international tourist visits, according to the United Nations World Tourism Organization (UNWTO), played a dramatic, if anguished, role, succumbing to German Blitzkrieg in 1940 and as the scene of the Allied onslaught against the Reich in 1944. Tourism bestowed meaning upon wartime events, helping contemporary and retrospective visitors contextualize the war into preexisting modes of understanding gained earlier in peacetime. In many ways, even if attenuated during wartime, tourism and the continuation of vacations provided a sense of normalcy to French people's lives, helping them survive and comprehend their wartime privations. Tourism in occupied France helped Germans solidify a feeling of cultural supremacy in being able to appreciate the French sites while claiming the superiority of the homeland, reflecting the power imbalances between victors and vanquished. Postwar battlefield, heritage, and memorial tourism helped many in France and elsewhere make sense of their struggles and in a sense their very survival.

The relationship of tourism and war is a large field inviting exploration on many different levels. Tourism imaginaries and on occasion tourism trajectories undoubtedly played a role in the activities, dreams, and aspirations of the "ordinary" Germans described by Christopher Browning and Daniel Jonah Goldhagen in their studies of complicity in the Holocaust. This concept was rooted in Hannah Arendt's description of Adolf Eichmann and the "banality of evil."[25] These were the many people who, in Arendt's words, "were terribly and terrifyingly normal."[26] If, as Goldhagen suggests, an eliminationist program directed against Jews had become "common-sense" for large numbers of Germans by the time of the Second World War, it is likely that tourism images had also become part of the "common-sense" for them as well and that these sets of images helped normalize the war and the behavior of which Goldhagen wrote. Such mental juxtapositions may partly explain why war is possible, why it starts, how it continues, and some of the effects it has afterward. Tourism and its images, in other words, especially in regard to France in 1939, had become so widely embedded in Western cultural values that they worked to integrate the experience of war into the worldview of those who fought, suffered, and even exulted, during and after the war. It was no accident that one of the victorious Hitler's first actions on defeating France in June 1940 was to tour Paris, ostentatiously expressing the altered power relationships of the time.

It is unlikely that it will ever be known to what degree, if any, the image of France as a tourism icon by the time of the Second World War may have helped save it from the fate of Poland, for example. Germans from Hitler down took pride in their having spared French tourist sites in 1940. And whether tourist imagery of Paris helped spare it, despite Hitler's order to destroy the city in August 1944, has been debated, but even here much of the postwar discourse has pivoted around the Paris tourism imaginary. Warsaw needed to be largely rebuilt after the war. Paris emerged relatively intact. Normandy suffered considerable damage during the spring and summer of 1944, but battlefield tourism since then has contributed to its economy and its cultural cachet. A seemingly unlikely mix, tourism, war, and France combined tell a story that is the subject of this book.

Despite the extensive literature on cultural tourism and on warfare and its history, there has been relatively little study of the interrelationships between the two. Magazines for enthusiasts, such as *After the Battle,* published in Britain, are devoted to the retrospective description of battlefield sites.

FIGURE 1. Cover of *After the Battle: Paris,* 1940–1944–1976, no. 14 (1976). Credit: *After the Battle.*

A Dutch website with listings of battlefields and other war monuments throughout Europe, WW2Museums.com, an initiative of STIWOT (Stichting Informatie Wereldoorlog Twee, or Foundation for Information on World War II), states: "WW2Museums.com is the place to plan your own battlefield tour along WW2 museums, monuments, cemeteries and other sights of interest in and outside Europe. Through WW2Museums.com you will be introduced to WW2 sights of interest that still can be visited today!"[27]

The slaughter of millions of people, combatants and noncombatants, and notably the willful genocide of the Holocaust which have marked the discourse relating to the war may be expected to continue to do so into the foreseeable future and, most probably, beyond. At first, the linking of the grave issues of war and genocide with the more pleasure-oriented and, some might argue, the seemingly more mundane or banal phenomenon of tourism might be surprising. In his *Society of the Spectacle*, Guy Debord called tourism "the leisure of going to see what has become banal."[28] It is generally considered a pleasurable pastime, associated with vacations and the kinds of activities that people choose to enjoy when they are not compelled by economic necessity to work. In 1986 Dean MacCannell differentiated between spectacles and sights, staged in different ways, the former more bounded in time and the latter, such as the Eiffel Tower, more temporally transcendent.[29] Both may become tourism sites, drawing the curious from near and far, exemplified in the crowds drawn to the streets of Paris to watch General de Gaulle's parade down the Champs-Élysées following the Liberation in August 1944. The "tourist gaze," to use John Urry's term, was not a function of distance traveled. Writing about "tourism, holiday-making and travel" in 1990, Urry commented, "On the face of it there could not be a more trivial subject for a book." He then explained that studying the tourist gaze could also offer insights into other aspects of human behavior.[30] In their earlier study of research themes related to tourism, Richard Butler and Geoffrey Wall also noted that its history could be studied "for the light which the knowledge of tourism can throw on other aspects of life."[31] The expansion in tourism documented by the UNWTO, together with the growing awareness among students of human behavior that the study of tourism, as Butler, Wall, and Urry suggested, does help shine light on social and cultural development in general, has led to increased attention to the subject.[32]

In broad terms, war-related tourism occurs in two forms, different in their own ways but also linked. First there is battlefield tourism, or *tourisme de mémoire* in which people visit past scenes of battle or other types of memorials and monuments to past wars. The second form of war-related tourism, less well studied, is that of people who went on vacations, travels, and

tours during wartime, or watched battles as they unfolded. This form of
tourism took place as thousands of German civilian and military personnel
were given tours of occupied France. The Second World War in France is
a striking case of both postwar and wartime linkages of tourism and war.
Battlefield tourism plays a major economic role in Normandy. Young German soldiers touring in occupied France may have become conditioned to
tourism as a leisure activity, contributing to the expectations and imaginaries
that underlay the tourism takeoff in Germany and elsewhere after the war.[33]

Tourism as Curiosity and Commodity

In a book titled *Le tourisme,* Marc Boyer, a French historian of tourism,
suggested that the most difficult task in writing about tourism was defining
the term. International agencies, he wrote, used the word in different ways,
and the specific countries of Europe also employed varying definitions in
assessing their tourist industries. The term had developed in early modern
England at the time of the Grand Tour. By the end of the nineteenth century,
it had spread into nearly all the European languages, including German, which
retained *Fremdenverkehr* (literally, commerce or traffic among strangers or
foreigners) but also had adopted the word *Tourismus.* For statistical purposes,
the League of Nations in 1937 defined a "tourist" as "anyone who, traveling
for his pleasure, leaves his usual place of residence for more than twenty-four
hours and less than a year; trips of less than twenty-four hours being
excursions."[34] In 1993 the UNWTO based its statistical studies of tourism
on the following definition: "Tourism comprises the activities of persons
travelling to and staying in places outside their usual environment for not
more than one consecutive year for leisure, business or other purposes."[35]

A distinction, however, must be made between a narrower definition of
the tourism industry, in which tourism has become a commodity and often
a means of political control, as argued by Theodor Adorno, among others,
and the act of touring or tourism.[36] The latter, however manipulated by
those in the industry, still channels a basic curiosity about the world. In its
broader sense, tourism is curiosity in motion, or the practical application of
aesthetic judgments. Whether in physically mobile or "armchair" and now
Internet tourism, people focus on their conceptions of the beautiful or the
interesting, framed, and at times manipulated, as Adorno suggests, in their
cultural contexts of time and place. The tourism industry may incorporate
power, evidenced, for example, in the organized tours of occupied France
provided to the victorious German soldiers by Nazi authorities after their
victory of 1940. Underlying all tourism, however, is curiosity and wonder.

Urry popularized the term "tourist gaze" for a sense of the looking in wonder that, he noted, has a long history in reference to the ways in which people encounter, assimilate, and understand ideas, material objects, and other people as they move around the world, observing and studying.[37] More recent scholars of tourism culture, including Rachid Amirou, Nelson Graburn, and Noel Salazar, have focused on "tourism imaginaries," in Amirou's words, the "totality of images and evocations tied to tourism," to the present. The tourism imaginary, he wrote, is extensive, embracing conceptualizations of "explorations, travels, pilgrimages, vacations, leisure, adventure, relationships to space, nomadism, wandering, and discovery, among others."[38] As Salazar states, "It is hard to think of tourism without imaginaries or 'fantasies'—the original Greek word for imagination, often used nowadays to denote more playful imaginaries related to things that are improbable or impossible."[39]

Based on the Latin notion of *curiositas,* tourism was deemed a reason to travel by the mid-fourteenth century. Petrarch wrote, "I know that in men's minds resides an innate longing to see new places."[40] As Mike Robinson, a British specialist in tourism research, wrote, "If one strips away much of the hardware of tourism and travel we find that the human imagination is at its core."[41] Tourist destinations, real and imagined, represent the aesthetic values present in a given culture at a specific time. Indeed, the cultural construction of tourist imaginaries, the values and images associated with the desire to visit, has become a significant field of academic inquiry.[42] The phenomena of tourism and the tourist imagination in Second World War France are products of the longer history of tourism and the aesthetic sensibilities with which it has been intertwined at least since the earliest humans began to wander around the world, gazing with curiosity at what they saw. In the words of one study of the relationship of tourism with aesthetics, "how we interpret what we see as tourists cannot be divorced from our own ideological underpinnings."[43]

In 1751 Alexander Gottlieb Baumgarten introduced the term "aesthetics," which he called the "criticism of taste," and established this field as a distinct area of philosophical inquiry.[44] Baumgarten's popularization of the term "aesthetics" coincided with the development of a vocabulary of tourism from the late seventeenth through the early nineteenth centuries in several European languages.[45] In its larger sense, tourism with its gaze and its imaginary encompasses "seeing," at least metaphorically, in addition to curiosity and aesthetics. Maurice Merleau-Ponty wrote, "Vision alone makes us learn that beings that are different, 'exterior,' foreign to one another, are yet absolutely *together,* are 'simultaneity.'"[46] Walter Benjamin suggested the relationship between seeing in this sense and tourism in his unfinished Arcades Project, in which he used the image of the *flâneur*, or stroller in the nineteenth-century arcades of Paris to lead him into an investigation of the social imaginary of modernity.[47] To Benjamin, tourism meant a show "where everything is done for money," although ironically, while he may have been describing the tourism industry, his own preoccupation with the *flâneur* reflected the more deep-seated tourist gaze or image.[48]

Discussing Urry's "tourist gaze," Kevin Meethan emphasized "the visual aspects of sightseeing as a fundamental and defining aspect of tourism" constituting "key elements in the tourist system."[49] In his book *The Art of Travel*, Alain de Botton, citing the eighteenth-century French writer Xavier de Maistre, discusses "receptivity" as the main component of "a travelling mind-set," with the focus on curiosity and seeing rather than distance covered in touring.[50] Tourism as curiosity and seeing relates directly to France during the Second World War. How many people may have looked out over the Normandy beaches as the Allies arrived in June 1944 with a touristic curiosity similar to what Benjamin had in mind will never be known. A tourist, after all, need not travel far, and of Paris it has been said that one may be a tourist in one's own city, as was Benjamin.

Tourism and Memory in France

In the form of visits to battlefield sites, such as in Normandy, and related museums and memorials, including death camps such as Auschwitz, the Second World War continues to be one of Europe's premier tourist paradigms.[51] Germany's expansion in the late 1930s and its military victories in the early years of the Second World War played a corresponding role, producing a new tourism imagery centered on Hitler and the images of the war. The Maginot Line, formerly a symbol of French resistance to a potential future threat from Germany, came to represent a head-in-the-sand mentality in the face of impending crisis. Because of its having been chosen as the site of Marshal Pétain's French government, which collaborated with Nazi Germany during the Occupation years, the town of Vichy, once associated only with luxury spas and vacations, was now seen to represent collaboration with a genocidal regime. In contrast, the Normandy beaches became symbolic of the victory of good over evil. As a subdivision of the sequence of paradigm shifts, war tourism, sometimes called battlefield tourism, although it extends beyond the battlefields themselves, reflects the institutional and personal articulations of tourism in the larger culture. This is especially visible in the case of Second World War France, as that country had already become a tourism icon in the years prior to the war in a culture of the West that was increasingly attuned to tourism during the late nineteenth and early twentieth centuries. France is not unique, as tourists have visited other, more recent war sites, including war-torn Baghdad, Afghanistan, and the demilitarized zone in Korea, among others. France, however, stands out in examining the connections between tourism and war, especially in regard to the Second World War, for three significant reasons: first, its role as a nineteenth- and twentieth-century tourism attraction and current world leader in international visits; second, the development of the field of cultural memory following the work in France of Maurice Halbwachs and more recently Pierre Nora; and third, the production of an extensive historical literature relating to the war and its interpretations since 1945.

Memory studies have assumed a growing place in the research of contemporary historians following the work of Halbwachs and others on cultural or "collective memory" and the creation of UNESCO World Heritage Sites in 1978.[52] The publication of the seven-volume *Lieux de mémoire* (Sites of Memory) anthology, edited by Nora in France in 1984–1992, intensified the focus on memory in France and elsewhere. His "sites of memory" may relate metaphorically to "places" within our memories rather than to specific itineraries on a Michelin road map. Nora and his colleagues emphasized, however, the role of physical locations, often war memorials or related monuments, in shaping memory and constructing political identity.[53] The broadening interest in "memory" in France led to a consecration of the work of Nora and his collaborators in 1993, when the phrase "site of memory" entered the *Grand dictionnaire Robert de la langue française*.[54] France's Caisse nationale des monuments historiques et des sites (CNMHS) in 1994 counted some fourteen thousand buildings and sites as historical monuments.[55] Books such as Henry Rousso's *Syndrome de Vichy*, first published in 1987, following the methodological approach toward collective memory by Halbwachs and Nora, have drawn considerable attention to ways in which the events of war, occupation, resistance, and liberation have been remembered in France.[56]

In his *Syndrome de Vichy*, Rousso discussed what he termed vectors of memory, such as films and history books. Although he did not highlight the issue of tourism, there were some references in his book and its sequel, *Vichy, un passé qui ne passe pas*, written with Eric Conan, to tourist sites as they related to how the Vichy experience had been seen. Two examples that stand out are the descriptions of the transfer of the remains of Jean Moulin to the Panthéon in 1964 and the turning of the site of the 1942 Vélodrome d'Hiver roundup of Jews for deportation to the death camps by the French police into an official memorial in 1993. Damaged by a fire, the Vélodrôme d'Hiver had been torn down in 1959. The convictions in 1987, 1994, and 1998 of Klaus Barbie, Paul Touvier, and Maurice Papon, respectively, of crimes committed during the war highlighted retrospective controversies and focused on French complicity and the role of Vichy in the Nazi Holocaust against the Jews, as did the publicity in 1994 surrounding then-president François Mitterrand's Vichy activity, and President Jacques Chirac's formal apology the next year.[57]

By the mid-1990s, the Second World War era had attracted enough study to become the second-most popular area for doctoral dissertations on France, behind only the 1789 Revolution.[58] Memory studies in the manner of Nora and his team were exemplified in France in the publication in 1995 of *Passant, souviens-toi: Les lieux du souvenir de la Seconde Guerre mondiale en France*, in which Serge Barcellini and Annette Wieviorka provided an extensive inventory and discussion of monuments to the war in France. They found a few monuments, such as the various memorials to Jean Moulin, which in their view expressed a unified memory, but most of the French monuments, they argued, represented divided rather than shared retrospection. Gaullist recollection was different from communist, and the authors also referred to the "conflictual" resurgence of the recollection (*souvenir*) of Vichy. The authors noted that much if not most of the French public was uninvolved in the historians' disputes about the war.[59] In 2010, Olivier Wieviorka published a study of France's "disunited memory" of the war. Emphasizing that the French maintained differing and competing sets of memory of the war, Wieviorka identified the memory of actual combat, the military campaigns of 1939–40 and 1944; that of the "yoke" of German occupation in northern France from June 1940 and in all of France from November 1942 through 1944; and the four-year rule of the Vichy government, which, while collaborating with the Axis powers, represented right-wing political positions deeply embedded in prior French political life. These experiences were subsequently honed by varying policies regarding the creation of public memory that Wieviorka traced from the end of the war to the present.[60]

Reassessing Second World War French Tourism

Despite the awareness in France and elsewhere of the political importance of cultural tourism, and the interest among historians and others in heritage and memory, particularly as they relate to the Second World War, the connection to tourism is rarely made. Occasionally a linkage may be found, as in a presentation by Josette Mesplier-Pinet, who, in addressing a conference titled "Tourisme Culture Patrimoine" in 2004, noted that cultural tourism, formerly concentrated on the beaux arts, was becoming increasingly less "elitist" and opening more to "new themes" that included military heritage (*patrimoine militaire*).[61] The attention given by historians to Vichy and the war years in memory has rarely addressed it in terms of touristic curiosity. Consequently there is little literature that addresses the reactions of tourists to the wartime monuments.[62]

The present volume draws the contours of the tourism phenomenon, highlighting the often unexplored ways in which it shed light on Butler and Wall's "other aspects of life" politically, economically, and culturally. Based on French and German archival materials, memoirs, films, the press, and personal interviews, it seeks to better understand the conflicts and competition between the nineteenth- and early twentieth-century French tourism narratives and the German-dominated tourism version of the Second World War that replaced it, followed by the Gaullist/Resistance account that followed the German after 1944. Documents from the archives of the German military offices in occupied Paris, kept primarily in the AJ/40 series in the Archives nationales (AN), testify to the tourism available to Germans, especially visiting military dignitaries, in Paris and the surrounding area. The German sources also shed considerable light in their many reports on Vichy policies and tourism in France. In addition, a large quantity of German material seized by the advancing Allied armies at the end of the war was microfilmed and made available by the National Archives in Washington, D.C. The collections T-77, T-120, and T-175, which contain materials from the Supreme Wehrmacht Command (OKW, Oberkommando der Wehrmacht), the Foreign Ministry, and the various police services, respectively, offer occasional glimpses into German tourism in occupied France. Captured German documentation gathered to prepare the cases against those on trial at Nuremberg after the war was collected in the archive of the Centre de documentation juive contemporaine (CDJC, the Center for Contemporary Jewish Documentation), since 1997 part of the Mémorial de la Shoah (Holocaust Memorial) in Paris, and made available to historians. In the decades since the war and the publication of my earlier book on the collaboration, French archives have opened more of their wartime collections and documents to the public.[63]

Memoirs of German officers such as Ernst Jünger and Gerhard Heller, stationed in Paris during the Occupation, and postwar films including *Is Paris Burning?* (1966) also offer evidence for Second World War tourism in France. Especially useful for an understanding of Vichy policies are materials from the beaux arts, sports, and tourism government services, AN series F21, F44, and F60, respectively. Some information was also gleaned from the material available prior to December 2015 in the Archives de la Préfecture de police in Le Pré-Saint-Gervais, just outside Paris. Whether the opening to the public in December 2015 of most of the police archives for the war years would bring any new revelations regarding the war and tourism remained to be seen at the time of writing.[64]

Wartime shortages led to restrictions on the use of paper, but tourism publications continued in France, although frequently in shortened format. The biweekly *Paris programmes: Guide de la vie parisienne* played a role for locals similar to the German *Wegleiter* in Paris. The *Bulletin de la Chambre de commerce de Paris* continued publication, occasionally addressing tourism issues during the Occupation, as did regional publications such as *La Bourgogne d'or* in Burgundy and *Lyon-Touriste,* the official organ of the Lyon regional Syndicat d'initiative. These publications are available in the BNF, which also holds collections of the tour guidebooks published during the war years, and the Bibliothèque historique de la ville de Paris (BHVP).

The large and increasing body of literature around the theme of memory in postwar France provides a context for the study of postwar tourism to wartime sites. Material documenting tourism after 1944 to these sites comes from a wide variety of sources reflecting the multiform nature of tourism itself, including the government tourism services in the F21 series mentioned earlier. Tour books published specifically for sites such as the Maginot Line and the Normandy landing beaches may be supplemented with more general guidebooks, including the Michelin *Green Guide* series, to help situate war tourism within the larger context of tourism in general. This literature has been augmented in recent years by the proliferation of websites, some for specific places, such as the martyred village of Oradour-sur-Glane; others for museums and libraries, such as the Invalides in Paris and the Caen Mémorial de la Paix; and yet others for more general assessments of tourism, such as those produced by the UNWTO.[65] Memorials and related ceremonies, as well as anniversaries, are regularly covered in the French and international press with articles that also shed light on their touristic aspects. The development of thanatourism, or "dark tourism," to sites such as the Vélodrome d'Hiver, the Drancy staging area for deportations to the east, and the Rivesaltes concentration camps, all related to the Holocaust in France, has produced its own literature, as have the many places associated with the Resistance and the activities of General de Gaulle. Tourist sites of pilgrimages for unrepentant Pétainists are addressed in the various issues of *Le Maréchal,* the periodical published by the Association pour défendre la mémoire du maréchal Pétain (ADMP: Association for the Defense of the Memory of Marshal Pétain), created in November 1951, shortly after Pétain's death.

Specialized periodicals, such as *After the Battle*, are also useful in studying war tourism. Cinema is important as well in forming people's images of sites related to the war and to tourism images in general. Films such as *Les visiteurs du soir* (1942), *The Longest Day* (1962), *Is Paris Burning?*, and *Saving Private Ryan* (1998), together with newsreels shown during and after the war, have undoubtedly been influential as key vectors of tourism. Publications statistics in the various French *Biblio* series offer a view of the relative ebb and flow of cultural interests as measured in book publications both during and since the war and may be viewed as a sample of interest in the war over time. Oral interviews, both with French men and women active during the war and with directors and conservators at *lieux de mémoire*" (sites of memory) and war-related museums in France enrich the available source material.

An examination of this wide range of documentation will show how tourism was manipulated and used during the war, under circumstances quite different from the tourism of the present. Different groups had their symbols, and on occasion the same symbol—for example, Joan of Arc or the Eiffel Tower—was used in different and competing ways. Armed with a knowledge of tourism's role in the production and evolution of symbols, we may now begin to appreciate more fully the subtle, and on occasion not so subtle, ways in which it contributed to the formation of political attitudes among French, Germans, and, after the Liberation, Americans and British Commonwealth subjects, evident in the changing tourist values of the wartime sites in a postwar era of reconciliation and European union.

A related subject for future study is the role of Italian tourism in Italy's occupation zone of France. When Italy joined the German war against an almost already defeated France in June 1940, it was rewarded with a slender zone of occupation in the southeastern part of the country, including the Riviera resort town of Menton. Shortly after the Italian occupation of 1940, the Ente turismo Costa Azzura di Mentone, Italy's Côte d'Azur Tourist Organization, began encouraging Italian tourism to Menton by supporting the distribution of food and other materials to the hotels there. One Menton hotel changed its name from Carlton to Albergo Bella Riva. Italian security services were concerned that spies and moneychangers might be hidden among the tourists. As Jean-Louis Panicacci indicates, there were relatively few Italian tourists in the Easter season, but more visited during the summer. Following the patterns of Fascist policy in Italy proper, local attempts were made to promote patriotism and youth, in the form of a youth colony and a monument to the fallen.[66] When the Germans occupied the formerly unoccupied zone of France following the Allied invasion of North Africa in November 1942, the Italian zone was extended to include Nice and the region of Provence to the Rhône River. Restrictions on public behavior included limiting the wearing of swimsuits to beaches and forbidding listening to music in public.[67] The Italians, however, were obliged to leave France when their government surrendered to the Allies in September 1943. The relatively limited tourism in the Italian zones remains to be more fully explored.

What is clear, however, is that tourism played a significant role during the Second World War in France and continues to be important in *tourisme de mémoire*. The Second World War as a tourist phenomenon may possibly have been the most photographed historical event ever. The many tourist imaginary–type photos taken of the Germans marching into Paris in 1940 and of General de Gaulle's triumphal entry into the city in August 1944 offer a hint of the extent to which the war in its many different aspects was photographed.

Accordingly, this book reassesses Second World War tourism in France by addressing the following points: (1) historical context, including tourism and war in France prior to the Second World War; (2) the war and what might be called "Big Tourism," the eyes turned toward Rommel and the Atlantic Wall, and German tourism in general in occupied France, 1940–1944; (3) French tourism during the war, attenuated but not eliminated; and (4) postwar *lieux de mémoire*. Normandy stands out, but France is littered with sites related to the war, with varying significations for those of differing political persuasions. It also addresses the differences between the curiosity of the tourist gaze along the Champs-Èlysées in 1940 and 1944 and the tourist industry's organization of site visits during and after the war. Finally, there is a quantitative assessment of postwar war tourism: Can we measure war tourism?

By the time of the Second World War, tourism had become deeply rooted in much of Western culture. The tensions between tourism in general as a "sacred journey," to use Nelson Graburn's term, on the one hand, and "superficial pleasures, entertainment, commodification," or "kitsch," on the other, remain a continuing conversation among students of the phenomenon.[68] These tensions become even more acute in the discussion of wartime sites such as the Normandy landing beaches, military cemeteries in France and elsewhere, and locales such as Auschwitz, where solemn rituals are juxtaposed with the sale of trinkets.[69]

The relationships between tourism and war have a long history. In his study of travel in antiquity, Lionel Casson mentions Romans on tour in Athens who also visited Marathon, some twenty miles distant, already by then a famous battleground site of the Greco-Persian wars.[70] Sites related to Napoleon's military campaigns, notably the scene of his final defeat at Waterloo in 1815, where spectators watched the battle unfold, have become attractions for latter-day tourists. Hotels and restaurants were built around the Waterloo battlefield, now in Belgium, and, in the words of Joyce Marcel, "changed the route of the 19th century British Grand Tour forever."[71] If we look back at tourism and the Second World War in France, Shirer's observation of German soldiers photographing Parisian tourist sites, the French pensioners vacationing in hotels in 1942, and the postwar transformation of Arromanches-les-Bains from spa to site of memory were hardly isolated examples of the interactions of war and tourism. This book proposes a closer look at the confluence of war and tourism, two of humanity's more extensive sets of activities, in France, a center of world culture in the mid-twentieth century.

CHAPTER 1

The Emergence of France as a Tourist Icon in the Belle Époque

The relationship between war-related tourism in general and Second World War tourism in France must be understood in the long-term perspective of France's history as a tourist destination for both foreigners and the French themselves. The Belle Époque period, taken broadly, from the late nineteenth century through the outbreak of World War I, produced a highlighting of France that was primarily a railroad-driven mechanism before the coming of the automobile. France became the center of a far-flung empire, and Paris, as its capital, had few rivals in both domestic and international tourism. Paris had been rebuilt under Baron Georges-Eugène Haussmann, the Eiffel Tower became a tourist landmark, and French gastronomy acquired a cachet that endures. The expansion of Paris under Napoleon III, together with the advent of the railroad and trans-Atlantic steamships, created the modern Paris that, during the Belle Époque years, became a focal point in the tourism imaginary of so many both in France and abroad. An added factor was the primacy of Europe, with its far-flung empires and commercial networks, including the French empire in North Africa, Southeast Asia, and beyond. The term Belle Époque became an acknowledgment of the centrality of France and its language and culture in the Western world.[1] Focusing on the *flâneur,* a kind of tourist, in the nineteenth-century arcades of Paris, Walter Benjamin named the city "the capital of the nineteenth century."[2] The centrality of Paris also translated into the tourism imaginary of so many within and outside France giving rise to the belief that to be a cultured person, one must have visited Paris. Extension of the railway system extended this imagery to much of the rest of France, although it would become even more widespread with the increased use of automobiles after the First World War. Belle Époque France, and Paris in particular, surged into the tourism imaginary with the invention and spread of film in the late nineteenth and early twentieth centuries.

Tourism in France from Its Beginnings through the Middle Ages

France has been a center for tourism since the creation of the modern French state in the early modern period and, in some ways, even before. Caves at Chauvet and Lascaux drew migratory visitors for religious pilgrimages and for their paintings. Rediscovered in 1940, the Lascaux paintings are approximately fifteen thousand years old. The Chauvet paintings, dated to some 35,000 years ago, were rediscovered in 1994.[3] Wartime heritage sites include Alésia, where the Romans defeated Vercingetorix and effectively extended their domain over Gaul. It is still marked by street names in France and has become a battlefield or war heritage site for today's tourists.

During the Middle Ages, Christian pilgrims on the road to Santiago de Compostela trekked across much of southwestern France, stopping at inns and undoubtedly gazing at sites along the way. Scholars such as the Benedictine monk Richer traveled from Reims to Chartres to consult books in the cathedral library there.[4] In his introduction to a study of medieval travelers, Noël Coulet writes that travelers are by definition admirers of all kinds of curiosities and discoveries that arouse their astonishment (*mirabilia* in Latin), although the modalities differ depending on time and place. As evidence, he tells the story of two late medieval German pilgrims, Hans von Waltheym and Hieronymus Münzer, passing through Provence on their way to Santiago de Compostela. Waltheym was able to gain access to tour the royal palace at Aix as well as the palace at Avignon, and Münzer, despite many guards, managed to see the young dauphin in Amboise.[5] Medieval battle sites also appear frequently in the anonymously written *Guide des chemins de France* (Guide to the Roads of France), published by Charles Estienne in 1552 and since then associated with his name. The *Guide*, for example, described Chalons-sur-Marne as a "stronghold in a flat countryside, beautiful needle-tipped bell towers, ancient and known for the battle against Attila, and as a merchant [center] for grains and textiles, watered by the Marne River."[6] Discussing the origins of the name Burgundy, the *Guide* traced the history of the German term *Burg* to fortified defenses against the Turks and the origin of the French term *bourgeois*. The name Burgundy was said to be a combination of *Burg* and Gundiochus or Gundion, the first inhabitant of the area and the creator of the fortresses.[7]

Medieval battlefield tourism continues at Crécy and Agincourt, while places associated with Joan of Arc and the military exploits she inspired have become significant tourist sites. The city of Rouen opened its own Historial Jeanne d'Arc in March 2015, complete with "bold scenography, decidedly modern via many multimedia displays."[8] The new Historial anticipated 100,000 to 150,000 visitors annually.[9] It exhibits items from all periods in Joan's life and includes a re-creation of the postmortem trial that exonerated her: "For an hour and fifteen minutes, you will be transported back to 1456 to the heart of the trial seeking to rehabilitate her, who had been burned at the place du Vieux-Marché twenty-five years earlier because she had been judged a 'heretic.'"[10] At Agincourt, a Centre historique médiéval (Medieval History Center) and battlefield that features the 1415 battle there, with an English-language website, are described as a "theme park."[11] In 2008, the Agincourt Center was reported to have attracted some 35,000 visitors.[12] The theme of the reenactment, according to Christophe Gilliot, director of the Center, was to celebrate the friendship between the English and the French.[13]

Tourism in Early Modern France

The development of the modern French state went hand in hand with that of an infrastructure for tourism. In approximately 1470, after the Hundred Years' War (1337–1453), a postal system was begun in France with horses and post stations about eight miles apart. By 1483, 234 postal stations existed. Postal horses and inns were offered for the use of mail carriers and other travelers. Not all travel, to be sure, is tourism or sightseeing, but the tourist gaze was most certainly present among those who moved along the roads, as it was with Waltheym and Münzer.

Johannes Gutenberg's invention of movable type ushered in an increase in the production of guidebooks, and the early modern period saw a surge in tourist manuals. Most significant for France was the publication of the *Guide des chemins de France*, which also discussed sites to visit and in many ways marks the beginning of French travel publications. It, like other Renaissance guidebooks, followed the model of the *Description of Greece*, written in the second century AD by the Greek traveler Pausanias. The first French road guide, the *Guide* outlined 283 itineraries in France and described local foods in a manner that made them, as Antoni Maczak wrote, "the prototypes of dishes later given star ratings in the Michelin guides."[14] It was designed to help pilgrims travel to Santiago de Compostela and Rome, to help the traveler "find his way," choose his inns and stopovers, and avoid the dangers of the road. Very much reflecting the perspectives of its time, the *Guide* became a prototype for later guidebooks to France. Estienne's book quickly sold out in 1552, was republished repeatedly, and was also pirated by other guidebooks during the second half of the sixteenth and seventeenth centuries.[15] With its road directions and site recommendations, it helped establish subsequent tourist images in France for both domestic and international visitors, images that, with all the differences between the mid-sixteenth century and later eras, constituted a model for guidebooks through the present. Old castles or fortifications were mentioned, such as sites in Calais from where, in good weather, one could see "the tail of England," and in the Champagne region, among others.[16] As Marc Boyer wrote, the *Guide* and its successors in the sixteenth and first half of the seventeenth centuries established the *corpus de videnda*, or the concept of itineraries with sites that must be seen.[17]

Estienne's guidebook appeared in a France in transition toward greater mobility. The emergence of the modern French state with the construction of better roads and canals together with improved domestic security during the seventeenth and eighteenth centuries, especially after the end of the religious wars in 1589, facilitated increased travel. Among the privileged, who wrote accounts of their journeys, were François Rabelais (1494–1553) and Michel de Montaigne (1553–1592).[18] Following the end of the religious wars with the accession of Henry IV in 1589, the new king and the duc de Sully, named high commissioner of highways and public works, began planning to modernize French roads, a process put into effect under Louis XIV.[19] In the 1620s a modern public postal service with set fees for the delivery of letters started to take shape. Cardinal Richelieu established post offices in the main towns, linked by postilions. Paris was linked with Provence in 1644.[20]

As travel became easier and more guidebooks appeared, Paris emerged as a leading destination in France for English and German visitors, followed by Lyon, Bordeaux, and Marseille.[21] Young and privileged English gentlemen visited France as part of their Grand Tour or *Bildungsreisen* (educational journeys).[22] Subsequent guidebooks in France included *Paris burlesque* by a Monsieur Berthod, also published in 1652, which focused on the turmoil, gossip, and thieves of the capital city.[23]

From the Enlightenment into the nineteenth century, the *Bildungsreisen* undertaken by aristocratic and middle-class travelers, largely male, represented an important stage in the development of tourism. Some traveled in

Italy or France in search of edification and discussed the knowledge acquired abroad and their experiences in literary works, travelogues, and travel novels. People journeyed in coaches, explored the countryside and cities, and visited landmarks in order to experience nature, culture, and art directly, on the spot, and to deepen their understanding of them. Others traveled in France, Britain, and Germany with the goal of learning about the technological progress and current developments in trade, agriculture, industry, technology, and manufacturing.[24] Beach and spa tourism developed as well, the latter exemplified by the visit of Madame de Sévigné to take the waters at Vichy in 1676 and 1677.[25]

In short, through the cultural shifts associated with the Renaissance and early modern periods, the guidebooks published by Estienne and others, the developments in roads and coaches, and the postal system, emblematic of the growing power of the state and enhanced pacification, France had developed a tourism self-image. By 1670, in a book praising the virtues of France, François Savinien d'Alquié wrote, quoted by Marc Boyer:

> France today is a kingdom so flourishing that all the nations on earth regard it as the Empire of the World because of its victories and triumphs and because there is not a sane person who does not strive to see this incomparable state. I am convinced that my work would not be unwelcome to the [other] nations if I made a summary of its [France's] delights.[26]

Sites visited by tourists included the late seventeenth-century Vauban fortifications along the western, northern, and eastern borders of France, declared World Heritage Sites in 2008 by UNESCO. Built by Sébastien Le Prestre de Vauban (1633–1707), the fortifications consist of twelve groups of fortified buildings. One such cluster, in Neuf-Brisach in Alsace, houses a tourism office.[27]

Tourism in France from the Revolution through the Late Nineteenth Century

The French Revolution focused attention on Paris, which supplanted Versailles as the political center of the country, and extended construction and expansion facilitated its emergence as a culture capital for both French and international tourists. Sites such as the place de la Bastille, where the old fortress had stood before being stormed and then destroyed in July 1789, attracted tourists, as did the place Louis XV, renamed place de la Révolution, and place de la Concorde, where King Louis XVI and Queen Marie-Antoinette had been executed. The Louvre Palace was taken over by the revolutionary state in 1791 and opened as an art museum in 1793, a step in the addition of museum culture to the French tourist circuit.[28] Revolutionary Paris became an attraction for activists including Thomas Paine, who wrote his *Rights of Man* there, and Anacharsis Cloots, a Prussian aristocrat who traveled to Paris, participated in revolutionary activity, and was executed during the Reign of Terror. Ultimately, locales related to Napoleon, notably the Arc de Triomphe, another military site, were added to his growing personality cult. Ultimately, Napoleon would be buried at the Invalides, to be visited by a triumphant Adolf Hitler in June 1940.

Battleground sites connected to revolutions have also drawn tourists. Locales connected to the revolutions of 1789, 1848, and 1871 have attracted secular pilgrimage and more general tourism. Examples include the site of the Bastille and the Mur des Fédérés in the Père Lachaise cemetery, the latter where Communard revolutionaries were executed in 1871. The Arc de Triomphe, commissioned by Napoleon in 1806 in Paris to commemorate his military victories, ultimately became one of France's leading tourist attractions, listed in tenth place by the French government, with some 1.75 million paying visitors in 2014.[29] The scene of his final defeat at Waterloo in 1815 has also become a tourist attraction. Even before the Battle of Waterloo, however, spectators observed Napoleon's forces at war. Writing about observers watching the fighting in Gaza in 2014, Jan Mieszkowski noted retrospectively that "at the beginning of the 19th century, warfare came to be understood as a theatrical performance, a clash of armies that should respect the unity of time and place as if it were a classical drama."[30] His article led to a discussion on the electronic network H-War in which one participant pointed out that the French had built reviewing stands for the Battle of Vitoria in Spain in 1813. Artillery cannon smoke, however, obscured much of the view of the fighting.[31] The development of a vocabulary of tourism from the late seventeenth through the early nineteenth centuries was capped in France by Stendhal's *Mémoires d'un touriste,* published in 1837–38. In addition to publicizing his travels through France en route to Italy, this book helped establish the usage of the word *touriste,* which had appeared in French earlier in the century.[32]

The discovery of the Rosetta Stone, brought to France and deciphered after Napoleon's Egyptian campaign of 1798, helping give birth to the field of Egyptology, also sparked interest in the Mediterranean, which emerged as a regional concept with the work of the early nineteenth-century French geographer Conrad Malte-Brun. Following the Napoleonic wars, English gentlemen retired to southern France (Pau) and Malta, helping to open the Mediterranean to increased tourism. The French takeover of Algeria, beginning in 1830, added a Mediterranean and North African dimension to the growing French tourism circuit. This interest grew after the 1859 Austro-Sardinian War, when the French acquired Savoy from Piedmont. The new acquisition enabled the French to develop the areas around Nice, Cannes, and Saint-Tropez, which together put the Riviera on the tourist map. Rail lines, extended from Paris to Nice in 1864, fueled the subsequent development of the Côte d'Azur, linking it with London and Paris and making the trips both faster and safer. Improved hygiene was also wiping out the diseases of the Mediterranean. The Côte d'Azur emerged as a tourist destination with British aristocrats often traveling to Hyères and Giens, in the Var, for warmer weather during the winter. They helped establish winter resorts on the Mediterranean, thereby creating the winter tourist "season."[33] The Mediterranean, open to European tourism, would take off as a destination in the twentieth century, adding a summer season to the winter season established in the nineteenth century.

Central to the tourist imaginary for France during the first half of the nineteenth century was Paris, which, in the words of H. Hazel Hahn, describing the cafés, hotels, and shops, emerged as the "capital of amusement." Until its gambling rooms were closed by the government, the Palais Royal was a center for a mix of men and women of different social classes and, as Hahn points out, "as the epitome of pleasure for all classes, a city within a city, but also [known] as vulgar and dangerous."[34] Improved streetlights and policing later made a return home after midnight relatively safe, turning the rough-and-tumble theater world of mid--nineteenth-century Paris, in which women were not allowed into the pit because of the frequency of brawls, into a theater culture that might attract tourists. Genres expanded to include popular subjects along with the rise of operettas and dances such as those featuring the cancan.

The development of the Tuileries Garden and the Champs-Élysées enhanced the allure of Paris, as did the fashionably dressed women seen there. According to *La Grande Ville,* quoted by Hahn, Paris by the 1840s was already "the center of the arts, sciences, fashion, and—one could almost say—of civilization."[35] The Second Empire reconstruction of Paris, engineered by Haussmann, and the development of electric street lighting in 1877 facilitated night tourism, turning the French capital from the "city of light" to the "city of neon."[36] Grand hotels such as the Ritz catered to women as well as men. The city became an attraction not only for visitors from abroad but also for local tourists—*flâneurs,* or strollers, exploring on foot. Discussing Paris during the Belle Époque years, the film historian Alan Williams writes: "In Paris an entertainment district had consolidated and expanded along the new boulevards, where one found everything from freak shows to wax museums to popular theatrical spectacles like that at the Châtelet. Along these wide thoroughfares, people of all classes strolled to observe each other and to contemplate the various attractions that solicited their patronage."[37]

One of the major changes in the tourist imaginary of France during the postrevolutionary years was the addition of gastronomy to the mix. The first restaurant in Paris, in 1765, was said to have been established as a revolt of the purveyors of bouillon (consommé with a meat stock that "restored" one's health), against the *traiteurs* (caterers whose guild held a monopoly over the sale of meats) and led to a proliferation of restaurants in Paris in the 1790s. Their numbers increased from fewer than fifty at the start of the 1789 Revolution to more than three thousand by 1820.[38] Restaurants in Paris varied from the most expensive—which became "musts," markers of social standing where members of an aspiring bourgeoisie vied to be seen—to the foulest soup kitchens, often serving recycled food to the poor.[39] The establishment of Delmonico's restaurant in New York in 1833 marked the emergence of French cuisine internationally and helped establish the French restaurant as a point of interest in the United States. Expatriate French chefs in London, such as Alexis Soyer—and, later, French-trained chefs including Charles Francatelli—helped inspire the gastronomic tour of France, which took off in the late nineteenth century.[40]

The French government also intervened to promote gastronomic tourism. In 1855 the Bordeaux Chamber of Commerce established a classification and rating system of place-names for local wines, the *appellation contrôlée*, to be used in the Paris World's Fair of that year. What Eric Hobsbawm referred to as the "invention of tradition" contributed to France's growth as a tourist destination.[41] Tied into this was the development of the concept of *terroir* (region, territory, land, place). In October 1906, the Touring club de France promoted regional gastronomy in its *Revue mensuelle* (Monthly Review), although systematically only after 1920.[42] Félix Urbain-Dubois, who popularized *service russe*, bringing dishes to the table in sequence to be served while still hot, in contrast to the older groaning board *service française*, published *La cuisine de tous les pays* in 1856, the first French international cookbook, which went through many subsequent editions and helped appropriate other international cuisines into the French culinary repertoire.[43]

Railways, Steamships, Gastronomy, and Grand Hotels in the Belle Époque

The late nineteenth-century development of railways and steamships, together with international hotels, such as the Hotel Ritz, established in Paris in 1898 and associated with César Ritz and Auguste Escoffier, together with spas at Vichy and

Évian, promoted an international French hotel cuisine. Using Urbain-Dubois's new restaurant service model, tourist circuits frequently adopted a semi-French service. French-style cooks, even if Armenian or Italian, traveled all over the world. The spread of electric refrigeration facilitated the storage of cheeses, the preparation of desserts, and the ability to chill wines. Pasteurization increased the safety of food consumption. Lower printing costs and better presses enabled the publication of menus, which emerged early in the nineteenth century. Menus themselves became collectors' items and a part of the gastronomic tour. The structure of tables also underwent change in the late nineteenth century with the emergence of the bistro and the milk-bar table. Increased use of knife, fork, and spoon at the same time all contributed to the enhanced prestige of French restaurants.[44] By the end of the century, Thomas B. Preston reported in the *Chautauquan* about the active role played by the French Republic in promoting tourism by supporting the culinary syndicates and the awarding of the titles of "chef" and "cordon bleu."[45]

The extension of the railroad network from Paris to Nice in 1864, already mentioned, plus the network of great train stations in Paris, completed with the construction of the Gare de Lyon between 1895 and 1902, timed to coincide with the Universal Exhibition of 1900, itself a major tourist attraction, solidified France as an international tourist destination.[46] An 1872 article found that railway travel and the increased tourist trade had driven up the price of stays in Saint-Malo and Saint-Omer for English visitors.[47] Gustave Flaubert's Emma, in *Madame Bovary,* written in 1856, wanted to take the train but could barely go anywhere. By 1890, a day train could take a traveler to almost any destination within France.[48] Increased travel by women and families and the introduction of *wagons-lits,* railroad restaurant dining cars, and the railroad hotel restaurant all came together.[49] In addition to the sites of Paris, pilgrimage destinations continued to attract travelers, many of whom were women. These sites included the increasingly popular Lourdes in southwestern France, known for the visions of the fourteen-year-old Bernadette Soubiroux in 1858. The military defeat of Napoleon III by Prussian forces in 1870 intensified pilgrimages, and 1873 was known as the "year of the pilgrimage," with treks to Chartres, Paray-le-Monial, and Lourdes, facilitated for increased numbers of people by the railways.[50]

Famous trains such as the Orient Express, which ran from Paris to Constantinople, beginning officially under that name in 1889, were additional draws for tourists to Paris.[51] Railway advertising posters themselves become collectibles, attracting a tourist trade to bookstalls and shops. The railways brought increasingly large numbers of people to Paris, whose older narrow streets were incapable of accommodating them. Streets were widened and extended, as in the case of the rue de Rivoli, which now ran from the Bastille to the place de la Concorde. Construction of the boulevards Saint-Michel, Sébastopol, Strasbourg, and Magenta facilitated the movement of traffic in the city. A new quarter grew around the recently constructed Opéra, and the areas around the Louvre, Élysée Palace, Hôtel de Ville, Palais Royal, and Tour Saint-Jacques were cleared and made more accessible. The city was expanded from twelve districts to twenty. In the words of the 1937 edition of *Les guides bleus Paris,* the *Blue Guide to Paris:*

> Paris became not only the capital of France but also the center of attraction for all Europe. The festivals staged there were of an unimaginable luxury; the sovereigns of England, Austria, Russia, Prussia came to visit. The Congress of Paris in 1856 marked the high point of imperial politics and the two universal expositions of 1855, and then 1867, were as the coronation of the Parisian apotheosis.[52]

Having moved to Versailles at the time of the 1871 Commune, the capital returned to Paris in 1879. The city's development continued under the Third Republic with the construction of the Palais de Trocadéro for the 1878 Exposition, replaced by the Eiffel Tower for the 1889 French Revolutionary Centennial Exposition and the Palais de Chaillot for the International Exposition of 1937. Another Exposition in 1900 produced the Grand and Petit Palais and the Pont Alexandre III over the Seine.[53]

In summary, the rebuilding of Paris, together with the coming of the railways and steamships, advanced gastronomy, and the extension of the French Empire into much of Africa and Asia, combined to make the Belle Époque the pinnacle of France's tourism history.[54] Trains brought people to sporting events, such as the first modern Olympics, held in Athens in 1896, and facilitated recreational bicycling and the first Tour de France bicycle race, staged in 1903. In addition, the railway network helped deliver the mail, which contributed to the development of urban tastes, tourism included, in large parts of Europe and North America. A near doubling in the extent of communal roads, from 331,000 kilometers in 1871 to 539,000 in 1911, made rural France more accessible to urban tourists and helped, in the words of Eugen Weber, turn "peasants into Frenchmen."[55] The launching of the White Star liner *Oceanic* in 1870 ushered in a new era of first-class travel across the Atlantic, and by 1890 steamships had reduced the time for the crossing to six days.[56] Health improvements in the late nineteenth and early twentieth centuries also helped tourism. Dietary ameliorations included a significant increase in per capita consumption of proteins as opposed to carbohydrates in France, as well as in other European countries.[57]

All these factors worked toward the embellishment of France as a tourist destination both locally and abroad. With the extension of the French and European railway networks and the advent of luxury steamships, and with few competitors for international tourism, France achieved the height of its cultural iconicity in the Belle Époque years.[58] As Dean MacCannell wrote in *The Tourist,* Paris had acquired a sacred status in the eyes of tourists, who were convinced that it was a "must see" in Europe. Once in Paris, the "must sees" included the Notre-Dame cathedral, the Eiffel Tower, and the Louvre, and within the Louvre, the Mona Lisa and the Venus de Milo.[59] He cited Alden Hatch's history of American Express: "Never was travel to Europe so pleasant as in the summer of 1914, never before and never again."[60] Russians, Scandinavians, and Germans, the last mentioned from an increasingly prosperous new Reich, visited Paris, which had little competition for the tourist, with few barriers across international frontiers. Mountains and beaches, formerly difficult to visit, became more accessible with the coming of railroads. Mountains, once seen as impediments to be avoided, acquired a positive attraction, fed by nineteenth-century romanticism. Postcards showing sites such as Mont Blanc and the beach at Deauville became popular. The beaches of Normandy became popular as well, and Deauville acquired its "season."[61] An article, "At Trouville," published by *Harper's Weekly* in 1890 reflected interest in the Normandy beaches, now accessible from Paris and other metropolitan centers by train.[62] The Eiffel Tower, constructed for the 1889 Exposition, which celebrated the centennial of the 1789 Revolution and became a tourist symbol itself, represented "La Grande France."[63] The 1890–1899 *Readers' Guide to Periodical Literature* included a separate subclassification for "Eiffel Tower," listing Minnie Buchanan Goodman's article, published in 1890, "Americans on the Eiffel Tower."[64] It was no accident that Hitler would be pictured with the Eiffel Tower as a backdrop in *Mit Hitler im Westen* (With Hitler in the West), a softcover photo album celebrating his military victory over France in 1940.

This was the period that would establish a French self-image that placed Paris and France meaningfully at the center of the world, creating the culture of tourism that would so heavily permeate both French and German, as well as Anglophone, tourist images during the Second World War. French became the international language of diplomacy and culture. The Union postale universelle, established by the 1874 Bern Treaty, chose French as its international language in 1911 and used it exclusively as its international working language until English was added in 1996.[65] French culture came to represent cosmopolitan sophistication, encapsulated in Paris, the Côte d'Azur, and France conceived as a whole. By the second half of the nineteenth century, the sites of Paris had so captured the tourist imaginary that Anne Jeanblanc, writing in *Le Point* in 2012, argued for a Paris version of the Stendhal syndrome, in which Stendhal had described experiencing an ecstatic feeling, "a fierce palpitation of the heart" so strong that he feared fainting, in proximity to the tombs of the great Florentines he had seen during a visit in 1817.[66]

By the beginning of the twentieth century, the world of tourist curiosity for the European upper and middle classes had increased exponentially. Technological and economic changes were accompanied by shifts in aesthetic perspectives from the 1880s through the Belle Époque as the coming of the camera and cinema helped move painting to the top of the beaux arts hierarchy, so that today "art" is often associated with painting. The visual, or seeing, emerged in ever more dominant presence, ultimately exemplified by the many German soldiers with cameras photographing tourist sites in Paris noted by William Shirer in 1940. Beginning in the 1890s and extending through the first decade of the twentieth century, Americans with deep pockets arrived in Paris to buy French paintings for private collections and American museums. Wealthy Americans such as Andrew Carnegie, Henry Frick, Andrew Mellon, Peggy Guggenheim, and William Randolph Hearst amassed impressive collections of paintings, a development reflected in the attention paid to museums by the tourist guidebooks at the turn of the century.[67] French preeminence attracted artists such as Mary Cassatt (1844–1926), who was raised in Pennsylvania in an environment that viewed travel as integral to education. She spent five years in Europe, learning drawing, music, German, and French, and eventually settled as an expatriate to paint in France.[68] The interest later expressed in French art by Hitler and Hermann Goering, among others, did not develop in a vacuum.

The twentieth century continued the rapid pace of the parallel transformation of aesthetics with tourism, evident in works such as Henry Adams's *Mont Saint-Michel and Chartres* and the coming of the automobile with the first Michelin guidebook in 1900.[69] *Mont-Saint-Michel and Chartres* helped popularize the hobby of stained-glass making and put the Chartres cathedral on the tourist map, helping produce a significant increase in tourism there.

Film and Tourism in the Belle Époque

The progression of film is yet another form of the linking of aesthetics with tourism. Film at the end of the nineteenth century played a role in the tourist imaginary for France, as sites that were already iconic grew more indelibly etched in the minds of increasing numbers of people. In his account of Hitler's visit to Paris in June 1940, Cédric Gruat notes that from its very inception, cinema focused on and magnified the appeal and attractions of Paris. Paris and the Parisian, he adds, became universally known with Max Linder and the films of the Belle Époque. Linder, whose dandy character could be viewed against a backdrop of Trocadéro or the Eiffel Tower, contributed to their tourism iconicity.[70] Charted by the Internet Movie Database (IMDb), which tracks films produced throughout the world in some half-dozen languages and lists some 3.5 million films from 1874 through the present, films offer insights into the tourist imaginaries of their era. Film titles, which can be counted in the IMDb, are important because audiences instantly recognize the association. Each title is a marker of cultural identity immediately recognizable by the audience, for example, *Murder in the Rue Morgue,* in which almost all non-French-speaking viewers will recognize that *rue* means "street," or films including the Eiffel Tower in their title. French terms such as *à la mode* and *à la carte* also appear frequently in the titles of non-French-language films during the early years, through the 1920s and 1930s. The early films listed in the IMDb are largely documentary. They include titles such as *Place de la Bastille, Cortège de tzar au Bois de Boulogne, Bois de Boulogne, Bateau-mouche sur la Seine,* and *La Gare Saint-Lazare,* all released in 1896. *Cortège de tzar au Bois de Boulogne,* directed by Georges Méliès, documented Tsar Alexander III's visit to Paris. *La Tour Eiffel* was filmed in 1900 and an English-language version, *Panorama of Eiffel Tower,* appeared the same year. As motion picture technology developed, more of a storyline appeared in films such as *La tragique amour de Mona Lisa* in 1910, *Shadows of the Moulin Rouge* in 1913, and *In the Latin Quarter* the following year.[71] The surge in the numbers of films about Paris during the first years of the twentieth century was due in part to the interest generated by the 1900 International Exposition in Paris.

The subjects of these films reflect the deepening tourism imagery of France in general and Paris in particular. Not surprisingly, films made during the years just preceding the First World War also suggest the arrival of the automobile, as beaches and islands are seen as destinations. Sites named in their titles include the Eiffel Tower, the Latin Quarter, Montparnasse, the Louvre, Maxim's or Chez Maxim's, Notre-Dame, the Moulin Rouge, Montmartre, the Rive Droite, the place de la Concorde, the Bois de Boulogne, the Champs-Elysées, the Champs de Mars, the Bastille, Les Halles, the Seine, and the Île de la Cité.[72] Films such as *French Can-Can,* made in the United States in 1898, suggested erotic tourism, another quality associated by some with France, and especially Paris.[73] Paintings such as Toulouse Lautrec's *Troupe de Mademoiselle Eglantine* in 1896, with its many reproductions, also highlighted the cancan, elevating its presence in tourism images.

The coming in the late nineteenth century of phonograph recordings helped create a music circuit in Europe, as most of today's opera houses were built from the 1860s onward. Begun in 1861, the Opéra Garnier in Paris was completed fourteen years later. Light opera and burlesque developed. The ballet *Giselle* took off in popularity as did the cancan in cabarets. The opera, together with the theater and cinema, the emergence of French gastronomy, the modernization of Paris's urban infrastructure, and the railways linking the city to the rest of France and Europe made France the focal point of the tourism imaginary for many around the world. France had become the center of a worldwide empire linked by steamships, which also brought tourists from North America. Late nineteenth- and early twentieth-century France experienced a true Belle Époque that was recognized as such at the time. The French tourism reality and images that would be so seductive to so many in the first half of the twentieth century, including the war years of 1939 through 1945, were in place when the Belle Époque came to an end with the war of 1914. Following the World War I disruption, tourism in France regained its development, aided by the increase in automobile use, which made the regions beyond Paris more accessible to increasing numbers of visitors, domestic and international. Greater accessibility of the regions contributed to an increased popularity of local gastronomy and the development of the regional hotel network, all enhancing tourist imaginaries of France.

War also played a role in the late nineteenth- and early twentieth-century expansion of tourism in France. Because of its unfortunate military situation, the town of Sedan became a tourist site for those interested in the 1870 and 1914–1918 wars. The scene of the Prussian victory over Napoleon III, which led to the fall of the Second Empire in 1870 and contributed to the unification of Germany the following year, Sedan is the location of the Château Fort de Sedan, which may be viewed on the website of the Office du tourisme de Sedan. A Panorama Room in the château features a large mural of the 1870 battle.[74]

The First World War and Tourism in France

First World War sites of memory have drawn substantial numbers of tourists. In addition to the desire to construct specific memories of the war, economic factors, especially important given the need for reconstruction in France after the severe destruction of the war, played a role in the campaigns by the Touring club de France and the Office national du tourisme to stimulate battlefield tourism. During the interwar years, the Michelin Tire Company and Thomas Cook's both promoted battlefield tourism with guidebooks to the sites. Covering much of northeastern France, the scene of so much of the fighting on the western front, the Michelin guidebooks depicted a people deeply wounded and a land heavily damaged but also the scene of heroic resistance against German onslaughts and successful French counterattacks, especially during the last weeks of the war. Sections describing the history of the specific areas were interspersed with suggestions for accessing them, often by automobile. Appeals to national pride and pilgrimage tourism were combined with the commercial interest of the Michelin Company in promoting the use of automobiles. Altogether, by the early 1920s, Michelin had published twenty-nine French-language guidebooks to battlefield sites together with twenty titles in English, of which three were devoted to the Americans' role in the war, and four in Italian plus one in German. Some 2 million copies were sold, indicating how visitors might recapture the trench experiences by touring the battlefields in their automobiles.[75] For example, the guidebook to the Verdun battlefields, published in 1921 by Michelin as part of its World War I series, shows Marshal Pétain as the honorary president of a committee charged with erecting an ossuary at Douaumont, site of the ten-month-long battle that lasted from February through December 1916. The Douaumont ossuary was to be located "in the center of the battlefield on a high point from where the eye can incorporate all."[76] At the end of the guidebook, a full-page notice indicated that the Michelin Bureau de tourisme would provide free of charge a detailed itinerary, indicating "good routes and good spots" for anyone planning a future trip by automobile in France or abroad. All that was needed was ten days' advance notice giving the tourism office a general sense of where the traveler wished to go.[77] The Michelin guidebook for Compiègne Pierrefonds, the site of the signing of the 11 November 1918 armistice, noted that it was also during the fighting at Compiègne that Joan of Arc was captured and taken prisoner by the Burgundians, allied with the English.[78]

A more recent World War I tourist site is the Historial de la Grand Guerre 1914–1918, opened in 1992 at Péronne, near the Somme River, another of the sanguinary battlegrounds of World War I. Described as an area in which "the First World War remains engraved on the soil," the Somme River region became a tourist circuit with six museums and memorials in close proximity. The Historial was described in a *Figaro* article published on Armistice Day in 2001 as the "natural point of departure" for a family tour of the area.[79] Unfortunately, the Péronne Historial's internationalist approach, which Friedhelm Boll, a historian at the Historical Research Center of the Friedrich-Ebert-Stiftung in Germany, praised in 2007 for promoting a message of peace, may have worked against the museum's success.[80] Reports showed a decline in visitors in the first decade of the twenty-first century. It was listed in eighth place among attractions in the Somme area, with some eighty thousand visitors in 2008.[81] It also had to compete with the newer Meaux Musée de la Grande Guerre, which opened on November 11, 2011. The Historial, together with many of the other museums related to the First World War, benefited from the centenary commemoration in 2014. Helped by a doubling of the number of adult visitors, the Historial attracted a total of 120,000 visitors in contrast to the 80,000 it had received during each of the prior years.[82] From its opening in 2011 through 2014, the Meaux museum received some 375,000 visitors, of whom 130,000 were counted for the World War I centenary anniversary year of 2014, up from 95,000 in 2013.[83] The somewhat lower figures for the Péronne Historial were presented in the French press as a battle between two war museums in which the Péronne museum was seen as a place of meditation and reflection, more oriented toward academics and a university clientele, with the new Meaux installation depicted more as a site for "understanding," oriented more toward the lower school grades, with more interactive technology and possibly a connection to the nearby Euro Disney as well.[84] The centenary of the 1914 war, however, also boosted attendance at Péronne, which rose to 120,000 in 2014 from approximately 80,000 for each of the preceding years.[85] Many of the visitors to both museums were schoolchildren brought in class visits to the sites.

Tourism Imaginaries in the Interwar Years

With an increase in tourism in the early twentieth century, its role as an economic force gained growing political recognition. In 1910 the French government established an Office national du tourisme, under the Ministry of Public Works, to encourage tourism. Legislation in 1919 helped organize spas, health resorts, and tourist centers. In 1929 a high commissioner and undersecretary for tourist traffic was named, and a ministerial commission was established to help regulate the tourist trade.[86] Interwar democratization of tourism was facilitated by the introduction of two-week paid vacations (congés payés) by the Popular Front government, paralleled by the Opera nazionale dopolavoro (OND, or National Recreational Club) in Fascist Italy and the Kraft durch Freude (KdF, or Strength through Joy) in Nazi Germany, as governments began to assume responsibility for promoting tourism and increasing its availability to broader strata of their populations. Tourism imaginaries, the domain of the upper leisured social classes in the Belle Époque years, became increasingly a part of the cultural images and expectations of middle- and working-class populations as well. Even if some of the tourism narratives would shift following the defeat of 1940, the basic structure was in place, to be further refined by the tourism of the *entre deux guerres,* the interwar years.

The period between the two world wars produced tourism images of France that became the property of many in the middle and working classes as well as the elites who had enjoyed the tourism of the Belle Époque. By the time of the Second World War, the imagery of France as a "must see" tourist destination, prized for its culture and its food, had been burnished in the interwar years, democratized by the increased availability of automobiles for domestic tourists and the beginnings of airplane flights for those from abroad. France remained in the center of the tourist imaginary for Americans who came to visit and stayed as expatriates, such as the Paris circle of Ernest Hemingway, Gertrude Stein, and Josephine Baker, among others, and for the German journalist Friedrich Sieburg, whose book *Gott in Frankreich? Ein Versuch,* first published in 1929, would evoke many Germans' images of France, to reappear again during the Second World War. Guidebooks such as the *Guides bleus* series spelled out in great detail the contours of the images of France. Soldiers, whether German in the years between 1940 and 1944 or Allied in the years that followed, could meaningfully see themselves as tourists in France.

With the spread of the telephone, electricity as a general source of power, the phonograph, and the inexpensive box camera, tourism, formerly largely restricted to small groups of social elites, expanded and deepened, ultimately becoming the single largest revenue-producing system of surplus value in many parts of the world in the second half of the twentieth century. Cycling and pedestrianism, or hiking in the countryside, increased, leading to a boom during the interwar years. Whereas prior to 1914 the automobile had been something of a fashionable plaything for the truly affluent, it became much more a means of transportation for the middle classes during the interwar years. Now available to young married couples, it emerged as the vehicle for family vacations in the mountains or at the seashore.[87]

The youth hostel movement and vacation colonies, as well as organizations such as the Touring club de France, increased exponentially in France. More roads meant more money for farmers, and trains meant more people moving at lower cost, creating more wealth across the country. France's *auberges de jeunesse* and Germany's *Jugendherberge,* their youth hostels, helped create local industries of hotels, taverns, and guidebooks. Larger numbers of organized wandering youth improved the level of safety overall, critical for the growth of tourism. Rather than wandering aimlessly, people clustered in villages, many in the mountains, such as Chamonix or Mont-Dore, creating safer concentrations in the countryside. The Touring Club worked to establish heritage (*patrimoine*) status at mountain lookout sites such as the Puy-de-Dôme observation terrace in the Auvergne in 1928 and the Aiguille du Midi, near Mont Blanc, in 1930. Mountain resorts such as Chamonix drew tourists for winter holidays, many taking part in ski vacations. Funiculars transported vacationers high up in the mountains on their way to the ski slopes, offering spectacular views. Grand hotels opened, as in the Val d'Isère in 1931. In his study of French vacations, André Rauch notes that the magazine *L'Illustration* in its issue of 23 December 1937, reported fifty-one express trains leaving the Gare de Lyon in Paris, transporting some 25,000 people, mainly skiers, to Saint-Gervais and Sallanches, near Mont Blanc. In one day, some sixty-nine trains headed for the Alps.[88]

In 1935, a Commissariat au tourisme was set up, extending the mission of the high commissioner and undersecretary for tourist traffic, established six years earlier. Paid vacations, together with the developing *auberges de jeunesse,* fostered touring in and becoming acquainted with the various regions of one's own country, even if relatively few traveled very far for their vacations.[89] The Dopolavoro in Fascist Italy and the Kraft durch Freude in Nazi Germany were both organized with agendas to enhance sentiments of national community through tourism. In Italy, working through the Ente nazionale italiano per il turismo (Italian National Agency for Tourism, or ENIT), the government promoted tourism from France and elsewhere. A pamphlet published in 1936, for example, took the form of a young Italian member of the Balilla, the Fascist organization for youth ages eight to fourteen, inviting a young French boy to visit Italy. Blending ancient and Renaissance sites with the "new" Italy of Mussolini, the pamphlet featured Florence, Venice, Genoa, Siena, Rome, and Naples, among other locations.[90] In conjunction with the KdF, Hitler promoted the Volkswagen, in theory a touring car for all Germans, though few were able to purchase one prior to the Second World War.[91] The *Autobahnen,* built with military objectives in mind, would later serve the interests of a growing tourist industry. Even the Soviet Union, despite its Marxist preoccupation with labor—at least in theory—created Intourist as a travel association during the interwar years. These changes across Europe nurtured local industries such as hotels, taverns, and guidebooks. Added to this mix were the youth hostels and student tours abroad.[92]

City people in France, even if a minority, left for vacations in the countryside, where in many cases facilities had not been updated to handle the new visitors. Vacationers themselves had to learn how to vacation.[93] As Julian Jackson points out, the tourism encouraged by the Popular Front "was not only a distraction it was also a discovery of France and French history."[94] During the years that followed, a plethora of scout, youth hostel, and Touring Club facilities, and *colonies de vacances*, corresponding to the German *Jugendherberge*, stimulated the tourist trade, especially among young people. More than five thousand *colonies* enrolled over 100,000 children in France.[95] Student exchanges, by contrast, were slower to develop. In 1929, only seven German students were studying in French institutions of higher education, and seven French students did the same in Germany.[96]

The interwar years produced the Paris that still dominates the tourist imagination in much of the world, the Paris of the years between Hemingway and Jean-Paul Sartre, of small automobiles and black-and-white films. Even during the First World War, the renown of Paris as a tourist site grew. As before the First World War, France as a whole, and Paris in particular, were reflected as tourist attractions in film. Before 1939, more films appear to have been made about France abroad than actually in France or other Francophone countries, according to the IMDb listings, meaning that much of the tourist imaginary of France depicted in cinema was international. Not surprisingly, given its centrality, Paris accounts for some half to two thirds of the films with place-names in their titles during this period.

With the end of the First World War, Anglophone films such as *Paris the Beautiful* in 1918 and *Paris at Midnight, So This Is Paris*, and *That Model from Paris*, all produced in 1926, and *They Had to See Paris*, in 1929, burnished the image of the city. It was the era of the films, the most important of which was *La madone des Sleepings* (The Madonna of the Sleeping Cars), released by Pathé in 1929 and based on Maurice Dekobra's 1925 novel of the same name. With a lurid cover, *La madone des Sleepings*, which could be found prominently displayed on virtually every bookstall, was a story of prostitution and romance on the French night sleeper, the Blue Train (le Train Bleu), inaugurated in 1922 to link Paris with southern France, the Midi. The Blue Train also gave its name to a restaurant that still exists in the Gare de Lyon.[97] In addition, it served large numbers of English tourists visiting the Riviera, encapsulated in English-language advertisements, such as one urging, "Summer on the French Riviera by the Blue Train."[98] European colonialism opened much of Africa and Asia to Western tourism during the interwar years, the great age of luxury steamships, regions increasingly accessible by steamship and rail, even if more Europeans "toured" these areas in the Paris pavilions of the 1931 French Colonial Exhibition than actually traveled to these faraway lands.[99]

The year 1926 saw the beginning of the *Guide Michelin*'s restaurant ratings, to be followed by its star system in 1931. Although there were earlier guides, with somewhat regular publication by the mid-nineteenth century, and the Touring club de France had promoted regional gastronomy, the *Guides Michelin,* especially with their star system, set the twentieth-century model for gastronomic tourism.[100] In addition to enhancing the tourism renown of the top restaurants of Paris, already on the tourist circuit since the Belle Époque, the coming of the automobile after World War I impacted the French gastronomic circuit by making the regions and their cuisines more accessible to more people. Regional gastronomy was touted with the publication of the twenty-eight-volume *La France gastronomique: Guides des merveilleuses culinaires et des bonnes auberges françaises* by Maurice-Edmond Sailland, better known as Curnonsky, and Marcel Rouff, from 1921 through 1928.[101] Curnonsky enjoyed tremendous success; his books on French regional cuisine helped put Lyon on the tourist map, and the French government honored him repeatedly. In the mid-1930s, the *appellation contrôlée* laws were extended, and the seventeenth- and eighteenth-century Chevaliers du Tastevins, or wine tasters with their colorful red costumes and pageantry, were reestablished in 1934 in Burgundy.[102] As André Rauch wrote, the tourist could travel to different regions to sample the local wine and food, "to savor the spirit of a region, to taste the soul of a country."[103] M. F. K. (Mary Frances Kennedy) Fisher (1908–1992), a young American writer, was able to drive through France in the 1930s and acquaint American readers with French regional cuisine.

With the increased accessibility of the regions, sunbathing also surged in popularity between the wars. The growing reputation of Deauville as a tourist attraction was reflected in the Jean Delannoy film *Paris Deauville* in 1934.[104] For industrial workers laboring indoors rather than outdoors, a suntan acquired a new meaning. Previously, the skin of workers had been bronzed by their agricultural labor in the fields, giving a lighter skin tone higher social prestige. Now, according to Marc Boyer, the shift in their workplace to factories gave outdoor tanning (*bronzage*) a special status, the appearance of returning to work after a vacation at the sea or in the mountains. The French now looked to Saint-Tropez, Saint-Paul de Vence, and Vallauris on the Côte d'Azur as leisure destinations.[105]

Film and Tourism in the Interwar Years

In addition to the films about Paris already mentioned, Charlie Chaplin wrote and directed the drama *A Woman of Paris,* an American film, in 1923. In France, Paris as a theme was highlighted by René Clair in *Paris qui dort* (Paris Asleep) in 1925, and *Sous les toits de Paris* (Under the Roofs of Paris), which appeared five years later. Marcel Carné's *Hotel du Nord* depicted the social ambiance in the neighborhood around the Canal Saint-Martin in 1938. *They Had to See Paris,* produced in 1929 and mentioned previously, is the story of an Oklahoma mechanic who suddenly acquires great wealth and is directed by his wife to go to Paris to gain "culture" and meet "the right kind of people." Tourist motifs are featured in 1920s films such as *Queen of the Moulin Rouge* and *Notre Dame d'Amour,* both in 1922, and *The Hunchback of Notre Dame* in 1923. Montmartre is well represented in the mid-1920s with titles that include *Das Spielzeug von Paris,* an Austrian film released in English as *Red Heels* and in French as *Célimène, la poupée de Montmartre,* both in 1925; and *The Girl from Montmartre* in 1926. In 1927, *Le Mystère de la Tour Eiffel* was produced. The year 1931 saw the appearance of *The Spirit of Notre Dame, Night in Montmartre, Faubourg Montmartre, Rive Gauche,* and *Der Raub der Mona Lisa* (The Theft of the Mona Lisa). The fictional Chinese American detective Charlie Chan visited in 1935 in *Charlie Chan in Paris.* Films such as *Rendez-vous aux Champs-Élysées,* in 1937 and *Remontons les Champs-Élysées,* in 1938 suggest a return to specific tourist sites from the grand period of the Belle Époque.[106] Not surprisingly, the film titles reflected the sites most frequently found in the tourist guidebooks.

The IMDb lists five films with "Folies-Bergère" in their title released during the interwar years. *Die Frauen von Folies Bergères* was a German film that appeared in 1927. Three years later, in 1930, Josephine Baker appeared in a short promotional film, *Le pompier des Folies Bergères* (The Fireman of the Folies-Bergère), the story of a firefighter who, after attending a show at the Folies, sees visions of naked women wherever he goes. In 1935, two films titled *Folies-Bergère,* and featuring Maurice Chevalier, appeared, one in France, the other in the United States. Last of the Folies-Bergère listings in the IMDb is *Bar aux Folies-Bergère,* released in 1938 in the United Kingdom.[107] Not least in spreading the fame of the Folies-Bergère during the interwar years were Josephine Baker's dance performances, one featuring a costume consisting of sixteen bananas strung into a skirt.

Beyond Paris, the IMDb lists films with titles including *A Visit to St. Michel, France,* shortly after the end of the war in 1919, and *Chartres* in 1923. The interwar films reflected the increasing mobility by train and eventually automobile within France. Four films, three in German, addressed Nice: *À propos de Nice* and *Nizza,* both listed for 1930; *Flucht nach Nizza* (Flight to Nice) in 1933; and *Blumen aus Nizza* (Flowers from Nice) in 1936. German interest also carried into the mountains, as in the film *Stürme über dem Mont Blanc* (Storms over Mont Blanc) of 1930. Film titles during the 1930s also referenced the Côte d'Azur, Biarritz, and Lyon.[108]

Americans in Paris during the Interwar Years

The interwar Paris mystique was the result in part of the Americans living there at the time. The lives and adventures of the Left Bank literary expatriate community, recounted in Hemingway's memoir *A Moveable Feast*, included James Joyce, Gertrude Stein, Josephine Baker, Sylvia Beach and her Shakespeare and Company bookshop, and others associated with the "Lost Generation," although they were not the only Americans involved with France and its capital. Discussing Stein, Shari Benstock wrote, "Paris provided a creative stimulus not available anywhere in America, not even in New York."[109] Flush with money, especially at a time when the French franc was largely devalued in contrast with the American dollar, Americans followed the increasing migration of Hollywood films and US advertising to France and elsewhere in Europe. Emblematic of the 1920s interest in France was the publicity surrounding Charles Lindbergh's transatlantic flight to Paris. As Brooke Lindy Blower notes, many used Paris as a jumping-off point to travel to other places in Europe. While some, she adds, came to start new lives in Paris, most came as tourists. Although the French tended to see their society as modern, the Americans visited in large measure to view the culture of the nineteenth century, specifically "art museums, cafés, picturesque streets, and wide boulevards."[110]

Americans of the Lost Generation helped in the "discovery" of the Côte d'Azur. Hemingway, John Dos Passos, and F. Scott and Zelda Fitzgerald toured from Montparnasse to Monte Carlo, effectively publicizing along the way Juan-les-Pins on the Riviera, "launched" by "the American Montparnasse Group."[111] The wealthy American Frank Jay Gould established casinos and spa towns along the Riviera. Hotels extended their seasons from winter to summer to accommodate the new tourists. Cannes in 1929 opened a summer casino and remained unrivaled in luster on the Riviera through the next decade.[112] Gould's wife, Florence, also hosted salons during the interwar years and after in Paris.[113] When the effects of the 1929 depression dimmed the Côte d'Azur casinos that had featured dancing the fox-trot, the Boston, and the Charleston, and films starring Douglas Fairbanks Sr. and Jackie Coogan, among others, the area's chief appeal became sunbathing.

A German View: Friedrich Sieburg and *God in France?*

Generally speaking, Germans admired French culture yet vilified what they saw as French decadence. By the interwar years, France had come to be seen as a land of romance and sex, as in the dancing girls of the Folies-Bergère.[114]

This interwar interest informed the views of would-be Francophiles such as the journalist and literary critic Friedrich Sieburg, whose *Gott in Frankreich?*, published in 1929, depicted the timelessness of "eternal" France while lamenting its unchanging backwardness. *Gott in Frankreich?* was translated the following year into French as *Dieu est-il français?* (Is God French?).[115] Republished in German in 1930, 1931, and 1932, with a new version and preface in 1935, two years after the rise of the Nazis to power, the book was also brought out in both German and French editions during the Occupation years and again in both languages in the 1990s. Sieburg's question "Dieu est-il français?" long retained a certain currency in France. It was quoted in *Le Monde* in 2001 and again in *La Tribune* in 2009.[116] According to Cecilia von Buddenbrock, Sieburg's biographer, *Gott in Frankreich?* established his fame as an author and marked the image of France in Germany for an entire generation.[117] Wolfgang Geiger, a student of images of France under the Third Reich, maintained: "Whoever is concerned with the image of France in the Third Reich must surely begin with Friedrich Sieburg. For a long time he alone and his representation of France attracted well-researched studies. Although it had already appeared in 1929, no other book influenced the Germans' image of France after 1933 also as *Gott in Frankreich?*"[118] In the words of Julia S. Torrie, "Perhaps the most prominent 'expert' on France was Friedrich Sieburg, whose work remained influential through the occupation."[119]

A journalistic account of the apparently profound national differences between Germany and France, *Gott in Frankreich?* is a significant example of the essentializing discourse that portrays another culture as the "other." Sieburg's writing has been described as *feuilleton,* meaning journalistic for the general reader, in a dilettante style, although he indeed studied the subjects about which he wrote. Yet he noted that his travel writing "did not in the least represent research and that it would be suggested not to represent it as such."[120] From 1921 through 1925, Sieburg contributed articles on theater to *Die Weltbühne* (The World Stage) and in 1923 went to Copenhagen, where he began to write for the *Frankfurter Zeitung.* In May 1926 he became its correspondent in Paris, where he emerged as the most prominent German journalist.[121] Sieburg later wrote that he had not gone to Paris from any inner desire but because the *Frankfurter Zeitung* had sent him there.[122]

Fascinated by France, he nonetheless saw its economy, politics, and culture as anachronistic. By the late 1920s, his politics aligned with the *völkisch* conservative revolutionary Tat-Kreis (Action Circle) around Hans Zehrer, who had participated in the Kapp Putsch, an abortive right-wing attempt to overthrow the newly established Weimar Republic in 1920. Sieburg greeted Hitler's rise to power as a positive sign of national self-consciousness but also a "fearful deception." His essay "Es werde Deutschland," published in 1932, in French as "Défense du nationalisme allemande," and in English as "Germany: My Country" the following year, which contained a passage criticizing anti-Semitism, was censored by the German government.[123]

During the 1930s Sieburg traveled to Africa, Portugal, and Japan for the *Frankfurter Zeitung*. Reflecting about the French on his travels in Africa, he regretted "the stubborn determination of this great people" who never were able to understand and improve relations with Germany in time.[124] In the interwar French quest for security from a potential German threat against the Versailles peace settlement through alliances and behind the Maginot Line, Sieburg saw the weakness of an antiquated French civilization as opposed to a vibrant and young Germany. He drew a sharp contrast between what he termed "static France" and "dynamic Germany," a concept dating back to the contrast between Roman-French and German ideas in Fichte's 1808 *Addresses to the German Nation*.[125] The French, he argued, were possessed of a pessimism that dated back to Pascal.[126]

The expression "to live like God in France" has a history that has been traced back to the Holy Roman emperor Maximilian I (1459–1519), who is said to have been envious of royal absolutism in France and possibly the lifestyle there as well.[127] The French translation of 1930 had established a French market for Sieburg's work, and he then continued writing for both German and French markets, although, as Margot Taureck notes, Sieburg's statement in the 1929 German edition regretting that France was no longer capable of creating political formations suited to the ideals of the modern world was omitted in the French translation of 1930.[128]

Sieburg depicted France much as a tourist circuit, and indeed, his view of France shared continuities with interwar and even earlier German views of France. He begins in Domrémy, the birthplace of Joan of Arc, who in the centuries since her having been ignored in Estienne's *Guide des chemins de France* had risen to an emblematic status in France. "All roads leading to the heart of the French being should begin with Joan," he wrote.[129] Employing the metaphor of the human body, Sieburg defined an itinerary of Paris that resembled the tourist circuit in place from the beginning of the twentieth century. The artery of Paris was the Seine; the heart was the Île de la Cité, on which Notre-Dame is situated; the lungs were the Bois de Boulogne and the Bois de Vincennes; the artistically curved nervous system was the network of the exterior boulevards; and the skin was the belt of roads around the city.[130] Using a reference later employed by Hitler and others, he described the Eiffel Tower as "a tower of Babylon in metal [built] in 1889," having become a garden decoration "a little out of date" in 1929.[131] In terms that would later be echoed by Hitler and propaganda minister Joseph Goebbels, Sieburg described Montmartre as "one of the most peaceful villages of France but also the most brilliant and perverted place in the world."[132] His depiction of France drew criticism in both France and Germany. Writing for *Le Figaro* in 1930, André Rousseaux described *Gott in Frankreich?* as non-objective, clichéd, and frivolous. In Germany, Paul Distelbarth in 1936 described it as a work of a "salon" milieu with scarcely any reference to the French people.[133]

In his essentializing portraits of "the Frenchman," Sieburg stereotyped the French, implying that they all bore the qualities he described. He also decontextualized French history by emphasizing France's forests and the countryside at the expense of its technological development. His perspectives were based on images of France already present in German culture, often disseminated in tourist literature. Germans had a long history of touring, even during wartime, as studied by Charlotte Heymel, who wrote about the personal diaries and travel accounts of civilians visiting the western front for various reasons during the First World War, with descriptions that often reflected stereotypes of Germany's enemies.[134] Sieburg's images of France fit clearly into the perspectives of the Comité franco-allemand (Deutsch-französische Studiengesellschaft), established by conservative circles in both countries in 1926, and at whose meetings he later gave presentations.[135]

Interwar French Tourist Images: The *Guides bleus*

Sieburg's vision of France, mixed as it was, as well as those of so many of the American expatriates and short-term tourists to that country, reflected the emergence of an image of France both domestically and internationally as a tourist mecca, in which the self-images of many there were intertwined with that of the country as a tourism center, creating, in other words, a self-referential tourism imaginary. This French touristic imaginary during the interwar years was encapsulated in tourism guidebooks, of which excellent examples were the *Guides bleus,* begun in 1910 as successors of the *Guides de voyage Joanne,* which had been published from 1841 through 1916. Catering to an extended tourism clientele, the *Guides bleus* were among the first to offer tourist routes based on roads for automobiles. André Rauch notes that they emphasized two characteristics necessary for a good tour. One was the choice of routes to maximize the use of time; the other was the cultural interest of "tourist curiosities," determining the time spent in gazing at them.[136]

The 1938 edition of the guide to France is a densely packed eight-hundred-page encyclopedia of roads, hotels, restaurants, and sites. Its title, *Guide bleu*

France automobile en un volume (Automobile Blue Guide to France in One Volume), makes clear its modernity in its focus on automobile tourism. The dust jacket touts it as a "sensational innovation for the automobile driver" that offers "all of France at hand [*sous la main*]." With hundreds of driving itineraries and thousands of sites mentioned, the *Guide* stands as a monument to France as a tourist image. Heavy emphasis is placed on itineraries and sites related to France's political and ecclesiastical history, but natural sites including seascapes, beaches, and mountain vistas are also enumerated. The word "picturesque" appears frequently in connection with old towns and rural landscapes. There are also references to local food and, occasionally, dress, festivals, and sports, as I discuss shortly. What emerges, however, from the totality of the *Guide* illuminates the process by which the history of France, especially in the political and ecclesiastical sequences, had been transformed into a constructed tourism itinerary, referred to as a "must see" by Dean MacCannell, by the close of the interwar years.[137] Whereas the 1552 *Guide des chemins de France* had stated as its mission to help religious pilgrims find their way to sacred sites, the interwar *Guides bleus* focused on leisure touring by automobile.[138] Published by Hachette, the 1938 edition for France contained 550 itineraries. Reflecting the centrality of Paris, the *Guide bleu*, like the *Guide des chemins de France*, began with a section on the capital, then divided the rest of France into seven zones: the north and east, Burgundy and Franche-Comté, Auvergne and the center, the Alps and southeast, the west, the southwest, and the Pyrenees.[139]

Paris, according to the *Guide bleu*, was the most densely populated city in the world, and despite the "incomparable diversity of its provinces," France was the most highly centralized country. The cultural, political, and economic center of France, "Paris has never ceased to hold this essential role at the head of Western civilization and its prestige of radiating throughout the entire world." Starting with the place du Châtelet in the center of Paris, the *Guide* highlighted the Île de la Cité; the Palais de Justice with the Conciergerie, where prisoners were held during the French Revolution; the Notre-Dame cathedral; and the Île Saint-Louis. Following the model of the *Guide des chemins de France*, the *Guide bleu* listed many Parisian religious sites, including Notre-Dame, the Sainte-Chapelle, and the Saint-Julien-le-Pauvre and Saint-Augustine churches, as well as more secular sites that might be said to have acquired a sacred identity, such as the Arc de Triomphe, the Panthéon, the Conciergerie, and the Invalides.[140]

Other recommended sites for visitors in the *Guide bleu* included Montmartre and the Sacré-Cœur basilica, itself built as a place of religious pilgrimage. The *Guide bleu* had little to say about Montmartre, except for a brief

reference to one flank of the butte, the "Montmartre of festivities," where
the nightclubs were located. At the summit of Montmartre, the highest point
in Paris, Sacré-Cœur, whose construction began in 1875, offered an immense
panorama of Paris.[141] Years later, Raymond Jonas addressed the irony of
locating the basilica in the same Montmartre district that helped give Paris
the reputation of "the Great Babylon," referenced by Sieburg, although, as
we have seen, Sieburg may have had the Tower of Babel in mind.[142] Sieburg's
trope of a modern Paris steeped in depravity in the image of the ancient city
of Babylon would reappear again during Hitler's visit to the city in June 1940.
The *Trésor de la langue française* mentions an earlier dictionary reference of
1838 to ancient Babylon as signifying in Scripture "a place of disorder and
crimes."[143] In *Le Club des valets de coeur,* in 1858, one of his novels centering
on the fictional character Rocambole, Pierre Alexis Ponson du Terrail has
another of the protagonists say: "Oh, Paris! Paris! You are the true Babylon, the true battlefield of intelligence, the true temple where evil has its
religion and pontiffs, and I believe that the breath of the Archangel of Dark-
ness passes eternally over you like the breezes on the infinity of the seas."[144]
Writing in 1863, Pierre-Joseph Proudhon complained that Paris had lost its
municipal authority under Napoleon III and that it had become a politically
impotent carnival. "Paris with all its luxury," he wrote, "is only a Babylon. It
will end as did Babylon."[145]

The religious pilgrimages to Montmartre—the Mountain of the Martyrs—
combined with the image of Paris-Babylon helped heighten the sense of
tourist frisson on the part of visitors from elsewhere in France and abroad.
Jonas points out that religious pilgrimage was often accompanied by more
mundane pleasures associated with leisure secular tourism in the quarter.
This was evidenced by the increased numbers of visitors to Sacré-Cœur during high season summer months and, ironically, during the 1889 Exposition
held to commemorate the centennial of the 1789 Revolution.[146] Continuing
its tour through Paris, the *Guide bleu* offered a brief history of the Trocadéro
Palace, noting that it was built for the 1878 Exposition and had been newly
remodeled for that of 1937. The Eiffel Tower, "for a long time controversial,
has become one of the essential elements of the Paris landscape and one of
the most universally known monuments."[147] Unlike in earlier guidebooks,
such as the *Guide des chemins de France,* museums play a significant role in the
1938 *Guide bleu.* An extensive, more than two-page discussion of the Louvre,
"our first national museum," leads the visitor, with reference to specific artists, through its halls and galleries.[148]

In the *Guide bleu,* most itineraries start from Paris with descriptions
of the roads, hotels, and restaurants en route. Maps of cities and towns

supplement the text. Again, churches, monuments, and museums figure prominently. Not surprisingly, World War I battlefields and monuments appear frequently in the section of the *Guide* on the northeast. It gives an asterisk, denoting a site worthy of special attention, to the Carrefour de l'Armistice, on the route from Beauvais to the 1918 Compiègne site where the armistice of November 1918 was signed. World War I battlefields described in the *Guide* include Meaux, the site of the French victory in the Battle of the Marne in September 1918; an American monument at the First World War battleground of Château Thierry; and the Argonne Forest battlefield. A paragraph is devoted to the history of the 1916 Verdun battle, followed by a full-page description of three battlefield itineraries at the site. A section devoted to the Auvergne and central France makes frequent reference to the waters of the many spas in the region, including Vichy, La Bourboule, and Le Mont-Dore, to name only three. Pilgrimages, both religious and more secular, continue to play a role in the *Guide*'s suggested itineraries. The two themes are juxtaposed with a reference to a religious pilgrimage along the "Route Napoléon," a suggested itinerary from Grenoble to Nice. Along this route, one might make a religious pilgrimage from the town of Gap to the church at Notre-Dame-de-Laus, where Benoîte Rencourel was said to have had a vision of the Virgin in 1664. There was a hotel near the church that accommodated pilgrims.[149]

Not surprisingly, as the *Guide* turned to mountain and beach destinations, more of its text addressed the natural attractions and related sporting activities at the various sites. Nice, it pointed out, had become a year-round destination with the development of its summer season added to its festivals. With excursions into the nearby Alps, one could visit Nice and pursue sports, including skiing and alpinism, according to the season. In its more detailed description of Nice, which parallels the relative proliferation of films made about the city during the interwar years, the *Guide* offered a long list of events that included costume balls, horse racing, and water festivals, among others. The *Guide* also devoted several pages to Corsica, which had become accessible by ferry. In the section on the southwest, the political history of France reemerges in Chantonnay, where, the tourist is informed, insurgents in the Vendée killed some six thousand defenders of the Republic in September 1793. Unlike the other sections, the last section of the *Guide,* devoted to the Pyrenees, describes itineraries beginning in Bordeaux rather than Paris. It mentions Biarritz as the most sophisticated seaside resort on the Atlantic Coast, with its notoriety dating to the Second Empire. Lourdes is characterized as "the most celebrated pilgrimage in Christianity" with more than 500,000 visitors annually.[150]

Paris: A Tourism Icon in Interwar France

The tourism iconicity of France that emerged during the Belle Époque and interwar years was due in large measure to the role played by Paris as a—or perhaps *the*—cultural capital, again to paraphrase Benjamin, in the tourism imaginaries of many. Paris imagery was expressed largely in its monuments, such as the Arc de Triomphe and the Eiffel Tower. The Paris that emerges in the *Guide bleu* series, exemplified by the volume devoted to the city published during the Exposition year of 1937, is a city that had grown since the Belle Époque and that, in the purview of the guidebook, now included the nearby suburbs as well. These, it noted, offered important attractions such as the Vincennes War Museum, the Saint-Denis basilica, the Sèvres Museum, and the parks in Saint-Cloud and Sceaux. It continued: "One can find there [in the nearby suburbs] many interesting remnants of the past, historic and literary memories of the past, and also visit urban achievements there, modern constructions, and remarkable technical creations, of which many are brought to light here for the first time."[151]

Like the *Guide bleu* for France as a whole, the edition for Paris emphasizes the uniqueness of the city, noting that François I had already called Paris "a world, not a city" in the sixteenth century. A description of the city dating to the late eleventh-century account of Jean de Garlande is mentioned in a note by G. Lenôtre, "Before Visiting Paris." The *Guides bleus Paris* also addresses Antoine de Rombise's *Voyage à Paris*, published in 1635, and *l'Ulysse français*, published eight years later. Lenôtre informs the reader that Paris possesses a unique charm recognized by the entire world, difficult to analyze because each individual is affected in his or her own unique way. The best way to see Paris, he continues, is to walk around and let one's imagination be swept away at virtually each step by the tragic or grand events that took place in its history, for example, "as one passes the old gate where Henry IV's carriage passed when the good king was assassinated" in 1610.[152] In his elegy to Paris, Lenôtre cites two Germans, Goethe and Alexander von Humboldt, the former praising Paris as a universal city, the center of all the realms of nature, all accessible for study, where Molière, Voltaire, and Diderot all lived and worked, and the latter saying that only in Paris did he feel really alive.[153] The spirit of Paris and its working people, who might appear unruly and ungovernable, Lenôtre writes, could be absorbed only slowly, and he criticizes tourists who spend a short time there, then return home and castigat it as the "modern Babylon" or the "House of Satan," after seeing just a small proportion of the city and not its majority of laboring people. Tourists, Lenôtre continues, wish to see only the "exterior" qualities of Paris. They no longer care about the factories that had been novelties in Rousseau's day, when manual labor was valued and industry was new, attracting more visitors than did palaces or museums. "The soul of Paris" is meaningful, Lenôtre concludes, only to the visitor who has spent some time in "the enchanting city." He ends by advising the tourist not to leave before "satisfying all the forms of his intelligent curiosity."[154]

Following Lenôtre's "Before Visiting Paris" section, the Guides bleus Paris offers a discussion devoted to "General Information," followed by six more chapters. The first presents a general description of the city in twenty-three different itineraries. Chapter 2 focuses on Notre-Dame and religious structures, chapter 3 on the Louvre and the main museums, and chapter 4 on "main collections or libraries." Chapter 5 is devoted to the principal cemeteries and catacombs, and chapter 6 to "Greater Paris," the nearby suburbs. The "General Information" section offers advice about the different seasons in Paris and the various ways of arriving in the city. An introductory chapter lists restaurants and hotels by category. Altogether, the "General Information" section is subdivided into chapters on topics including theaters, music halls, cinema, shows, painting, music, fashion, religious sites, "intellectual Paris," tourism, sports, and monuments, among others. Contemporary art is highlighted, as in the note that Paris attracts foreign artists such as Pablo Picasso and Kees van Dongen, who with others had formed the École de Paris, and that Igor Stravinsky was playing an innovative role in music similar to Picasso's in painting.[155]

Fashion was another "must see" in Paris. In the words of the Guides bleus Paris, "There is no domain in which Paris is more a universal capital." Although the new meridian may pass through Greenwich, the guidebook continues, "the meridian of fashion still passes through the rue de la Paix." Several couturier houses are then listed.[156] The chapter on religion lists current houses of worship, and "intellectual Paris" devoted to bookstores, newspapers, lectures, and courses that one might take. The "tourism" chapter focuses on tourist associations where the visitor might obtain information. The Touring club de France; the Club alpin de France; the Centre national d'expansion, du tourisme, du thermalisme et du climatisme; the Bureau national du tourisme; the Union des fédérations des syndicats d'initiative de France, colonies et protectorats; and the Union national des fédérations all are mentioned as covering one aspect or another of tourism.[157] A number of these organizations, however, especially the last, are depicted as more oriented toward promoting the tourism trade as a whole than catering to the individual visitor, bringing to mind again the differences in analyzing the interests of the tourism industry on one hand and, on the other, the aesthetic perspectives of the many varied individual tourists as they imagined and viewed the various sites.

Similar to the *Guide bleu* for all France, the *Guides bleus Paris* is replete with descriptions and histories of the various sites it includes. Assembled by a team, the *Guides bleus Paris* is a wealth of information and factoids of all sorts about Paris and its history as of its publication date. One learns, for example, that the Odéon theater and the Palais Garnier opera house were the only two completely freestanding theaters in the city. One of its longer passages describes the Jardin des Plantes, including a map of the botanical gardens and a discussion of famous people, including Marie-Antoinette, who visited. In its description of the nearby area, the *Guides bleus Paris* mentions the mosque, but only in passing, choosing instead to describe in greater detail several of the historic houses around it. It describes the venerable Les Halles quarter as evoking more than any other part of the city the old commercial Paris and adds that the Saint-Eustache church is the city's second-most beautiful, behind only Notre-Dame. In one of its many literary references, the *Guides bleus Paris* mentions that the food market at Les Halles inspired Émile Zola to call it the "ventre de Paris [Paris's stomach]." In another literary reference, the *Guides* notes that Victor Hugo evoked the area around the rue Saint-Martin, the scene of a republican insurrection against the government of Louis-Philippe in 1832, in his novel *Les Misérables*.[158]

Not surprisingly, given the then recent experience of the First World War, the *Guides bleus Paris* devotes considerable attention to military monuments, such as the Hôtel des Invalides, described as "the most glorious place in Paris," which held the army museum and Napoleon's tomb, and the Arc de Triomphe. The Champs-Élysées receives considerable attention as the center for much of the high-end shopping, and because it, and seemingly all the major avenues, lead to the "enormous mass" of the Arc de Triomphe, which rises above the place de l'Étoile. The visitor is advised to get a map to see how the twelve major boulevards radiate from the arch, or to view them from an airplane if one is unable to climb the steps to the top. The arch, the *Guides bleus* continues, is at the center of the urban design of the entire region. In the few pages devoted to Montmartre, the *Guides* noted vast changes in the quarter since the end of the First World War. For some, the name Montmartre evoked a community of artists, for others its "nocturnal pleasures," and for yet others a feeling of religious piety—"the place where the spirit breathes," in the words of Maurice Barrès, quoted in the *Guides*, which also mentioned the construction of the Sacré-Cœur basilica following the war of 1870. Montmartre, however, was changing. The place du Tertre, the old village's public square, with its ancient trees and provincial allure, was still picturesque, but it was already being invaded in the evenings by luxurious automobiles awaiting the diners in the neighboring restaurants there, the *Guide* indicated with an apparent tone of regret. The Montparnasse section of Paris was described as being akin to Montmartre, a special sort of place. It had now become (in the 1930s) a center for artists and avant-garde groups, a kind of "cosmopolitan Bohemia" with as many nightclubs as in Montmartre. In contrast, the southeastern section of the city was the place to visit to see elements of the "new Paris." Specific mention was made of the then new Air Museum and the Air Ministry.[159]

In contrast to the western side of Paris, the east had only commercial and working-class neighborhoods to show the tourist, but the *Guides bleus Paris* still recommended a walking itinerary there to see "the delicious stopping point" at the Buttes Chaumont and "the most illustrious of Parisian necropolises," the Père Lachaise cemetery. The sites considered are wide-ranging, including, for instance, the boulevard du Temple, near the place de la République in eastern Paris. The most "curious part" of this boulevard, according to the *Guides,* disappeared with the creation of the place de la République. It was nicknamed the "Boulevard of Crime" because of the "horrific dramas" performed in theaters there.[160]

The final section, devoted to "le grand Paris," reminds the reader that the suburban area had grown considerably from the time of the First World War through the coming of the economic depression in the mid-1930s, and together with a lack of planning, this had made the suburban area too "chaotic" and had contributed to a disenchantment among people living there. The description of the suburbs was, accordingly, to be less detailed than that of Paris proper. Nonetheless, there are extensive sections on the Bois de Boulogne and the Saint-Denis basilica. Vincennes was especially interesting for the tourist because it housed an important castle, the Château de Vincennes, and its park, the Bois de Vincennes.[161]

The *Guides bleus* books on France and Paris in the late 1930s show a country that had become a major tourist destination for both domestic and international travelers and one in which there was a real awareness of this identity, a "tourism imaginary" in the sense of Rachid Amirou and Noel Salazar. An English guidebook, *The Land of France,* published just prior to the war in 1939, and reviewed in France in 1941, stated that "France is inquestionably [sic] the finest touring country in the world."[162] To the economic benefits were added the enhanced status in the minds of many that came with the identification of a country that "one had to visit" to be considered culturally sophisticated in much of the Western world and an awareness of this status in France itself. The capstone of this process was the staging of the International Exposition of 1937 in Paris, at the time of the publication of the two tour books just discussed. Perhaps Ossip Pernikoff, the head of a tour company in France and technical attaché for tourism and transportation for the 1937 Exposition, best expressed this sense of enhanced imagery in the title of his book, published in 1938, *La France, pays du tourisme* (France: Country of Tourism).[163]

CHAPTER 2

Two 1940 Sites as Symbols

The Maginot Line and the Compiègne Railway Car

Events that took place with the French defeat in 1940 affecting the course of the Second World War along the Maginot Line and in Compiègne in northeastern France had complex and often subtle interrelationships with France's history and status as a tourism icon even before the war, then again as the war unfolded, and in subsequent *tourisme de mémoire*. The Maginot Line became famous as the series of fortifications along the Franco-German frontier that were intended to block any German military advance into France.[1] W. Somerset Maugham, on a tour through wartime France in the spring of 1940, visited one of the forts, or casemates, along the Maginot Line, which he called "that great machine."[2] After describing the good morale of the soldiers there, he added, "The war correspondents have said all there is to say about those wonderful and truly awe-inspiring constructions, with their lifts that take you deep underground, their endless passages with their useful trolleys, their electric plant and their air-conditioning, the great stores of food, their armaments and their vast supply of ammunition."[3]

With the German victory in 1940, the Maginot Line changed in meaning almost overnight from an expensive state-of-the-art network of defensive fortifications to a site of touristic curiosity on the part of the victorious Germans. Touring the newly taken fortifications was said to be "all the rage" among the Germans in June 1940; Hitler himself visited on the thirtieth of that month. Officers and journalists who followed him were given guided

Figure 2.   German Soldiers at the Maginot Line following the French defeat, June 1940. Heinrich Hoffmann, *Mit Hitler im Westen* (Munich: Verlag Heinrich Hoffmann, 1940), p. 111. Author's personal collection.

tours. To increase the impression of size, these visitors were transported slowly on the underground railway running beneath the forts. Luftwaffe officers were said to have wept openly after seeing how little damage their bombs had done.[4] Within months, however, the Maginot Line appears to have lost interest for most of the Germans, as the installations there began to deteriorate. The Maginot Line itself lost military significance when it became clear in the fall of 1940 that the center of warfare would soon move elsewhere, though in Germany books continued to be published about the line well into the war.[5]

The Maginot Line: From Military to Tourist Site

The fortresses of the Maginot Line gained new meaning after the French defeat when the phrase "Maginot mentality" came to symbolize both in France and elsewhere a kind of head-in-the-sand mindset in which one retreated behind a supposedly impregnable and expensive wall, which failed, however, to protect against disaster.[6] As early as July 1940, during the Battle of Britain, *The Economist* stated, "The efficacy of blockade is a mirage, a delusion comparable to the Maginot-complex that bemused and enervated France."[7] Anthony Kemp, a postwar historian of the line, referred to it as "with the exception of the Great Wall of China . . . the greatest system of permanent fortification ever built and probably the last," which emerged as a postwar symbol of what had gone terribly wrong.[8] An article of March 2011 in Le Point described the first two years of François Mitterrand's presidency as representing a Maginot mentality when France adopted a go-it-alone socialist policy, breaking with the United States and the European Union; and an article in Le Monde the following June suggested that because products were made with components from many different countries, the discussion of free trade versus protectionism for France had become "as obsolete as the Maginot Line, a wonder of the defensive art that the German armies superbly ignored in 1940, to the stupefaction of the French General Staff."[9] Shortly after the 13 November 2015 terror attacks in Paris, an article appeared in which Alain Bauer, a criminologist, addressing six individuals who had left France for Syria and returned unmolested, maintained, "Today we are in a Maginot Line cycle." He saw the French as very good at surveillance of French people and foreigners in France but not beyond its borders. For Belgium, the situation was exactly the reverse. The result was a network of porous frontiers that could no more contain a potential threat from beyond France's borders than did the Maginot Line in 1940.[10]

The line, however, has become significant, in the words of the historian Michaël Seramour, for the development of "contemporary military tourism," a judgment echoed in a study by the European Institute of Cultural Routes (EICR), an initiative launched in 1999 by the National Sites and Monuments Service of the Grand Duchy of Luxembourg. The EICR and Seramour gave a figure of some 300,000 visitors annually to the fortresses in 2007 and 2009, respectively.[11] Dedicated to "discovering the history of European fortification in time and space," the Luxembourg initiative sought to promote the preservation of, and by extension tourism to, the sites of "defensive architecture, from the Roman frontiers to the Maginot line or the Atlantic Wall." In the words of the EICR portal, "If one refers to statistics, tourism related to military heritage is in full expansion."[12] Now one may visit several of the Maginot Line fortresses virtually.[13]

The Maginot Line's shift from military to tourism use occurred during the 1950s, when France's changed military situation made the fortifications obsolete for defensive purposes. With the onset of the Cold War and the creation of NATO, the French military had begun to modernize the fortresses with the goal of containing a potential Soviet invasion, but the war in Algeria beginning in 1954 necessitated a redeployment of their resources.

The successful testing of France's first atomic bomb in February 1960 further rendered the Maginot Line irrelevant to French military defense needs as France shifted from a strategy of conventional defense to one of nuclear dissuasion. Progressively the French military gave up the idea of remilitarizing the Maginot Line. Various options, including converting some of the fortresses into missile bases, were discussed during the 1960s, but gradually the army ceased maintaining them.[14]

Many of the fortresses along the line were opened for tourism, and they have attracted war veterans from Germany as well as France. Some of the smaller parts of the fortifications were auctioned and found interested buyers in Germany.[15] As early as 1950, notes Seramour, the fort at La Ferté (Ardennes) was opened to the public following the construction of a monument to honor 107 of its defenders who had suffocated during a German attack on the night of 18–19 May 1940.[16] Searchers found the remains of the last seventeen of the French defenders in 1973. The fort at Fermont near Longwy was repaired by the French army shortly after the war and then abandoned in 1964. It subsequently came into the possession of private societies. In 1976 the Association de l'ouvrage du Fermont obtained access to the fort and opened it to the public the following year.[17] A series of television programs in 1965 brought the Maginot Line's new status to the attention of the French public. The army maintained the Simserhof fortifications in the Moselle department and established a museum there in 1966 with an extensive collection of artillery, shells, and related military materiel.[18]

The resignation of General de Gaulle as president in 1969 and his death the next year contributed to the turning of a page in postwar French history in which non-Gaullist representations of the wartime past, while hardly new, acquired greater currency than at any other time since 1944. The release in 1969 of Marcel Ophuls's film The Sorrow and the Pity (Le chagrin et la pitié), which dealt with the war as experienced in the city of Clermont-Ferrand and questioned the vision of a united France resisting the Nazis, showed footage of soldiers bunkered down in the Maginot fortresses in 1939 and 1940. In 1970, the government began selling some of the Maginot fortifications. Guidebooks were published in both French and German, and tours of the fortifications were used to promote Franco-German reconciliation in a postwar political atmosphere very different from that of the Occupation years.[19] In 1972, the commune of Marckolsheim acquired its local fortification, restored it, and opened it to the public. A series of histories of the line in the 1970s by Roger Bruge, starting with his Faites sauter la Ligne Maginot (Blow Up the Maginot Line) in 1973, which maintained that the forts had served France well in 1940, forcing the Germans to circumvent rather than attack them directly, gave a boost to tourism there.[20] The Bambesch fort, near Metz, then recently opened to tourists, received nearly ten thousand visitors in 1973.[21]

Following the discovery of the last defenders of La Ferté in 1973, the French government and the veterans of the German unit that had fought against them placed plaques in their honor at the site. Several of the soldiers were buried in a small military cemetery opposite the road from the bunker in which they had been entombed. A memorial ceremony is held each year for them on the Sunday closest to 19 May, the day they died in 1940. In the early 1970s the fort was bought by the Comité du souvenir des défenseurs de Villy-La Ferté (Committee to Remember the Defenders of Villy-La Ferté), which opened it to tourists.[22] During the mid-1970s, additional forts along the line, abandoned except by scavengers who removed copper from them, were purchased by private associations, sometimes in conjunction with the local municipalities, and opened to the public.

Public interest in the Maginot Line continued to develop in the 1970s with private organizations raising funds and, often in conjunction with the military authorities, restoring many of the forts. Hackenberg, the largest of the Maginot fortifications, near Metz, was the subject of a 1976 guidebook, published in both French and German. Hackenberg, it noted, had taken five and a half years to build. It reached ten kilometers in length, and at its deepest point extended ninety-six meters into the earth.[23] Published with the aid of the Association Amifort, a private group that administered the site, the guidebook described an extensive tour that included a ride on the fortification's underground railway and a climb to ground level from which the surrounding countryside could be observed.[24] In 1979 the association managing the Fermont fortification established a museum there and received an award for its work of historic restoration.[25]

The audience intended for the restored Maginot sites was clearly different from that of the official war monuments such as Oradour-sur-Glane, a village whose inhabitants were massacred by the SS in the summer of 1944. Rather than the sense of national unity sought in the Resistance sites, or mourning and victimization associated with Oradour, the Maginot fortresses gave the visitor an uncanny sensation, described in 1979 by Paul Gamelin, who wrote several books about them: "On a visit one day to an abandoned fortification, alone or in the company of others, one gets the feeling of being in another world. One could imagine being a person from the year 2000, who, having escaped a cataclysm, traveled to discover the past and visited caverns where there had lived a generation that has disappeared."[26]

Two Maginot fortresses were given official protection in the 1980s.[27] Interest in the Maginot Line appeared to mount. Tourism and commemorative activity at the fortifications tripled between 1980 and 2003, according to Seramour, and they had become major tourist attractions in both Alsace and Lorraine. In 2003 the Lorraine forts drew some 250,000 visitors.[28] Claude-Armand Masson's 1942 Maginot Line memoir was republished in 1985 and sold in souvenir stands at the sites, for example, at the Fermont fortification. Tour guides were often local volunteers, some of them war veterans. The French authorities continued to consider what to do with the fortifications. Fermont remained the property of the French army, which occasionally held military maneuvers on its grounds, as in a demonstration of 150 helicopters of the Air Mobile Division on 14 July 1986 in the presence of President Mitterrand.[29] By the late 1980s, an Association des amis du Simserhof (Association of the Friends of Simserhof) was organizing tours of the fortress.[30] As in the case of Normandy, the Maginot Line saw a proliferation of museums. Several of the restored fortifications set up museums, each claiming to be "the museum of the Maginot Line," with collections similar to that at Simserhof. The authors of the *Guide de la Ligne Maginot* (Guide to the Maginot Line) cautioned tourists that none of the museums had received the official imprimatur of the Ministry of Culture. According to the *Guide,* the three most important of the museums were at Simserhof, Fermont, and Hackenberg. The intended audience for the fortifications and their museums was largely veterans and war enthusiasts, and, not surprisingly, there was considerable interest in the Maginot Line among Germans in the 1970s.[31]

Increased tourist visits to the Maginot forts may have been stimulated by the creation of a Vichy tourist circuit, renewed interest in Lyon's Hôtel Terminus, and, to a lesser extent, the publication in 1987 of the *Guide de l'homme de droite à Paris,* subtitled, in English, *Paris by Right,* by Francis Bergeron and Philippe Vilgier, all evidence for a shift in attitudes whereby sites associated with the defeat and the "other side" were losing their taboo status. In 1988 the British monthly magazine *After the Battle,* which features stories about historic battlefields and what has become of them, published a map of the Maginot Line showing some twenty-five fortifications, including four along the Franco-Italian frontier. Of the twenty-five forts, ten were open to public touring, attracting some 200,000 visitors annually.[32] Those open in 2007 were estimated to have received some 300,000 visitors in total annually.[33] More recent global figures for the totality of the fortresses are not readily available but indicate some consistency in that the Lorraine tourism office counted some 90,000 visitors to four Maginot forts in 2013.[34] In neighboring Alsace, the Schoenenbourg fortress on the Maginot Line was listed as the fifth-most-visited *lieu de mémoire* in 2014, with 36,338 entries.[35]

FIGURE 3.   The casemates at the Fermont fortification along the Maginot Line, June 1993. Photo by author, 1993.

Authenticity and preservation are also issues for the Maginot fortifications, where the rise in interest since the 1970s may most reflect shifting perspectives on the war. More than the other sites, the Maginot Line addressed both the aging French and German veterans of the war and, as the German plaque at La Ferté indicates, symbolized reconciliation among them. A group of tourists ascending from the Maginot Line fortification at Fermont was seen to be more solemn than when they entered the site earlier.[36]

The Armistice Railway Car at Compiègne

Of equal significance in the course of the war in 1940 was the railway car where the 1918 armistice ending World War I had been signed. It would shift in meaning in 1940 and again after 1944, as did the Maginot Line. The idea to stage the signing of the 1940 armistice between Germany and France in Rethondes, in the same railway car, at the same clearing in the Compiègne forest, undoubtedly came from Joseph Goebbels, who, as German propaganda minister, stage managed it and is said to have boasted often of it to his press division assistant Hans Fritzsche.[37] For Goebbels's propaganda machine, the image of righting the earlier "injustice" done at Compiègne was heaven sent. His diary entry of 26 May describes the developing German victory as history's judgment against France for centuries-long tyranny exerted against Germany.[38] Goebbels, whose diaries are an excellent example of the kinds of source material that history can offer for the understanding of tourism, stopped to see the Compiègne site of the 1918 armistice, which had been reconstituted by the Germans as the setting for dictating their terms to the defeated French in June 1940.[39] To the Nazi leadership—and many other Germans as well—the Compiègne railway car represented the humiliation of a country whose armed forces, they believed, had been betrayed by a variety of domestic enemies, including socialists, democrats, and Jews. The French had maintained the car in place during the interwar years as a monument to their victory over "the criminal pride of the German Empire."[40] Goebbels and Hitler both looked upon the Compiègne site as a place of "shame" and also of German "national uprising," all represented in the tourist symbol of the forest clearing and the railway car created and then transformed.[41] Heavily involved in the preparations for the Compiègne meetings, with much telephoning from Berlin, Goebbels was keenly interested in the propaganda effects of the ceremony. "The shame is now extinguished," he declared. "One feels as if born anew."[42] Screening his own production of the weekly German newsreel *Die deutsche Wochenschau*, Goebbels remarked: "Unimaginable. The war in living pictures. Gripping, the scene in Compiègne. This is history!"[43] Goebbels made certain that the event was open to the world press, including William Shirer, who told the entire story of the armistice signing, complete with Hitler's gloating, vengeful, and angry expressions. Having learned of the planned ceremony, Shirer arrived at Compiègne several days in advance. Aware that the Germans had planted hidden microphones in the railway car, he listened in on the negotiations and was then the first to release them to the public.[44]

After the signing of the armistice, Goebbels had the car moved to Berlin, where it was displayed to German crowds for several weeks near the Brandenburg Gate before being garaged and eventually destroyed during the Allied advance on Germany in 1944.[45] The prominent presentation of the railway car in Berlin and the crowds of visitors it attracted attest to the German leadership's sense of the importance of the Compiègne scenario and also their use of tourism to embellish their own political narrative. Hitler's personal photographer Heinrich Hoffmann put together several photo-essays extolling the German victories of 1939 and 1940, and his *Mit Hitler im Westen*, which chronicled the victory in France, included six photographs of the proceedings at Compiègne, enhancing even more the prominent role of the armistice ceremony in the minds of the Nazi leaders.[46]

Of all the connections between touristic considerations and military and political decision making during the war, it may be that the decision to grant defeated France an armistice at all at Compiègne was the most portentous.

Apart from some vague ideas about a future French-German border that returned Alsace-Lorraine to Germany, Hitler had no immediate follow-up strategy after the magnitude of his 1940 victory over the French and certainly none for the occupation of that country. Admiral Erich Raeder argued for a Mediterranean strategy of going through Spain into Gibraltar and North Africa, cutting Britain off from most of its empire, thereby forcing the British to make peace. German forces would then have been freed for the planned attack against the Soviet Union. There is evidence to show that General Francisco Franco of Spain was ready to enter the war on Germany's side in June, but Hitler did not pursue this option.[47]

By stopping their offensive when it was in high gear and accepting an armistice with the French, the Germans missed a chance to settle things decisively in the west. Because of their agreement with France, which also meant supporting Pétain's government, the Germans were unable to make a pact with Spain that would have enabled them to take Gibraltar and close the western Mediterranean to the British.[48] Franco appears to have been ready for such an arrangement in June, but Hitler delayed, and by the time he met the Spanish leader in October, British resistance had stiffened. No longer certain of a quick German victory in the war, Franco raised the ante.[49] The German decision to give France an armistice that neither offered the Western powers a generous peace nor brought Spain into the war to help defeat the British was probably made within the three-week period of military victory in May and June 1940. As a German officer put it in July of that year, "The offensive was so rapid that it killed the war."[50] During this time, Hitler and his immediate entourage seem to have been at least partially preoccupied with thoughts of vengeful touring, deciding whether to force the French to accept an armistice at Compiègne, to tour Paris after his victory, or, even earlier, to tour the trenches on 6 June in northern France, where he had fought as a soldier in the First World War.[51] Seemingly a minor affair, the German touristic celebration in Compiègne, Paris, and elsewhere helped postpone any further serious German offensive either against England or to the south until it was too late. In his diary at the time of being informed of the armistice plans, General Franz Halder, the head of the German army's general staff, complained of "dilettante interference" in military planning."[52]

General Walter Warlimont, deputy chief of the German army's operations staff, pointedly commented later that following his great victory over the French, Hitler went off to tour World War I battle sites with two former comrades from his unit of the time. He then followed this with a tour of Paris.[53] The implication that Hitler and his entourage had been distracted by war tourism was clear. Hitler subsequently wrote enthusiastically to Goebbels about his visit to the World War I trenches and had himself photographed there for Hoffmann's album of the 1940 campaign.[54] Compiègne and Paris may not have been the only example of touristic interests distracting the Nazi leaders from the task of planning the military and political sequels to their victory. In a review of five books published about World War I, Philipp Blom mentions Hitler's 2 July 1940 tour to the World War I battlefield at Langenmarck in Belgium. Blom points out that this battle, better known in France and Britain as Ypres, resulted in the loss of some two thousand German soldiers but that it had been propagandized in Germany as a great victory. Hitler, who had served in the Bavarian infantry at Langenmarck in 1914, now wished to celebrate his 1940 triumph, and, in Blom's words: "The German military elite symbolically declared an end to the First World War. Victory at Last."[55]

Compiègne, already on the memory circuit as the site of the 1918 and 1940 armistices, acquired renewed meaning after 1 September 1944, when American forces liberated the armistice clearing. By the following 11 November, the anniversary of the World War I armistice, German prisoners of war had restored the clearing. A ceremony took place that day in the presence of General Pierre Kœnig, commander in chief of the French Forces of the Interior (Forces françaises de l'Intérieur), French and American soldiers, and veterans of World War I. Scouts lit fires on braziers, and the area was set ablaze. All that was left standing was the statue of Marshal Foch, which Hitler had also spared in 1940—according to one subsequent French account, to allow Foch to survey the destruction of his work rather than out of respect for the man who had signed the armistice with Germany in 1918.[56] The "shame of June 1940" was extinguished by fire four years later. With Foch's railway car having been destroyed, a similar one was found in Romania and refitted to replicate the original. In all other respects the clearing was restored as it had been on 11 November 1918. By 1946 the site had become a designated place of pilgrimage, but according to Le Monde at the time, this was due in part to the tourists arriving from reasons of curiosity or commerce.[57]

Compiègne had also been the location of a prison camp at Royal-Lieu, where thousands of members of the Resistance had been interned during the Occupation. In addition, it had witnessed the first contingents of the "so-called Relève," a 1942 scheme in which one French prisoner of war in Germany was released for every three skilled French workers sent there to work.[58] In 1948 war veterans and groups of former prisoners of war, under the patronage of President Vincent Auriol and Minister of Veterans and War Victims François Mitterrand, requested the creation of a monument at Compiègne to commemorate those who had fallen for the liberation of France.[59]

The touristic focus in Compiègne, however, continued to be the restored armistice clearing. In 1950 the conservator of the Carrefour de l'Armistice (Armistice Crossroads) defined the purpose of the site:

> More than ten years have passed since Hitler's profanation of a site surrounded by the respect of all the French.
>
> At the armistice clearing the outrage is effaced. A new force is born in the remembrance of 11 November 1918 and comes to sustain our hopes across the clouds that might again rise over the world.[60]

Occasionally questions of "authenticity" were raised regarding the restored Compiègne clearing, where annual celebrations commemorated the 1918 armistice, often in the presence of the president of the republic, but with a replica railway car. A curious German visitor was told by other Germans living in Paris that seeing the Compiègne railway car was not worth the trip and that it was not even the original car but a copy "for the tourists, naturally," a comment that calls to mind the "staged authenticity" that Dean MacCannell described as so common in tourist settings.[61] As Serge Barcellini and Annette Wieviorka note, however, little is ever said of the other—the 1940—armistice that was signed there.[62] A Picardie tourism website accessed in 2010 mentions the clearing in Compiègne, referring to both armistices as well as the museum that "exhibits the famous railway car" but does not mention that it is a replacement.[63]

Together, the Maginot fortresses and the Compiègne railway car represented the stunning military defeat of France which surprised so many in 1940. Each became a *site de mémoire* for German visitors during the four-year occupation that followed, becoming tourism sites that spoke to the victory and perceived glory of the Third Reich, representing a shift in tourism paradigms from the interwar years. Both remained tourism sites after the Liberation of 1944 but with different meanings related to the Allied victory and the liberation of France. The events at both sites in 1940 ushered in a period of German military occupation, often called *les années noires* or the "dark years" in France.[64] Military defeat and occupation, however, would not end tourism in France, as the events of 1940 through 1944 would show.

CHAPTER 3

The French as Tourists in Their Occupied Country

War-related tourism does not take place only after the fact at memorials and monuments; it goes beyond battlefield tourism to include tourism during the warfare itself. As the example of the 1942 Michelin guidebook for the Auvergne shows, tourism continued in France between 1939 and 1945 although clearly there were changes and restrictions. For many in France, despite war, defeat, and military occupation, life went on with leisure activities that often included tourism. The paid holiday program of 1936 remained in force during the war, and many took advantage of it. The tourism imaginaries that had been developed in French culture over the decades that preceded the war continued and were expressed in many ways, not the least of which was touring in rural France to discover the French "soul," encouraged by the Pétain government's National Revolution. Tourism officials also planned for a reconfigured future postwar tourism industry, promoted by government corporatist economic programs.

The very "ordinariness" of activities such as tourism during the war is a reminder that while many suffered, and worse, in battle or concentration camps, others carried on as usual, postwar plans were made, and the cultural value of tourism, so prevalent in the early twentieth century, did not disappear. To what at first glance might seem a surprising degree, tourism in a variety of forms continued even under the stressed conditions of war and occupation in France.

While limiting the possibilities for tourism, the war and Occupation by no means stifled tourist curiosity. Enforced mobility, political pressures, and the sometimes romanticized visions of travel and adventure all contributed to maintaining the desire to tour. Manifestations of tourism during the war included a cult of monuments and visitations (Joan of Arc and Napoleon were examples); an active cinema, which flourished in part because of the lack of American competition; a vogue for the rural and village past in France, in which excursions to relevant sites were encouraged; and a preservation movement that focused on historic houses and other treasures of the *patrimoine*. Ex-soldiers, *maquis* (Resistance fighters), and even collaborators who fought alongside the Germans, in part as a way of escaping the boredom of the Occupation, evoke much of this in retrospective stories.

The *Drôle de Guerre* and Tourism: September 1939– May 1940

The coming of war in September 1939 slowed tourism by imposing curfews in Paris and elsewhere. Jean Berthelot, adjunct director of the SNCF (Société nationale des chemins de fer français, the French railways) later recalled:

> [Those] behind the lines were asleep in the comfort of a false security. We wanted to make the bourgeois understand that we were at war by prohibiting the circulation of private cars on weekends. . . . The majority of the Council [of Ministers] wished to spare the country all unnecessary inconvenience. It seemed that to sustain morale in the rear, it was best to disturb as little as possible the cherished habits of the interwar period.[1]

Trains were requisitioned to transport some 600,000 residents of the border areas of Alsace and Moselle from potential danger to safer locations in the southwest, while others traveling north and east were filled with soldiers headed toward the front. Hotels were requisitioned for use as hospitals for the wounded.[2] In the southeast area bordering Italy, the casino in Juan-les-Pins received 2,500 mattresses in the event they were needed to house refugees from an Italian attack.[3] As the *drôle de guerre*, or "phony war," dragged on from September 1939 through May 1940, the restrictions imposed did not prevent affluent Parisians from taking vacations on the Riviera. With the French apparently well defended behind their Maginot Line in the fall and winter of 1939–40, they appear to have behaved much as usual. The Touring club de France continued to publish its monthly bulletins through 1939 and into 1940 but focused more on war preparations, the protection of French monuments and museums, and ways in which the club could serve as an intermediary between the French touring public and the military authorities. Restricted in size following the declaration of war in September 1939, the club's monthly bulletin reported in October that the Touring Club had been receiving six hundred new members and 3,700 letters per day at the outset of the war. Adjusting to the war situation, the club was using its connections with people in the hotel trade to secure accommodations for some three thousand displaced persons whose homes in eastern France were threatened by the combat. France was now officially under a state of siege, requiring individuals to obtain identity cards to travel freely within the country. Those wishing to travel to the military zones of operations would henceforth need safe conduct passes, and the club assisted in procuring these as well. The club also helped collect gasoline from its members for military use.[4]

Reports from the administrative council of the Touring Club indicated continued involvement in outdoor activities such as camping, hiking, and bicycle, automobile, and mountain tourism, as well as sailing. The club also engaged in activities to support the war effort, including the creation of a committee of women who collected and sorted through books to be shipped to soldiers at the front.[5] In February 1940, the French Touring Club awarded its *grande médaille* to the Touring Club of Finland to honor that country's struggle "for the safeguard of its independence, threatened by barbarians."[6] At its administrative council meeting of 7 May 1940, the Touring Club was preparing publications to celebrate the fiftieth anniversary of its founding.[7]

Tours through the French military defenses, however, came with restrictions. The war correspondent Roland Dorgelès, who is said to have coined the term *drôle de guerre,* for the war in the west in 1939–40, complained that while visiting the French forces near the line of fire in Lorraine, he and those with him were treated like "schoolchildren or tourists," allowed to travel only in escorted groups.[8] The phony war, however, took a dramatic turn with the German western offensive that began on 10 May 1940. Even as late as 9 June, Vassili Souk-homline, a Russian expatriate writer who lived in Paris through February 1941, noted that hope still existed that the French would somehow stop the onslaught before it reached the capital, and that at 6 p.m. the terrace at the Café de Flore was filled with both French and foreigners drinking their apéritifs. Nearly all the habitués in Soukhomline's circle of acquaintances were there.[9] By 15 June, however, things had changed with the large-scale flight of civilians and military personnel to the south. Soukhomline was now seeing thousands of frightened people from all walks of life fleeing Paris and the north and using every conceivable type of transportation.[10] So different from the vacation travel of the Popular Front, the flight of thousands of refugees nevertheless evoked in some the metaphor of tourism. Recalling trains packed with refugees fleeing toward the south, Dorgelès described "these thousands of tourists with neither jackets nor ties, shirt sleeves rolled up to their elbows, their wives crimson at the doors, reclining chairs [*chaises longues*] tied on the roof, who had less the allure of fleeing from the enemy than from the heat."[11]

Even in the desperate and frequently chaotic exodus, the kind of touristic curiosity that later had people gazing toward the Atlantic Wall and the Normandy coastline was already evident. Maurice Toesca, an official in the Paris police prefecture and a writer who left the city with so many others in the June 1940 flight, was in the town of Laval, west of Paris in the direction of Brittany. In his diary he described how he "watched the war" as the first German motorized forces arrived.[12] As the German troops began pouring, seemingly unimpeded, into northern France, a Major Paleirec, in charge of the French army censorship agency, exploded with rage in a comment that would presage the Germans' behavior following their victory:

> What a war! Enemy motorcyclists arrive in a village. They stop at a gas station, fill up in the most peaceful manner in the world—it is even said that they pay!—and they then proceed farther without otherwise being stopped! Is there no one to blow up the reservoirs, to cut the routes? No one to speak to them for the country? . . . No, they arrive as tourists and are fed amicably. It is almost as if they are given the restaurant's menu for another time! . . . Then they go to the bistro, quench their thirst, pay for their food, and leave again, smiles on their faces, as simply as they had come! I have never before seen this."[13]

Even after the panicked flight that came to be known as "l'Exode" (the Exodus), when tens of thousands of terrified French civilians and soldiers fled south in the face of the advancing German forces in May and June 1940, some looked on the flight as an adventure. Addressing the generalized panic, the historian Robert O. Paxton noted that "many adolescents . . . remembered the exodus as a holiday lark, a kind of impromptu camping trip in which one could discard conventions, as during Carnival."[14] Robert Cardinne-Petit, who served with the French military censorship agency and fled with the government as it moved from Paris first to Tours, then to Bordeaux, and subsequently to Vichy, recalled how, amid the confusion and sense of disaster, he and a colleague wandered through the streets of Bordeaux, making a tour of the city.[15]

Vichy: "Queen of Spas" and Provisional Capital

The choice of the spa city of Vichy as the provisional capital of France following the June 1940 defeat also encapsulated elements of tourism. Vichy was in the unoccupied zone, therefore free of German troops, although not far from the demarcation line and connected by good railway service to Paris. As a spa resort, it possessed large hotels with extensive telephone networks suitable for government use; it was not the fiefdom of any of the leading French political figures; and the Auvergne region in which it was located offered a relatively plentiful food supply.

Pétain was especially pleased by Vichy when he visited it, and Pierre Laval, a longtime republican political figure instrumental in creating the new government, approved it as it was close to his own village of Châteldon. As the historian Michèle Cointet points out, another factor was that the French government already owned much of the property in the town, regulated the use of the spas, and controlled the licenses of many of the establishments such as the Grand Casino.[16]

Touristic curiosity and spectacle accompanied the formation of Pétain's government as it was establishing itself in Vichy in July, described in a comment by a witness:

> All day long, whoever the occupant of the palace [the Hôtel du Parc], a crowd of onlookers, seated on iron chairs, patiently watches the entry into the Hôtel in the hope of seeing high-level personalities come and go. The crowd was inspired more by curiosity than by patriotic fervor or fear. It resembles what, at the time of the arrival of the Germans, excited people about the quality of their materiel.[17]

"But Paris will always be Paris"

The swift German victory and subsequent occupation of three-fifths of France, including Paris, changed the tourism landscape in fundamental ways, as the occupying authorities would use France in general and Paris in particular as a recreation area for their soldiers and privileged civilians, to be addressed in the next chapter. A sort of "ordinariness" or spirit of "life goes on" characterized many aspects of life in occupied France, including finance, fashion, film, and theater. The sense of normalcy in Paris that the Germans wished to showcase was sought by many among the local population as well, as they straggled back from the south to resume their lives in the occupied city. Returning to Paris after having been demobilized in the summer of 1940, Philippe Boegner recalled having been most struck by the "banalization," of the German presence, the way in which most Parisians accepted it in a mood of accommodation, which he believed augured a long occupation.

An officer in the French army's photographic service who experienced the May–June 1940 defeat and then followed the government to Vichy,

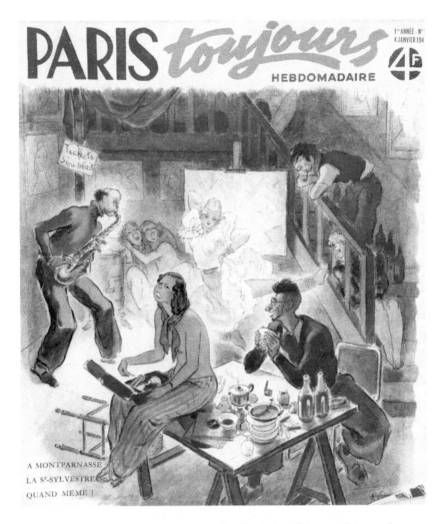

FIGURE 4. "Paris Forever!" "In Montparnasse, New Year's Eve, all the same!" A magazine cover proclaims the attractions of the capital even under German occupation. *Paris Toujours,* 4 January 1941. Author's personal collection.

Boegner was demobilized in late July. Fifty years later he offered an eyewitness account of occupied Paris. Boegner pointed, for example, to freshly installed signposts at major intersections, allowing German visitors to more easily find their way through the streets of Paris.[18] Boegner's observations are reminders that the history of the Second World War includes not only the perpetrators and victims but also, as Philippe Burrin later recognized in the French case, the "accommodators," the many who got by and made their peace with the war on many different levels.[19] The sense of continuity and "live while you can," so prominent in the summer and fall of 1940, or of

Figure 5. "Life is beautiful again, since one can dine 'with wine' for 9.50 francs in Paris in August 1940," reads the caption under a photo of two German soldiers strolling by, in *La Semaine*, 15 August 1940. Author's personal collection.

accommodation by those just trying to get by, was expressed in a 1976 film by André Halimi, rereleased in 1994, *Chantons sous l'Occupation* (Singing under the Occupation).[20]

Indeed, as the weeks passed during the summer of 1940, Boegner observed the city gradually return to life. The café patios along the Champs-Élysées again filled with patrons who watched the daily German military parades down the avenue with the comment "it's the circus," and turned their chairs away but, in Boegner's words, "not without having observed what was going on around them." Observing the Germans' military parades and attending their concerts, the Parisians had become, in effect, tourists watching spectacles in their own city. The expression "Paris sera toujours Paris" (Paris will always be Paris) made the rounds throughout the city as its inhabitants began to note that many of the Germans wanted only to discover the "real Paris." Theaters and cinemas reopened. The expression "we must live" permeated conversations.[21] The numbers of films made in France and recorded in the IMDb, not surprisingly, dropped during the Occupation years, but Paris remained prominent.[22] A police report of 29 July 1940 indicated that ten Parisian dance clubs had reopened during the previous week, bringing the total of functioning dance clubs to thirty-seven. Musical shows were also reopening, and more were expected with the coming of the fall season in September.[23]

The weekly magazine *Paris Programmes,* in many ways a local parallel to the *Wegleiter,* appeared on 26 September 1940. Its lead article, "Paris veut vivre" (Paris Wants to Live), declared that only a few weeks earlier the city had an air of desperation: "To open the window was to open one's veins." Suddenly, however, the city—like a convalescent hungry for sunlight, hope, and work—had revived and a miracle had been achieved.[24] The magazine covered theaters, music halls, cinemas, restaurants, concerts, expositions, museums, and a more general category called "luxuries of Paris." In his gastronomy column, Pierre Andrieu, who later wrote the gastronomy sections for the Odé guidebooks, which were translated into German, advised his readers that present difficulties did not have to obscure the French cuisine that Bismarck and the Germans had come to appreciate after their victory over France in 1871.[25] A listing for the restaurant Chiberta, near Étoile, stated that "at its bar you will find *tout-Paris élégant* [all of elegant Paris]." Listings were divided by neighborhood: the Champs-Élysées, the Grands Boulevards, Montmartre, Montparnasse, and the Latin Quarter. A sense of the hope of the guidebook's publishers was expressed in an advertisement for Gypsy's, a cabaret in the Latin Quarter: "Paris remains Paris, the Temple of French Gaiety." The last page and the inside back cover contained the rubric "Where to go today."[26] As with the *Wegleiter,* the message of *Paris Programmes* was clear: life in occupied France was to return to "normal," and tourism was an important component of that. In the second issue of *Paris Programmes,* the "Paris veut vivre" feature informed its readers that the curfew had been extended from 11 p.m. to midnight and that the horse races had been reopened.[27]

Not all went smoothly at the various sites listed. In October 1940, the Paris police reported two "melees" among locals and German soldiers in Montmartre nightclubs and in the Pigalle Métro station, where a German soldier attacked a wounded French war veteran. A German military patrol intervened in the last episode, helping the wounded veteran and stopping the German soldier, described as "very excited" (*très excité*).[28]

Changes in the Tourism Landscape as Narratives Shift

In the transfer of political power that followed the defeat of 1940, France witnessed the development of new cultural sites and the revision of older ones. Within the first weeks of the new Vichy government's existence, these sets of symbols bifurcated along the split between the Free French Resistance on the one side and Vichy on the other. The Cross of Lorraine and the Strasbourg cathedral acquired new signification in the culture of the Free French, whereas the town of Vichy acquired new meaning for both the Vichy government and the Resistance. All became highly charged code words in French political discourse, as did Joan of Arc, whose sites and images were used by both sides, and the entire city of Paris itself, declared an open city to spare it in June 1940 and the site of high political drama in 1944.

Not surprisingly, the armistice and subsequent occupation conditions imposed by the victorious Germans upon the French took a heavy toll on the tourism industry. Some 150,000 railway cars were confiscated by mid-September 1940, according to Jean Berthelot, newly appointed secretary of state for communications.[29] In September 1940, the German military authorities demanded that all 1938 to 1940 models of all passenger cars (*voitures du tourisme*) of fourteen horsepower or less in Paris and its suburbs be presented to them for inspection.[30] In addition, curfews enforced by the occupation authorities restricted evening activities for many in France and especially in Paris. Hotels were often requisitioned by the Germans for the use of their personnel in the unoccupied as well as the occupied zone, as in the case of an unnamed establishment on the Corniche in Marseilles mentioned in a French police report.[31]

The last prewar *Michelin Guide* for France as a whole appeared in 1939, and the guidebook did not reappear until the spring of 1944, when a special edition, based on the 1939 edition, was published in Washington, D.C., by the Allies to provide their forces with maps of French towns.[32] Michelin, however, continued to publish roadmaps of France, such as one that appeared in 1942.[33] The Michelin France series was resumed only in 1945, with its stars rating system reappearing in 1946 and 1947, as the French hotel-restaurant industry returned to its prewar norms.[34] If wartime restrictions limited tourism, the tourism imaginary continued, fed by publications such as the *Almanach François,* a guide for households, which in 1941 included an article titled "Où aller en vacances?" (Where to Go on Vacation?). The choices among seacoast, mountains, and countryside, according to the magazine, were difficult. Key to the decision making, it continued, should be atmospheric pressure. Higher elevations contained less oxygen, whereas the seacoast contained the highest levels. At sea level, breathing would be the slowest and the blood would be the richest. Those with emphysema, heart problems, and rheumatism were advised to avoid these areas. They were, however, acceptable for those with tuberculosis, provided they were shielded from high winds. The lowlands were recommended for convalescents, those with respiratory problems, and heart patients, all of whom were advised to avoid the mountains. No specific destinations were mentioned.[35]

Parisians who could no longer drive were still able to visit expositions of automobiles in September 1940. Lack of fuel severely restricted automobile use in France, but a variety of ersatzes were employed, notably the *gazogène*, a gas generator that burned fuels such as wood, coal, or charcoal, often attached to the rear of the car.

FIGURE 6.   Some of the various ersatzes used for transportation in gas-starved Paris. *L'Illustration* 5093 (19 October 1940), cover. Author's personal collection.

In 1941 the *Almanach de la Bonne Presse,* a Catholic publication, in an article on the installation and use of *gazogènes,* featured an illustration of an automobile equipped with a large trailer transporting its *gazogène.* The article noted that car owners had often been reluctant to convert to *gazogènes* because they made for heavier vehicles with a less comfortable ride.[36] The tourist imaginary was present, however, even in the *Almanach,* which included an article encouraging visits to fortified churches that dated to medieval France and to the Paris catacombs.[37]

When lack of fuel removed most private automobiles from the roads, the French toured by bicycle, whose care and maintenance was later featured in the "tourism" section of the 1943 *Almanach Hachette.*[38] At one point in January 1941, General Otto von Stülpnagel, in charge of the German forces in France, complained that too many of the French were being allowed to cross from one zone to another and that approval should be given only for travel that was in German interests and not for private trips.[39] Stülpnagel's admonition seems to have gone unheeded as group requests to cross the zonal line continued to be granted, although with restrictions. In April 1941, for example, the Paris Ski Club petitioned to allow its ski racing team to travel to an Easter competition in Chamonix. The Ski Club was favored as having been "German-friendly" even before the war, having invited German teams to compete in French races even over the objections of the French sporting associations of the time.[40] Hotels also suffered as a consequence of the defeat and occupation. Some had been requisitioned for troop use prior to the French defeat; German occupation personnel requisitioned others for use thereafter. Government subsidies to hotels to house the unemployed were reduced with the Occupation, and hotel owners were worried about fuel for heating during the coming winter. Food supplies for the hotels were also endangered because of the lack of transport.[41]

While many saw their travel restricted to armchair tourism or visits to the cinema or libraries, others still managed to go farther afield. Parisians continued to take vacations, but the coast was off limits to them, so they headed inland instead. Ongoing tourism was exemplified in the report, mentioned in the introduction, by a Monsieur Clauzel, the head the Hotel Committee in 1942, indicating that some 400,000 pensioners with paid vacations, dating from the French legislation of 1936, had found lodgings in two thousand hotels recommended by his service in 1942. An additional 500,000 vacationers were helped as well. Summer vacationers were to be sent on *séjours de remplacement* (replacement visits) to the interior of France with the coast, where they usually went, closed by the war. The Loing River valley in central France, not far from Paris, and the Aube department in the Champagne region were attracting visitors, as was the department of the Basse-Pyrénées, which, according to the author, was drawing the smart set.[42]

Most of the vacationers, according to Clauzel, found guesthouses (*pensions*) costing some fifty to seventy francs per day; luxury hotels accounted for only 6 percent of accommodations involved in his committee's efforts to find spots for vacationers. Menus in the *pensions,* although not abundant, given the circumstances, were of good quality and bore the *marque du terroir.* His office planned to remain open into the autumn of 1942 to aid those seeking places for winter sports. Lastly, and perhaps unknowingly anticipating a later twentieth-century trend, Clauzel predicted an expanding opportunity for the French hotel trade among retirees with pensions in 1943. Especially in winter, retirees would wish to visit the smaller provincial hotels that were heated by woodstoves.[43] On the other side of the tourism equation, and reflecting a negative view often found in more recent commentaries, Suzanne Sauvan, writing about the Haute-Bochaine in the French Alps in a geography periodical in 1942, excoriated the effects of tourism, which she believed were turning France's rural areas into suburban developments with garish red corrugated metal rooftops.[44]

A Michelin tourist guidebook for the Auvergne region, published in 1942, returned to the theme of the unavailability of automobile touring, noting:

> Paris, May 1942, friend reader, today your car is asleep in your garage, but you can still take a vacation. If the Auvergne tempts you, this guide will lead you there. You will no longer find programs for the long trips and excursions that the car would enable you to do, but the train, the bus, the bicycle, back in style, even your legs, reaccustomed to walking, give you the ability to circulate everywhere.[45]

With the expectation of increased bicycle usage, the Paris authorities imposed one-way directional limits on some of the cycling lanes.[46]

Vichy's "Return to the Soil" and the "Rediscovery" of the Countryside

Tourism and interest in it, although naturally attenuated by the coming of war in 1939 and the Occupation in 1940, continued in a variety of ways, including a restructuring of the industry in an attempt to incorporate the *étatisme,* corporatism, and the "return to the soil," all aspects of Vichy's National Revolution. Christian Faure has shown how this agenda was carried out in the emphasis on regional and national folklore in Vichy's cultural politics and the related tourism promoted by the Pétain government.[47] In a study of tourism in France, Marc

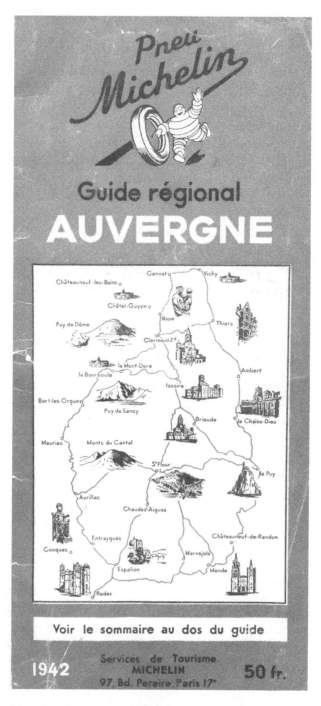

FIGURE 7. A tourism guidebook to the Auvergne region, published despite the war and Occupation. *Guide Michelin rouge régional Auvergne 1942* (Paris: Michelin Services du Tourisme, 1942), AGFA-1ZOKOP3© Michelin 2017. Author's personal collection.

Boyer points out that many of the French during the Occupation years experienced mobility, even if not of their own choosing and under severe conditions of restricted transport. Places of refuge and pilgrimage could be agreeable, as in the case of the Côte d'Azur, which served as a refuge for many but was also a prized tourist area.[48] Jean Berthelot, presiding over the task of rebuilding and modernizing French railway networks in 1940, later wrote of plans to construct new train lines in the tourist routes of the Côte d'Azur, the Maures and Esterelle cliffs, the cliffs from Nice to Menton, the Var line, and the route along the coast from Nice to Cannes, as well as rebuilding the Roya bridges. His ministry would also provide funds to extend the Promenade des Anglais in Nice to the Californie peninsula. Confronted on 4 December 1940 by local officials in Nice concerned about the city's future with a threat of possible Italian annexation, Berthelot asked rhetorically, "Would I spend 100 million [francs] if this area were not going to remain French?"[49] His response appears to have provoked the anger of the Italians, as they reported it back to the Germans, who apparently told Laval to reprimand Berthelot. The French countryside was rediscovered by many hungry urban dwellers, who sometimes found good food in the rural homes of previously neglected parents or other relatives. Health benefits of the countryside were also rediscovered. Despite the hardships, many of the French, Boyer argued, retained pleasant memories of these experiences, and these sentiments encouraged them to tour in ever larger numbers after the war once conditions had improved. The stunning success of the first postwar Salon de l'Automobile auto show in 1946, and the surge in automobile touring in the years that followed, were due in no small part to the experiences of so many of the French during the war.[50]

Although only a minority of eligible workers took advantage of their paid vacations to travel after 1936, Boyer notes that the public considered them a right.[51] Despite the economic hardships of the Occupation and its own moralistic agenda of "Travail, Famille, Patrie"(Work, Family, Country), with its emphasis on work, the Vichy government extended the paid holidays, set at fifteen days in 1936, by an additional day for those on the job five years or more.[52] In March 1942 the Hotel Industry Committee (Comité d'organisation professionnelle de l'industrie hôtelière), Vichy's professional association for hoteliers, established an office in Paris where workers and employees could find appropriate hotels or *pensions* in the country for their summer vacations.[53] A report by the Hotel Association emphasized the social benefits of tourism and sought to help ensure that hotels and other guest establishments had enough food available to feed their clients. Arguing in favor of the proposal, the Secrétariat d'état aux communications, the French government office now in charge of tourism, maintained that "vacations are a physiological necessity, which the government has just consecrated by a legal obligation."[54]

As in general, tourism took many forms in occupied France. Vichy's National Revolution was based in part on a "return to the soil" program that promoted a cult of the rural and village past in France in which excursions were encouraged, as was a cult of monuments and visitations, such as those related, for example, to Joan of Arc, who became a focal point in the creation of memory for many different political movements, collaboration as well as Resistance. A national committee for folklore promoted a renaissance of interest in the provinces, and the government encouraged restoration of old country homes as part of preserving French heritage.[55] This policy resulted in part from limitations on access to Paris, in the occupied zone, but it also reflected a genuine promotion of a "return to the soil," in the spirit of the idyllic pastoral stories of the writer Jean Giono and a rejection of the image of cosmopolitan urban life as unhealthful and arguably of dubious moral caliber as well, a rejection of the Paris of the Folies-Bergère. A regional committee for tourism was established in Nice in June 1941, and the Vichy government supported a Regionalist Exposition at Toulouse, as well as organizations such as Jeune France, the Chantiers de la jeunesse, and the Compagnons de France, all of which attempted to interest young people in the village and rural traditions of provincial France. One publication, in support of Vichy's "return to the soil" movement, argued that to "make men," the youth of France needed to return to nature and the countryside. Women's roles were as mothers and homemakers.[56] Articles in newspapers such as L'Œuvre extolled handicrafts in the Musée des arts et traditions or showed how "80 little Parisians" had become "apprentice peasants" in the countryside.[57]

Reflecting the values of Vichy's National Revolution, Lyon-Touriste noted that foreigners would be invited to see the "French soul," meaning rural France, rather than the France of luxury, by implication the case before the war.[58] The Hôtelier Alpin, a regional hotel trade publication, encouraged the discovery of less well-known French regions, asserting in March 1943 that whereas foreigners came to France to visit Paris, the Riviera, and the Basque coast, they should be urged to visit all of France. Tourism, unlike agricultural and industrial products, it maintained in an argument heard elsewhere as well, was an inexhaustible resource.[59]

The Organization of Tourism in Vichy France

With the military defeat of May–June 1940, the Touring club de France turned its attention to helping refugees and attempting to regroup in the unoccupied zone. German authorities demanded Touring Club photographs of Alsace and Lorraine, apparently to be used in their annexation of the provinces.[60] As of July 1941, the Touring Club was again allowed to publish its *Review* but, because of the shortage of paper, with fewer pages than previously. The club reported the loss of half of its membership, either in the provinces of Alsace and Lorraine, now annexed to Germany, or in the colonies, as well as those members in German prison camps. The division of France into occupied and unoccupied zones meant that in the unoccupied zone, cut off from the office in Paris, the Touring Club needed to function somewhat autonomously. A general secretariat annex had been set up in Lyon. Because of the limitations on transport, the club was limiting its activity to camping and to bicycle and pedestrian tourism. Following the "new" political directives, the club was forming youth groups to become "nurseries of tourists and defenders of the beauties of France."[61] In late 1942 the president of the Touring Club reported that the organization had dropped from 346 agents at the beginning of the war in 1939 to 107. With automobile use severely restricted, the club now organized garages for bicycles. In collaboration with the government, it set up youth brigades to clean historic monuments, and another affiliated group, the Jeunes équipes de la vieille France, was to be organized under government auspices to clean and maintain historic monuments as well. The club's leadership feared that tourism organizations would be subsumed within the new youth organizations being created by the Vichy government, and the club president promised to do all that was possible to maintain the "material advantages and special conditions accorded to "travels and sojourns" (*déplacements et séjours*).[62]

A major task ahead was said to be to ensure that tourism was not absorbed into the new organizations being developed for sports. The Touring Club wished to make certain that the government would give the same material support to travel (*déplacements*) and visits (*séjours*) as to sporting activities.[63] In addition to supporting what it could of tourism in metropolitan France, the Touring Club looked across the Mediterranean, increasing its membership in Algeria as of June 1942. Clubs in Algiers and Constantine were to be linked with one in Tunis. The club planned to support the establishment of trails, tracks, refuges, and vacation homes in Algeria and Tunisia.[64] Additionally, the club supported the Comité national du folklore, whose mission in keeping with Vichy policy was to stage events that highlighted French folklore.[65]

As noted earlier, the division of occupied France into several military zones meant German permission was required to travel within much of France. Children away at school wishing to spend their vacations with their parents residing in another zone needed special permission from the German military authorities to cross from one zone into another.[66] The German military authorities allowed children to travel to vacation colonies (*colonies de vacances*), but not if these were "youth camps," consisting of members of the Compagnons de France and the Chantiers de la jeunesse, youth groups organized to mobilize the youth in favor of the Vichy government and, in the case of the Chantiers, to provide activity for unemployed young men demobilized from the army after the 1940 defeat.[67] French schools continued to organize vacation colonies for their pupils, but they now had to identify to the German authorities the leaders of these groups, together with the numbers of pupils, their activities, and the sites for their vacations.[68] Propaganda gain was not far removed, as in the case of the Germans approving a vacation colony for the young girls from poor families in the Paris suburbs that had been hit by English bombs. The Frenchwoman in charge noted that there would be approximately eighty girls ranging in age from ten to fifteen, that their activities would be "scholarly" rather than religious or political, and that none of the children were Jewish.[69] In contrast, a similar request from the École Notre-Dame de Paris for the use of the Grand Mesnil château in the Chevreuse valley as a school vacation colony for Easter, Pentecost, and other school holidays from March through October 1943 was denied "for military reasons."[70]

In La Valette, a town of about five thousand inhabitants east of Toulon, the mayor and the town council organized local vacation colonies, one for boys and one for girls, as a place to keep children off the streets. The effort, according to the mayor in his postwar memoirs, was supported by the Secours national, a private charitable organization controlled increasingly by the Vichy government. It involved some 250 children for a month at a time in August and September 1941.[71] The vacation colonies continued in the summers of 1942 and 1943, but the circumstances of the war prevented their being established in the summer of 1944.[72] The Auberges françaises de la jeunesse, which functioned as an umbrella organization under the Vichy government, including young men and women from the Scouts, the Touring club de France, the Catholic youth groups, and several others, claimed that "thousands" of youth had made what were essentially camping trips along three itineraries: the Alps, the Auvergne, and the Garges du Tarn, all in the unoccupied zone. Its goals were described as "the geographical and human discovery of the country," and in their forays its followers were advised to avoid the cafés and main roads and seek out instead historic châteaux and rural panoramas.[73] During their treks into the countryside, the young people camped in some hundred or more hostels (*auberges*), all in the unoccupied zone.[74] "Given the low cost of lodging, the hostels will become the refuge of the vagabonds," stated one of the group's brochures in 1942.[75]

A report from the head of the Service des voyages de vacances (Vacation Travel Service) of the French Education Ministry described a program whereby some 6,500 people were registered for interzonal convoys for Easter 1942. *Trains spéciaux aux grandes vacances* (special trains for major vacations), when available, needed to be reserved, and some eight hundred to nine hundred personnel were needed to organize the 5,676 students and maintain order during the trips. This travel, also described by Jean Guéhenno, who accompanied a group of students on one such trip in 1942, was restricted to students going home to visit their parents for the holiday.[76]

There was also consideration of closer liaison among German, Italian, and French tourism organizations during the war, but a suggestion to this effect, made to Elmar Michel, in charge of the German economics office in occupied Paris, by Fritz Gabler, the leader of the German professional hotel organization, gained no traction. Following a visit to Paris, Gabler suggested that in his capacity as president of the International Hotelkeepers Alliance, he might approach his professional colleagues in France for closer collaboration, as he was proposing in the case of his Italian colleagues. Michel, however, opposed such Franco-German collaboration in the hotel trade on the grounds that the French organization was not ready for "closer ties" and that it needed first to complete a process of reorganization, presumably to become more structurally and ideologically aligned to the German New Order.[77] Addressing the same topic, Hermann Esser, the author of the official guidebook for the German pavilion at the 1937 International Exposition in Paris, and undersecretary for tourism in the Reich Propaganda Ministry from 1939 through the end of the war, also called for postponing plans for closer international cooperation. Hitler, he noted, had expressly ordered that resolving international organizational cooperation issues be postponed until after the war.[78]

L'État français and the Travel Industry

After the initial shock of defeat in the summer of 1940, tourism picked up in Nice as the casinos reopened in the spring of 1941 with some of the larger hotels run by German or Italian interests.[79] A letter written to the *Petit Dauphinois* in Grenoble, intercepted by the French police in August 1943, complained of moneyed clientele enjoying expensive wines, with cost of no concern to them, in the Savoy spa hotels "at the most somber moment in our history." Winter sports, the letter continued, were a pretext for unspecified wealthy clients to spend extensively on food and drink in the name of health cures at the spas. The writer, secretary of the Comité social of the Château

Feuillet factory, demanded that the spa hotels be closed, or at least that they be used for local factory workers who were truly ill. Instead,

> Vichy published a decree facilitating the restocking of the hotels, the number of trains [presumably leading to the hotels] was increased. It is not necessary to write to you of the bitterness of the workers before this way of acting. And one speaks about suppressing the class struggle!! No, truly, it is not with this spirit that one will make the National Revolution.[80]

A follow-up report indicated that although the hotel managers at the popular winter spas at Val d'Isère and Saint-Bon had kept to the legally set rates during the 1942–43 season, they had charged excessively high prices for food and wine to make up for the costs of these items, which they had acquired in illegal markets. "The clientele in these two stations had been effectively composed of very wealthy persons, of whom several [were] Israelites, who paid without questioning the prices asked of them." Sanctions were suggested.[81]

Anti-Jewish restrictions put in place by the Vichy government also affected the tourism and travel industries. The Hotel Committee, which worked closely with the government's tourism department, was charged with the development of policies regarding agencies owned by Jews for possible "Aryanization" in 1941.[82] A committee was established to determine whether such properties were to be ceded to non-Jewish owners or closed altogether. The committee was also to recommend how much money should be paid to the "provisional" non-Jewish "administrators" to cover their costs of management and/or liquidation.[83] A government survey of travel agencies noted that from 1938 through 1942, fourteen had had their licenses revoked. Of the fourteen, ten were identified as run by Jews.[84]

The impact of the war on the organized travel industry was severe. The same report that addressed the closing of Jewish-owned travel agencies listed some 117 agencies, of which 78 had closed since 1938. Of those that continued to operate in 1942, the monetary turnover of most was less that year than prior to the war, in many cases considerably less. American Express, for example, had closed by 1942, although it was still listed with a turnover of 995,466 francs, as contrasted to 15,024,713 in 1938. A handful of agencies including the state railways and Danubia, based in Paris; Depeche et Petit toulousain, based in Toulouse; Indépendant du Midi, based in Perpignan; Kuoni in Nice; and Rivoire et fils in Saint-Étienne saw substantial increases. Apart from those based in Paris, these agencies were all in the zone unoccupied by the Germans at the time the list was drawn up. Those in Paris may have benefited from the closing of large numbers of competitors, as well as increased travel between France and Germany by military in addition to civilian personnel.[85] As Richard Vainopoulos and Sandrine Mercier note, however, in their study of "received ideas" about tourism, it was on 24 February 1942 that the first legislation regulating travel agencies, and the requirement for them to be licensed, was promulgated in France.[86]

Uncertain where to construct the state apparatus in charge of tourism, and desiring to integrate it somehow into what was to be a new corporate economic structure in France, the Vichy authorities moved it around, a pattern that continued into the postwar years as well. The governmental office in charge of tourism, the Commissariat général au tourisme, created as part of the Ministère des travaux publiques (State Secretariat for Public Works) in 1935, was downgraded in a law of 15 October 1940 to a Service du tourisme, which functioned under the Secrétariat d'état aux communications (Ministry of Communications). A decree in late December 1940 reorganized France's travel agencies into a corporation under the Délégué général au tourisme as part of the restructuring of the French economy begun the previous August.[87] The newly formed Comité d'organisation professionnelle des agences & bureaux de voyages was to license travel agents, survey and improve the training of tour guides, supervise the mandatory insurance of travelers' luggage, and coordinate the promotion of tourism by chambers of commerce and travel agents. It was to study the possibility of organizing a corporative entity for travel agents as well as a center for their training.[88] Regulations subsequently adopted included, for example, the prohibition on travel agents' publicizing verbally or in any other way tendentious or unverified information concerning the history, art, sciences, or economy of countries visited by their clients.[89]

A September 1941 memo from the Ministry of Communications argued that while tourism was not an administrative matter, the state could not abandon to "the fantasy of private interests the development of this essential element of French *patrimoine.*" It called for a "tabula rasa" of France's tourism structure to create a *faisceau* (cluster) of all private interests into an organization headed by the state, functioning in the national interest. Included in this new corporatist organization was a Hotel Committee (Comité de l'hôtellerie) to administer the supplying, administration, and training for hotels; a committee for travel agencies to maintain standards for the profession, create travel circuits, and organize international exchanges; and a Committee for the Organization of Spas (Comité d'organisation du thermalisme) to coordinate professional interests in its area under the communications and health ministries.[90] Under the guidance of the Communications Ministry, the Union des fédérations des syndicats d'initiatives (U.F. ESSI, Union of the

Federations of Chambers of Commerce) would publish books guiding tourists to French sites. The Touring club de France and the Club alpin (Alpine Club) would also contribute to the expansion of tourism in France. The prewar number of state functionaries involved in the tourism industry would be reduced from fifty to ten in what was said to be a move toward greater efficiency.[91] What was not said was that wartime and occupation conditions had, of course, greatly diminished the activities of the tourism industry. The problem of a duplication of effort had already been aired. Bernard Chenot, the *commissaire du gouvernement, délégué général au tourisme* (Government Commissioner and General Delegate for Tourism), argued that many spas, especially those that allowed gambling on their premises, more properly fell under the jurisdiction of the tourism authorities than that of the Health Ministry. Nice, Cannes, and Deauville were examples of sites classified as "thermal stations," or spas, which, however, should fall under the purview of tourism rather than health, unlike the spa at Berck, a tuberculosis cure site.[92] In 1942 the Commissariat général au tourisme was reestablished as part of the Ministère des travaux publiques.[93] Henry de Ségogne (1901–1979), a noted alpinist and the leader of the first French expedition in the Himalayas in 1936, and also a friend of Antoine de Saint-Exupéry, became its head. After the war, he would play an active role in the protection of French cultural heritage.[94]

Vichy's reorganization of France's tourism structure included the establishment of regional committees for tourism (Comités régionaux de tourisme) and associated local organizations that, in the words of Georges Mathiot, vice president of the Fédération des syndicats d'initiatives "Lorraine-Vosges-Alsace" (Federation of Chambers of Commerce for Lorraine-Vosges-Alsace) and president of the Syndicat d'initiatives de Bussang, a small town now in the Vosges department, "transformed" its tourism infrastructure. Following Vichy's blend of *étatisme* and regionalism, the new legislation meant that the state would be involved in all private tourism organizations, even the most local.[95] Not all in the tourism field were happy with the new legislation. The leadership of the Touring club de France worried that their organization would somehow lose its autonomy in a new Union nationale des associations de tourisme, an umbrella organization being formed to group together different tourism organizations under the control of the secretary of state for tourism. Maintaining that it was an organization "uniting on the national scale tourists practicing diverse forms of tourism without distinctions of specialties nor regions of residence," the Touring Club decided to maintain what it could of its autonomy vis-à-vis the state, while admitting that it would be difficult to do so.[96]

Vichy decrees of 12 January 1942 and 5 June 1943 authorized the establishment of a Comité régional du tourisme in each region, in which the prefect represented the governmental *commissaire*. The minister of public works and transport selected members of the regional committees whose task was to coordinate the development of tourism in their respective areas. They were to evaluate and coordinate tourism advertising. Their power was to recommend policy to the *secrétaire d'état aux communications*, and presumably, after the tourism function was transferred, to the minister of public works. Final authority, as with many of the Vichy political structures, rested with the minister.[97]

During the Occupation, however, a number of tourist offices closed, including the prewar Union touristique automobiliste et hotelière de France, known as "UTAH," which provided information to automobile drivers and was authorized to give *triptyques automobiles* (triptych road maps, as offered by automobile clubs). After June 1940, the sign for UTAH continued to adorn the building, which, however, had been converted into a restaurant and bar, cited by the French police for having violated curfew regulations.[98] Some among those who favored collaboration with Germany took the German Kraft durch Freude program as a model for France. A Monsieur Fremont, having worked in Germany and returned to France in November 1941, gave a speech at a Montrouge meeting of the Rassemblement national populaire (RNP), a collaborationist political party, where he praised the KdF for its organization of inexpensive sports, theatrical and literary evenings, and excursions. It was, he reported, a true ministry of leisure, a model to be copied in the new France that was to be built along National Socialist lines.[99]

Planning for a Better Future

Despite closures, restrictions, and other hardships, those in the industry hoped and planned for better times. A writer for *Lyon-Touriste*, which reduced its issues from three to two annually at government orders, hoped that the elimination of almost all "tourist movement" as a result of restrictions was only momentary.[100] In the spirit of Vichy's emphasis on regionalism, a proposal was put forward in November 1941 to the minister of public works, under whose domain tourism matters now lay, for the construction or installation in Paris of a "Maison du tourisme" (House of Tourism) to encourage tourism to the regions by promoting their architecture, folklore, and stage productions.[101] Another governmental initiative in favor of tourism even under difficult conditions was the establishment of French tourist offices abroad, in Switzerland, Spain, and South America, in late 1941 and early 1942. Given the wartime conditions, the offices were opened "not to invite tourists to visit France, but to bear witness that the land of France is ready to welcome them in better days." The offices were to be discreet and more focused on economic activity than politically high profile. The SNCF, the French state railway company, for example, received subsidies for offices in Madrid, Barcelona, and Seville. Currency exchanges were supported in Lisbon, Buenos Aires, Rio de Janeiro, and Montevideo. The Foreign Ministry also supported this policy of a French tourism presence on the international scene. Promotional activities included exhibitions of photographs by the Service du tourisme, together with films of France's landscapes.[102]

In November 1942, the Paris Chamber of Commerce adopted a report, written by Jean Truillé, arguing for the need to modernize French freeways (*autostrades*) to enhance commerce after the war. In a section devoted to tourism, Truillé saw negatives and positives. He wrote that that use of freeways would deprive tourists of the variety of sites in French villages and the countryside. Tourism in France, which was unparalleled in its attraction, he argued, would be harmed. Future freeways, however, could be used by commercial traffic, freeing the smaller, more picturesque roads of France for tourists. In addition, freeways would allow tourists to travel quickly to places of interest and then tour locally, just as railways already did. In any event, the French road system, he concluded, required modernization, even if it brought both benefits and losses to tourism.[103]

Others looking to the future included Gaston Mortier, the president of a French hotel trade organization, who welcomed the "very modern" phenomenon of "intellectual tourism."[104] His book *Le tourisme et l'économie nationale: Un passé encourageant . . . Vers un meilleur avenir* (Tourism and the National Economy: An Encouraging Past . . . Toward a Better Future), published in 1941, asked rhetorically why one should write about tourism now when preoccupations were of a "higher order." He replied that the present period was suitable for meditation so that the French tourist industry would be ready for brighter "normal" times in the future.[105]

Some in the French tourist industry looked to the new corporatist emphasis of the Vichy government to propel a "tourism revolution" (*révolution touristique*), in Mathiot's words. In a book published in October 1945 but written largely under occupation conditions and German censorship, Mathiot traced the development of government institutions with regard to tourism during the Occupation. He noted that the war in 1939 had led to governmental requisitioning of hotels for military personnel, severely impacting tourism in France even before the German occupation the following year.[106] To Mathiot, there was a difference between state intervention in tourism, which he favored, and politics, which he opposed. The state had intervened, he argued, with the creation of paid vacations for workers in 1936. Workers on vacation quickly learned to "leave their posters and flags at home" and allow the local residents to live in peace. The locals, in return, learned to accept workers peaceably on vacation. "In matters of tourism, sites, and monuments," he concluded, "politics has no place."[107] All that was needed, he added, on 30 June 1944, while the battle to liberate France was in progress, was for the state to provide sufficient funding to the tourism industry.[108] Mathiot's comments are all the more interesting because of his role in 1945 in Alsace, a region that had been annexed by the Germans after 1940, and the circumstances under which he wrote his book.[109]

Government Policy and the Hotel Industry

One of the important early and continuing issues confronted by the hotel industry was the attempt by the Vichy government on both practical and moral grounds to limit the consumption of alcohol. In a study of Vichy's restriction on apéritifs, Sebastien Cote found a significant rise in alcohol consumption in France between the 1910s and 1939. As part of the Daladier government's 1939 *redressement national* (national recovery), provisions incorporated into the new Code de la famille included limitations on alcoholic consumption, especially apéritifs. Here, as in other areas of policy, Vichy followed programs initiated by Third Republic governments prior to the war. Vichy, Cote notes, followed an established government policy when, on 23 August 1940, it required that the alcoholic content in apéritifs and bitters be reduced from 18 percent to 16 percent. The president of the Hotel Committee in 1941 asked that wine-based apéritifs be allowed to contain 18 percent alcohol.[110] Wines and digestive liqueurs were not affected. Cote saw the Vichy legislation as political because the apéritifs restricted included pastis, which had been illegal under the Third Republic but had been legalized in 1938 by the Popular Front government of Léon Blum. By restricting the bitters and anise-flavored drinks, Vichy could now pose as a more morally pure government, placing the blame for the decadence that it claimed led to the 1940 defeat on the Third Republic. To Cote, the legislation was more for show than designed to produce real social reform.[111] Again in 1941, the Hotel Committee expressed concern that reductions in the availability of wine, together with increased taxes on it, would adversely affect their industry. While paying respects to the expressed desire of Marshal Pétain to combat alcoholism, members of the committee hoped that this policy would not be pursued at the expense of their industry.[112] In a subsequent meeting, the

Hotel Committee noted that the government's anti-alcohol policy sought to reduce the number of establishments selling such drinks from one for eighty inhabitants of France to one in four hundred. Concerned about the loss of a precious *patrimoine* built up over a long period, the Hotel Committee recommended compensation for any alcoholic beverage retailers who were to lose their licenses.[113]

The Hotel Committee was also delegated with determining the various categories of restaurants, mentioned earlier as an issue that sometimes caused problems with the Germans, and also deciding which restaurants were to be assigned to each category. Restaurants classified as "exceptional" were those that offered "perfect cuisine" and "luxurious service," and were limited by government fiat to a select few. As of September 1939, to be classified as "exceptional," hotels had to offer service considered "palatial."[114]

Politics were not far beneath the surface in the Hotel Committee's professional bulletins. Writing in the January 1942 newsletter for the Yonne department, René Hure looked back to the start of the organization's subcommittee on food distribution established by a decree of 9 August 1940 to regulate the allotment of foodstuffs to local hotels. He hoped publicly that the new year would bring "peace and the liberation of our country," the return of hotel industry workers then in German prisoner of war camps, and an unspecified reform of the hotel corporation.[115] German censors blocked the publication of the newsletter, leading to extensive deliberations.[116] In August 1942 the Germans granted permission to the Hotel Committee to publish its professional bulletins, which were considered official notices of the French government.[117]

In language borrowed from official Vichy manifestos, the May 1942 bulletin of the Rennes region described the hotel administrator as a "human person exercising the functions of a leader [*chef*], a consciousness of his duty, and desire to serve," whose role was to "assure the life of the country and prepare its recovery [*redressement*]."[118] As in the January issue, much of the attention was devoted to the distribution of food to hotels and the regulation of the hours when they could serve various items. Hotels that had been requisitioned by the Germans and dining rooms set aside for them were fully outside the regulatory purview of the French agencies. In establishments serving French and German clientele, orders from the German authorities were to treat both sets of patrons equally. The hoteliers and restaurateurs had to deal with complex and shifting rationing regulations. Beer, for example, could be served only in officially licensed *débitants de boissons* (beverage distributors). Coffee, in short supply because metropolitan France was cut off from its sources in Madagascar and the Ivory Coast, could not be served in the summer months, from June through August. Tea was unavailable, and the limited chocolate supplies were carefully regulated. An allotment of chocolate had been promised to the Rennes hospitality industry, but no one seemed to know when it would arrive. In addition to food restrictions, the bulletins addressed the details of the hotel trade, transmitting official directives for social security contributions for employees, and the various contributions made to their national health and life insurance programs. Hotel owners and managers were advised to accept German requisitions, their only avenue of redress being to contact their prefect, who might intervene with the local German military command post. In addition, the government offered to pay some of the costs of repairing hotels and replacing furniture damaged in the 1940 military operations.[119]

Virtual Tourism in Occupied France

For those unable to travel, tourism imaginaries remained active, stimulated by publications that continued during the Occupation. *Sciences et voyages,* whose mission, in collaboration with the Club des explorateurs, was to educate those "who want to learn the customs of people around the world," continued to function, although German approval was required. *Sciences et voyages* also sponsored lectures, such as one by a Miss Marion Senones, who spoke on the "salt route" to an audience at the Palais de Chaillot in Paris in December 1941.[120]

In addition, restrictions on travel may have contributed to the significant increase in film attendance and reading that occurred in occupied France. A hint of the magnitude of this kind of tourism can be seen in the 510 documentary films produced in France between 1940 and 1944.[121] According to Jean-Pierre Rioux, attendance at movie theaters increased from 200 million in 1938 to 304 million in 1943. Requests for the loan of books from municipal libraries in France rose from 1.2 million in 1931 to 2.23 million ten years later.[122]

The Southern Zone and the Later Stages of the Occupation

The German occupation of the southern zone in November 1943, which occurred while conditions were worsening and food was becoming ever harder to acquire for most of the French, offered travel opportunities for those who had not wished to or could not obtain the needed German permission to cross (*Ausweiss*) zones, and many Parisians traveled south to visit

FIGURE 8.   Agfa-Isopan advertisement for film to take on vacation in 1942. Inside back cover, *L'Illustration* 5180 (20 June 1942). Author's personal collection.

relatives or just to get away from the city. In his account of wartime Paris, published in 1946, Pierre Audiat wrote that at vacation time the trains were packed, with lines beginning at 5 a.m. Parisians took hotel rooms near the railway stations to be first in line for the trains the following morning. The struggle for tickets was intense.[123]

An article in a 1943 issue of *La Bourgogne d'Or*, a publication whose subtitle invoked literature, the arts, regionalism, history, archaeology, and tourism, made its political views clear in referring to a France "contaminated by internationalism and the Jew, no longer a republic but Marianne, the Notre-Dame of bistros."[124] Although on a reduced scale, *La Bourgogne d'Or* continued publication through the end of 1943, evoking the culture and folklore of the region. Under "Notes bourguignons," in what turned out to be its last wartime issue, the periodical reported that Beaune had just been named a "town of art and locality of artistic and picturesque character."[125] Deficiencies in transport by the first half of 1944 led *Lyon-Touriste* to suggest that the local population of Lyon should use the opportunity to rediscover their city by foot.[126] In yet another case of the politicization of tourist symbols, a report in *L'hôtelier français* stated that Paris authorities were threatening to close the "American bars" because of their name. The *Hôtelier français* article, appearing ironically in retrospect one day before the Normandy invasion, reminded its readers and the authorities that these bars were "clearly French and Parisian" and that they had no connection with the United States.[127] Another irony, perhaps, was a recommendation made the same day by the Touring club de France's administrative council to relaunch its Comité de tourisme gastronomique (Gastronomic Tourism Committee), suspended in 1939. Discussions had been going on among some of the members of the previous committee, and the council determined that the time was ripe to consider its principles and activities for the postwar world.[128] As the war continued, the German occupation exactions became heavier, and travel was impeded not only by the requisition of hotels and trains but also by shortages of electricity that, for example, affected the Paris Métro. By the spring of 1944, many of the subway stations were closed, and by March of that year, train service had been curtailed to the hours from 8 a.m. to 10 p.m. Fares increased as well.[129]

Pilgrimages and Tourism

Pilgrimages, in older forms related to Church sites and, in newer forms, to *lieux de mémoire,* also characterized the Occupation years. Religious pilgrimages, a legacy of premodern tourism, surviving in the hajj and pilgrimages to Benares and Santiago de Compostela, took place as well in occupied France.[130] Such pilgrimages undoubtedly date back to early humans, who traveled with a sense of curiosity, visited sacred sites, and imparted religious signification to the places they discovered. The fictional pilgrims of Chaucer's *Canterbury Tales* and the real ones on the road to Santiago de Compostela encountered trinkets, exchanged stories, and stayed in inns, however spartan, in the

Middle Ages.[131] In his study of daily life in the Loire River valley during the Occupation, Robert Gildea mentions several religious pilgrimages, including one to Béhuard that took place on 8 September 1942 at the site of a shrine to Mary, on an island in the Loire. Some of the pilgrims, he indicates, walked great distances to reach the shrine.[132] In a religious pilgrimage to Vue, not far from Nantes in northwestern France, on 26 July 1942, several hundred young people among some five thousand pilgrims were found by the German authorities to be wearing what they termed "Gaullist" symbols in red, white, and blue, as well as crosses of Lorraine. In the spring and summer of 1944, the Return of Our Lady of Boulogne, a months-long celebration, described as the "great event" by Gildea, was centered on a statue of Mary and three copies of it believed to have entered Boulogne in the seventh century. The festival was a pilgrimage that crossed central France with processions held at Richelieu, Loches, and Chinon, as well as Angers and Tours.[133] These events coincided with the Liberation, and it appears that the statues did more traveling than the pilgrims, several of whom, however, had come from some distance to see the icons.

Annual pilgrimages from Paris to Lourdes were suspended in 1940 because of the military mobilization of their organizer, Father Gérard Sébastien Deryckère. The zonal demarcation line blocked pilgrimages from Paris in 1941 and 1942, but a small pilgrimage took place in 1943 following the German occupation of the formerly unoccupied zone. Once more in 1944, there was no Paris-Lourdes pilgrimage.[134] Despite increased travel difficulties, a crowd of pilgrims, estimated at sixty thousand, trekked from Lourdes to Paris, from March 1943 through June 1946. Through war-torn France the procession moved, passing, for example, through La Roche Bernard on 6 August 1944, shortly after the town had been riddled with gunfire during a battle.[135] The Touring club de France also lent its imprimatur to Lourdes as a destination with its support of the Musée pyrénéen de Lourdes, which opened in 1921 at the old Lourdes fort, which had been leased by the club to house the museum. In a lengthy report of July 1943, the Touring Club endorsed the museum's work encouraging exploration of the Pyrenees.[136]

The transfer of the remains of Napoleon Bonaparte's son Napoleon II to the Invalides in December 1940 also offered a pilgrimage site, with new meaning after Hitler's gesture of repatriating the body. For some of the French committed to the Axis cause, the tomb of "l'Aiglon" (the Eaglet), as Napoleon II was known, became a pilgrimage site representing the greatness of France together with Franco-German collaboration. More than thirty years after the event, Jacques Schweizer, a young Paris lawyer who had headed the wartime Jeunesse de l'Europe nouvelle (JEN), recalled a pilgrimage to the site in September 1943 to demonstrate support for the German cause.[137] In 1969 the postwar French government, wishing to put the affair behind them, had the remains placed in their present location in the lower level of the Saint-Jérôme chapel under the dome of the Invalides.[138]

"Join the Army, See the World"

How many French volunteers joined combat formations on either side in a "join the army, see the world" spirit can never be known. Frenchmen volunteered for German military organizations, such as the Légion des volontaires français contre le Bolchévisme (LVF, the Anti-Bolshevik Legion) and the Waffen-SS française, both units of French volunteers who fought alongside the Germans against the Russians, sometimes out of curiosity to see the world, as in the case of a veteran who was moved to do so by a Paris Métro recruiting poster.[139] A small but significant segment of recruits to the pro-German cause consisted of young romantics whose prewar years had been spent in the youth hostel movement in quest of adventure and camaraderie on the roads of the French countryside. They came from the secular youth hostel movement, the Centre laïc des auberges de jeunesse (CLAJ), a lay splinter group from Marc Sangnier's more Catholic denominational youth hostel movement. The Centre laïc attracted a large number of the sons and daughters of the white-collar bourgeoisie, teachers in particular. During the mid-1930s, many of the young CLAJistes were drawn to the writings of Jean Giono. In his accounts of rural folkways, Giono provided a focal point for middle-class urban youth in quest of spiritual values that they believed lay in the countryside. A pacifist, Giono opposed war against Germany, and many of the CLAJistes shared this sentiment.[140]

Marc Augier was active in the hostel movement and during the war joined the Waffen-SS. The son of a cement plant owner, Augier was born in 1908 in Bordeaux. To Augier, the youth hostel movement represented a spirit of one for all, all for one, combined with a romanticized aristocratic spirit in which what might be called today "adventure travel" played a key role. He became a journalist and from 1935 to 1940 edited the Centre laïc's newspaper, in which he described his own mountaineering treks into the Swiss Alps and winter ski trips to Norway.[141] Chosen to represent his organization at a world youth congress at Vassar College in Poughkeepsie, New York, in 1938, Augier opposed what he perceived as a communist attempt to turn the meeting into an antifascist event. He emerged as a militant anticommunist.[142]

Upon his demobilization following the French defeat in 1940, Augier joined Schweizer in establishing the JEN as a youth affiliate of the Groupe collaboration, led by the writer Alphonse de Châteaubriant.[143] Plainly, Augier saw in Nazi Germany the camaraderie and emphasis on love of nature he had prized in the hostel movement, and he criticized the official youth organization of Vichy, the Chantiers de la jeunesse, for being insufficiently political or too "Boy Scoutish." By late 1941, the JEN was organizing camping expeditions to Germany. Augier's comment, referred to earlier, about the JEN's camping expedition representing a future leisure culture of conquest rather than decadence, expressed in the pro-German language of the day, indicates the direction in which his own tourism imaginary was moving.[144] Looking for a larger field of action, however, he joined the Anti-Bolshevik Legion and later edited its publication, *Le combattant européen*. Service in the Legion, Augier stated, represented "grandeur and the sense of adventure."[145] Believing that the Legion effaced the stain of the 1940 defeat, he proudly recalled being saluted by uniformed Germans in the streets of Berlin. With the incorporation of the Legion into the newly formed Waffen-SS Charlemagne division in June 1944, Augier became a political officer.[146] He seems to have viewed the German invasion of the Soviet Union as a grand travel adventure. *Les partisans,* his account of his involvement in the Anti-Bolshevik Legion, published in 1943, reads like a travelogue, with occasional references to his prewar travels and adventures. The entry of the French volunteers from Polish into Soviet territory, he wrote, reminded him of travel books he had read: "With our entry into the old [Soviet] Union, thousands of fires and thousands of men made an offering that peacetime travelers never received. And there I detected suddenly in the wind a fragrance I know well for having been impregnated with it lavishly in Finnish Lapland: that of the overheated essence of Nordic pine."[147]

Augier wrote that the battle in the Soviet Union was leading to the unification of the world. He wrote of trying to inspire his comrades in the Legion with a slogan, "travel with the Kommandateur Line," a takeoff on the peacetime advertisements he recalled such as "Sail with the French Line," "Visit the fjords of Norway," "Spend 1 May in Moscow," or "Take the Cunard Line, the most comfortable." He continued:

> All the refinements of civilization were reunited on the ships, the trains ran on the steel of the rolling mill, but the steel of the rail supported the weight of the sleeping cars and cradled our sleeping happy travelers. But this great work of peaceful travel led to what end? To move the nostalgias of some lovers, to detach from themselves those obsessed who imagined only a tour of the world at 250 pounds, to transport beyond hostile frontiers a small number of armaments agents, to

promenade at the cost of all the princesses of the political delegates and ambassadors. But the peoples did not travel; the peacetime economy could not invest so gigantic a capital.

The war economy has given birth to the biggest enterprise of world travel. From 1914 to 1918, my farmer visited the east of France, Italy, Greece, the Dardanelles. Without the war, this man would never have taken off his clogs. In 1932 and in 1936 I wanted to visit the Soviet Union. Two requests for a visa remained unanswered. Peacetime economy. In 1942 I came from Smolensk to Paris in two and a half days with my pay book [*Soldbuch*] and a little square of paper, the special identification card [*Sonderausweiss*], [serving] as my passport. At the same time, tens of thousands of men from all countries go and come without any more difficulty from Petsamo to the island of Crete, from Rostow to Douarnenez. War economy. All is taken care of by the Kommandateur Line . . . and the dormitories in the railway stations and the hot soup in the soldiers' homes [*Soldatenheim*], and en route the feeding, the showers, the anti-parasite struggle, the distribution of new clothing upon exiting the USSR.[148]

Augier saw a parallel between camping and soldiering. "As an old nomad," he wrote, "I can appreciate these things." Nevertheless, he added, there was nothing in common between the soldier planting his tent and the camper planting his. The camper, a city person, sets up his tent as late as possible in the evening with the intention of moving the next day, whereas the soldier sets his up more permanently in the hope of staying put. The reason, Augier maintained, was that camping was a movement of nomadic, rootless (*déraciné*) city dwellers, whereas the "European" armies—in other words, the Germans and their allies—were composed largely of peasants, who moved only because of force or war publicity. Because of nostalgia for the land, however, the peasant soldiers wished to stay put, and each time they set up camp hoped to remain there.[149]

Adventure tourism characterized a trek made across the Sahara by several French travelers, one of whom wrote about his trip in *Jeune force de France*, a semi-monthly periodical published in occupied France by Jean-Marie Balestre, who, like Augier, ended up in the French Waffen-SS.[150] Describing his trek through the desert, Marcel Montarron is asked at the outset whether he is a "sporting type," as the journey will be hard. He describes the searing heat of day and the cold of night as he and his companions make their way from Algeria to what was then French West Africa, now Mali. En route he asks rhetorically, "Where are the Pullman cars that we are shown crossing the dessert like racing cars on the advertising posters?" Instead, he and his companions bounced around in an old Berliet-Diesel truck that felt like a furnace as they crossed the Tanezrouft into Mali. There he found Frenchmen building bridges, dikes, and channels, knowing only from occasional newspapers of the events in the world, but who, he wrote, were maintaining the grandeur of imperial France.[151]

Nostalgia for a time when moral choices were clear and life was dangerous occasionally appears in memoirs of Resistance activists as well, such as those of Henri Frenay, recalling his underground organizational and journalistic activities. Lucie Aubrac, a teacher in public and a Resistance agent in secret, wrote of taking her students for day tours of Roman ruins near Lyon to emphasize France's historic ties to the grandeur of Rome.[152] Finally, during the war, select French visitors had the opportunity to tour Germany. The visits to Germany of prominent pro-German literary figures such as the writer Robert Brasillach and others have been well documented.[153] Lesser-known French visitors, however, also had similar opportunities. A group of French participants in a professional training meeting in Dresden in May 1943 was offered the opportunity, which appears to have been accepted, to visit sites in the city's surroundings. Appropriate sleeping car arrangements needed to be made.[154] Even some of the French conscripted into the STO (Service du travail obligatoire), the labor service in which thousands of French workers were forced to labor in Germany, often under abysmal conditions, had their tourism moments. The son of an acquaintance of Jean Guéhenno's had been drafted into the STO, and Guéhenno had the opportunity to read his letters from Germany to his mother back in Paris. Stationed in April 1943 in the small town of Belzig in Brandenburg, not far from Berlin, the son described the town as the prettiest village in the world, with lakes, forests, and meadows. Berlin was not far away, he said, and one could go there as a tourist ("en touriste!").[155] The letter writer was lucky enough to return to Paris in the fall of 1943, but having been worked nearly to death in Belzig, he arrived home with a heart condition and horrific stories of his experience there.[156]

Anti-Jewish and Anti-Masonic Exhibitions

Vichy also sponsored traveling anti-Jewish and anti-Masonic exhibitions, somewhat in the manner of touring circuses, one in the Petit Palais in Paris in October 1940 described by Vassili Soukhomline as having brought Masonic artifacts taken by the Germans from the offices of the Grand Orient of France to show that Hitler had "liberated" France from the Judaeo-Masonic-English plot to dominate the world. Visitors, according to Soukhomline, were few, and the exposition made little impression on the Parisians, "already skeptical by nature."[157]

Olivier Barrot and Raymond Chirat itemized several additional such expositions. In May 1941, a Vichy-sponsored exposition called "La France européene," promoting France's role in the German New Order, drew some 635,000 visitors to the Grand Palais in Paris, and an anti-Freemason exposition offering free admission at the end of that year at the Petit Palais in Paris attracted some 1 million of the curious. The Palais Berlitz hosted "Le juif et la France" (The Jew and France), which had a "resounding success" in September 1941.[158] In May of the following year, an anti-Bolshevik exposition took place at the Salle Wagram in Paris. These shows attracted the curious but, as Barrot and Chirat write, they quickly grew wearisome to all but a minority of those committed to the Axis cause.[159] Writing in general about museums and expositions, Marc Chesnel reminds us that in all types of expositions, "the collection of objects is gathered to be presented to the public to which it is oriented, meaning, in what interests us here, the tourist clientele."[160]

The Battle for France and the Arrival of the Allies

Issues of tourism surfaced even during the military campaign that raged across France during the summer of 1944, when in July a local sub-prefect in Puy-de-Dôme in central France closed the Château de Barante, "forbidding all visits of the premises by foreigners and tourists, who up to now have come in sufficiently large numbers."[161] With the liberation of almost all of France during the spring and summer of 1944, interzonal barriers disappeared and gradually tourism could begin to assume something of its pre-Occupation form, although the French were still focused on the war in late 1944 and certainly until the German defeat in 1945. The Seine River bridges in Paris, already invested with tourist significance, acquired new appeal among tourists interested in seeing the sites where street fighting took place during the liberation of Paris in 1944. Plaques eventually marked the spots where Resistance fighters were killed in action. Tourism symbols gained new meanings as Vichy cultural constructions were replaced by those of the Resistance, both Gaullist and communist. These often became embroiled in what have been called "battles for memory."[162] Even while the war continued after the liberation of France, the Touring club de France called for a meeting of all concerned organizations, public and private, to join together to ensure the preservation of France's artistic *patrimoine*. Sponsored by the "French Touring Club Welcome Committee," a meeting was to be held with a Colonel Webb, head of the Anglo-American mission in France, on 7 December 1944.[163]

The departure of the Germans in August 1944 was followed by the arrival of the Allies, and although the political equation had changed, many of the same issues related to tourism remained, specifically those dealing with foreign soldiers, determining and preserving the *patrimoine,* and planning for a reinvigorated tourism industry. Once the material situation improved in the years after the war, tourism and the tourist industry would surge in a manner unprecedented in the earlier twentieth century. In another paradigm shift, the postwar tourism narratives again would change. One of the more significant aspects of Second World War tourism in France, however, was that of the Germans during the four-year Occupation, which is considered next. German tourism during the Occupation also had roots in the tourism imaginaries of prewar France, as the success of Friedrich Sieburg's work amply demonstrated. It surely played a role in the postwar expansion of tourism as well.

Chapter 4

German Tourism in Occupied France, 1940–1944

Even with the deprivations endured under wartime and occupation conditions, tourism remained a catalyst for cultural change. An examination of German tourism and French acquiescence to it in occupied France illuminates its role in expressing and deepening the inequalities in the political and economic relationships of occupier and occupant. Tourism and the tourist imaginaries, in other words, are manifestations of the relationships of power that Walter Benjamin saw expressed in the medium of film and that others see in today's tourism relationships between the wealthier and poorer countries of the world.[1] While many in occupied France suffered deprivations, one group stands out as privileged, namely, the German occupation personnel for whom France became a prized billet, a place for rest and relaxation, and, for many, a place to exercise the tourism imaginary that had developed over the preceding generations in Germany as elsewhere. Appealing to this sensibility in a guidebook translated into German in 1943, Pierre Andrieu wrote that France's restaurants justified the "much-spread-about expression," quoting Sieburg, that "[the amenities of Paris] let you live like God in France [lässt sich leben wie Gott in Frankreich]."[2] Despite roundups and exterminations of Jews and other targets of the Third Reich, and increased death rates in France, the war years saw a continuing German curiosity about France, and many young soldiers stationed there were provided with tourism opportunities they otherwise would not have had. An article in a June 1942 issue of the *Wegleiter* extolled the benefits of wartime tourism, arguing that the war had made young Germans acquainted with the political and "natural" characteristics of peoples about whom in times of peace they could learn only in books.[3] German wartime tourism in France undoubtedly contributed to the increases in postwar tourism in general. Instances of the German tourism imaginaries of France ranged from the stories and photographs of Hitler's quick tour through defeated Paris in June 1940 to General Dietrich von Choltitz's account of his role in saving the city during the German retreat in 1944.

Perhaps most dramatic for France was its future in the event of a German victory. Flush with triumph in July 1940, Hitler made clear his lack of interest in a collaborationist France, even one ruled by a friendly authoritarian government. Looking ahead, he declared in a comment showing a contemptuous view of tourism as a concept shared with so many others before and since:

> Germany will not conclude with France a chivalrous [generous] peace. Germany does not consider France an ally, but a state with which accounts will be settled at the time of the peace treaty. In the future, France will play in Europe the role of an enlarged Switzerland and will become a country of tourism specializing eventually in certain fashion productions.[4]

Shelley Baranowski, who has written extensively on the tourism program of Nazi Germany's Kraft durch Freude (KdF, Strength through Joy), commented, "Although the tourism arising from the Wehrmacht's invasions and its relationship to KdF's troop entertainment programme deserves further study, the acquisition of Lebensraum unquestionably offered vast opportunities for realising personal ambitions and making concrete the imperial ambitions that KdF promoted."[5]

Nazi Germany and Tourism

The importance attached to tourism in Nazi Germany, despite whatever views Hitler may have held personally, was manifested in the establishment of the KdF program, which promoted paid vacations and tourist excursions for German workers, both within Germany and beyond its borders. The official guidebook for the German pavilion at the 1937 International Exposition in Paris, prepared by Hermann Esser, an early close associate of Hitler, and in 1937 Bavaria's economics minister, extolled the virtues of tourism, inviting visitors to come see the improvements made in Germany "since Adolf Hitler took over the reins of government," the "huge and beautiful buildings" in Berlin, Munich, and Nuremberg, as well as improvements in German resorts, the national highways, and more intensive use of spas.[6] By the time of the Second World War, tourism as a concept was so well established in the minds of many Germans that when the Luftwaffe launched a bombing campaign against cultural targets in the spring of 1942, including the historic British cities of Exeter, Bath, Norwich, York, and Canterbury, which followed a British raid against Lübeck, the attacks became known as the "Baedeker raids," after the popular German guidebooks. Baron Gustav Braun von Sturm, a spokesman for the German Foreign Office, claimed that the Luftwaffe would work its way through the Baedeker tourist guide.[7]

Not all German tourism in France, however, was of the innocent kind depicted in Sieburg's interwar best-seller, extolled in the 1937 Exposition guidebook, or indicated in the Baedeker guidebooks. Otto Abetz, a former German representative to Franco-German youth congresses, who spoke excellent French with a Parisian dialect and was married to a Frenchwoman, frequented Montparnasse coffeehouses in the late 1930s in efforts to meet journalists and political figures. Abetz had worked during the 1930s to promote Franco-German tourism with a small group of pro-German Frenchmen, including Fernand de Brinon, the first French journalist to interview Hitler after his accession to power.[8] Brinon had helped create in 1935 the Comité France-Allemagne, a French reconciliation committee, which engaged in cultural activities and sponsored youth tours to Germany.[9] His activities in Paris were supported by the German embassy there.[10] Having worked with the KdF in Italy and France, Abetz was expelled from France in 1939 on suspicion of espionage.[11] He enjoyed a triumphal return after the 1940 German invasion as "ambassador" to occupied France. The activities of Abetz, who was subsequently sentenced in France after the war to twenty years' hard labor and released after five, and Brinon, who was executed for wartime collaboration, highlight the relationship between tourism and espionage, an underexplored area of tourism studies.

By the time the Second World War began in September 1939, the Nazi KdF program had so conditioned the vacation and tourism expectations of Germans that the official suspension of vacations in view of the wartime situation had to be lifted. Reduced tourism activity continued in a sort of "deceptive normalcy," in the words of Hasso Spode, a specialist in German tourism history, until it was progressively eliminated in 1943 following the Battle of Stalingrad and the turn to "total war," or, in Goebbels's words, "first victory, then travel."[12] Following its victory in June 1940, the Wehrmacht conducted thousands of tours for Germans in occupied France, and American soldiers succeeded them as tourists after the Liberation. Second World War tourism in France is often construed as consisting of the Moulin Rouge and the exclusive Maxim's restaurant in Paris, where German occupation soldiers spent leisure time, or the large hotels in the Alps and beach resorts near Nice, many of which remained open during the war years.[13]

Tourism Opportunities and Images

Clearly interested in tourism in occupied France after 1940, the Germans used it as a rest and rehabilitation zone for their soldiers from other fronts and offered visits there as rewards for others, military and civilian.[14] German organizations such as the Deutsche Arbeitsfront (DAF, or German Labor Front) and KdF, together with a special unit of the Wehrmacht, organized tours for Germans in France. Despite paper shortages, the German occupation authorities sponsored the publication of tour books for their personnel in occupied France and photo and other travel literature related to France for popular consumption back home in Germany. Frequently produced by local French with German support, the tourism publications, such as the *Wegleiter*, contributed to the Nazis' attempts to promote popular stereotypes and engendered the creation of the kind of kitsch that has often been seen in their cultural attitudes generally.

In a battle of images, German propaganda was dominant through much of the Second World War. One of Hitler's first acts after the defeat of France in June 1940 was to tour Paris with his personal photographer, whose photo of him with the Eiffel Tower in the background became iconic. Hitler's visit and the priority he placed on it reflected tourism images that were echoed by Goebbels, Ernst Jünger, and thousands of other German visitors, described by William Shirer and sometimes called the "tourists in uniform" mentioned in the introduction to this book.[15] The *Wegleiter* expressed essentialized German imaginaries of a naughty Paris and backward France.

Subtle but profound tourist images of France among Germans from Hitler down may well have played an important role in political and military decision making, specifically, as we have seen, in the decision to grant France an armistice in 1940 at the site of the 1918 armistice at Compiègne which ended World War I, the use of Paris as a tourist destination during the occupation of France, and, if not the actual saving of the city from destruction by German forces at the time of its liberation in August 1944, the discourse around that topic. Emphasizing what they wished to promote as their own high level of cultural and artistic sophistication, the Germans proudly claimed that they had preserved French cultural monuments, such as the city of Paris and Rouen cathedral, during the fighting in 1940. The way in which Paris was saved from destruction in 1944 had touristic overtones, a story famously told in the book *Is Paris Burning?*, published by Larry Collins and Dominique Lapierre in 1965, and made into an award-winning film the next year.[16]

Hitler Tours Paris, Goebbels Follows

Despite the obvious differences between a soldier sent abroad and a civilian taking a trip for pleasure, the relationships between touristic interest and the military were clearly understood by the Germans during the Second World War. Hitler's whirlwind tour of Paris was filmed and photographed by Heinrich Hoffmann, his personal photographer, in late June 1940.[17] His visit to Paris was virtually unescorted and took place in the early morning hours to avoid potential security problems. Economics adviser Albert Speer and court sculptor and artist Arno Breker, who had lived and studied in Paris, were summoned to accompany Hitler on his tour. In his memoirs years later, Breker recalled the diligence with which Hitler had prepared for the tour. Hitler, he wrote, was fully familiar with the layout of the Paris Opéra, "its exact measurements and a thousand other details."[18] At one point during the tour near the Carrefour Saint-Michel, Hitler pointed out a cupola and asked Breker if it was the Tribunal de Commerce. Calling upon his experience of having lived in Paris, Breker corrected him, telling him it was the Institute, presumably the Institute de France. As they passed the building, Hitler turned to Breker and pointed to the inscription on the building, which read "Tribunal de Commerce." Breker notes, "This little insignificant incident proved how intense the preparation for his visit had been."[19] He recalls that on visiting Napoleon's tomb in the Invalides, Hitler decided that a grand gesture to promote Franco-German reconciliation in the future would be to authorize the return of the remains of Napoleon II, known in Germany as the Duke of Reichstadt, then buried in the Capuchin vault in Vienna, which would later take place under strained circumstances in December 1940.[20] Toward the end of his tour, as he gazed upon the Sacré-Cœur basilica and the view of Paris from Montmartre, Hitler thanked destiny for having allowed him to visit this city "that has always fascinated me." Although the French government had withdrawn from Paris, declaring it an open city to forestall conflict there and secure its preservation, he stated that he had given orders before and during the fighting to save it whether or not the French declared it open. By 8:15 in the morning the tour was over.[21]

The photograph of Hitler, together with Speer and Breker on either side of him at Trocadéro with the Eiffel Tower in the background, was used for

FIGURE 9.   Hitler at Trocadéro in Paris with the Eiffel Tower in the background, photographed by Heinrich Hoffmann just after the German military entry into the city in June 1940. Heinrich Hoffmann, *Mit Hitler im Westen* (Munich: Verlag Heinrich Hoffmann, 1940). Author's personal collection.

the cover of Hoffmann's *Mit Hitler im Westen,* published in September 1940. *Mit Hitler im Westen* is a tourist album of the German victory in the West. The photograph, an iconic image of Hitler's victory in 1940, has been reproduced repeatedly in Germany and elsewhere.[22] It is a highly unusual photo because it was taken at dawn rather than dusk, a rare hour for tourist photos of the Eiffel Tower. Late afternoon is usually preferred for tourism pictures because of the warm-colored shadows, making photography relatively easy. Few tourists manage to catch the soft light of the predawn hours. Hoffmann's book also featured pictures of the German leader crossing the Rhine bridge at Kehl to enter "German Strassburg" and then touring the cathedral there.[23]

Isolating the role of Hitler in the victory, the *Mit Hitler im Westen* cover focused on him and excluded Speer and Breker. Testifying to the centrality of Paris as a tourist destination, it was used to glorify Hitler's role in the military victory over France.[24] Roger Langeron, the Paris police prefect at the time, wrote that Hitler traveled around the city "as a tourist," and claimed to have had him followed by Paris agents—"imprudent enough!" Hitler also took a walk down the boulevard Saint-Michel, but as Langeron noted, it was early in the morning and the streets were deserted so no one noticed.[25] Although Hitler expressed joy at having had a chance to visit Paris, a place he said he had always wanted to see, his touristic assessment of the city, which was based on its architectural monuments, was mixed at best. He praised the Invalides and the Madeleine but criticized the Panthéon and found Sacré-Cœur "ghastly." Except for the Eiffel Tower, he later wrote, Paris possessed nothing that made it stand out as a city in the way that the Coliseum did for Rome.[26] Given Hitler's pretense at architectural sophistication and his clearly defined ethnocentric biases, his comments should not surprise.

The images of Paris in *Mit Hitler im Westen* give a rather pedestrian view of the French capital. They reflect the touristic imaginaries of interwar Paris depicted in the guidebooks of the interwar years, with a narrative of the German military victory of 1940 superimposed. Three German fighter planes are flying over Paris in one photo, apparently prior to the German entry into the city. A caption identifies the Arc de Triomphe.[27] Additional photographs show Hitler and his entourage looking down at Napoleon's tomb in the Invalides, Hitler and his party descending the steps of the Church of the Madeleine with the Corinthian columns behind them, and Hitler and his group emerging from the orchestra section inside the Paris Opéra. Given his interest in architecture, Hitler was also shown gazing up to admire massive French cathedrals in Laon and Strasbourg, cities captured in the course of the German western offensive.[28] Hitler, for whom much was corrupt in the French capital, invoked the nineteenth-century image, repeated by Sieburg, of Paris as "Babylon."[29] Nonetheless, he admired its architectural monuments and told his entourage, "I thank Providence to have been able to see this city whose magical atmosphere has always fascinated me."[30] Discussing the German filming of Hitler's June 1940 visit to Paris, Cédric Gruat emphasizes the role played by military monuments in creating an almost fictional back-drop for the imaging of the German leader in Paris, simultaneously a "decor, museum, and imaginary" city. The Arc de Triomphe featured prominently in the film, as did the Madeleine, conceived originally as a temple to the glory of the Grand Army in 1806 before being converted into a church in 1845.[31] Shortly after Hitler's tour of Paris, the cover of the first issue of *Signal*, the German magazine published throughout occupied Europe during the war, bore a picture of German military planes flying past the Eiffel Tower.[32]

Goebbels followed quickly thereafter with his own tour of Paris. His itinerary followed that of Hitler. Describing Paris as a "magnificent city," during a morning visit Goebbels saw the place de la Concorde, place de l'Étoile (splendidly laid out: his comment), the dome of the Invalides, Napoleon's tomb (deeply moved—despite all, a great man), Notre-Dame, the Madeleine (somewhat absurd architecture for a church), and Sacré-Cœur (which disappointed him very much). He preferred Montmartre, "where I would like to live for a few weeks," and its view of Paris. The Chamber of Deputies building was a "stable," the Luxembourg Palace looked a bit better, and, finally, the Quai d'Orsay, then and now home of the French Foreign Ministry, was notable as the site where anti-German policies had been fashioned. In the afternoon he visited Versailles, symbolic as the center of government under Louis XIV and the site where German unity had been achieved in 1871 and its World War I defeat sealed by the peace treaty of 1919. Finding the château desolate but apparently quite beautiful in normal conditions, Goebbels commented that the Hall of Mirrors, scene of the events of 1871 and 1919, was now good for a barn. Nonetheless, the sequence of French kings named Louis had been great men. After watching his newsreels with soldiers at the Trianon palace, he revisited Montmartre at twilight. "Below lay the darkening Paris, this enigmatic [*rätselhafte*] city."[33]

Hitler going to see the World War I sites, the trenches, and planning a new armistice at Compiègne, the site of the old one—equally unsuccessful—and Goebbels dragging the Compiègne railway car back to Berlin both unwittingly gave evidence to an old and shortsighted, if not petty, German view of France. Each of them made his blitz tour through occupied Paris, offering a grudging admiration combined with vengeful contempt, not dissimilar to the tone of Sieburg's prewar descriptions. At a time when total victory over France lay within their grasp, neither visited the forward lines along the channel or the Atlantic or even tried to see, let alone seize, the French fleet in Toulon. Naïvely they accepted a view in which France was at once contemptible and grand, and this view may have inadvertently spared France the kind of destructive "polonization" that occurred elsewhere during the war.

Occupied France in the German Tourist Imaginary

Nazi leaders' touristic perspectives on France were based on images already present in German culture. The sites visited by Germans, starting with Hitler at the top, reflected those commonly seen in the Stendhal paradigm that had characterized popular tourist images of France since the second half of the nineteenth century. Philippe Boegner described a crowd of Germans enthusiastically viewing a performance of Georges Bizet's *Carmen* at the Opéra-Comique during the summer of 1940. Out of curiosity, Boegner went to the performance, observing that "the Germans have always loved Bizet." He remembered having been to the Scala theater in Berlin in 1934, where a performance of *Carmen* in the presence of Hitler and other dignitaries "surrounded by a sea of green and brown," referring German military uniforms, had evoked an enthusiastic response from the entire audience. Beniamino Gigli, "the greatest tenor since Caruso," appeared on a stage decked with Nazi flags and gave the fascist salute, to which Hitler responded, and the hall was filled with shouts. As Gigli began to sing, the audience fell silent. "That evening," Boegner remembered, "I could not hold back my tears in hearing sung 'La fleur que tu m'avais jetée.' In this hyper-Nazi auditorium, Bizet and his two Jewish associates Meilhac and Halévy provoked an enthusiasm that I can still hear six years later in leaving the Opéra-Comique."[34]

The interwar image of France as a land of romance and sex, together with good food as enjoyed at Maxim's, and the good life in general, expressed in Sieburg's *Gott in Frankreich?*, had become common currency by 1940. Sieburg's book was republished in both German and French during the Occupation, although Sieburg was later described by a French observer as a "petty bourgeois" with only a "conventional" knowledge of France and a latecomer to Nazism.[35] The very "conventionality," or perhaps banality, of Sieburg's touristic appreciation of France and the fact that he and his work were honored in both France and Germany during the Occupation years make him a good point of reference for understanding the kinds of images of France that the Nazis would later favor.

Germans arriving in France in 1940 were thus primed to perceive the country as a backward but delightful counter-model to German modernity. Their 1940 victory had confirmed German superiority in the minds of many, but, as Julia S. Torrie notes, France's charms remained, and tourism was a key to enjoying them.[36] Robert Gildea writes, "Many [German soldiers] came to France as sexual and gastronomic tourists as much as soldiers."[37] As early as October 1940, Marshal Gerd von Rundstedt reminded his forces that they were occupying a largely hostile country in which much of the local population still hoped for a turnaround in the fortunes of the war. Although an English invasion was improbable, he warned of coastal landings that might attempt to bolster England's military prestige and perhaps take some prisoners. The coastal defenses along the Atlantic, he ordered, had to be reinforced and remain alert in order to thwart any would-be English landing in the winter of 1940–41.[38] Rommel, placed in charge of the construction of the Atlantic Wall coastal defenses, made it clear that he expected the war to be won or lost on the beaches along the Atlantic.[39] What focused tourist gazes and imaginaries, or the "receptivity" of "a travelling mind-set," to refer again to the words of Alain de Botton, was newsreel film of Rommel on tour along the Atlantic Wall shown during the war in theaters through-out France and much of Europe. Although one might hesitate to call Rommel a tourist in the sense of a participant in a Cook's tour, Scott McCabe in an essay on the concept of the tourist reminds us that the *American Heritage Dictionary* offers as one of its definitions "a brief trip through a place, as a building or a site, in order to view or inspect it: The visiting prime minister was given a tour of the chemical plant."[40] Not a participant in the tourism industry, Rommel nevertheless reflected the curiosity enveloped in the tourist gaze, as did so many others who looked with wonder at the spectacle of the Atlantic Wall.

How many aerial photographs and gazes were directed during the war toward the Atlantic Wall, or how many people in France watched newsreels of General Rommel touring the fortifications will never be known.[41] Interest in the coast can only have been immense as Allies and Germans, military and civilians, looked toward the wall in anticipation of the outcome of the war.[42] Ernst Jünger, a German officer and writer stationed in Paris, wrote on 4 May 1944, "The landing occupies everyone's attention; the German command, as well as the French, believe it will take place one of these days."[43] A mammoth undertaking that employed thousands of workers and was run by the Organisation Todt, the Atlantic Wall, in an allusion reminiscent of an earlier description of the Maginot Line, was described by the magazine *L'Illustration* in 1943 as comparable in history only to the Great Wall of China.[44] A cartoon published shortly after the Liberation in *Le Parisien Libéré*, pointed to the significance of the wall in depicting a pile of rubble marked "all that remains of the Atlantic Wall."[45] Of equal importance in the creation of the tourist imaginary were the numbers of people who watched the various tanks, trucks, and wagons of all types roll down highways and village lanes, often depicted in the German newsreels of 1940 and their American counterparts of 1944.

"Tourists in Uniforms"

Beyond the extensions of the tourist gaze were the physical visits, "tours" in the more restricted and perhaps conventional sense of the term associated with the tourism industry, of Germans in France between their arrival in June 1940 and their expulsion in the summer of 1944. It took little time for Germans to follow Hitler's lead and begin touring occupied Paris, as Shirer noted in June 1940.[46] En route to take up his duties as one of the French representatives to the Armistice Commission, whose task was to negotiate with the Germans at Wiesbaden details of Franco-German economic relations, Jean Berthelot, on 27 and 28 June, reported German soldiers in Paris taking photographs of sites recommended by Baedeker.[47] Pierre Audiat described the German soldiers during the first days of the Occupation as traveling throughout the city day and night, with free access to the Métro, taking photographs. "At any moment, the strollers in green [the color of the German uniforms] would stop in front of a monument or a scene that they found interesting and click; often the Parisians found themselves in their photos without knowing it." German military personnel by the thousands, both men and women, were to be seen everywhere in Paris, "tourists in uniform," in Audiat's phrase.[48]

The wartime Germans strove to preserve the French tourist infrastructure that had been established during the Belle Époque and interwar years, which served them as it had others before. German documents show an interest in keeping top Parisian restaurants, often reserved exclusively for them, well stocked and maintaining clean brothels for German soldiers.[49] Local French were allowed to sell postcards and souvenirs near the Hôtel des Invalides, but the Germans carefully monitored them.[50] Setting the mark-franc exchange rate at an artificially favorable twenty to one, when, according to Vassili Soukhomline, the rate should have been closer to ten to one, the Germans could easily buy up French goods at enforced low prices. In a form of legalized pillage, German authorities encouraged their subordinates to buy as much as they could, turning occupied France into a vast bazaar for their personnel, who shipped a wide variety of goods back to Germany.[51] Occupied Paris became a rest and rehabilitation center for their soldiers. One may only speculate as to what Hitler and his associates had in mind as the ultimate fate of the Parisians. In fact, just as the Otto list of censored books for occupied France banned *Mein Kampf*, so the French were not to know what Hitler was planning for the future. Provisionally, Paris was apparently to be the primary amusement park of German Europe. German Blitzmädchen, women's auxiliaries sometimes known as "gray mice" because of the color of their uniforms, were encouraged to shop in occupied France for now inexpensive goods often unavailable at home. Soukhomline recalled that in late June 1940, "every day, tens of buses filled with soldiers and brassy blonde German women in mouse gray uniforms stopped in front of Notre-Dame, the Invalides, and other monuments of the city: the German Kraft durch Freude organization made visits to the marvels of the capital for its new tourists."[52]

Bastille Day, the fourteenth of July, was celebrated in 1940 with a German rather than the usual French military parade of past years, and this time the place de la Concorde was filled with Nazi flags. German filmmakers circulated around l'Étoile and the Champs-Élysées, photographing the exercises of their compatriots. The château at Fontainebleau was made available for German official functions, such as a supper for thirty dignitaries held in the Guard Hall with General Walter von Brauchitsch, in charge of the German military in the summer of 1940, presiding. Toward 2 a.m., a torchlight tour through the museum there ended the evening.[53]

Part of the Germans' effort to re-create a sense of "normalcy" in occupied France consisted of strict orders within weeks of their arrival in Paris to all military personnel to be on their best behavior, as not just Paris but France in general became a beehive of German tourist activity.[54] Lille, for example, situated in the "forbidden zone," an area in northeastern France closed to the return of French refugees and considered by the Germans for possible annexation to the Reich, has been described by the historian Étienne Dejonghe as "a city where one is entertained" with leisure activities having a normalizing quality. Luxury restaurants flourished, as did *salons de thé* with "young welcoming women" for German officers. "In brief, Lille was the city of pleasures where the occupiers re-created a German micro-society where one made holiday."[55] In his wartime memoirs the French writer Alfred Fabre-Luce described Paris in 1941 as a rest and rehabilitation center for the Germans.[56] Orders were given to soldiers not to shoot their weapons in the air. A high command complaint about German soldiers and their officers visiting the "worst dance halls" in Montmartre stated that "this behavior of German soldiers is fully counter to all expressions of *national dignity*. It contradicts as well the *order given by the Führer himself* that *Paris should not become an Etappenstadt* [city of military malingerers]."[57]

Hitler's orders against allowing Paris to become an *Etappenstadt* were reiterated in the June 1941 edition of the *Wegleiter*, which quoted the "well-known words of Hitler: 'I do not want Paris to become an *Etappenstadt*'" and added that this goal had been achieved.[58] The reality, however, was quite different. Within a month of their arrival in Paris, Hitler's order notwithstanding,

German military officials were complaining of the sexual tourism by their men, specifically in the dancehalls of Montmartre. August von Kageneck, a German soldier aged eighteen, arrived in Brie, France, shortly after the June invasion and had the opportunity to visit several sites in the country. He later wrote that most of the German soldiers were the sons of farmers and had never left their villages prior to the war. They had learned about France in school but had never visited there. One infantryman from Hamburg, who entered Paris by bicycle, wrote that he had never seen so beautiful a city. To many, the Métro was a new and wonderful discovery, as few German cities possessed underground railways.

Others climbed the Eiffel Tower and carved the names of their wives into its beams. The Hamburg soldier wrote, "We were shown a series of things that we knew only in our wildest imaginations." He also found his way to a brothel and noted: "Ah, soldiers. They always find a brothel more readily

FIGURE 10.   Soldiers at the Eiffel Tower, June 1940. Deutsches Historisches Museum, Berlin.

than a church." Von Kageneck mentioned an Austrian lieutenant, stationed in a small town in the Allier, who spent four days visiting Paris and much preferred it to "crude and ugly" Berlin. The lieutenant vowed to return to Paris, whose broad avenues, trees, sumptuous houses, and monuments reminded him of "our Vienna": a city with allure, taste, and elegance.[59]

Local merchants took advantage of the German presence to sell their wares at what were described as extra-high prices to German soldiers near the Eiffel Tower.[60] Although German soldiers were limited to purchases of fifty francs per person, not a large amount, they were able to buy silk stockings, no longer available at home, and chocolate and coffee, which had also become hard to find in Germany. "Wine and champagne flowed freely."[61] During the early period of the Occupation, especially before Resistance activity began to make the streets less safe after the German invasion of the Soviet Union in June 1941, Paris was a cushy billet, much in demand among German personnel.[62] Von Kageneck described the summer of 1940 as a "honeymoon" between the German soldiers and the French civilians. On the occasion of the reopening of the Paris Opéra, an elderly French civilian, apparently of an upper social stratum, approached General Kurt von Briesen, who commanded the Thirtieth Infantry Division, telling him that his soldiers were better propagandists for Germany than its propaganda minister, Goebbels.[63] As the historian Henri Amouroux wrote, Germans enjoyed Paris during "the first sixteen months of the Occupation, before the entrance of the United States into the war, well before Stalingrad, when it was not foolish to believe that the German army would be able to keep all of Europe in obedience indefinitely."[64] This was the time when Germans could enjoy the pleasures of occupied France in conditions that, it seemed, would never end, paralleling the so-called "happy time" in the war at sea, when German submarines could attack Allied shipping virtually at will, from 1940 through early 1942.[65] By late 1940, the German demand for shopping, touring, and other vacation visits to Paris was so high that the military authorities ordered a curtailment. Study trips to Paris were ordered canceled for January 1941.[66]

Nor were German tourists confined to Paris or even France. Officers and soldiers on leave, along with German civilian personnel, so crowded the trains to Brussels in early 1941 that military officials complained that there was a shortage of housing for them. Overnight trips to Brussels were to be curtailed, and conferences and courses were not to be held there for German personnel based in Paris.[67] In Paris itself, restaurants such as Maxim's on the rue Royale and La Coupole on the boulevard Montparnasse attracted German officials and those French who collaborated with them. "Each tourist site bent to the Nazis' habits and customs," wrote the historian

Christine Levisse-Touzé. Accordingly, the Montmartre neighborhood, with its Sacré-Cœur butte and basilica, fascinated many of the Germans, including Hitler and Goebbels. A cultural and tourist center during the interwar years, Montmartre catered to German soldier-tourists with many sought-after canteens. La Mère Catherine, a restaurant in Montmartre, offered a no-frills menu in French and German. The Cercle de l'Union Interalliée, an exclusive private club on the rue du Faubourg Saint-Honoré, was taken over by the Germans for their officers' exclusive use and renamed "Kasino." Less chic establishments, too, such as the Brasserie Wepler on the place de Clichy, catered to the soldiers and worked to create a feeling of home for them.[68]

Beyond Paris, von Kageneck recalls the comments of an infantryman in a mounted unit stationed in Auteuil, next to the Bois de Boulogne just outside the city. His unit had been put in charge of the thoroughbred horses belonging to locals who had fled Paris prior to the Germans' arrival, and the soldiers were now living, evoking Sieburg's phrase, like God in France. Other soldiers, in the Eighteenth Army, were stationed in the small towns surrounding Paris. The staff of one division occupied the Trianon Hotel in Versailles, where a plaque commemorating the 1919 peace treaty was removed by order of a general, only to be replaced in 1944.[69] Summing up the experiences of the German "tourists in uniform" in the early days of the Occupation, von Kageneck wrote that their memoirs indicated surprise, enthusiasm, and a strong desire to experience "the thousand refinements of a country that seemed to be a paradise on earth." To von Kageneck, the soldiers were "tourists." A grenadier of the Nineteenth Infantry Division stationed near the armistice demarcation line along the Cher River, wrote: "None of us who experienced that 1940 summer in France will ever forget it. The billeting was good, the drudgery [tasks] agreeable, the population correct [in its behavior toward the Germans], later nothing but friendly, the countryside magnificent."[70]

The *Wegleiter*: Where to Go and What to See

The biweekly *Wegleiter* first appeared almost a month to the day from the German entry into Paris. In addition to its tourism tips, the *Wegleiter*, distributed free at German civilian offices and military posts, offered vignettes of Parisian life written by German soldiers. Although the magazine was published in German, its first issue contained prefaces in both German and French. The German-language preface noted the exemplary behavior of the occupying forces, which, it claimed, had contributed to the reopening of restaurants, clubs, theaters, and museums. Similar in format to today's *Pariscope*, the *Wegleiter* stated that its goal was to assist the non-French-speaking German

Figure 11. The biweekly German guide describing what to do in Paris for the period 28 February through 14 March 1942. "The German Guide: Where in Paris?" *Der deutsche Wegleiter* 39 (28 February–14 March 1942). Bibliothèque nationale de France.

soldier with excursions and purchases. The French-language preface, written by the local publishers, justified a German-language guidebook, which, it said, would contribute to the return of prosperity in Paris and help give "our old adversaries" an enhanced appreciation of the uniqueness of the city.[71] A list of recommended sites that might have been taken from the interwar *Guides bleus* started with the Arc de Triomphe, followed by the place de la Concorde, the Madeleine, the Opéra, place Vendôme, the Louvre, Notre-Dame, the Palais de Justice, the Luxembourg Palace, the Panthéon, and the Hôtel des Invalides and Dôme des Invalides, then, listed separately, the Eiffel Tower, Trocadéro, Sacré-Cœur, and the Vincennes zoo.[72] The second issue carried an article on the reopening of the Folies-Bergère, noting that Paris was beginning to live again. It also directed the attention of its readers to the German embassy, an elegant building dating to 1714, which had been bought by the king of Prussia in 1818 and redecorated in Empire style, becoming the embassy in 1871.[73] The magazine contained advertisements for racetracks, fashion boutiques, theaters, restaurants, and nightclubs, and noted, for instance, in September 1940, the reopening of Luna Park, a popular amusement park in Paris. In September 1940 the Deutsches Verkehrsburo (German Tourist Office) began offering travel information in the occupied zone in France and from there to Germany. Travel information was also available for German military and civilian personnel in Paris and the occupied zone.[74] Tourist sites occasionally changed, as exemplified by the Luxembourg Palace, which had been opened for visits but was closed early the following October because it had been taken over for use by the Luftwaffe staff.[75]

Shortly after the arrival of the German forces in France, guidebooks for them began appearing. The *Deutscher Soldaten-Führer durch Paris* (German Soldiers' Guide to Paris), which described Paris as the most beautiful city on the European continent, and appears to have been hastily translated from a French original, was quickly made available to German troops.[76] French writers sometimes competed for the German tour book market, as in the case of one author who complained to the military authorities that the *Deutscher Soldaten-Führer* had been plagiarized from his own *Kleiner Führer durch Paris* (Little Guide to Paris) and had cut into his market.[77] In 1941 German censors rejected a proposed book with the same title—possibly the same book—as being too clumsily translated from its original French text.[78] The *Deutscher Soldaten-Führer,* like most of the guidebooks, accused of plagiarism or not, focused on architecture, offering detailed measurements of the height and breadth of structures such as the Arc de Triomphe, Trocadéro Palace, the Eiffel Tower, the Invalides, Napoleon's tomb, the Institut de France, the Saint-Germain-des-Prés church, the Luxembourg Palace, the Panthéon, and

FIGURE 12.   A tour book memento of Paris for German soldiers published after the German victory in 1940. *Kleiner Führer durch Paris für Deutsche Soldaten Ernnerung an Paris 1940,* cover. Deutsches Historisches Museum, Berlin.

the Cluny Museum. The Louvre was praised for its size, described as "the most brilliant gigantic palace in the world."[79] Tourist attractions ranged from the Fontainebleau château, taken over for use by the German army command, to Parisian restaurants, some reserved exclusively for German use, to "sound-and-light" shows, and revues featuring nude women.

Another small guidebook, hardly more than a listing of sites, published in October 1940 began with the place de la Concorde, followed by the Champs-Élysées, the Parc Monceau, and the 1937 World's Fair's German Pavilion, which it described as "the most beautiful building of the 1937 Exposition. A masterpiece of modern German architecture. An example of the progress of German art and German science in all fields during the last few years."[80] The *Pariser Zeitung*, a German-language daily newspaper, and the *Guide Aryen*, a bilingual brochure in French and German, steered the Occupation soldiers to tourist attractions that included the Louvre, reopened in October, the Moulin Rouge, and Longchamps racetrack.[81]

Napoleon as a Tourist Attraction

The Germans gave extensive publicity to sites related to Napoleon, especially his tomb at the Invalides. Hitler was photographed there during his June tour of Paris, and Goebbels visited as well, writing his ruminations about the French emperor in his diary. In late 1940 Hitler decided to transfer the remains of Napoleon II, the Duke of Reichstadt, from the Capuchin vault in Vienna, where they had been placed following his death in 1832, to the Invalides.[82] According to Arno Breker, Hitler had decided on this repatriation during his June tour of Paris. It was to be a symbolic and inexpensive act of magnanimity on Hitler's part toward the French and seems to have been suggested by Foreign Minister Joachim von Ribbentrop, seconded by Otto Abetz. Goebbels expected the gesture to be received with great thankfulness, and the German press in France praised Hitler's "chivalry."[83] The transfer was made on 15 December 1940, the centennial anniversary of the transfer of the remains of Napoleon I from Saint Helena to the Invalides in Paris, in a cold, snowy nighttime atmosphere made especially tense by the fact that two days earlier, Marshal Pétain had dismissed Pierre Laval, his prime minister, perceived as the architect of Franco-German collaboration.[84] Given the severity of the winter and the restrictions of life under the Occupation, the event also became the butt of jokes at the time, such as "they take our coal and send us ashes."[85] One letter addressed to Hitler and delivered to the military command in Paris praised the return of the ashes as a step toward French-German rapprochement and maintained that 90 percent of the French would look favorably upon Germany if not for three factors: the call for the "elimination" of France in *Mein Kampf*, the present hunger and suspension of industry in France, and the German annexation of Alsace-Lorraine. More than a "theatrical gesture" was needed.[86] A French guidebook, translated into German and published in 1941, nevertheless praises the initiative of the German government in reuniting Napoleon and his son.[87]

Another popular figure on the German tourism circuit was the composer Richard Wagner, who had spent considerable time in France. German visitors were directed to a plaque in honor of the composer on the house in which he had lived in the Paris suburb of Meudon, where he had composed his opera *The Flying Dutchman*. Wagner's *Tannhäuser* was first performed in Paris, and there the composer wrote the text for *Die Meistersinger*. The German tourist literature on Wagner in France generally focused on the difficulties he encountered there, either material or, emphasizing the alien qualities of French culture, spiritual and stylistic.[88]

Tours for Military Officers

For the German military brass, occupied France offered a wide variety of tourist possibilities. The army staff in Paris arranged tours for visiting individuals and groups. A Major Hebeler of the German Army Command requested a tour guide for a visiting group of thirty university professors in late September 1940, and others were requested for a visiting *Gauleiter* in early October.[89] One example of the difficulty in separating military or business travel from what might be called "pleasure tourism" in general is the story of the *Gauleiter*, whose visit began with a "short tour" of Paris en route from the railway station to the hotel. The first and second days of a four-day visit included meetings with other military personnel, but time was found on the second day for visits to Fontainebleau, Versailles, part of which was kept open to the public, and the Trianons, and on the third day a morning trip to Villacoublay, with a possible afternoon visit to Reims or the time to be spent "at leisure." A further trip to Reims was planned for the fourth day.[90]

An unnamed German general, apparently visiting Paris in October 1940, received two loge seats for a show at the Casino de Paris. Additional recreational spots recommended to him included the Sheherazade and Monseigneur, both nightspots near the Casino de Paris, where one could also dine. The local officer arranging the visit had secured tickets to *Aida* and Massenet's *Thaïs* at the Paris Opéra and *Carmen* at the Opéra-Comique so he could offer his general a choice, adding in his letter forwarding the tickets, "I enclose a copy of the *deutsche Wegleiter*, in which I have marked several good restaurants (pages 26–28)."[91]

A report listing entertainment possibilities for the German military command officers in December 1940 in Paris once again reflected the establishments that had acquired tourist iconicity before the war. Included were visits to the Opéra to see grand opera, comic operas, or ballet, depending on the day of the week, together with a meal at L'Impératrice on the Champs-Élysées. Tickets to new revues at the Folies-Bergère could be obtained through the military command in Paris, along with table reservations at the Sheherazade, described as a "decent, very clean, intimate locale." Also on the list was the Casino de Paris, whose revue was said to be second only to the one at the Folies-Bergère. Together with a visit to the Casino, a meal at Maxim's could be included. One could go to hear the songs of Lucienne Boyer, a popular cabaret singer, at Chez Elle, on the rue Volney 16, where a meal was served at 8 p.m. followed by the performance from 9 to 11:00. Lastly, the Bal Tabarin, a nightspot in Pigalle featuring the cancan, was slated for a reopening on 12 December 1940.[92] Looking back on the Occupation years, Arno Breker wrote:

> Maxim's during this time was a festival for the eyes every night, such as I have never seen it before or after the Occupation. Fragile images such as a breath of waving lace, the nuanced forms and appearances evoked Monet or Renoir. The fantasy, the extravagance was so striking that the pampered ambassadresses gave out exuded only an ephemeral destiny. Thus did the grand art of makeup triumph.[93]

An internationally known restaurant before the war, Maxim's was turned over to the Berlin restaurateur Otto Horcher and served wartime exotica such as leeks and apples, as well as cauliflower and cheese, bread, wine, and a variety of other foods not generally available to most of the French population.[94] If French tourist sites offered a range of pleasures to German officers, enlisted men and civilians visiting on assorted missions were also given opportunities to enjoy the local sights and sounds. The French who collaborated with the Germans also occasionally had the opportunity of dining at Maxim's. Marcel Déat, the head of the collaborationist Rassemblement national populaire political party, recorded at least two occasions when he dined there in 1941.[95]

Organized Tourism for the Germans

By late summer 1940, the German military authorities had established a special tourism unit of the Wehrmacht, the Abteilung I c, Besichtigungen (Unit I c, Visits). The magnitude of their touring operation in occupied Paris is expressed in a claim in the Wegleiter that by May 1941, some 1 million Germans had been given tours of Paris.[96] During the eight-day period from 22 through 29 September 1940, the Abteilung I c organized visits for some 9,300 soldiers, or an average 1,162 per day, of the Armee-Ober-Kommando (A.O.K) 2 in occupied Paris.[97] A count of the figures taken from the daily registers available in the French Archives nationales for a seventy-seven-day period from 9 October through 29 December 1940 shows an average of 2,910 visitors signed up per day for group tours of Paris by the Abteilung I c. The total of 224,104 visitors for the seventy-seven days, if extrapolated to the ten months from the beginning of July 1940 through the end of April 1941, comes to over 800,000 visits, thus approximating the *Wegleiter*'s claim. Not all those signed up necessarily participated in the tours, but the figures represent an enormous German effort at organized tourism in occupied Paris during the war.[98]

Soldiers taking part in the group tours of Paris, which lasted from approximately 11 a.m. to 7 p.m., were expected to maintain military discipline, especially in Montmartre, to avoid "harmful influences," according to a *Wegleiter* article on the Abteilung I c. Tour guides were Germans already resident in Paris, and each group of at least one hundred was provided with a guide paid by the army. If a given group of soldiers had coupons for gasoline, they might hire a bus; otherwise the group was led through the Métro, on which all German personnel were allowed to ride free of charge. Coffee and a snack were provided by the German Red Cross in a restaurant requisitioned for this purpose; the soldiers were forbidden to break ranks and enter any of the local cafés.[99] Neither the documents in the Abteilung I c file nor the *Wegleiter* article provide detailed itineraries of the tours, but the *Wegleiter* photos show groups of German soldiers near the Notre-Dame cathedral, in front of the Invalides, and at Napoleon's tomb. The *Wegleiter* article concludes by noting that German soldiers were also shown the "social backwardness" of France, thereby becoming all the more thankful for "what is being done today in this area in the new Germany."[100]

In addition, the Germans, following their interwar program of "Jeder einmal in Berlin," created an organization called "Jeder einmal in Paris" (Everyone in Paris Once), with offices in the Palais Bourbon, the former (and postwar) home of the French Chamber of Deputies. The organization's expressed goal was to offer all German troops in France a holiday in Paris, arranged in rotation by army unit.[101] Tours were also run by the Deutsche Arbeitsfront (DAF, German Labor Front) as part of the KdF program in occupied France. Advertised as using "comfortable and modern buses," the ten different tours listed were (1) Old Paris, (2) Modern Paris, (3) Paris by Night, (4) Versailles and Malmaison, (5) Fontainebleau, (6) Paris—the City of Revolutions, (7) The Birthplace of Paris, (8) From Gothic to Modern Paris, (9) The Louvre, and (10) Châteaux and Castles of the Loire. A 1941 brochure advertised these excursions as "culture tours" aimed at building bridges of understanding between the Germans and French. Each tour returned to its starting point, the Paris KdF offices, where aperitifs or coffee, depending on the hour, were offered along with discussions of what the visitors had seen. The tours showed striking continuities with the common Paris circuits of the prewar and immediate postwar years, but they also reflected a shifted paradigm with visits to locales related to Germans in France such as Wagner and in the narratives constructed around the tours.

The itinerary for Tour 1, "Old Paris," listed the Champs-Elysées, place de la Concorde, rue de Rivoli, place du Carrousel, the Left Bank, Cité, Notre-Dame, place Saint-Michel, the Luxembourg Gardens, the Panthéon, the Saint-Paul quarter, place des Vosges, the Bastille, the grand boulevards, the Opéra, rue de la Paix, and Vendôme. Special stops were made to view the interiors of Notre-Dame, the Panthéon, and the Opéra. Tour 2, "Modern Paris," focused on the Grand and Petit Palais, the Alexandre III Bridge, the Invalides (including a stop at Napoleon's tomb), the École Militaire, the Eiffel Tower, Pont d'Iéna, Palais Chaillot (site of the 1937 World's Fair), and the avenue Jean Chiappe, named for a high-ranking Vichy official killed when the airplane in which he was traveling was shot down in 1940. The avenue, which leads to Trocadéro, was renamed in honor of Georges Mandel after the war. The "Modern Paris" tour also included the Bois de Boulogne, avenue Foch, the Arc de Triomphe (with a stop to visit the Tomb of the Unknown Soldier), the outer boulevards, place Clichy, Montmartre (where the Sacré-Cœur basilica was emphasized), place Blanche, place Pigalle, Trinité, the Saint-Lazare railway station, and the Church of the Madeleine (with a stop to visit its interior).[102]

The tours of Montmartre included visits to unnamed "artistically and culturally significant" Paris nightspots. In a description reminiscent of Goebbels, Versailles not only evoked the brilliance of Louis XIV but also symbolized the apogee of German power in 1871 and the depths of that power in 1919. Malmaison was important as the place where Napoleon had spent "the best days of his life." The Fontainebleau tour included the atelier of François Millet in Barbizon, described as "the cradle of modern French art." Although the itinerary for the "City of Revolutions" tour mentioned that Paris had known upheavals since the fourteenth century, it emphasized Robespierre's house, the place de la Concorde, where the guillotine had stood, and other sites related to the 1793–94 Reign of Terror. The "Birthplace of Paris" tour focused on the early history of the city and the Îles de la Cité and Saint-Louis, the "Gothic to Modern Paris" tour emphasized architectural sites drawn from tours 1 and 2, the Louvre visit included a lecture about the history of the museum, and the "Châteaux and Castles of the Loire" trip, restricted to the summer months and subject to the availability of transport, highlighted France's "river of destiny." Reflecting the Nazi view of "blood and soil" which extolled rural as opposed to urban life, the Loire tour description depicted the rise of Paris as having led France to decline, the implication being of the city as a den of iniquity in a reprise of the Paris Babylon motif. The future of France, according to the brochure, in a perspective that fit the Nazi "blood and soil" cult but also the Vichy "return to the land," would depend on its ability to regain a connection with its "uncorrupted countryside."[103] A *Wegleiter* article in 1941 with the title "Paris as Not Seen in Baedeker" again evoked the German guidebooks, as had the "Baedeker raids" over England, attesting once more to the currency of the name. "Baedeker" represented common tourist sites, whereas the *Wegleiter* article advised its readers to avoid the beaten track of the popular guidebooks. In another example of the changed tourism paradigm of power relationships after 1940, the article also highlighted the blighted regions of suburban Paris, while at the same time extolling some of its less well-known sites such as the place des Vosges.[104] German tour books in general, however, directed visitors to the sites visited by Hitler and Goebbels and the itineraries described in the DAF prospectus discussed earlier.

Many of the kinds of problems encountered by the German authorities as they developed and regulated their tourism in occupied France were of a kind normally associated with tourism in peacetime, namely, the securing of tour guides, the regulation of tourist shopping, and the control of sex tourism, the last an issue especially among the soldiers of a conquering army. Demand for tours organized by the Besichtigung unit in Paris in September 1940 was so high that it was a struggle to find enough qualified tour guides. One of the unit's officers, Hauptmann Robert Weiss, complained that the guides were being asked questions that required a historical knowledge beyond what should be expected for tours that cost the visitors at the most five Reichsmarks (roughly $12.50 at the time). The best possible guides had been reserved, he reported, for officers' tours. An art historian had been requested to guide a tour of officers later in September, but the Besichtigung office had been told that none were available.[105]

As is so often true with tourism, commercial concerns were not far beneath the surface in occupied France. Officers had to ensure that sufficient numbers of touring German soldiers shopped at the Soldatenkaufhaus, a store set up by the German authorities with a monopoly on sales to German soldiers in Paris and a mandatory stop on Abteilung I c tours there. Figures kept for the numbers of visitors to the Soldatenkaufhaus showed them in the tens of thousands. Officials reported, however, that too many of the men were not being taken to the shop. This led to complaints against refractory tour guides, one of whom, Rudolf Krell, was dismissed for having advised the soldiers under his tutelage that they could purchase better goods at lower prices elsewhere in Paris.[106] In a letter to the military command post in Paris, Krell complained of having been fired as "unsuited for the touring service" by Hauptmann Weiss. He argued that the soldiers had enjoyed his tours, that, in addition to the prescribed itineraries, he had taken them to historic sites such as Roman roads where military supplies had been brought in, the German Institute, the house where Voltaire died, the Pont-Neuf, the École des Beaux-Arts, and Paris's sixth-century churches. Referring to the shortage of tour guides, Krell insisted that he must have been let go in error.[107] The reason for Krell's dismissal, however, seems to have been his disparaging remarks about the Soldatenkaufhaus.[108]

Sex Tourism during the Occupation

Sex tourism also became an issue early in the Occupation. The German authorities focused on preventing the spread of disease. Within a month of their arrival in Paris, German officials determined that local French brothels lacked proper hygiene and were insufficiently supervised by the governing authorities. Select brothels in larger cities, under medical supervision, were made available to German military personnel, though access to them was forbidden to French civilians other than the prostitutes themselves.[109] The best-known brothels in Paris were Le One Two Two, at 122 rue de Provence on the Right Bank, and Sphinx on the Left Bank, both out of the price range of ordinary soldiers. Germans were forbidden to frequent brothels other than those especially designated for them; signs were to be posted outside brothels indicating that they were either restricted to German soldiers or forbidden to them. Jewish and other "alien race" prostitutes were not allowed to serve German personnel, nor were bordellos permitted to serve as hotels for travelers. Prostitutes were to be examined twice weekly by local doctors under the supervision of German hygiene officials, and those who were deemed healthy were issued numbered inspection cards which they were to present to their clients. Women who were found to have diseases were transferred to civilian French hospitals, where they were to be treated until cured. Collaboration with mayors and other French civilian personnel was deemed essential in this matter.[110] General von Brauchitsch noted that the longer German forces were in occupied territory, the more sexual issues would arise. In occupied France, he ordered that the troops be taught "self-discipline," especially those who were married.[111] In her book *Wehrmacht et prostitution sous l'Occupation,* Insa Meinen emphasized the inequalities in the status of the French prostitutes and their German clients. When the German military conducted roundups in the streets in their attempts to control prostitution, the French prostitutes were invariably sanctioned, never their German male clientele.[112] In their attempts to control the sex trade, however, the German authorities decreed on 26 March 1941 that any of their soldiers developing gonorrhea would be subject to a six-week prison sentence.[113]

Control of nightclubs also became politicized during the Occupation. In one incident, in which German officers were frolicking with the women of a brothel, the officers decided to start up a nearby pickup truck. In the truck was a concealed delayed-action bomb. It exploded, killing three of the women and two German officers. "Heldentod" (hero's death), remarked one of Jean Guéhenno's friends, sarcastically recounting the incident.[114] A German sea captain in Rouen in July 1942 maintained that trusted French informants had reported that the German police had acquired a personal interest in keeping certain nightclubs open there. These nightspots, he added, were "like mushrooms sprouting from the earth."[115] Michèle Cointet points out that a combination of Nazi legislation against nightclubs in Berlin as decadent and Vichy's moralistic anti-alcohol and anti-homosexual policies elsewhere in France made the Parisian clubs all the more attractive to German personnel and their French allies. Clubs such as L'Étincelle, in Montmartre, advertised the "prettiest models" in its show; a transvestite starred in a show at the Folies-Bergère in 1943; and the Lido and Bal Tabarin, among others, offered sex shows and luxurious food. Following years of economic depression and mobilization for war, it was hard for local nightclub owners to turn away the Germans, a suddenly prosperous clientele.[116] For many Germans the attractions of Paris offered erotic tourism imaginaries as well as practices. As Alan Riding writes, the sight of half-naked women dancing in the reopened nightclubs in the summer of 1940 and thereafter for many soldiers "was the best reason for going out at night." The *Pariser Zeitung,* which began publishing in January 1941, offered tips on where to go, suggesting that the Tabarin offered the most erotic show.[117] For those who could afford pricier entertainment than that offered by establishments listed in the *Pariser Zeitung* and the *Wegleiter,* there was *Pariser Nächte* (Paris Nights), a guide for officers.[118] Riding writes that "numerous gay bars in occupied Paris were popular with German soldiers," despite the official prohibition of homosexuality. Robert Hugues-Lambert, a French actor, was arrested in Le Sans-Soucis, a gay bar, and ultimately died in a German concentration camp.[119]

Gastronomic Tourism in Occupied France

French food, especially at the top restaurants of Paris and other cities, some of which were legendary by the 1940s, also attracted German personnel, mostly officers who could afford it. Wartime food scarcity in France led to a complex system of rationing and related governmental regulation of restaurants and their prices, about which the Germans occasionally complained because they did not wish to have limits placed on what they could consume in local establishments. Some restaurants were taken over exclusively for German use and were therefore exempted from the French restrictions, while others, such as Maxim's, although nominally under French authority, had no restrictions on what they could stock, as they were also frequented by Germans. A note from the German military administration to French officials in May 1941 demanded more choice for the Germans in restaurants.[120]

By August 1940, restaurants patronized by prostitutes, Jews, or "colored" were to be marked with signs by the French police and were declared off limits to German military personnel. After several French restaurant owners complained of a consequent loss of clientele, the German authorities relented, but according to one of their reports, interesting in retrospect for the light it sheds on local attitudes of the time, many of the restaurant owners posted such warning signs voluntarily.[121] Muslim ("Mohammedan") restaurants in Paris, located largely in "dubious" neighborhoods and not highly regarded, according to one German military report, were also declared off limits to German military personnel.[122]

As the Occupation wore on and the presence of the Germans grew, a growing number of restaurants were taken over for their use. In December 1941, the increased numbers of personnel in the Organisation Todt's (OT) office on the Champs-Élysées, with 304 *Reichsdeutsche* (German citizens) there, led to a request for additional inexpensive local dining options for them. The nearby Café Marignon was proposed on the grounds that Fritz Todt himself, the head of the OT, had visited and approved it, and that in the mornings its only clientele were French profiteers.[123] Supervision of Parisian restaurants was divided between German and French authorities, and the restaurant classifications shifted over time. As of August 1941, the restaurants categorized as *hors classe* (exceptional), meaning that they were reserved for Germans and their guests and, accordingly, exempted from French government food restrictions, were Carton, Drouant-Gaillon, Lapérouse, Maxim's, and La Tour d'Argent in Paris, and Le Coq Hardi in Bougival, the last so designated in November 1941.[124] At the end of January 1942, twenty-six restaurants in Paris, of which one was the restaurant at the Ritz hotel, were declared *hors classe*.[125]

A not uncommon tourism phenomenon, the customer who is cheated on a restaurant bill, also was in evidence in occupied Paris. In a written complaint to the German military authorities in January 1943, General Friedrich-Carl Hanesse of the Luftwaffe accused the restaurant Lapérouse of overcharging him. The proprietor had penciled in a higher price than allowed by the French government price regulations and had charged the excess as "drinks" in his books. Because Lapérouse was one of the *hors classe* restaurants frequented by Germans, the proprietor claimed that he had been allowed to go beyond the legal price limits, but when confronted, he backed off and apologized to General Hanesse. He was then let off with a warning to stick with one set of prices.[126]

A small sample of the nationalities of Parisian restaurant owners, if not the type of cuisine served, is offered by a list of those having committed infractions against the various ordinances set up by the French authorities. Resulting from four months of inspections, from January through April 1942, made by the French police, the list was given to the Germans to keep them posted on the suppression of infractions in Paris. One hundred twenty seven restaurants were referenced, of which twenty-eight were found innocent of any infractions. The nationalities, listed only for the remaining ninety-nine, included eight-four French owners, nine Italians, two Spaniards, and one each Albanian, Turkish, Yugoslav, and Chinese.[127] The infractions included stocking forbidden food items and substituting them for items listed on the menu. One restaurateur who was charged with this contravention defended himself by arguing that the twelve guests to whom he had served illegal, presumably black market poultry and charcuterie were Germans. The inspectors determined that the guests in question were indeed German, with the exception of two Frenchwomen who, however, were accompanied by the Germans.[128] The dossier does not indicate whether the restaurateur's defense was successful. According to information obtained by the Germans from the French Economics and Finance Ministry, restaurant profits for the various categories in 1941 increased by a factor of from two and one-half to ten times since 1939.[129]

In early 1943, a quarrel broke out within the German military administration over who had authority in monitoring the restaurants in Paris. The security services complained that they were charged with enforcing price limits and related economic regulations in French restaurants but that a certain OKVR (Oberkriegsverwaltungsrat, or chief administrator) Lippert had intervened to block a three-month closure of the Restaurant Pierre, found by the Paris police to have violated the regulations. Politics immediately came into play. In a written report, Lippert claimed that a French acquaintance had approached him with Pierre, the proprietor, complaining that anti-collaboration circles within the French Economics and Finance Ministry had targeted his establishment. Pierre was said to be a loyal supporter of the Vichy government. Lippert claimed to have contacted the German military and diplomatic authorities when it had appeared that the security services would not intervene on behalf of Pierre. The subsequent complaint from Helmut Knochen, in charge of the SD (Sicherheitsdienst, or Security Service) in Paris, led to a review of the lines of German authority over local restaurants. Some sixty restaurants in Paris taken over by the Germans to serve their personnel were under the direct supervision of the military command. The French authorities, who reported to the German military authorities, supervised the remaining restaurants. Four restaurants were given *hors classe* status: Maxim's, La Tour d'Argent, Lapérouse, and Au Canneton.[130]

Most restaurants in occupied France, however, saw the imposition of severe restrictions on foodstuffs and prices, and the majority of Parisians, and French in general, could only gaze in from the outside while they struggled to find enough to eat under increasingly dire circumstances as the war went on. Ernst Jünger described how the Germans felt, enjoying sole and the famous duck at the Tour d'Argent while "watching at their feet with diabolic satisfaction, like gargoyles, the gray ocean of rooftops under which jostle the starving masses. In times like these, to eat well and to eat a lot gives a feeling of power."[131] In a report to First Secretary Rudolf Schleier of the German embassy in Paris in June 1943, Dr. Felix Grosse, an embassy official, reported that the food situation was especially dire in Bordeaux, which had recently been occupied by the Germans. One Bordeaux restaurant, in the Hotel Splendide, was open to Germans and also served French people without demanding ration tickets. Grosse noted, "It has been brought to my attention from different sides that these facts do not make an especially good impression in French circles."[132]

The plight of the average housewife in securing enough to eat, in contrast to the luxury restaurants in France, even made it into the German press. A newspaper clipping sent to the German embassy in Paris pointed to the social contrasts between affluent and needy in France but blamed the hardship facing the average citizens on France's inability to govern itself in an egalitarian way. Nothing was said of the economic resources taken from France by the Germans. The article recalled German suffering during the 1923 inflation and implied that now it was the turn of the French.[133]

Tourism Publications for the Germans

By 1941, with the Occupation having settled into more of a routine, a variety of tourist publications had become available to the Germans. A tract titled "Die schönste Erinnerung an Paris und Frankreich" (The Most Beautiful Memory of Paris and France), printed in August, showed drawings of an attractive young woman in French peasant costume standing at the seashore with sailboats in the background, and a view from a café up the Champs-Élysées toward the Arc de Triomphe, with another attractive young waitress in the foreground. The perspective is of someone, presumably a visiting German official or soldier, writing notes in a diary with a glass of red wine on a café table.[134]

    In addition to the guidebooks written explicitly for the German audience, French-language tourism literature was translated into German. Notable among the latter were the guidebooks edited by Doré Ogrizek and published by Odé in Paris. These include *Paris, Frankreich Nord und West*, published in 1941 and restricted to those parts of France then occupied by German forces.[135] *Paris und Umgebung,* also published by Odé in 1941 and devoted to Paris and its surrounding area, discussed eighteen sites in the capital, followed by an additional six in the region. Odé's leading ten, in order of presentation in 1941, were place de la Concorde, the Champs-Élysées, place de l'Étoile, the Arc de Triomphe, Trocadéro, the Eiffel Tower, the École Militaire, the Invalides, Montmartre, and the Opéra. The Invalides is noted for containing "the mortal remains of the great Corsican," and mention is made of the return of the remains of Napoleon II so that "father and son [might] rest next to each other."[136] Suggested trips farther afield included the Bois de Boulogne, whose racetracks and fashionable houses were mentioned; Versailles, noted as the site of the proclamation of the German Empire in 1871 and the signing of the peace treaty half a century later; Fontainebleau; Vincennes; and Compiègne. At Versailles, the château had been reopened to the public during the fall of 1940, but only the historic painting rooms in its north wing could be visited. The Vincennes area included Champigny-sur-Marne, where Württemburg and Saxon forces had fought against the French in the 1870 war, and Le Bourget airport, where Charles Lindbergh had landed after his transatlantic flight of 1927. Compiègne was mentioned as the site of the armistices of 1918 and 1940. Comments about the Versailles château paralleled the reviews by Goebbels and the DAF tour brochure.[137] Subsequent guidebooks compiled under Ogrizek's direction and published by Odé included *Paris Frankreich, und Provinzen* published in 1942 and 1943, after the Germans had occupied all of metropolitan France in November 1942.[138]

Ogrizek worked with the German Zentrale der Frontbuchhandlungen (Central Office for Book Dealers at the Front) and later used his connections to help publish a series of color photo books of several countries by Saar-Verlag in the French-occupied zone of Germany after the war.[139]

German Soldiers Photograph France

German-sponsored tourist activities included photography, painting, and French classes organized by the military authorities.[140] More photographic essays, in addition to a picture book on châteaux, followed Hoffmann's 1940 *Mit Hitler im Westen*. Von Kageneck mentions a book published in 1942 with an introduction by General Ernst von Schaumburg, the German commanding officer in Paris, which contained reproductions of paintings and drawings from an exhibition, "Luftwaffe Art of the Front," with texts by German soldiers. The paintings in the book included countryside scenes from Brittany, Normandy, and Burgundy, along with "picturesque corners" of Montmartre, as well as churches and cathedrals. Schaumburg's introduction exhorted the German soldiers in France to respect the local châteaux and cathedrals. Addressing the German soldiers in France, he wrote:

> For you the stay in France has become a major event. Few of you are capable of expressing by pen or brush what is offered before your eyes. But several have this gift and it is their works that bear witness in this book to the impressions that the German soldier serving in the Occupation force has experienced in this country, a country whose destiny has so often mixed with his in heavy and bloody wars.[141]

A collection of "visible reminders" of the soldiers' tours of duty in France, a book titled *Soldaten fotografieren Frankreich* (Soldiers Photograph France) juxtaposed 153 photographs of France with kitschy sentimentalized stories of German soldiers stationed there. Photographs of Paris featured the Seine and its bridges, Montmartre, including Sacré-Cœur, the Eiffel Tower and Trocadéro, the Tuileries, and the place de la Concorde.[142] Soldiers on duty in Paris were provided a studio where they, including "Mädchen in Uniform" (women military personnel), were provided with the materials for painting in their leisure hours. From 7 to 10 p.m., approximately twenty soldiers, some on leave from the Russian front, would sketch and sculpt. As of late 1943, a German press report estimated that two thousand soldiers had practiced their art in Paris. In the words of the report, which summarized in part German touristic views of Paris, the participants in the art program "absorb in this way a bit of the atmosphere of this city, which is a city of painters, as scarcely any other city in the world."[143] In addition to reflecting the power relationships in which the Germans were the masters, the normalcy of these activities was designed to give a human face to the war.

Germans as *Kulturvolk* Appreciating "the French"

As Ian Buruma writes, "Paris, unlike the other European capitals under Nazi occupation, was meant to look normal."[144] An exhibition in 2008 of photos taken in occupied Paris by André Zucca and published in the German magazine *Signal,* which show Parisians strolling in the streets and parks and in general enjoying the benefits of what appears to be normal life, evoked renewed discussion over the degree to which people in France suffered during the Occupation, something that clearly varied depending on the individual, whether Jewish, communist, or other perceived enemy of the New Order.[145] The Germans clearly sought to impose a façade of normalcy and at the same time show themselves to be cultivated admirers of the treasures of French culture, even if these were also essentialized as somehow alien, to be appreciated but also serving as reminders of the primary loyalty and affection among the Germans for the *Heimat* (homeland).[146]

The efforts to promote German tourism in occupied France reflected a Nazi desire to present the Germans as *Kulturvolk,* demonstrating their "high culture" in a sophisticated appreciation of French tourist sites. At the same time, such efforts drove home the message that "the French"—invariably stereotyped—were not like the Germans, and the latter should study the former to appreciate all the more their own homeland. Tourism in occupied France offered the Germans a chance not only to escape the war on the eastern front after June 1941 but also to imagine themselves as a powerful and cultivated people, well able to value the art and architecture of France—see Hitler—without, however, losing sight of the uniqueness and preciousness, if not the superiority, of their own homeland. Once more, the images of tourism expressed and intensified the pattern of military and political power in occupied France. Stereotypical depictions of the French in the *Wegleiter* and other German tourism publications, replete with vignettes of Parisian life written by German soldiers, praised the "grandeur" of French art and culture while making it clear that poverty and "degeneracy" were also rampant in France. The construction of a German self-image through tourism in the *Wegleiter* reinforced the notion of German superiority, paralleling the colonizer/colonized dichotomy elsewhere in the world. Tourism was to be another weapon, engendering a greater appreciation of and nostalgic longing among the German soldiers for *die Heimat* which no foreign attraction could quite match.[147] In his diary of *les années noires* (the dark years), Jean Guéhenno recorded finding in a street urinal between the Panthéon and the Lycée Henri IV an inscription in Gothic letters that read "Heimat, süsse Heimat" (Home, sweet home). In a reference to the Germans' green uniforms, he wondered whether it might have represented a secret confidence "of one of the innumerable green 'tourists' who come to visit the Panthéon."[148] Frequent and casual references to "eternal" France, such as those of Sieburg, focused on unchanging stereotypical images of national character rather than on historical development, in ways similar to those of Western books and museums that sometimes objectify "eternal" Asia or Africa, ignoring regional differentiation and historical change. In an article portraying the French as a people without historical development, a *Pariser Zeitung* writer noted that the changing face of Paris over the centuries did not obscure the continuity and unchanging nature of the French.[149]

Emblematic of the German views of occupied France was another *Wegleiter* article, "The Face of France," whose author, Private Dr. Rehbein, was listed as editor of the magazine, on a roster of leisure activity centers for German military personnel in Paris that included cafés, restaurants, movie theaters, a soldiers' chorus, and cruises on the Seine.[150] Rehbein wrote that he had learned more about "the secrets of foreign homes" in several weeks as a soldier than one could in many years during peacetime. Moving through the Champagne country, he quickly dismissed "a few overdone and tasteless modern things," focusing instead on the sights of "eternal" France, those that might have been seen "by our fathers and older comrades" in 1914. He cited the "eternal" chimneys, which gave the look of castles to the poorest huts, the dark-colored wallpaper printed to give the impression of costly fabric, the decorated furniture, old-style artisanal works—everything, in his words, that those who loved tradition would like. Rehbein found certain sites, however, hard for a German to appreciate, specifically the "famous splendor" of Versailles, which left him and, he added, many of his compatriots perplexed and cold. Understanding Versailles, he wrote, necessitated a comprehension of the impersonal nature of the French language, which, in contrast to German, did not allow for the expression of one's innermost feelings. Wandering through Paris reminded Rehbein of Mozart, who had never felt so German as while in the French capital. In words that echoed earlier evocations of the homeland, he wrote, "One must be a German to warmly love his fatherland and at the same time to be able to comprehend how beautiful and great a foreign [country] is."[151]

The propagation of these images made the Germans winners twice over: they could conceive of themselves as highly cultured people of the world and at the same time appreciate their good fortune in being German. Tourism, in other words, played a highly sophisticated role in enhancing an image of Germany that the Nazi leadership wished to promote not only to the world but to themselves as well. Consequently, although the Germans hardly treated the French kindly during the war, France was not relegated to the position of occupied Poland and other eastern European countries. Three examples illustrate this difference on the symbolic level. First, Hoffmann's *Mit Hitler in Polen,* the photo account of the German conquest of Poland in 1939, unlike its companion volume, *Mit Hitler im Westen,* showed no identifiable Polish tourist sites, with the possible exception of the old city of Gdansk (Danzig), considered a German city anyway. Second, German soldiers stationed in France were encouraged to learn French, whereas those on duty in Poland were said to have less need to know the local language.[152] Third, whereas in November 1940 the Germans ordered a cessation to their daily military parades at the Tomb of the Unknown Soldier in Warsaw, they expressly continued the same tribute in Paris.[153] Even more strikingly, the tourism message of German superiority subtly evoked in France was paralleled by a more brutal practice elsewhere during the war when the KdF organization arranged tours of the Warsaw Ghetto, where Germans could smugly feel superior to the ragged and disease-ridden Jews. German "execution tourists" took pictures of the mass killings of Jews and others in eastern Europe, where, in the words of Richard Evans, "negative tours" enabled Germans to maintain a sense of superiority over their enemies. The Russians found snapshots of mass executions on the bodies of dead German soldiers during the war.[154] Ian Buruma writes of the Nazis treating the Warsaw Ghetto, which they filmed, as "a type of zoo, with special tours laid on for curious visitors, who were permitted to lash out at the wretched denizens with whips for their amusement."[155]

Germans and Art Tourism in Occupied France

The German tourist circuit in Paris, described in the *Wegleiter,* is echoed in the memoirs of the German officers, such as Jünger and Heller, and the artist Arno Breker, whose accounts also provide a good sense of what they did in France.[156] Retrospective stories by both German and French former soldiers, *maquis,* and even collaborators who fought alongside the Germans in part as a way of escaping the boredom of the Occupation evoke much of the tourist scene in occupied France. A variety of tourist adventures have been the subjects of memoirs occasionally nostalgic for the "beautiful days of the Occupation." Encouraged by Otto Abetz, Nazi Germany's ambassador to occupied France, Breker brought his work to Paris. French luminaries from the worlds of the fine arts, letters, and cinema paid highly publicized visits to Germany. German tourist itineraries can also be followed in postwar films, which are copious in their descriptions of occupied France, such as *Is Paris Burning?*, or *The Longest Day*. To these may be added the accounts of witnesses such as Jean-Paul Sartre and Simone de Beauvoir.[157]

The artistic life of Paris continued during the Occupation—for those who were not Jewish or other enemies of the regime—and served as a magnet for Germans such as Heller, an officer in charge of censorship in occupied Paris, and Jünger, the novelist also stationed in Paris. In a memoir of his experience in Paris under the Occupation, Heller writes of having become friendly with the French writer Jean Paulhan, with whom, he wrote, "I truly discovered the beauty of this great place Paris, its grand perspectives, and at that time, its marvelous silence."[158] In preparation for an exhibition of Breker's sculptures at the Orangerie in May 1942, Heller was sent to Collioure, a small Catalan town in southern France, to accompany Breker's old master Aristide Maillol, who lived there, to Paris. As in the case of so many business trips before, during, and after the war, Heller combined work with tourism. Stopping at Toulouse, where he had studied in 1934–35, he also visited the Côte Vermeille, the Catalan coast along the Mediterranean in southern France, where he was enchanted with "a little fishing port whose picturesqueness had been completely preserved."[159]

Even Pablo Picasso and Henri Matisse, who represented the Nazis' much-maligned *entartete Kunst* (degenerate Art) of the moderns, were allowed to work. Both Heller and Jünger paid visits to Picasso in Paris.[160] Matisse, whose work had been declared "degenerate" prior to the war, was officially invited to visit Germany in 1941 and was not molested even though he declined.[161] The sparing of Picasso and Matisse, indications that the Germans themselves did not always take their art theories seriously, gives a sense of the continuing tourist awe of France on the part of the Germans, from Hitler down.

Jünger, a member of the advancing German forces in 1940, had been impressed with the Laon cathedral. He was stationed in Paris during much of the 1940–1944 period, during which he kept a journal, later published.[162] Well aware of the misery of so many of the French, as has been seen, Jünger described in his memoirs the high lifestyle of the German officers. Paris, to Jünger, was the capital, symbol, and citadel of a grand style of life and ideas, transmitted through the centuries. Having visited Paris during the interwar years, he found it even more brilliant during the Occupation than before. In 1941 he considered staying on in Paris, this city that, through no effort of his own, now lay open to him.[163] More than a year later, reflecting on an afternoon's walk with a female friend through Paris, from l'Étoile along the rue du Faubourg Saint-Honoré and ending at place du Tertre and Sacré-Cœur, Jünger wrote that the city had become for him "a second spiritual fatherland, the ever deeper image enveloping all that is dear and precious to me in the old civilization."[164] Heller, who appreciated Jünger's taste for Paris, described him as wandering throughout the city, with the same love of humble houses as of grand monuments, of grand perspectives as well as narrow streets and old cemeteries. "As did I he wandered the city in all directions, day and night, during these four years [1940–1944]."[165] In words that might have been written by any tourist visiting Paris in 1900, 1940, or now, Heller wrote:

> Whether at the Comédie française to see again the *Femmes savantes*, *Le Misanthrope*, or to discover Cocteau's *Renaud et Armide*, whether at the place du Tertre, at the Brasserie Lorraine, at the place des Ternes; or on the rue Mouffetard; whether at Père-Lachaise or in the little cemetery near Trocadéro; in the garden at Palais-Royal or at Bagatelle; Paris was for us as a second spiritual fatherland; the most perfect image of what was preserved of old civilizations, now gone. I felt as Jünger did, and many times with him, this atmosphere of happiness and amorous joy given off by the old stones as well as the river and sky of Paris.[166]

Once again, Heller's emphasis on the "old civilization" by implication extols its opposite, presumably the modern and dynamic world of Nazi Germany. In addition, as Ahlrich Mayer writes, the quotidian bureaucratic activities of Germans like Jünger and Heller, combined with the attractions of Paris, enabled them to avert their gazes from the German occupation policy in France that dictated privations for most of the French and the rounding up of Jews to be sent to the extermination camps, as well as the war against the Soviet Union.[167] Jünger's expression in his diary of the power he felt dining in the top restaurants while aware of the food privations in occupied Paris, and of the embarrassment he felt as a German officer seeing Parisian Jews wearing the yellow star, made him something of an exception among the German chroniclers of life in occupied France.[168]

Mayer's words hold for Arno Breker, who had accompanied Hitler on his tour of Paris in June 1940 and was the sole German artist to mount an exhibition of his work in occupied Paris. Speaking to French journalists in May 1942 at the Orangerie, Breker said: "As an old Parisian . . . I ask instantly to be treated as if this exhibition were taking place in normal circumstances, that is to say, in times of peace. This exhibition should not be considered a consequence of the Occupation and I will vouch for anyone who would publish a sincerely negative critique."[169]

In his memoirs, Breker also recalls making a trip through Burgundy on Hitler's orders during the summer of 1942. As Breker tells the story, Heinrich Himmler had come up with a plan to transfer the German-speaking population of the Tyrol, an Italian province, to Burgundy and to incorporate the region into Germany. The plan seemed too far-fetched even for Hitler, who wanted Breker to visit and report back his impressions. Breker planned his trip with Speer and Marshal von Rundstedt at a lunch "chez Francis, the king of French gastronomy," in the Coq Hardi restaurant at Bougival. There Francis helped plan the trip. At Beaune, Breker toured the hospice and the churches and, in the company of Speer, dined well and enjoyed good Burgundy wine. In his memoir, he takes credit for having helped quash Himmler's plan and having kept Burgundy French.[170]

As evidenced in Breker's Orangerie exhibition, the Germans made much of their interest in art, as well as architecture and historic preservation in occupied France. A Kunstschutz (Commission for the Protection of Art) directed by Count Franz-Wolff Metternich was established to evaluate and protect the French art that came under German control in the Second World War. During the 1940 campaign, General Günther Hans von Kluge was said to have saved the Rouen cathedral by burning down small houses in its vicinity to create a firewall around it. Almost immediately after June 1940, châteaux such as at Versailles and Fontainebleau were made available "for the enjoyment of German soldiers."[171] That Kunstschutz activity in occupied France was considerable may be seen by consulting its publications referenced in the French archives. Notable is a book by Paul Clemen, *Deutschen Kunstschutz im Kriege*, a two-volume work on World War I, which was described as making good propaganda today, meaning during the Second World War, and being informative regarding dealing with the artwork of enemy states. Other items included reports by Dr. Hans Möbius and Count Metternich.[172] German tourist interest extended also to French châteaux and other works of art, which the Occupation authorities claimed to be protecting under the Kunstschutz organization, although in many cases this was barely disguised spoliation.[173]

From August 1940 through the spring of 1941, some twenty-four German photographers, under the direction of Count Metternich, were said to have taken nearly twenty thousand photographs of French artistic treasures and historical monuments to be made available throughout German universities.[174] Some of these photographs were used in a book by Erhard Göpel on Normandy published in 1942 by a German army unit command and distributed by the Pariser Zeitung.[175] Plans were made to establish a German art-historical office in Paris, to be headed by the art historian Alfred Stange, director of the Art History Institute of the University of Bonn. The task of this office was to be the promotion of the appreciation of German art in France; a focus on German influences in French art, especially in cathedral design; and the facilitation of the work of German scholars in France.[176] Although Goebbels received a directive from Hitler on 13 August 1940 to organize the return of all German cultural items from the occupied countries of western Europe, competing German bureaucracies and the lack of a central plan of action stalled the program, and none of the artworks on various "return lists" were brought to Germany from France.[177] Ultimately, it was decided to have the Deutsches Institut in Paris handle cultural matters in France and postpone the establishment of an office dedicated to art history until after the war.[178]

The French archives hold a copy of a report of a professional tour to Paris made in June 1942 by Professor Joseph Buchkremer, the master architect for the Aachen cathedral.[179] A church architect and art historian, Buchkremer focused on the similarities between the pillars of the Aachen cathedral and others that he saw in the Louvre, the main purpose of his trip, but he also toured and commented on life in general in occupied Paris. He found France on the whole inferior to Germany, hardly surprising given the circumstances of his trip, and noted few automobiles on the streets of Paris, but commented favorably on the well-made-up Parisian women. The Petit Trianon was especially "romantic." Buchkremer concluded his report by hoping that after the end of the war he would be able to return to Paris with help, presumably German, to "return our stolen treasures" taken from the cathedral in Aachen, arguably by the French revolutionary armies in 1794. Of special interest is the inclusion in Buchkremer's material of some thirteen pages on the Massif Central torn from *La France touristique*, a prewar French guidebook, along with previous reports from German art historians touring occupied France.[180]

In Göpel's 1942 book on Normandy, 47 percent of the photographs were of churches with an additional 22 percent showing châteaux. There were two pictures of German troops and a view of Rouen with a pontoon bridge over the Seine built by German Pioneers in 1940. The text, which included chapters on the geology, history, and art of the province, was sprinkled with references to the "Germanic" Norman character and concluded with an admonition to the German troops to avoid the mistake of the early Normans and not lose their identity among the foreign peoples they conquered.[181] The Normandy tourism paradigm centered on German racial identity articulated by Göpel would shift again to one of Allied freedom after 1944.

FIGURE 13. Sketchbook of Joseph Buchkremer, master architect of Aachen Cathedral, "Trip to Paris," with drawings of Charlemagne's tomb in Aachen Cathedral and the Eiffel Tower, 15–25 June 1942. Joseph Buchkremer, Dombaumeister, "Reise nach Paris, 15.-25. Juni 1942," AN, AJ/40/573.

Art and architecture in Normandy and elsewhere in France were in theory to be made available to soldiers as well as officers and other highly placed officials. A widely distributed notice, apparently intended for all German military personnel in France, announced two tours to the châteaux of the Loire Valley in the summer of 1943. For a total cost of 250 francs, or 12.5 marks at the then current exchange rate, visitors could participate in either of the two tours, each limited to thirty people, with a promise that more such trips would be organized if demand warranted.[182] Connections between the fine arts, museums, and tourism characterized the activities of many of the Germans concerned with French art during the Occupation years. Magdeleine Hours, who worked in the paintings and archaeology department of the Louvre, recalled that while the museum had been emptied of most of its artworks, especially in the later days of the Occupation, bare display pedestals were kept on hand to be brought out on occasion when the Occupation authorities organized tours of Paris for soldiers on leave from the eastern front.[183]

Germans as "Protectors" of French Art

Just as Hitler claimed to have saved Paris in 1940, a German wartime photo-essay book devoted to French châteaux was written by Hans Hörmann and Franz Albrecht Medicus as a result of their travels in France. Hörmann, a specialist in historic architecture who served as art conservation (Kunstschutz) officer in France, and Medicus, then head of the military administration in Paris, expressed in their book a view of benevolent German historic preservation in France. The book, published in 1944, highlighted the picturesque historic as opposed to modern industrial character of France, enabling the Germans to articulate a self-image of chivalric generosity and historic preservation. The châteaux, they wrote, had been placed "under German protection." According to Medicus, the most creative and original form of French art was the country's architecture. Noting that the book was intended to introduce the German soldiers to the French châteaux being protected by the Germans, Medicus emphasized the generosity of the German soldiers, who instinctively, he argued, had placed "sacred" artistic monuments under their protection as they overran France in 1940. Citing Goethe's injunction to preserve historic treasures, Medicus maintained that the Wehrmacht had lived up to the ideals of the great writer. Hörmann added that in 1940, German soldiers had protected the châteaux at Amboise and Blois from destruction in the heat of battle. In his introduction, Hörmann indicated that the French influence on the building of châteaux in Germany, such as Potsdam's Sans Souci, was sufficient reason for Germans to be interested in French castle architecture today. Sans Souci, however, he continued, showed how the Germans took French influences and made them their own. "In place of the artistic ideal of Versailles [there arose] the spirit of Potsdam." Versailles, the apex of French château construction, once again came under German criticism. As in the case of France in general, German perceptions of the château were mixed. On the one hand, it represented great art and architecture to be admired and had been selected as the site of the proclamation of the German Empire in 1871. On the other, however, it symbolized a kind of "soulless" grandeur incompatible with the idealized German spirit and, of course, also the 1919 peace treaty that sealed Germany's defeat in World War I. Hörmann confined his comments to the political, the events of 1871 and the "so-called peace treaty of 1919." Now on the circuit was the Saint-Germain-en-Laye château, scene of another 1919 "so-called peace treaty with Austria," and Fontainebleau, now doubly a site of tourist interest because of its prewar history as well as its being the location of the German military leadership meetings held there shortly after the victorious campaign of 1940.[184]

In 1943, Hörmann, placed in charge of the group responsible for the protection of art (Beauftragter für Kunstschutz), toured a France now fully occupied by the Germans. During trips through what had been the unoccupied zone, Hörmann, as had Buchkremer, wrote detailed reports on his travels and took photographs.[185] In a trip to Périgueux and the Vézère Valley in February 1943, Hans Möbius, an archaeologist also working for the Kunstschutz, visited and photographed the Lascaux caves, which had been discovered two and a half years earlier. Reporting to the Army Command, he described at length the grotto of Combarelles with its paintings of animals, the Cap Blanc shelter with reliefs of wild horses, and the museum at Les Eyzies.[186]

The German Kunstschutz staff appears to have taken some steps to protect French art building up to and during the 1944 military campaign in France. German approval was obtained by the French director of museums to requisition a quarry in the town of Sèvres in order to store boxes containing more than six thousand fragile ceramic artifacts from the Musée national de Sèvres in the event of Allied bombings or invasion.[187] A request for antiaircraft batteries to be placed in the town and park of Versailles in April 1944 took note of the artwork there, which it said would be protected to the greatest extent possible.[188] A German press release in June 1944 praised the Wehrmacht for having carefully spared the Rouen cathedral during the fighting in that town, just as it had done four years earlier during the Battle of France.[189] Kunstschutz correspondence also included the arrangements to transfer the Bayeux Tapestry from a depot in the Sources château to a more secure location in the Louvre in Paris. The move took place during the night of 27–28 June.[190] The other side of the equation concerning art was the notorious plunder of French artworks by Goering and others during the Occupation years. The legacy of this pillage continued long after the war. In 1997 a new tourist circuit was created of museums in and around Paris displaying some 987 artworks taken by the Nazis during the Occupation. After the war these works came into the possession of the French government, which only in the mid-1990s attempted to locate the original owners and their heirs.[191]

Tourism and the Resistance

Following the German invasion of the Soviet Union, tensions mounted in occupied France. In December 1941, attacks against German soldiers in France were beginning to change the atmosphere, and Jünger found extended curfews dimming the activity of Paris.[192] That month, assaults on German police officials led to the closing of sections of Paris to nonresidents, which also inhibited tourism in the city. Civilians and military personnel touring Paris were required to do so in groups authorized by the military command. Early in 1942, the *Wegleiter* published an article featuring cemeteries in the Paris area where German soldiers lay buried and adding them to the German tourist circuit in France. A cemetery at Pantin held the remains of German soldiers from the 1870–71 war, another in Ivry for soldiers from the 1914–1918 war as well as some sixty who had died while entering Paris in 1940. A photograph showed the burial at Ivry of a German soldier who had been recently shot, presumably by partisans, in Paris.[193]

As Resistance activity following the invasion of Soviet Russia increasingly threatened Germans in Paris and elsewhere in France, soldiers were warned in March 1942 that "terrorists," the word used for those resisting Vichy and the German forces, were on the hunt for arms. Soldiers were ordered neither to walk on quiet backstreets at night nor to leave weapons in theater and club checkrooms. They were to be especially careful with pistols in the public rooms of hotels and other places accessible to French personnel.[194]

German officials, however, continued to promote tourism when they could use it to enhance their propaganda. A group of some one hundred Germans returning from the United States in May 1942, after the American entry into the war, were given a holiday of several days in the "best hotel" in Biarritz, where they were provided with concerts, visits to the cinema, and tours of the area.[195] In January 1943, the "total war" effort announced by the German government, following the defeat at Stalingrad and the increase in Resistance activity, caused more restrictions in tourism in occupied France. The military command in Paris was directed to close nightclubs and exclusive restaurants to German military and civilian personnel in Paris. An officer reporting this policy was of the opinion that such restrictions would also please the local French population, who, in any case, were in no position to avail themselves of such entertainments. A report included with the note added, however, that as of the beginning of 1943, some sixty-nine establishments in Paris were officially open until 1 a.m., with another twenty-one open until 5 a.m. Although as many as half of these could be closed as far as the Germans were concerned, they still wanted to keep some of them open as places of relaxation for soldiers on leave from the war zones, as well as Luftwaffe and navy personnel.[196] With their occupation of the former Italian zone in September 1943, the Germans took over Nice and the Côte d'Azur. In his history of tourism in Nice, Robert Kanigel described the entry of the Germans into the city:

> The Germans tried to come across as benign. They sent out photographers to snap soldiers at tourist spots—gesturing meaningfully beside the Emperor Augustus's monument at La Turbie; or mingling with street urchins; or camera in hand, strolling along the Promenade, flanked by beach umbrellas and sidewalk merchants. If the Germans were just tourists, the photographs as much as said, why fear them?[197]

The Germans briefly enjoyed the hotels and resorts of Nice, but the increasing pressure of the war changed things quickly. Hotel receipt taxes (*taxe de séjour*) declined from 190,000 francs in December 1943 to 14,000 in May 1944.[198]

Mounting wartime difficulties were taking their toll on the Germans elsewhere in France as well. An eight-page supplement in 1943 to a Grieben tour book of Paris, published originally in 1938, reflected the growing insecurity of German personnel in occupied Paris, where increasing numbers of Métro stations were being closed because they could not be secured against Resistance attacks. An addendum to the 1943 Grieben guide noted that German citizens needed special passes to enter occupied France, and those visiting Paris were required to register with the local command offices within twenty-four hours of their arrival. There the visitor exchanged his or her German food coupons for special ones used in Paris and was assigned living quarters. France, it was noted, was now on Central European Time.[199] Germans there were advised to get to trains early because of heavy use and to avoid Le Bourget airport, which was closed to passenger traffic.[200]

Gastronomic tourism, however, did not cease merely because the war was turning badly for Germany. The 1943 Grieben guide advised that wartime food restrictions did not prevent the Parisian restaurants from setting a good cover and named several of them maintained specifically for Germans, along with a list of cabarets.[201] Sites now closed included the châteaux at Chantilly,

Compiègne, Saint-Germain-en-Laye, Maisons-Laffitte, and Vincennes, along with the Eiffel Tower, the catacombs, and the sewers. One could, however, still visit select sections of the Louvre, the Musée de l'Homme, the Opéra, the Rodin Museum, the Palais de la Découverte, and the Vincennes zoo. Regional sites still available for touring included Fontainebleau, Malmaison, and, at Versailles, the park and the few remaining open rooms at the château.[202] German military personnel and *Urlauber* (vacationers), who had traveled previously in both directions between Germany and France during the war, faced new luggage restrictions in late 1943. Such travelers, said to have sometimes carried as many as three to six suitcases on military express trains going to and from Germany, were criticized for exposing the trains to derailments and increased vulnerability to air attacks. Passengers henceforth would be limited to what they themselves could carry.[203] The business-as-usual mentality of some under the worsening conditions came to the attention of Jean Guéhenno, who described an Allied bombing run that struck the Renault plant in Billancourt, just outside Paris, in April 1943. Several bombs hit the Longchamps racetrack, which had been equipped with antiaircraft positions. The dead and wounded were quickly gathered together, and then the bell sounded for the first race. Bets were placed.

> Did one not need to keep the bets of the survivors and the dead to know who would win the Vulcan or the Almanzor? . . . This little fact shows well enough the level of our degradation. The P. M. U. [*pari mutuel urbain*, pari-mutuel betting] is eternal. At the same time as the list of victims, the newspaper this morning publishes "the racing results."[204]

Even the *Wegleiter,* which generally adopted a business-as-usual approach itself, reflected the changed conditions. Describing an exhibition on the Champs-Élysées on behalf of the newly created French unit of the Waffen-SS in early 1944, the *Wegleiter* called the famous avenue the symbol now of a fighting Europe.[205]

August 1944: Is Paris Burning?

Eyes that had for so long turned toward the coast in anticipation of an Allied landing now focused on Normandy during the first weeks of June 1944, when Guéhenno noticed fewer Germans on the streets of Paris. "Those whom one encounters around Opéra no longer have that air of pretentious strollers [*flâneurs farauds*] that they still had even a few months ago."[206] Little in the German publications in occupied France gave any hint of an impending withdrawal as Allied forces swept across the country in the summer of 1944.

As Pierre Audiat noted, German military and civilian personnel, up until August of that year, continued to frequent the same cafés in as elegant a style as before. Buses transporting German auxiliaries into the center of Paris operated as they had since 1940, although there seemed to be more activity now that the war had again reached France.[207]

A columnist in the *Pariser Zeitung* of 8 August, without mentioning his own forced withdrawal, wrote wistfully of Normandy's having grown on him after several years' service there. Already he seemed to miss Normandy's calvados, trees, wind, and brooks.[208] Writing that "cities are women, tender only to the victor," Ernst Jünger visited the terrace of the Sacré-Cœur basilica at almost the same time for a nostalgic final look at occupied Paris.[209] As the Allied forces drew closer to Paris and the Resistance there rose against the Germans, street fighting broke out while a largely impatient population awaited the arrival of the Free French. "Curiosity [seekers] and onlookers," in Audiat's words, even during this time of hunger, bombardments, and reprisals, marked the days before the liberation of Paris. The terraces of cafés, when open as they were on restricted schedules, were filled with people watching military convoys and ambulances carrying the wounded from the Normandy front. The Germans, exasperated by the insouciance of the Parisians, could do nothing, as their own propaganda had worked to create a business-as-usual mentality all throughout the Occupation.[210]

Resistance newspapers began to appear in a city that, in the words of an observer, Victoria Kent, was quiet as people avoided the streets. "Paris is on vacation," she wrote. "No more traffic, no more police, hardly any bicycles, and the few Germans who are on the streets are well armed and in cars. I see them pass like a little summer cloud. Who can now delay our liberation?"[211] Audiat also sensed a vacation atmosphere, as Parisians waited impatiently for what most hoped would be their liberation. Crowds gathering at the gates of the city to watch the comings and goings of the Germans guessed whether they were heading toward the eastern front or coming from it: "From time to time, an order from a German officer, furiously trying to regulate the traffic under idle and sometimes ironic gazes, regrouped or dispersed the onlookers who quickly infiltrated and regained the lost ground. Another distraction was to go to see the Germans auctioning some of the material they could not transport."[212] By 19 August, Resistance groups had begun to take control of parts of Paris, "surrounded by the curious, great and small," who kept gazing at them, often in envy. Children especially were happy to be out of school, and the city took on a festival air anticipating an imminent liberation.[213] When the forces of General Philippe Leclerc finally arrived at the

Porte d'Orléans and Porte d'Italie on the southern extremities of the city on the evening of 24 August, crowds gathered to watch and welcome them.[214]

Just as the onset of the Occupation had been accompanied by tourism motifs in the decision to make the defeated French return to the Compiègne site of the 1918 armistice to receive the terms for the pact of 1940, as well as in Hitler's early visit to Paris, its close was also marked by an event with important tourism implications: the failure of the retreating Germans to destroy the city in August 1944. The story that the local German commander in Paris, General Dietrich von Choltitz, disobeyed Hitler's order to level the city and spared it instead has been retold many times, including in *Diplomacy*, a French-German film released in 2014. Notwithstanding this recounting of the story, recent commentary has called this account into question. Lionel Dardenne, assistant curator of the Museum of the Order of the Liberation in Paris, and Ian Buruma have argued that von Choltitz lacked the means to destroy Paris and question whether the dramatic meetings with Pierre Taittinger, head of the Paris municipal council, and Raoul Nordling, the Swedish consul in Paris, occurred in the way that von Choltitz had indicated.[215]

In the story as told by von Choltitz in his memoirs, published in 1951 and retold notably by Larry Collins and Dominique Lapierre in *Is Paris Burning?* in 1965, Hitler had ordered the city destroyed, but after a dramatic conversation with Taittinger, who visited him to plead for the city, von Choltitz, realizing the hopelessness of the German military position, relented.[216] According to the story, Hitler made clear to General Walter Warlimont in August 1944 that the Seine had to be held at all costs and, to that end, Paris was to be defended. Ordering the bridges over the Seine mined and prepared for destruction and the paralyzing of the city's industry, Hitler, probably in a mood of bitterness in response to the iconic status of Paris, told Warlimont and the other generals gathered at his headquarters: "Why should we care if Paris is destroyed? The Allies, at this very moment, are destroying cities all over Germany with their bombs."[217] Then, again according to the story, when Taittinger became aware that von Choltitz had the resources to destroy the city and intended to do so to slow the Allied advance, he took the general out to his balcony at the Hotel Meurice and showed him the peaceful rue de Rivoli, with an attractive young woman riding by on her bicycle, children sailing their boats in the Tuileries pond, the Invalides across the Seine, and the Eiffel Tower in the distance. Pointing out the Louvre with its gardens, and noting the symmetry of the place de la Concorde, Taittinger said to von Choltitz:

"Often it is given to a general to destroy, rarely to preserve. Imagine that one day it may be given to you to stand on this balcony again, as a tourist, to look once more at these monuments to our joys, our sufferings, and to be able to say, 'One day I could have destroyed all this, and I preserved it as a gift for humanity.' General, is not that worth all a conqueror's glory?"

Von Choltitz . . . turned to Taittinger, his voice softer now. "You are a good advocate for Paris, Mr. Taittinger," he said. "You have done your duty well. And likewise I, as a German general, must do mine."[218]

Having determined that the destruction of the city would be a criminal act, von Choltitz, in his own account, finally ignored Hitler's order. After a brief imprisonment and exile, von Choltitz had every reason subsequently to burnish his role in the story of the sparing of Paris. In an article on touring the sites of America's "good war" in France, Geoffrey M. White suggests that the story became "a synecdoche for World War II as a story about the liberation of Europe," reflecting a narrative of American triumph.[219] The accuracy of the story, retold by Collins and Lapierre, however, may be less significant than the tourism iconicity of Paris around which it is constructed. Either von Choltitz saved Paris because of its intrinsic value or he fabricated a story he knew would resonate with large numbers of people in France, Germany, and elsewhere, and thereby rescue his reputation, otherwise damaged by his involvement in Nazi atrocities in eastern Europe. Either way, the story is a testament to the power of the Paris tourism imaginary. On 25 August, the day of von Choltitz's surrender, however, another narrative attested to Paris's continuing tourism iconicity. From the balcony of the city hall, the Hôtel de Ville, General de Gaulle expressed in his own way the iconicity of Paris when he called out, "Paris brisée, Paris martyrisée, mais Paris libérée" (Paris broken, Paris martyred, but Paris liberated).[220] A new narrative, focusing on the "heroic week" and a new tourism paradigm, would begin, reflecting the changed military and political realities following the Liberation. Wartime tourism would be succeeded by *tourisme de mémoire*, or heritage tourism, with its own shifting power relationships and images.

CHAPTER 5

The Liberation, 1944

Normandy and Paris

The shift in paradigms that followed the end of the war is evident in the emergence of the 1944 Normandy landing beaches as a major tourism attraction, with enhanced symbolic meaning, often depicted as the victory of good over evil. Pictured as a center of superior Nordic culture during the German occupation, Normandy now became an emblem of freedom, democracy, and liberation. Small peaceful villages that before the war had been devoted to coastal fishing became, first in 1940, the locus of German activity in preparation for a possible invasion of Britain and later for defense of "Fortress Europa" against the Allies, and then, after the Allied invasion of 1944, focal points of tourist activity with economies transformed accordingly. Significant for the revenue it brings to the region, and fed in part by a postwar proliferation of *lieux de mémoire* as tourist sites, the Normandy battlefield circuit attests to the success of the French in exploiting its tourist potential.[1] Within months after the 1944 Liberation, even while the war continued, the Touring club de France was in contact with the head of the Anglo-American mission in Normandy, asking him to "safeguard French artistic *patrimoine*" there, as well as with Raoul Dautry, newly installed as minister of reconstruction and urban development, asking him to protect tourist sites in Normandy.[2]

From War Sites to Tourist Sites

Shortly after the end of the war, suggestions circulated among French tourism officials that recent battlefield sites, in Normandy in particular, would become popular tourism destinations. The Commissariat général au tourisme, the agency charged with overseeing the industry in the postwar provisional government, was to design a circuit of the landing sites to train tour guides who would then be made available to travel agencies. To ensure their competence and independence, these guides were to be trained by the agency, which would also organize special Normandy tourist circuits for them.[3]

A tour through France, Germany, and England by seven American journalists in the spring of 1946 included a visit to Normandy, where one of the journalists, L. R. Blanchard, described the heavy Allied bombing of targets there, including churches. The Rouen cathedral had been heavily damaged in a bombing raid, and Le Havre, he added, had been bombed 104 times, with thirty thousand people rendered homeless.[4] Although there has been some discussion of Americans coming to understand only recently the extensive damage done by Allied bombing raids in Normandy, Blanchard makes it clear that this was not the case.[5] He saw far more extensive damage in Norman cities, where he reported "acres of ruins," than in the countryside. "Where wide, stone bridges once stood are the Army's [prefabricated portable] Bailey bridges," he added.[6] Blanchard also visited American military cemeteries, including one at La Cambe, the only one of several, as he put it, within easy reach of the traveler. La Cambe, which held the remains of more than 4,500 American soldiers, he argued, was typical of all American military cemeteries in Normandy, with fresh flowers and marble memorials erected by the French.[7] During the years after the war, the remains of many of the American dead were repatriated and others were moved to other military cemeteries, including one established in 1954 at Colleville-sur-Mer, dedicated two years thereafter, also in Normandy. La Cambe retained a German military cemetery. As will be seen later, the messages given by the cemeteries at La Cambe and Colleville-sur-Mer were very different from each other and would become sources of controversy in the early twenty-first century.

Blanchard also visited Caen, which he described as a ruined city with thousands of homeless and hundreds living in a shelter under the walls of a church.[8] Writing from Granville in Lower Normandy, he advised, "This is no year for touring France." The weather was cold, the provincial hotels unheated, and the better of them were still being used by military forces. Old cities with ancient walls, "picturesque courtyards," and narrow streets made France an attractive tourism destination, but the visitor would have to put up with a "complete lack of the comforts most travelers have come to expect." Food, when available, however, was good, and the French knew how to make much from little.[9] With or without comfort for the tourist, Normandy by the late 1940s was launching a new career as a war *tourisme de mémoire* destination for Americans as well as the French.

On 22 May 1945, Raymond Triboulet, who had been named the first subprefect of liberated territory in Normandy on 15 June 1944, created a committee charged with organizing commemorations of the landings. Wishing to preserve the material remains of the invasion, he helped secure the *loi Triboulet* of 21 May 1947, which created an annual celebration of the Normandy landings.[10] This law became part of a long history of French classification of military fortifications as official historic sites beginning with the Amiens citadel in 1840.[11] Michelin published its first battlefield map of the landing sites in 1947.[12] In the 1950s there were two museums in Normandy devoted to the landings. A 1988 guidebook to the landing beaches in Normandy listed eighteen relevant museums, of which eleven were in the Calvados department, four more in La Manche, and another three in "others."[13] By 2009 there were over thirty such museums or other sites, a proliferation that occasioned a comment in a book review of a history of the military struggle in Port-en-Bessin referring to "the potted guide one might buy at the entrance to any of the Second World War museums that dot the Normandy region."[14]

Gaullist Narratives and the "Liberation Circuit"

As Olivier Wieviorka wrote in his history of divided memory of the war years in postwar France, the early commemorations in Normandy focused more on the coast than on the interior of the region, where so much of the bloodshed and destruction occurred, and highlighted the Western Allies to the virtual exclusion of the Soviet contributions to the victory. The commemorations also tended to privilege the Anglo-American role in contrast to the suffering of the local population. The paradigm Wieviorka described remained dominant into the 1980s.[15] By the late 1940s, the Gaullist narrative of the war was securely in place.

A "Liberation Circuit" tour, a three-day itinerary organized in 1948 by the Compagnie française de tourisme (French Tourism Company), focused on the Allied landing beaches, offering an account of the 1944 liberation of France, which itself assumed touristic iconicity and highlighted Normandy on the tourist map. The illustration for the "Liberation Circuit" included a Cross

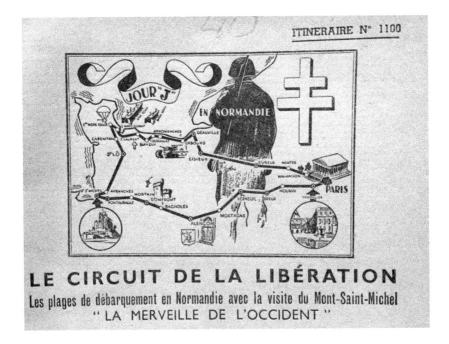

FIGURE 14. A 1948 tour guide to Normandy battlefields ("Itinéraire no. 1100, Le Circuit de la Libération"), in *Horizons de France et d'Europe* (Paris: Compagnie Française de Tourisme, 1948). Author's personal collection.

of Lorraine, a soldier, and the inscription "Jour 'J' " (D-Day). En route from Paris to Normandy, the tourist visited Alençon, "liberated 12 August 1944 by the tanks of the glorious Leclerc Division," a reference to General Philippe Leclerc's Free French forces. Battlefield sites to be visited on arrival in Normandy on day one included a thicket near Mortain where a panzer division had been annihilated while trying to cut off the Americans. On day two, visitors saw more battlefields and bombed towns, as well as the Utah and Omaha landing beaches. On day three, the tour stopped at Arromanches, site of a British-built artificial port, and Courseulles, liberated by Canadian tanks. Courseulles was followed by a "pilgrimage" to Bény-Riviers, where more than two thousand Canadian soldiers lay buried. Caen, described as a "martyred city," had suffered seventy days of nearly uninterrupted bombing, during which three-quarters of the city had been destroyed, some eight thousand of ten thousand buildings having been demolished. Finally, on the return trip to Paris, there was a visit to Évreux, whose town center had been "devastated in 1940 by German artillery" and where, on 30 August 1944, General de Gaulle's provisional government had installed its first Republican

FIGURE 15.   Remains of the artificial harbor built by the British for landings in Arromanches. Photo by author, 2009.

Regional Commission, a local government agency. Another of the French Tourism Company's Normandy itineraries featured the artificial port at Arromanches.[16]

Commercial factors also shaped the development of tourist sites of remembrance, as seen in the proposal of a local committee to erect a monument to the Resistance in Le Havre, on the English Channel, in 1961. A private committee, noting Le Havre's popularity with both French and foreign tourists, argued that the proposed monument would attract visitors drawn to the other tourist spots in the city. At the same time, it suggested, a memorial would bring in new tourists who would also visit the other local sites.[17]

Normandy Tour Guides and Anniversaries

Significant anniversaries were also key in the development of war-related tourism, as exemplified in the case of the Normandy invasion sites. A guidebook to these locales, prepared for the twentieth anniversary of the invasion in 1964, contained a preface by General Pierre Kœnig, who claimed it to be the first of its kind. No longer, he wrote, would those wishing to tour the battlefield need to do extensive preparatory research, as now everything had been put together in one accessible guidebook intended especially for war veterans, families coming to pay respects to their dead, and, "naturally, tourists traveling these regions heavy with history."[18] In addition to a brief history of the events leading up to the Normandy invasion, the guidebook listed seven touring itineraries, one relating to the landings of the British parachute troops, another devoted to events from the Battle of Cherbourg to the Battle of Caen, plus five other tours, each focusing on one of the landing beaches: Sword, Juno, Gold, Omaha, and Utah. The book concluded with a chronology and a bibliography.

An explicit function of the 1965 *Guide bleu* for Normandy was to help make the battlefields and historic monuments of the Second World War accessible to the tourist.[19] The 1967 Fodor guide, published in the United States, referred to Normandy as a "maritime Garden of Eden." Normandy, it continued, was a natural corridor between France's transatlantic ports and Paris, but this feature, an asset in peacetime, turned out to be a liability in war. The guidebook described briefly the battle that took place in 1944, highlighting the "Mulberry" artificial harbor at Arromanches and the first of the symbolic milestones marking "Liberty Way," the route taken by the American armies, at Sainte-Mère-Église. Mention was made of "miracles of reconstruction" that had restored the ports of Cherbourg and Le Havre, with the latter available for free tours from the local Syndicat d'initiative (Tourist Office).[20]

A 1993 guidebook to the Normandy landing beaches by Stephen H. Chicken, an engineering officer in the British Royal Air Force, encouraged "anyone interested in D-Day to visit Normandy." Travel to France was easy, and the local people were friendly, but, the author warned, "please remember, as you study this period of history, that war does not consist of machines killing other machines but men killing other men. A visit to any of the war cemeteries in Normandy is a sobering experience."[21] The issue of authenticity in the sites was clearly on the author's mind as he counseled the reader to visit the Museum of Normandy Wrecks near Port-en-Bessin because the objects in its collection, salvaged from the waters off the coastline, were "real examples of the equipment which was attempting to land on 6 June 1944, rather than replicas or similar marks of vehicles."[22]

Another anniversary guidebook was *The Visitor's Guide to Normandy Landing Beaches: Memorials and Museums,* published in England in 1994 for the fiftieth anniversary of the invasion. Some twenty museums in the Normandy area were described as focusing on the invasion, in addition to one in Portsmouth. The Portsmouth museum housed the Overlord Embroidery, completed in 1968 after five years' labor, modeled after the Bayeux Tapestry, depicting William the Conqueror's successful invasion of England in 1066. In addition to the twenty museums in Normandy, *The Visitor's Guide* identified 177 memorials, not including the many streets and squares named in commemoration of the events of 1944.[23]

The fiftieth anniversary of D-Day was also the occasion for the promotion of tours not just to battle sites in France but to the staging areas in England as well. A supplement to *Travel + Leisure* included features such as "The Great Crusade," "London at War," and "The Friendly Invasion." BritRail offered a "pass through history" discounted rate starting at the equivalent of $28 per day, and a short article advised readers where to find more information on "Seeing D-Day Sites."[24] Tours were organized in Plymouth, Torbay, and other towns in southern England that had been training sites for the landing forces prior to June 1944 and from which the invasion forces had departed. Advertised in a leaflet published jointly by the Plymouth Marketing Bureau and the English Riviera Tourist Board were exhibitions, memorial services, 1940s music concerts, yacht and powerboat races, fireworks, a "Miss 1994 Competition," and a variety of other events lasting from 2 April through 31 October 1994.[25] Writing about the fiftieth anniversary in 1994, Mary Blume of the *New York Times* noted:

> The number of veterans and tourists expected to visit the battle sights this spring cannot even be estimated. "I would be talking nonsense if I even tried to give you a figure," said Jean-Claude Demais of the Comité Regional de Tourisme de Normandie at a recent press conference. Piety, nostalgia and hard-nosed Norman practicality have brought three départements together to coordinate festivities with a view not only to a short time gain in bleak times but to ensure, with the opening of the Channel tunnel, a steady flow of tourists in coming years.

Blume mentions tour operators' brochures proclaiming, "The 82d Airborne Division Association presents . . . The Invasion of Normandy 50 Years Later!," and featuring "a QE2 cruise to Cherbourg including Second World War era big bands, movies and newsreels and the presence of Dame Vera Lynn and the 91-year-old Bob Hope." Reports surfaced of British veterans who had made reservations years in advance being displaced by hotels in favor of a higher-paying American tour operator.[26]

Touristic Promotion of Normandy Battle Sites

In her essay "Gratitude, Trauma, and Repression: D-Day in French Memory," Kate C. Lemay notes a significant increase in both French national and regional governmental promotion of tourism to the Normandy battlefields.

The Lower Normandy authorities organized tours with historical indicators and, in 1997, the Société d'études touristiques et d'équipement des loisirs (Society for Tourism Studies and Leisure Facilities) set up eight battlefield tourism itineraries with guideposts along the roads to explain the sites and point visitors to the next ones. American veterans returning to visit the sites increased "memory tourism," sometimes in collaboration with local authorities. Lemay mentions Agnès Bouffard, the mayor of Hiesville, as especially involved in promoting commemoration activities with American veterans in her area, in particular on the 6 June anniversary of the landings.[27] A brochure published in 1994 by the Comité départemental du tourisme du Calvados (CDT, Calvados Departmental Tourism Committee) mentioned eight special itineraries "illustrating the major phases of the battle and including places of memory, historical sites, and different museums." Four of these, "Overlord—Assault," "D-Day—The Shock," "Objective—A Port," and "The Encirclement," were new as of 1994. Altogether, twenty "principal sites and museums" were listed, together with an additional eleven "other museums and sites." Included in the brochure was a flyer with a quiz consisting of twenty-one questions to test the visitor's knowledge of the Battle of Normandy. Winners were to receive prizes.[28] Among the veterans returning to see the places where they had fought were two British commando officers captured in a reconnaissance raid and interviewed personally by Rommel on 20 May 1944. Forty years later, one of the officers, George Lane, visited La Roche Guyon to view again the spot where Rommel had interrogated him.[29] As the years passed, however, Toni and Valmai Holt observed in their *Visitor's Guide to Normandy Landing Beaches* that it was younger people, many having studied the battle accounts in school, and family groups who toured the area "to see where dad, or granddad, fought or where history was made."[30]

In 2009 a "Normandie Pass" offered discounts for visits to twenty-six D-Day museums in the region.[31] Normandy had many other tourist attractions, such as the Bayeux Tapestry, which, according to the director of the Musée mémorial de la Bataille de Normandie (Memorial Museum of the Battle of Normandy) in Bayeux, also drew people to the D-Day story. The Musée mémorial was officially inaugurated on 14 July 1981.[32] One display in the museum included a telegram sent by the United States War Department to the parents of a twenty-year-old soldier killed in action in Normandy on 30 July 1944. The picture of the soldier, one of four brothers serving in the war at the time, is just below it. "At that moment *Saving Private Ryan* was very close to me," wrote one visitor to the site.[33]

In the British landing sector, the Musée du débarquement in Arromanches-les-Bains, the site of the artificial harbor constructed to facilitate the landings, was one of the first D-Day museums. Established as a private venture in 1953, it was inaugurated the following year, on the tenth anniversary of D-Day, by President René Coty.[34] By the early 1960s, the Musée du débarquement was attracting over 200,000 visitors annually, according to paid entrance figures.[35] Frédéric Sommier, its director, indicated that it drew about 400,000 visitors in 2004, the sixtieth anniversary of D-Day, but normally attracted some 300,000 annually. The war, he added, had entirely transformed the tourism face of Arromanches-les-Bains, turning it from a spa town—hence its name—to a *lieu de mémoire*. He depicted his museum's clientele more as "tourists," in quotes, than the visitors to some other places, such as the Mémorial at Caen.[36] In 2011, the Musée hosted 331,100 paid visitors, according to the *Annuaire statistique de la France,* placing it in fourth place among the sites with entrance fees in Lower Normandy. Just ahead of it, in third place, was the Mémorial–Cité de l'Histoire pour la Paix (Memorial Museum–Center for History and Peace) in Caen, with 371,000 visitors in 2011.[37] More recent renovations by the regional government of earlier museums built by the Comité du débarquement included a museum at Pegasus Bridge in 2000, the Airborne Museum in Sainte-Mère-Église in 2011, and the erection of new exhibits at the Utah Beach museum, also in 2011.[38]

The Caen Memorial-Museum of Peace

Heavily damaged by fighting in 1944, Caen, the principal city in Lower Normandy, was chosen to house the Mémorial–Cité de l'Histoire pour la Paix, established in 1988, as a Memorial-Museum of Peace, an impressive structure containing exhibits, a library, a bookstore, and meeting rooms for activities related to the history of the war, as well as larger issues of war and peace.[39] Not surprisingly, the heavy bombing and occasional misbehavior of Allied troops in Caen and elsewhere in Normandy, described by L. R. Blanchard in 1946, contributed to mixed memories of the campaign for the locals, as well as to some of the more historical recent literature related to it.[40] The Mémorial–Cité in Caen has been described as a museum with a scenography "based on emotion, the mise en scène seeking to mobilize passions, sentiments, emotions—in this case the memories of the spectators—while the historical content seeks to mobilize reason."[41] To Shannon L. Fogg, an American historian of France, "a month spent studying at Le Mémorial de Caen and visiting war sites throughout Normandy cemented my love for the period and for France."[42]

According to paid entrances figures, the Mémorial–Cité receives approximately 380,000 to 400,000 visitors each year. In 1994, the fiftieth anniversary of the D-Day landings, some 600,000 persons visited the Mémorial. One of its strengths, according to Claude Origet du Cluzeau in a study of cultural tourism, is the activity of the staff in personally soliciting the visitors to familiarize them with the goals of the institution, with interpretive centers, in the English and American style, without, however, using the term "interpretive center."[43] Comparing the Caen Mémorial to other Second World War sites in Normandy, Marc Pottier, its educational and research director in 2009, stated, "We are more oriented to reflection, more demanding of the visitors."[44] The Caen Mémorial is also situated on a tourist access route to Mont Saint-Michel, so it attracts a substantial "tourisme d'autoroute, de passage" (transient, highway tourism), in Pottier's words.[45] It was said to be just behind Mont Saint-Michel as the second-most-visited tourist site in the Normandy region.[46] More recently, the Mémorial continued to attract roughly 300,000 to 400,000 visitors annually. In 2010 it renovated much of its exhibit area to devote more space to the Holocaust. Its maps and explicative panels relating to the Second World War were updated and made more interactive to appeal to a younger audience, especially as many of its visitors are students on school field trips. Responding to the increased focus on the twenty thousand civilian deaths and destruction in Caen and Saint-Lô, the Mémorial opened a new space devoted to the Battle of Normandy.[47] From 2010 through 2013, the Mémorial received approximately 350,000 to 370,000 visitors annually, a figure that jumped to 438,000 in 2014, the seventieth anniversary of the Normandy landings. This figure, however, was down from the 557,000 counted during the sixtieth anniversary in 2004.[48] As Philippe Gay, Calvados tourism director, noted, "Anniversaries are always big tourist years."[49] The American military cemetery at Colleville-sur-Mer in Normandy attracted between 1 million and 1.5 million visitors for each year from 2010 through 2013 and 2,126,940 visitors during the anniversary year of 2014, of prime economic importance for the area.[50]

Tourism and Memory in Normandy

Connected to the issues of D-Day tourism in Normandy are the fraught questions of meanings and interpretations, together with how the events of the war should be remembered in the construction and design of monuments and museums. On the one hand, a German guidebook published in 1997 noted that much of the former Atlantic Wall had been turned into memorials to specific military actions, mile markers, and cemeteries for the fallen on both sides. In addition to the remembering came the reconciliation, expressed in signs along the tourist route that bore German as well as British names.[51] On the other hand, addressing suggestions that increased tourism might glorify or trivialize war, Elisabeth Raffray expressed concern about "accusations made against all development of such a *patrimoine* that would promote 'war tourism'" in Lower Normandy.[52]

Although the Caen Mémorial has international understanding and peace as its main theme, Friedhelm Boll found a contradiction in its message. World War I sites, such as Verdun and the Péronne museum at the Somme, spoke unambiguously to the need for peace and international reconciliation, in Boll's view. An international message of peace was conveyed by the use of three languages, French, English, and German, at Péronne, and the burial of German as well as French soldiers at Fort Douaumont, near Verdun. Both Péronne and Verdun highlighted the sufferings of the ordinary soldier in the trenches, a sentiment that included German as well as French and English troops.[53] Normandy, however, he argued, presented a different image, and not only because the Second World War was closer in time than the first to the observer. Tourist brochures from the Normandy landing sites invited visitors to recall the history of the battle that began the liberation of Europe from the scourge of Nazism, maintaining a continuity of the spirit of the war, unlike, Boll writes, the sites of the First World War. Films in the Caen Mémorial reproduced the sights and sounds of the 1944 landings with vivid visual and acoustic effect. In Boll's words, "The war is present as in scarcely any other museum site."[54]

Computer war games that focused on D-Day maintained this sense of conflict, and Boll also noted a sense of triumphalism more than reconciliation conveyed at the American military cemetery at Colleville-sur-Mer. Rather than a site of sadness and introspection, Boll found the American cemetery a place of power and triumph. The motto at the German military cemetery in nearby La Cambe, "One wins no peace through war," would have been fully out of place in the American cemetery. He tells the story of a group of Polish, German, and French students visiting the landing sites in a German bus and twice being insulted along the way. In another incident, this one at the American cemetery at Colleville-sur-Mer in 2005, a young Frenchwoman asked three female students, German, French, and Belgian, overheard speaking German, "Vous n'avez pas honte de venir ici?" [Aren't you ashamed to come here?]. Boll was sufficiently struck by this question that he used it as the title of his essay.[55]

Boll's reflections, both on the incident at Colleville-sur-Mer and, more generally, on the Caen Mémorial, demonstrated the power relationships in tourism that had shifted from a German -dominated model during the Occupation to one structured by the Allies in the postwar years.[56] The Caen

Mémorial, in his view, gave out a contradictory message. It calls for peace and reconciliation, Boll acknowledged, emphasizing the work it does in its exhibits and pedagogical programs promoting Franco-German friendship, European unity, and international reconciliation and peace. He saw an incongruity, however, between these peace initiatives and the selling of war toys in its gift shop, a practice justified by the need to raise funds for the Mémorial. The tensions between the messages seeking to promote international understanding and the commercial imperatives of battlefield tourism in Normandy were especially jarring to Boll, who sensed an anti-German feeling there despite the official friendship between France and the Federal Republic. He concluded that memory of the Second World War in France focused on the 1940–1944 Occupation and was accordingly centered on French-German relations, whereas in Germany, memories of the Holocaust, the war in the east, and the concentration camps played a larger role than the occupation of France. To Boll it was the English and American monuments in Normandy that leaned too heavily on reliving the war and lacked the messages of reconciliation present in most of the French and German sites. "Dubious 'souvenirs,'" which, he maintained, too often dominated pacifist pedagogy, could lead only to the creation of hostile feelings toward Germany, which was at variance with the spirit of the Mémorial. An indication of this was the exclusion of official German participation in D-Day anniversary celebrations for sixty years.[57]

Tourism to the Normandy battlefields was stimulated by films such as Darryl Zanuck's *The Longest Day* in 1962 and Steven Spielberg's *Saving Private Ryan* in 1998, both of which highlighted again the sites related to D-Day. The latter film was described in France as "the memory of the century as theme park."[58] The tensions Boll felt in the Normandy messages, and especially those in the Caen Mémorial, reflect the continuing problems with conflicting memories of the past, especially with regard to the war. He is clearly not defending either German Nazism or the German occupation of France but arguing instead that an effective work of reconciliation and the building of a united Europe require a dialogue of peace rather than war. His argument reflects what other historians, such as Henry Rousso, have seen as the "fractures" in memory, the many different ways in which successive historical, political, social, and cultural groups construct the past in their own memories.[59] The involvement of the tourist industry in influencing these conflicts of memory through the propagation of images in Normandy and elsewhere is one of the many ways in which tourism and the tourism imaginary in relation to war have become such an important part of contemporary culture.

Debates over narratives of the Normandy battle continue and undoubtedly impact tourism there. In 2009, President Barack Obama visited Omaha Beach for the D-Day anniversary. Serge Halimi, writing in *Le Monde Diplomatique,* noted that in his entire speech there, Obama devoted only fourteen words to the Russian role in the Second World War victory. The D-Day images, he wrote, represented a victory of liberal democracy and global capitalism, reflected in the shift in polls of Parisians inquiring who they thought had contributed most to the victory over Nazi Germany. In August–September 1944, with the war still in progress, 61 percent had selected the Russians, 29 percent the Americans. Responding to a similar poll sixty years later, 58 percent of the French said that the Americans had contributed the most to the victory, in contrast to 20 percent who picked the Russians. Pointing to the combined effects of Hollywood and the American victory in the Cold War, Halimi emphasized the selective mechanism of memory and the fact that its contours are shaped by the events of the present.[60] By the time of the 2011 anniversary of the landings in Normandy, the battle and its imagery had become so commonplace in France that the satirical newspaper *Le Canard Enchaîné* lampooned an article in the newspaper *Ouest-France* that covered a speech given in Normandy by Jeannette Bougrab, secretary of state for youth and community service. According to the *Canard Enchaîné* article, which joked about the *Ouest-France*'s reporting of the speech, Bougrab reportedly spoke about the landing at "Obama Beach" and its role in liberating the "American continent."[61] For many Americans, tours to the Normandy landing beaches with narratives extolling American involvement in the liberation of France evoked memories of the "Good War," as the Second World War came to be known in popular American culture. The focus on the American role in the Normandy landings, catered to by the local French, appears to have impacted tourism there. Commenting on the seventieth anniversary of D-Day in 2014, Delphine Lefèvre, co-director of Normandy Sightseeing Tours, said: "We plan visits to Normandy with driver-guides. The landing sites make up 85 to 90 percent of our activity. The French generally come by car and have little use for our services, as do also the British, who cross the channel with their personal vehicles. Our main clientele remains the Americans, who appreciate benefits of this type."[62]

As Geoffrey M. White writes, "Many Americans who travel to the D-Day landing beaches and military cemeteries in Normandy seek, and find, an emotion-filled landscape dense with iconic signifiers of American agency in a war of liberation."[63] In all, the Normandy landing sites received approximately 5 million visitors annually, of whom 40 percent were international, according to Philippe Gay, Calvados tourism director, in 2014. Of these,

1.5 million visited the American military cemetery at Colleville.[64] The contrast between the message of triumphalism at the American cemetery and that of international peace and reconciliation in the German cemetery at La Cambe could hardly be more striking. La Cambe's conservator noted that after the fiftieth anniversary of D-Day in 1994, increasing numbers of British visitors referred to the Germans buried there as "adversaries" rather than "enemies."[65]

The reach of the Normandy battlefield tourist imaginary also extends beyond the borders of France. In an essay on "atomic tourism" to the Manhattan Project facilities in Oak Ridge, Tennessee, one of the sites where the earliest nuclear bombs were developed during the Second World War, Lindsey Freeman focuses on the Secret City Festival there, illustrating the shift in the town's economy from physics to tourism. Held annually in June beginning in 2003, the Secret City Festival includes a reenactment of the Normandy landings, which, Freeman writes, "was one of the most popular performances of the two-day event." Freeman continues:

> It is nearly a hundred degrees outside as soldiers in period dress invade "Normandy." Artillery is on display from tanks to guns to grenades. Smoke blankets the battlefield as ersatz soldiers scamper across the grounds, taking and giving orders, grunting, clutching their chests and dying with dramatic flair. The medics are there too, scooping up the injured and attending to wounded brethren. This resurrected battle carried out on home soil is peculiar for a place that was actually a haven from fighting during [the] Second World War, where neither bayonets nor grenades but microscopes and Geiger counters were daily wielded.[66]

Brittany: A Paucity of War Tourists

In contrast to the Normandy tourist battle sites, those in Brittany, equally a part of the German Atlantic Wall, languished as the curious gazes toward the Atlantic Wall dissipated quickly after the German withdrawal. Looking at the destruction at Saint-Malo in Brittany in 1946, L. R. Blanchard speculated that it might never be rebuilt. If it were indeed reconstructed, he expected it to lose much of the charm it had acquired over the centuries as the home of Sircouf the pirate, Chateaubriand the writer, and the explorer Jacques Cartier. In Nantes as elsewhere, he noted, German Occupation soldiers had generally behaved correctly toward the local French population, but this had not always been true of the American soldiers, whose behavior on occasion drew complaints from the local population. Recent historians have also cri-tiqued the behavior of the American soldiers.

Gérard Le Marec, the author of a guidebook to Resistance sites in Brit-tany in 1987, emphasized the importance of the region in the construction of the Atlantic Wall and the many casualties among those who resisted. He called for a more comprehensive construction of memory, and by extension tourism, to include workers who struck during the construction of the wall, various kinds of saboteurs, and those living in pockets of the region that the Germans continued to hold until the end of the war in May 1945, long after the liberation of the rest of France. All of this, he maintained, justified a more intense development of memory and, accordingly, a more developed tourism program.[67] Lacking the drama of the fighting in Normandy and sub-sequently Paris, Brittany, despite its many Resistance sites, did not emerge as a center for war memory tourism.

Liberated Paris and New Tourist Sites

In addition to the liberation of most of France, begun in Normandy, the year 1944 saw the expulsion of the German occupation forces from Paris, a series of events that also created additional tourism sites. Postwar tour-ist literature about Paris often evoked the August 1944 insurrection against the Germans that broke out shortly before the arrival of General Leclerc's liberation forces as the Germans were preparing to withdraw from the city. Paris, it will be recalled, had not been destroyed despite Hitler's order to the contrary during the German retreat. In 1945 the Committee for Paris Tour-ism (Comité de tourisme de Paris) published an illustrated English-language account of the liberation of the city, informed by the Gaullist Resistance narrative of the events and at the same time specifically addressing the role of tourism in the event. Alexandre Parodi, a key figure in the Parisian insur-rection, wrote the introduction.[68] On 26 August, Parodi joined General de Gaulle in the march down the Champs-Élysées that celebrated the liberation of Paris. Not long after the Germans fled eastward, Parodi wrote, emphasiz-ing the element of tourism spectacle:

> The lorries of the *Wehrmacht* reawakened the interest of the onlooker and made him forget his cares, made him an interested spectator, an adversary. The main thing was to be in the street, to enjoy the spectacle, to discuss it. . . . As the week advanced, Paris counted more passers-by; soon they did not pass but stayed, living in the streets, the women with folding stools and knitting. [Paris] liberated, welcomed the Allied

soldiers, old companions in arms, whose approach had made possible, *but not accomplished*, its liberation.[69]

Of twenty-nine identifiable sites photographed for the book, four showed the city hall; three each the Latin Quarter; the Police Prefecture headquarters, where the insurrection had begun; and the place de la Concorde. There were two photos each of the Notre-Dame cathedral, where General de Gaulle had attended a mass amid shots ringing out shortly after the liberation; the Opéra; and the Arc de Triomphe. Parodi's account of the liberation of Paris contrasted with the communists' version in the construction of Resistance tourist circuits. French communists paid special attention to other sites, such as the police headquarters from which the August 1944 Resistance insurrection that had accompanied the liberation of Paris had been launched. The Gaullists focused on symbolic national sites such as the Arc de Triomphe and events such as the renewal of the celebration of the 11 November World War I armistice in Compiègne in 1945.[70] Similarly evoking the liberation of Paris, an English-language guidebook, published in 1947 by the Franco-Allied Goodwill Committee, featured the Arc de Triomphe on its cover and assured its readers that "Paris, the most beautiful city in the world, [had] emerged from the battle intact."[71]

In contrast to the perspective published by the Goodwill Committee, Ossip Pernikoff, the author of *La France pays du tourisme* in 1938, found the city to have been "decapitated" by the loss of many of its bronze statues, routinely melted down by the Vichy government for German war needs during the Occupation.[72] With American support, Pernikoff assembled a group of volunteer supporters to restore the Paris statues, cautiously making certain, however, to use only materials that had no potential value to any future invader.[73] Requests for government funding to replace statues destroyed by the Germans continued in France as late as 1962.[74] Although most of these requests went unheeded, there were many memorials to greet the tourist throughout France. As Gérard Le Marec noted in his guidebook to Resistance sites in Brittany, the tourist could expect to find plaques, steles, and monuments in every village.[75] As is often the case with relationships between tourism and memorials, tensions between commemorative and tourist considerations arose in the fate of a statue of Léon Gambetta, one of the founders of the Third Republic in the 1870s. Prior to the war, the statue had stood in the Cour Napoléon, a courtyard at the Louvre in Paris. During the Occupation, however, the Germans had melted down its bronze decorations. A sound-and-light show was planned for the 1954 tourist season at the Cour Napoléon, but the Gambetta statue stood in the way. In the name of "urban planning," which meant, among other things, the development of tourism in Paris, French authorities removed the statue. A patriot of the 1870 Franco-Prussian war, Gambetta, who at least in statue form had survived the German occupation of 1940–1944, fell to the postwar tourist trade.[76]

Expressions from personalities in French political life as different as Pierre Taittinger of the Paris municipal council, the communist leader Rol Tanguy, Parodi, and Pernikoff all spoke to the continuing centrality of Paris in French life. French and foreign tourists alike were expected to feel the weight of "eternal France" in their visits to its capital. The liberation of Paris was one of many wartime events that gave rise to Resistance sites that would be integrated into postwar memory narratives. Sites related to General de Gaulle would come to mark the Resistance narrative, which sometimes existed in tension with locales associated more with communist imagery. Holocaust sites such as the Vélodrôme d'Hiver and the former staging area at Drancy, from which Jews and others were sent to the camps in eastern Europe, formed tourism itineraries. On the other side, those who sought to promote the story of Vichy and the collaborationists also created their sites and itineraries, and the city of Vichy wrestled with its image as the capital of the pro-Axis government of Marshal Pétain.

CHAPTER 6

Sites of Memory and the Tourist Imaginary

How cultural memory and tourist imaginaries were expressed differed in the construction of sites of memory and, consequently, tourism circuits by various groups emerging from the war, including the diverging Gaullist and communist narratives of the Resistance, which often focused on victims of German and Vichy rule. Other narratives emphasized sites specific to anti-Semitism and the Holocaust. Sites established in the immediate aftermath of the war honored General de Gaulle, the Resistance leader Jean Moulin, and the communists. Occurring prior to the reconciliation with the new Federal Republic of Germany, the establishment of these sites was often marked by admonitions against future German aggression. Their construction and related tourist itineraries after the Liberation reflected what Henry Rousso called the Gaullist effort to create a unified "resistancialist" (*résistancialiste*) memory of the war, according to which virtually all France had resisted the German invaders. As an example, he cites a monument, located near Fontainebleau, to Georges Mandel, the Third Republic minister assassinated by Vichy's militia (Milice) in July 1944. As Rousso notes, the inscription states that Mandel had been "murdered by the enemies of France." These enemies, Rousso continued, were unidentified: "They might have been not *miliciens* but Germans, and in the mind of today's casual tourist they probably are."[1] Efforts to perpetuate a unified Resistance image through the sanctification of places of memory as tourist sites began within months of the Liberation. Because governmental approval was needed to erect public monuments in France, all such proposals, even if supported by private funding, required state sanction. One proposal, in mid-1945, was to erect a monument at the place Saint-Michel in the heart of the city, recalling those who had died during the August 1944 fighting to liberate Paris.[2]

Sites of Trauma

Sites such as the Glières plateau in Savoie in southeastern France, where Vichy's Milice and German forces killed some 120 of 450 *maquisards* in March 1944, have become honored *lieux de mémoire*.[3] A visit to Glières became an annual ritual for Nicolas Sarkozy during his presidency. A 2011 photograph, for example, shows Sarkozy paying his respects, accompanied by Bernard Accoyer, president of the National Assembly.[4] In 2014 his successor, François Hollande, chose instead to honor Tulle, where he had been mayor, and where the SS Das Reich division had killed some hundred inhabitants following the D-Day landings in June 1944.[5] Hollande also visited Mont-Mouchet, the site of a museum that honored the Resistance fighters killed there by the Germans shortly after the Normandy landings in June 1944.[6] When he was elected in 2017, Emmanuel Macron visited the martyred village of Oradour-sur-Glane, which he wished to have added to Glières as a pilgrimage destination.[7]

A memorial dedicated to those who fought and died at Glières in 1944 was listed in 2011 on a tourism website as a stop during a tour of local built heritage there, but with only a one-line mention, and it was not highlighted in the manner of some of the Normandy sites.[8] Reflecting the evanescent nature of Internet websites, this web page had completely changed by early 2016. One local website in 2011 mentioned a hotel overlooking the plateau and the Resistance monument where "you can recollect the life of the *maquisards* thanks to historic pathways."[9]

Postwar tourism is, of course, more than battlefields. It involves burial sites and scenes of trauma and, in the case of the Second World War, often former concentration camps. Places associated with suffering, such as the contested site at Mont-Valérien and Oradour-sur-Glane, were transformed into monuments, and new locations, such as the Monument to the Martyrs of the Deportation on the eastern tip of the Île de la Cité in Paris, became tourist destinations as well as *lieux de mémoire*.[10] Not surprisingly, narratives of de Gaulle and the Resistance play major roles in the creation of tourism sites, with those related to Pétain and Vichy, as will be seen, often muted and contested. In *La mémoire désunie* (Divided Memory), Olivier Wieviorka traces

the history of ways in which war-related sites were given Resistance signification after 1944 as succeeding governments, following de Gaulle's lead,
portrayed a France united in resistance to the Nazis.[11]

The post-Liberation connection between the establishment of Second World War memorials and tourism in France was articulated as early
as June 1945 in an issue of *For You,* a locally published guidebook for
English-speaking soldiers. The article encouraged service personnel then
in France to join the French in visiting the ruined town of Oradour.[12] By
the mid-1950s, a restored European prosperity, the rise of a peaceful Federal
Republic of Germany, and the easing of immediate postwar passions began
to lend more historical distance to the sites connected with the war.[13] Tourist meaning, however, continued to be contested among the different French
political groups. The Resistance narrative of General de Gaulle was joined by
other versions of the wartime experience. Sites related to the Jewish Holocaust assumed increased visibility with the trials of Klaus Barbie, Paul Touvier, and Maurice Papon in the 1980s and 1990s.[14]

De Gaulle Tourism Itineraries

General Charles de Gaulle, as a larger-than-life figure, has been seen as the
voice of resistance in 1940, the liberator of France in 1944, and the shaper of
the Fifth Republic in 1958. From a tourism perspective, his greatest monument
is arguably the Charles de Gaulle Airport, opened and named for him in
1974, located in Roissy, near Paris.[15] According to one American observer in
1985, General de Gaulle "looms in the French memory somewhere between
a George Washington and a Thomas Jefferson."[16] Four days after de Gaulle's
death on 9 November 1970, the place de l'Étoile, the circle in which the
Arc de Triomphe is located in Paris, was renamed place Charles de Gaulle;
as one of France's primary tourist sites, it draws millions of visitors annually. As Pascal Ory noted, the practice of renaming streets and other public
roadways characterized all of France's revolutions and restorations since
1789.[17] The year after de Gaulle's death, his Paris headquarters were turned
into the Fondation Charles de Gaulle, a library and documentation center
for his career, similar to American presidential libraries but more unusual in
France. His home, La Boisserie in the village of Colombey-les-Deux-Églises
(Haute-Marne), became a national museum. A monumental Cross of Lorraine, the symbol of the Free French of 1940, was erected near the village.[18]
As time passed and the memory of the general faded, tourism to Colombey
declined. A museum devoted to his life was planned in 2001, expressly with
the hope of reinvigorating the *tourisme de mémoire* which had been on the

wane there in the late 1990s.[19] It was officially inaugurated 11 October 2008 in the presence of German chancellor Angela Merkel and President Sarkozy.[20]

Continuing interest in de Gaulle in the mid-1980s was exemplified in the publicity concerning the discovery of a 1942 film script, titled "The De Gaulle Story," written by William Faulkner at the request of President Roosevelt.[21] According to a French report at the time, the Fnac bookstore in Paris stocked nearly four hundred titles on de Gaulle, more than on anyone else except Napoleon.[22] The city of Paris sponsored the celebration of the centenary of de Gaulle's birth in 1990 with a sound-and-light show along the banks of the Seine. During events held throughout that year, many of his former political adversaries paid tribute to his enormous role in the history of the twentieth-century in France and throughout the world. The house in Lille in which de Gaulle was born was classified as a national monument in 1990 and came under the ownership of the Fondation Charles de Gaulle. On its website, the Fondation provides extensive information on visiting the house, officially under the jurisdiction of the Nord department since January 2014.[23] The birthplace comprises two sections, the house itself, transformed into a museum, and a portion of it, "La fabrique d'histoire" (The Making of History), a multimedia center dedicated to education about nineteenth- and twentieth-century history, oriented primarily toward children ages six through eleven. The house was fully restored in 2005.[24] A website link to "La fabrique d'histoire" proposed four ways to visit the home where the general was born: (1) an "emotional visit" focusing on all the rooms of the house, (2) a "playful" and "didactic" visit of discovery using the multimedia center to learn and to play games, (3) an audiovisual visit to view and discuss things in the projection room, and (4) an *évènementielle* (eventful) visit to the temporary exhibitions and thematic programs.[25] As with many other war-related museums, General de Gaulle's house has been arranged with the education of visiting schoolchildren in mind.

Additional official sites dedicated to General de Gaulle included the Historial Charles de Gaulle, inaugurated in 2008 at the Invalides.[26] Bayeux is especially important on the de Gaulle tourist circuit because it was the first major town liberated in the Normandy offensive, and it was there that de Gaulle made his first significant public speech on French soil following the Normandy landings. Bayeux is home to several monuments in addition to the Musée mémorial de la Bataille de Normandie (Memorial Museum of the Battle of Normandy), which developed among the plethora of Normandy landing museums mentioned earlier. It hosts the Musée Mémorial du Général de Gaulle (Memorial Museum of General de Gaulle), situated in a building dating from the fifteenth through seventeenth centuries, the former residence of the governors of the region. The building was used in June 1944 as the seat of the Liberation government as it began to extend, or reextend, the Republic over all of France.[27]

Although the French Resistance narrative focuses largely on General de Gaulle and, to a lesser extent, Jean Moulin, whose remains were removed to the Panthéon in 1964 and who figures as a personage of nearly universal veneration, there are other sites as well. A double museum established in 1994, the fiftieth anniversary of the Liberation, honors Moulin and General (later Marshal) Philippe Leclerc (Philippe Leclerc de Hauteclocque), near the Montparnasse railway station in Paris. As the Free French military commander of Equatorial Africa, Leclerc led the Free French forces into Paris in August 1944. He would also lead the French forces in the liberation of Strasbourg the following November. The transfer of Moulin's remains to the Panthéon in 1964 became one of the relatively few images that reflected a nearly unified memory of the war.[28] Both museums display artifacts from the war, with the two sections focusing on Moulin and Leclerc, respectively.

Strasbourg: From Site of Conflict to European Capital

The Leclerc Museum, not surprisingly, focuses on the liberation of Strasbourg in 1944, in which General Leclerc redeemed his earlier vow not to rest until the city had been retaken for France. Although the city has long been a tourist site, with its historic Cathédrale Notre-Dame-de-Strasbourg (Liebfrauenmünster zu Strassburg), dating back to the twelfth century, Strasbourg's meaning in another tourism paradigm shift transitioned with the changing military fortunes in 1940 and 1944. As a focal point of Franco-German enmity, Strasbourg switched back and forth between France and Germany. The capital of Alsace, acquired by Louis XIV in 1681, Strasbourg was lost to the Germans in 1871, regained in 1918, and lost again in 1940. Heinrich Hoffmann's *Mit Hitler im Westen* shows Hitler crossing the Rhine Bridge at Kehl to enter "German Straßburg" and then touring the cathedral there.[29] In 1941 General Leclerc vowed "to stop [fighting] only when the French flag again flies over Metz and Strasbourg," an oath he redeemed on 23 November 1944, when he led Free French forces into the city.[30] Having emerged as a sacred site for the Free French in 1944, postwar Strasbourg was reincarnated as a European capital of friendship and reconciliation. In this role postwar Strasbourg had a history very different from that of Compiègne, a site reflecting continuing Franco-German enmity.

A 1947 Michelin map titled "The Battle of Alsace," republished in French and English in 1992, included a history of the battle, together with a list of twenty-one historic sites. It described the liberation of Colmar as "an example of the splendid spirit of cooperation which existed between the French and American armies." In its section on the history of the battle, the text declared, "Over four years of occupation had not diminished the Alsatians' spirit of resistance and their faith in France."[31] Strasbourg's iconicity, however, changed dramatically with the establishment there of the Council of Europe in 1949 and the European Parliament later.[32] In 1949 it was chosen as the seat of the Council of Europe, a supranational organization to promote human rights and improve cultural and social life in Europe.[33] The city emerged in the late 1950s as one of Europe's "capitals," subsequently the home of the European Parliament (of the European Community, now the European Union). The Palais d'Europe, opened in 1977 in Strasbourg, became the seat of the regular plenary sessions of the European Parliament and with its surrounding buildings became the center of the city's "European quarter," buttressing Strasbourg's claim to be a "capital of Europe."[34] The central historic part of the city was declared a World Heritage Site by UNESCO in 1988, the first French city to be so designated.[35] By 1990, the European Parliament in Strasbourg welcomed 450,000 visitors annually, more than the city's famous cathedral.[36] At a meeting in Edinburgh in 1992, Strasbourg was confirmed as the seat of the European Parliament. Tourist literature in Strasbourg promoted the city as a European capital and, focusing on its dual French and German heritage, a site representing the overcoming of a long history of Franco-German hostility.[37] In 2010 the Strasbourg Tourism Office's website described the city as "Strasbourg: the European capital," and appealed to its modern architecture to generate tourism interest:

> New York, Geneva and Strasbourg are the only cities in the world which are home to international institutions without being national capitals. The choice of Strasbourg as the European capital following the Second World War is no accident. The city stands as a shining symbol of reconciliation between peoples and of the future of Europe. Discovering Europe's institutions is also a great opportunity to admire some marvellous examples of contemporary architecture.[38]

The European Parliament's monthly commute between Brussels and Strasbourg, however, produced an unintended impact on tourism in the Alsatian city. European officials, their staffs, and lobbyists so filled Strasbourg's hotels during their weeklong stays there that the prices increased. In 2010 the parliament had to hire a tourist boat to accommodate the additional staff.[39]

Mont-Valérien: A Conflicted Site

In contrast to the relative unanimity in France over the sites related to de Gaulle, Moulin, and Leclerc, debate over the commemoration of the war erupted in the deliberations as to the kind of memorial to erect at Mont-Valérien, in the western suburbs of Paris, where the Germans would lock up resisters and hostages in a chapel, then take them at daybreak to be executed in a nearby clearing. The bodies were then buried in nearby cemeteries. Many of the Mont-Valérien victims had been communists. The number of those shot remains in dispute, with estimates running as high as 4,500. Gaullists and communists, however, disputed the significance of the site, the former wishing to celebrate annually the anniversary of General de Gaulle's call to resistance of 18 June 1940, and the latter focusing on the clearing where the victims were shot.

In 1945 General de Gaulle signed a decree to establish a commemorative monument at Mont-Valérien. Writing about post-Liberation commemoration in France, Gérard Namer indicated that de Gaulle, out of office after January 1946, worked to organize war commemorations around his own role. At the inaugural ceremony, on 18 June 1946, the anniversary of his

FIGURE 16.   Tour bus at the memorial to Resistance fighters killed at Mont-Valérien, near Paris. Photo by author, June 2009.

first radio address from London to occupied France in 1940, he lit an eternal flame to honor the memories of the fifteen war victims who had been buried there the previous 15 November. Namer points out that two of the fifteen had been deportees, rather than Resistance fighters as such, but that at the ceremony the following June, there was no mention of them.[40]

A private initiative, in 1947, sought to construct a *via dolorosa* linking the Tomb of the Unknown Soldier under the Arc de Triomphe to Mont-Valérien, a stretch of more than four kilometers. Steles inscribed with the names of some ten thousand victims were proposed for the route. This proposal, as well as many others, was blocked by the government, which argued that a Mont-Valérien monument should be a public rather than a private venture.[41] Disagreements between Gaullist and communist Resistance veterans and their supporters stymied action on a Mont-Valérien memorial from the late 1940s into the late 1950s. With the return to power of General de Gaulle in 1958, a compromise was reached in the design of the memorial and the crypt, featuring both the Cross of Lorraine and the clearing in which the victims had been shot. De Gaulle inaugurated Mont-Valérien as a *lieu de mémoire* on 18 June 1960, the twentieth anniversary of his first radio address from London to occupied France, underscoring again the importance of anniversary commemorations in the construction of war-related tourism.[42] A large bronze bell was added in 2002 inside the chapel opposite the lists of names of those executed.[43] By 2010 the Mont-Valérien memorial had opened two interpretive pavilions together with a permanent exposition devoted to the Resistance prisoners who had been executed there. The execution sites were restored as well.[44] In early 2016 a virtual visit was made available online.[45]

Preserving a Site in Time: Oradour-sur-Glane

Focusing on the attempts to maintain the ruins of Oradour-sur-Glane, destroyed during the 10 June 1944 Nazi massacre of some 643 men, women, and children, Sarah Bennett Farmer evaluated the problems of trying to preserve the town exactly as it was when destroyed, in order to convey the horror of the atrocity, as opposed to accepting the inevitable deterioration of the ruins, caused by time and weather, necessitating intervention to create something other than the wreckage of the 1944 massacre. Analyzing the layout of the various sites—the ruined town, the cemetery still in use, and the new town—Farmer constructed a "topography" of memory.[46] She described plans to make the site available to "pilgrims," "visitors," and "tourists," situating the pilgrims in a tradition of Christian visitors to holy sites.[47]

In contrast to Compiègne, where the French government promoted dramatic change in the touristic symbolism after the war, it tried to preserve inviolate the ruins of Oradour as they had been following the 1944 massacre. Blanchard and the group of American journalists visiting France in the spring of 1946 stopped at Oradour. It had already been determined that the town would be preserved "in blackened nakedness, . . . a perpetual source of shame to those of Nazi connections."[48] In 1946 and 1947, the French government moved to protect the ruined town, along with the Struthof concentration camp in Natzweiler in Alsace and Omaha Beach in Normandy.[49] Oradour was to be preserved exactly as it was when the massacre ended. Despite the attention paid to maintaining Oradour as a site of memory, the martyred town was not entirely successful in fulfilling its role in the years after the war. Saving the ruins from the ravages of time and weather required intervention, which necessarily altered the wreckage. Such unavoidable change, a problem for all historic preservation, called into question what Dean MacCannell termed the touristic "authenticity" of such sites.[50] Trials of some of the Germans, as well as Alsatians conscripted into the Waffen-SS, kept passions high in the 1950s, but as time went on, Oradour's visibility diminished. A 1976 guidebook to French pilgrimage sites failed to mention it. The guidebook, more than two hundred pages in length, listed only one place related to the Second World War, Saint-Martin-de-Vercors, the site of a pilgrimage route created to honor the Resistance martyrs of that town in 1948.[51]

The increased publicity of the war years and the Holocaust brought about by the Barbie, Touvier, and Papon trials led to a renewal of interest in maintaining Oradour as a memorial. In 1989, Jean Claude Peyronnet, president of the Conseil général of Haute-Vienne, proposed the creation of a memorial center, the Centre de la mémoire–Oradour-sur-Glane, to President Mitterrand. The project was launched officially in 1992 with the support of the Ministry of Culture, the Ministry of War Veterans, and the European Community. Opened to the public in 1999 near the entrance to the *village martyr* (martyred village), by 2002 the center had received some 300,000 visitors, who were able to view the permanent exhibition as well as temporary exhibits.[52] The Observatoire régional du tourisme (ORT, Regional Tourism Office) for the Limousin region reported Oradour to be the most-visited paying site in the area, with nearly 100,000 admissions. Having analyzed articles from the French and international press for the years 2003 through 2008 concerning tourism destinations in Limousin, the ORT found Oradour to be in first place, with eleven references. When some two thousand people in France were asked to name tourist sites in Limousin, Oradour was the only one that received unprompted responses. When respondents were given a list of sites in the region, Oradour received the highest level of recognition among those queried.[53] Oradour maintained its position of primacy in attracting visitors in Limousin, being the only site to attract more than 100,000 visitors in 2014, and "more in particular [for] the Center of Memory," in the words of a Regional Tourism Committee report. The 2014 figure, according to the report, represented a 60 percent increase over that for 2011, attributed to a special exhibition in 2014 commemorating the seventieth anniversary of the massacre there.[54] Although the varying figures over the years may well reflect different methods of counting tourists, the Center of Memory remained consistently the number-one regional attraction.

Despite Franco-German reconciliation after the Second World War, however, German touristic images of wartime France engendered controversy in the 1990s. A DuMont tour guide to the Limousin region of France, published in Germany in 1992, created a stir in its account of the sites of two massacres of French civilians by the SS. On 9 July 1944, the Das Reich division, on its passage from southern France to fight in Normandy, also committed atrocities in the town of Tulle, where, after a Resistance attack, they hanged ninety-nine hostages and deported an additional 149, of whom 101 died in concentration camps. According to the DuMont guidebook, some seventy to eighty German soldiers had been taken prisoner previously, then "massacred" by guerrillas. In retaliation, the German forces, according to the account, sought out non-locals and other suspects, whom they then hanged as resisters.[55] In addition, the Oradour massacre was explained as a consequence of the German forces having found the corpses of wounded soldiers attacked the previous day by the Resistance. The German soldiers were also said to have discovered weapons hidden by the Resistance in houses in Oradour. Consequently, they shot most of the men, considered to be partisans, and burned the houses down. "Many of the women and children, locked in the church, died in the fire. The ruins and burned-out remnants of the walls are today an enclosed ghost city [Geisterstadt] and a well-organized, much-visited tourist site."[56]

The DuMont versions of both the Tulle and Oradour incidents were at odds with virtually all other historical accounts of the massacres in the two towns, and its translation into French caused a sensation in Limousin, whose regional council president protested to the publishers of the guidebook. In 1996 Maria-Anna Hälker, speaking for DuMont, apologized and promised "appropriate corrections" in subsequent editions.[57] The Limousin incident was not the only example at that time of German tourist guidebooks rewriting the history of the Second World War in France. A tour guide being prepared for publication in Germany, covering the northern portion of Alsace, said nothing about the war years, never even mentioning Hitler. The president of the general council of the Bas-Rhin department (Alsace) moved to block its publication and distribution on the grounds that it was transmitting to the public an "unconscious revisionism."[58] As of 2016 Oradour had become a tourist site, with some 741 reviews listed for it on TripAdvisor in January 2016. In the words of one reviewer: "This World War II memorial will repay a visit, but you will gain more if you read up on the history before you go. The reason the school children and most adult[s] are quiet is then clear. There is adequate car parking, and an information area with toilet, shops and the counter to buy tickets."[59]

Deportation and the Holocaust: Memorials and Tourism

Unlike Mont-Valérien and Oradour, the Mémorial des martyrs de la déportation (Memorial to the Martyrs of the Deportation) in Paris was a site newly created as a place of contemplation to honor those who had been deported to Nazi concentration camps, especially the estimated 200,000 who never returned. The Mémorial stands on the Île de la Cité, just behind

FIGURE 17. Memorial to the Martyrs of the Deportation on the Île de la Cité across from Notre-Dame cathedral. Photo by author, 2009.

the Notre-Dame cathedral, one of the most visited tourist sites in France. Its architect was Georges Henri Pingusson, and it was built by the Réseau du souvenir (Network of Memory), which donated it to the French government in 1964. General de Gaulle inaugurated the memorial on 12 April 1962. Carved deep into the ground, with only a small opening allowing one to view the Seine through a narrow slit in which is placed sharp metal bars evoking a concentration camp, the underground monument contains the remains of an unknown person who died in the deportation. On the walls are engraved verses from poems by Robert Desnos, who died as a deportee, Paul Éluard, and Louis Aragon. An atmosphere of silence is designed to evoke a sense of those who disappeared in the network of the concentration camps.[60] The contrast between the silence of the memorial, carved into the island, and the lively comings and goings of the thousands of visitors to the nearby Notre-Dame cathedral could hardly be more striking. Admission to the memorial is free, so there are no counts of visitors, but to all appearances it draws very few in contrast to the cathedral. A French Senate report in 1997 noted the "weak promotion" of the site and the fact that, unlike many other sites of memory, it lacked a facility there to accommodate groups of schoolchildren.[61]

Other sites related to Jewish memory were constructed almost immediately after the war, such as one in Paris, where, in 1948, the Union of Jewish 1939–45 Veterans dedicated a monument to Jews who had died in the war and in the Resistance.[62] The Mémorial de la Shoah was begun in 1953, when the first stone was laid for what was then called the Tomb of the Unknown Martyred Jew at 17 rue Geoffroy l'Asnier in Paris.[63] It was inaugurated in October 1956.[64] In 1974, the tomb was reconsecrated as the Memorial of the Unknown Martyred Jew. Public commemorations are held there annually on the anniversaries of the Warsaw Ghetto uprising and the 16–17 July 1942 Vélodrôme d'Hiver roundup of Jews for ultimate deportation to the extermination camps.[65] Commemorating the seventieth anniversary of the Vélodrôme d'Hiver roundup in 2012, François Hollande, the first president to visit the site since Jacques Chirac, who had visited and formally acknowledged French complicity in the Holocaust in 1995, stated, "The truth is that the crime was committed in France by France." As Le Monde reported, he blamed France itself and not the Vichy government, as had been the practice prior to Chirac's acknowledgment.[66]

The Drancy apartment buildings, used as a staging point for the deportation of Jews to the east, were completed after the war and are still intact and inhabited. Although Drancy was also used to hold homosexuals, Roma, and others determined to be "undesirables" by the Vichy government, the majority of its inmates were Jews. From Drancy, trains left for Auschwitz beginning in March 1942. Some 77,000 French Jews were deported, including 11,204 children.[67] In 1976, a Memorial to the Deportation was created there by the sculptor Shlomo Selinger to commemorate the French Jews imprisoned in the camp. In 2001 Drancy was declared a historic monument and placed on a tourism circuit of "heritage days" (*journées du patrimoine*) the following September.[68] A small museum and the memorial may be visited. During Passover, on 11 April 2009, swastikas were painted on a railway car used to deport Jews and the commemorative stele that formed part of the memorial.[69] In 2012, once again on the seventieth anniversary of the beginning of the deportations to the concentration camps, François Hollande inaugurated a building at the Drancy site, created as a monument by the Fondation pour la mémoire de la Shoah.[70]

Many of the camps involved in the incarceration and deportation of Jews and other enemies of the Nazis and Vichy have become tourist sites, especially for the young. In April 2010, the organization Cercil (Centre d'étude et du recherche sur les camps d'internement dans le Loiret at la déportation juive, or Circle for the Study and Research of the Internment Camps in the Loiret and the Jewish Deportation), together with the Fédération française de cyclotourisme (FFCT, the French Federation for Biking), organized the "first trek through the sites of memory [*lieux de mémoire*]" in the Loiret. Thirty young people, divided equally among French, Germans, and Poles, hiked to the Jargeau, Beaune-la-Rolande, and Pithiviers concentration camps as well as other *lieux de mémoire* in the Loiret department. Guided by members of the Cercil and FFCT, the young people heard lectures at the various stops along the route.[71]

In 1997, the discovery in a public trash container of archival documents pertaining to the Rivesaltes concentration camp highlighted that site, near Perpignan, capital of the Pyrénées-Orientales department in southern France adjacent to Spain and the Mediterranean. Among the departments of France, Pyrénées-Orientales ranks third in tourism. The discovery of the documents intensified efforts by the Association des fils et filles des déportés juifs de France (Association of the Sons and Daughters of Jewish Deportees of France) to have the camp declared a site of memory. The camp had been used in 1939 for Republican Spanish refugees; in May 1940 to incarcerate German and Austrian citizens, of whom half were Jewish refugees; and then during the Occupation as a staging area for rounded-up Jews, many of whom were eventually deported to the extermination centers in the east. After the war, it housed "displaced persons" and in 1963 held more than 1,300 *harkis,* pro-French Algerian Muslims who had fled in fear of their lives after Algerian independence. In 1997 the camp housed illegal immigrants on their way to forced repatriation.[72] Under Christian Bourquin, president of the Conseil général of the Pyrénées-Orientales region, the regional and departmental administrations agreed to pay for 80 percent of the costs of reopening the camp, with the remainder to come from the national government. By the early twenty-first century, the camp had become a Holocaust memorial, the first in southern France. From the opening of a portion of the Rivesaltes camp during the *journées du patrimoine* in 2005, the site attracted 4,500 visitors annually and, with the planned museum, hoped to draw 100,000 each year, many of whom were expected to be schoolchildren. In 2006 Bourquin stated: "The camp is in very good condition, exactly like it was in the 1940s. Everything is still there. You can see the barracks."[73]

The civic aspects of memory preservation were highlighted in the planning of Rivesaltes, Gastineau and Rosso later wrote, but the economic advantages of enhanced tourism played a significant role for the departmental governments.[74] Sarah Wildman, writing for the travel section of the *New York Times* in 2007, described the planned memorial and educational center at the camp as

a place that already draws visitors who come to pay homage to the persecution faced by those who were considered undesirable: Spanish Republican families and International Brigades fleeing Franco at the end of the Spanish Civil War; foreign Jews rounded up by the Vichy French government; Roma, or Gypsy, families; Algerians who fought alongside the French during the French-Algerian war; and others.

Funded by the Fondation pour la mémoire de la Shoah, the International Red Cross and Red Crescent Museum in Geneva, and the United States Holocaust Memorial Museum in Washington, DC, the project was estimated to cost 18 million euros and was the subject of considerable controversy in the local press. "Meanwhile," wrote Wildman, "visitors continue to drift to the site, pulling off the A9 auto route between Perpignan and Rivesaltes, following the signs to the camp and turning on to the tiny Route d'Opoul, where modern windmills barely turn in still, hot air."[75]

By 2010, the Musée mémorial du camp de Rivesaltes (Rivesaltes Internment Camp Memorial) was still working on putting together the memorial. In the meantime it organized traveling exhibitions, including one at a Saint Louis synagogue in the United States, in which Denis Peschanski, a French historian and specialist on the Second World War and the Holocaust and a member of the committee organizing the layout of the site, presented a lecture.[76] To avoid polemics over the reconstitution of camps such as Rivesaltes, the

French government appointed well-known and highly respected people to the various organizing committees. Peschanski was one example in the case of Rivesaltes, along with Robert Badinter, a former justice minister. Construction of the museum was begun in 2012, and an endowment fund started the following year, based on private donations. After Bourquin's death in August 2014, Prime Minister Manuel Valls announced that the government would support the project in collaboration with the regional authorities. In October 2015 the Mémorial du camp de Rivesaltes opened to the public in a three-day series of ceremonies beginning with a speech by Valls and several other cabinet members.[77]

A process similar to the turning of the Rivesaltes camp into a site of memory was under way at the concentration camp at Les Milles, near Aix-en-Provence, with a museum opened there in September 2012. Serge Klarsfeld, an internationally known documentalist of Nazi depredations in France, was selected vice president of the committee organizing the restoration of the camp.[78] In October 2015, UNESCO created a chair of education for citizenship, human sciences, and shared memories there in the presence of President Hollande, who gave a speech on the occasion.[79]

Touring the Other Side: Vichy

Tourism also extends to the "other side," Vichy and the collaboration, although often, not surprisingly, in a more muted tone, representing the perspectives of political minorities. Examples of such tourist locations include the city of Vichy itself, the provisional capital and scene of so much of the drama during the Occupation, and the sites related to the life of Marshal Pétain, still visited and honored by a small number of supporters. The shifting tourist iconicity regarding wartime France is best illustrated by Vichy's attempts to reinvent itself as a tourist destination with the decline in its spa trade after the war. Local leaders at the time struggled with the stigma of the association of their city with pro-Nazi collaboration, even as visitors came to tour the sites associated with the Pétain government. The notoriety of Vichy is such that Alain Carteret, a local historian of the town, recorded in 2006 that its name drew more than 2.87 million hits on Google, far fewer than "sex," with 7 million, but more than most if not all other small cities in France.[80]

Clearly, the name Vichy has lived on in a kind of infamy, to paraphrase Franklin Roosevelt's reference to another theater of the Second World War.[81] As an object of tourist curiosity, Vichy must have first aroused interest when, shortly after the inception of the government there, people both in and outside France began collecting postage stamps with the motto "État français" and other related memorabilia by the second half of 1940.[82] Negative connotations of the name appeared not long after the transfer of the government to Vichy in July 1940. Vichy was criticized by General de Gaulle as the center of everything treacherous. By the fall of 1940, the collaborationist Marcel Déat was also denouncing Vichy, in his case as clerical and reactionary, unwilling to make a "real" revolution to align France more closely with the Axis powers.[83]

Only with the awareness that the Vichy government would be defeated and itself become history, or *passé,* a symbol of "what went wrong" in Second World War France, did the city become a historical curiosity for tourists, a process that undoubtedly began when, in recognition of the Allied victory, the inquisitive started to visit sites associated with the collaboration. Mila Parély, a film actress who appeared in *La règle du jeu (The Rules of the Game,* directed by Jean Renoir), recalled how officials descended on Vichy in 1940, expelling all those taking the waters, then fled again in 1944, leaving the city in a "lamentable state." They left a terribly negative memory conflating the "Vichyssois," the innocent residents of the city, as much victimized as anyone else in France by the war, with the "Vichystes," who either served in Pétain's government or had ideological affinities with it.[84] As a term, "Vichy" came into disrepute early in both French and English. An Escoffier cookbook published in English in 1941 changed the name of vichyssoise to "Crème Gauloise," and in 1943 a New York restaurant listed it as "de Gaullesoise."[85]

At the time of the Liberation, the vice president of the Lorraine-Vosges-Alsace Chamber of Commerce noted that the Vichy-Cusset-Bellerive metropolitan area had increased in population from 30,000 to 130,000 as state functionaries streamed in after the 1940 armistice. The requisition of large hotels for state use had, he argued, hurt Vichy tourism, although he did not comment on the additional income brought into the area by the newly arrived state officials.[86] In September 1944 the municipal council of Vichy requested that any allusion to the Vichy regime be stricken from the French language.[87] To place the Pétainist pilgrimages within the larger context of tourism to Second World War–related sites in France, and contrast the references to Pétain after both world wars, it is instructive to note that the first issue of the Michelin guide that appeared after the Liberation, compiled in October 1944 and published in the spring of 1945, made no mention of the Occupation in its section on Vichy. This was in stark contrast to Michelin's post–World War I guidebooks to the battlefields of France. The sole reference to Pétain in the 1945 Michelin guide was an indication of a "rue Maréchal Pétain" on a map of Vichy.[88] Even local Resistance leaders had difficulties in restoring the good name of the town. In November 1944 the municipal council protested again, this time against what it called the undeserved opprobrium associated with the term "Vichy government."[89]

During the 1950s, the Association pour défendre la mémoire du maréchal Pétain (ADMP, Association for the Defense of the Memory of Marshal Pétain), based in Paris and seeking to restore the favorable memory of Marshal Pétain, sought to convert locales associated with his life into tourist sites of pilgrimage. It worked to turn his wartime apartment in Vichy's Hôtel du Parc, which had since been converted to private residences, into a small museum. Supporters erected a plaque to the effect that "here the marshal worked for France." Local Resistance veterans' organization protested and removed the plaque, hindering all attempts to set up the museum. They also confronted those who visited ritually each 11 November to lay wreaths there to honor Pétain.[90]

In April 1959, General de Gaulle, newly installed as president of the Fifth Republic, visited Vichy, which he called the "queen of spas." He acknowledged the unusual nature of his visit in view of recent history, thereby mixing together the two associations of Vichy with its spa and its wartime role. De Gaulle emphasized, however, that the French were "one people" and that the divisions of the past should be laid to rest. Discussing what he called the "astonishing" speech of General de Gaulle, which included the cry "Vive Vichy!," Henry Rousso noted that in view of the negative connotations still associated with the name Vichy in 1959, one of de Gaulle's ministers had spoken of an "exorcism."[91] The ADMP's organ, Le Maréchal, took de Gaulle's message as a justification for the reburial of Pétain at Douaumont, where in his will in 1938 he had asked to be buried. The reburial would be the corrective for a victim who had "improperly suffered" from the divisions to which de Gaulle had alluded.[92]

During the 1970s the Pétainists moved their commemorative activities from the Hôtel du Parc to the celebration of a mass at the Vichy Saint-Louis church on each succeeding anniversary of Pétain's death. Again, confrontations resulted and, although the Church pleaded for the Pétainists to be allowed at least to have their mass, enough commotion was raised in 1978 to require intervention by the CRS (Compagnie Républicaine de Sécurité), tasked with crowd control. The bishop stopped the celebrations.[93] To add to the difficulties in restoring the name of Vichy, the term "Vichyite" in America had come to be used in 1979 to refer to any collaborator generically, in the negative sense of the term, as in the New York Review of Books' reference to "a collabo, someone who picked the wrong side, a 'Theban Vichyite' in Antiquity."[94]

Tensions around the use of the name Vichy continued, with fluidity in the use of the name and related terms long after the war, as shown in a 1984 reference to Parisian and "Vichyssois" collaborators.[95] The conflict around the name, however, may have worked as advertising to increase rather than decrease tourism to the town. In addition to problematic symbolic associations faced by Vichy, the four-year interlude during which it served as the capital of France came at a time when the town's spa trade was in decline from a record number of 129,600 cure seekers in 1931 to 19,009 in 1983.[96] Many among the spa clientele were military and colonial officials, the latter having the right to a six-month vacation every ten years, which they often spent at Vichy's spas. The decline of the French colonial system beginning in the 1930s and marked definitively by Algerian independence in 1962 was a severe blow to the spa trade in Vichy. By 1977, only 26,822 visitors came for the waters. In a study of Vichy's tourism in 2001, Christian Jamot pointed out that in addition to the decline in spa tourism by colonial officials after 1962, French insurance no longer considered spa cures medically justifiable, putting an additional crimp in the trade. By the early 1990s, spa tourists were down to about 12,000 per year, a figure that held steady with only a slight increase at the beginning of the twenty-first century.[97] From 11,685 spa tourists in 2000, the figure rose to 22,768 in 2012, according to figures supplied by the Auvergne Rhône-Alpes Regional Chamber of Accounts (Chambre régionales des comptes), the result at least in part of increased diversification of the tourist industry there, with a new emphasis on sports and business tourism.[98] As a commentator put it in 1985, however, Vichy suffered from a past that was neither pardoned nor forgotten. A bookseller there noted that the suggestion of creating postcards picturing the Hôtel du Parc had brought threatening phone calls. Recalling the slow dissipation of the bad reputation of the Second Empire, he observed, "It takes the French a century to recognize their past."[99]

Visiting Wartime Sites in Vichy: The Pétain Tour

Influenced possibly by the decline in spa tourism and an increasing tourist interest in wartime sites, in 1987 the Vichy Tourism Office created a "Sites vichyssois du Régime de Pétain" (Vichy Sites of the Pétain Regime) circuit, where twenty-five francs bought a two-hour tour guided by a history student. Tourist curiosity about the wartime sites came, according to Eric Conan, largely from Germans and Americans. Before opening this circuit to tourists, however, the government tested it on the *renseignements généraux* (police intelligence services) as well as local Resistance veterans, winning the support of both. The tour was approved despite objections from the management of the Hôtel du Portugal, former seat of the Gestapo in Vichy. It continues to be offered during the summer months.[100]

In 1988 Marc Ferro, a historian with no partiality toward the Pétain government, invited to lecture in Vichy about a new biography of the marshal he had written, was not allowed to speak in the town because of allegations that even to speak of Pétain in Vichy was a step toward rehabilitating him. The next year, Vichy's socialist mayor, Claude Malhuret, fatalistically complained that even trying to restore the good name of the town could be interpreted as revisionist history seeking to justify the collaborators.[101] During the same year, 1989, the Michelin Company published its first *Green Guide* for all of France. Its sole reference to Vichy's role during the Second World War in its entry for the city came in a sentence noting that Vichy was marked by having been "the seat of government of the French State (12 July 1940–20 August 1944), having withdrawn there with a liberty very much watched over when the suddenness of defeat had plunged France into a stupor."[102]

At the least, the town of Vichy attracted crews making films about the war and the Occupation. Pierre Beuchot's *Hôtel du Parc* was released in 1992, and the following year Jean Marbœuf's *Pétain* premiered. Much of Marbœuf's film was shot inside the Aletti Palace Hôtel, known as the Hôtel Thermal during the war and used for a variety of purposes, beginning with its service as a hospital in 1939 and 1940 prior to the defeat of France. During the Occupation, it housed several government offices, including those of the commander in chief of the military forces, the Finance Ministry, and the War Secretariat.[103] Currently owned by the American Westin chain, the Aletti is now the only hotel used by the government during the war that has not since been converted into private residences. Addressing the making of Marbœuf's film, Eric Conan focused on the irritation of Vichy city officials who believed their city had been singled out for a historical opprobrium that it did not deserve. Visitors who came to Vichy for its spas, including Germans and Americans, were also curious about its wartime sites, notably those of the various ministries in 1940–1944, the Commissariat for Jewish Questions, and the headquarters of the paramilitary Milice. City officials came to view wartime tourism as a potentially profitable market.[104]

As of June 1992, the only memorial that could be found in Vichy commemorating the history of 1940–1944 was a plaque on the opera house alluding to the eighty parliamentarians who had voted on 10 July 1940 against the granting of constituent powers to Marshal Pétain. The plaque reads: "In this room, 10 July 1940, 80 parliamentarians by their votes affirmed their attachment to the Republic, their love of liberty, and their faith in victory. Thus ended the Third Republic."[105] The plaque is on a wall inside the main lobby of the building, making it visible but not accessible from outside. John Campbell argued in 2006 that by evoking the minority of deputies who voted against handing full powers to Pétain rather than mentioning the overwhelming majority who voted to liquidate the Third Republic, this plaque "can only be explained in terms of extreme denial."[106] In August 1992, another plaque was unveiled at the entrance to the Hôtel du Parc to commemorate the Jews deported from unoccupied France to concentration camps in central and eastern Europe.[107] This plaque, erected by Serge Klarsfeld, was occasionally vandalized by "Negationists and Revisionists," those denying the reality of the Holocaust. It was moved from the entrance to the Hôtel du Parc to a spot along the park on the esplanade across the street and, as of 2010, had remained undisturbed since 2002.[108]

During the mid-1990s and continuing into the present, Vichy town leaders and spokespersons have been trying to escape the opprobrium associated with their town's Second World War history. A *New York Times* article by Jessica Burstein at the end of 2015 quoted the city's longtime mayor, Claude Malhuret, as "perplexed and slightly defensive over how to respond to the enduring stigma." Despite the development of the Omnisports Parc, a large sports center, and the transformation of the casino into a convention center, "ghosts of the war years linger." In a veiled reference to the ADMP, Burstein mentioned a triathlon in August 2015 "that took the runners past the Hôtel du Parc, where Pétain's office has been carefully preserved by an organization dedicated to enshrining his memory."[109] Long after the city had been rebuilt materially, its citizens had to endure opprobrium for something that, according to a local historian, had not been their fault.[110] Under "Vichy," the English-language 1994 Michelin *Green Guide* for France was barely more expansive than its predecessor of 1989. After discussing the town's early history, the guidebook states that "more recently, Vichy gave its name to the government of the French State, the regime led by Marshal Pétain which ruled the country under close German supervision from 12 July 1940 until 20 August 1944."[111] In 1997, critics of the right-wing National Front, which had gained control of the city government in Toulon, referred to the "Vichy-ization of spirits" (*vichysation des esprits*) of daily life in their city.[112]

The town of Vichy continued to face a battery of problems in reconstructing its tourist trade in the early twenty-first century, including defining whether it should try to attract elderly tourists for its spas, business tourists for conventions, or younger visitors with families for its sports facilities. Jamot pointed to a lack of nightlife and fine restaurants as inhibiting tourism to Vichy but said not a word about the Second World War.[113] Alain Carteret alluded to the memory of its role in the Second World War as a "continual theme that, as much as it interests journalists, does little for the readers," by which he meant the vast majority of newspaper readers in Vichy and, presumably, France as a whole.[114] INSEE (Institut national de la statistique et des études économiques) figures for the Pays de Vichy-Auvergne, an area that includes Vichy plus ten neighboring communes, registered 188,468 tourist arrivals in 2007 and 85,515 for the first half of 2008, lower probably because of an economic downturn at the time.[115] These figures are not specific to the town of Vichy, let alone its war-related sites, but they offer a perspective that supports Carteret's view that, despite the continued arguments about "Vichyssois" and "Vichystes," the town suffers little from its association with the Pétain government.

By the early twenty-first century, life and tourism continue in what might be called a relatively "normal" sense in Vichy. In its section on Vichy, the 2011 Michelin *Guide vert* makes no mention of the war years. A small number of people, such as those in the ADMP, which acquired Pétain's former offices in the Hôtel du Parc, continue to call for the marshal's rehabilitation in France and maintain the struggles of the 1940s, but a general reconciliation, high-lighted by de Gaulle's visit and the effects of time, have transmuted Vichy and the arguments around it into items of curiosity.[116] The process of "nor-malization" or "historicization" for the wartime Vichy period is likely to take some time, however, and may need to await the passing of most of those who experienced the war and the finding and publication of their memoirs. In 2001 Alain Carteret called for the creation of a museum in Vichy devoted to its history, including the wartime period, "the object of a strong demand for information on the part of tourists." The failure to create such a museum, he maintained, stemmed from confusion between a museum dedicated to the 1940–1945 period, which risked opening old wounds or being perceived as pro-Pétain, and a museum that exhibited the entirety of Vichy's "glorious past."[117] In a tone favoring tourism to Vichy, Carteret wrote:

> In no case should a museum of Vichy be limited to the dark episode of the last world war. First, the "Vichy capitale" period left nothing worth noting. It left only damaged hotels and facilities. Following and above all because the beautiful history of Vichy is situated earlier (Napoleon III and the Belle Époque) and afterward (since Pierre Coulon's [rede-signed] baths at the Lardy University Center). To interest the largest number of people, without restarting the past ("which isn't past," according to the title of a book by Henry Rousso in 1994), the museum should be general. It should address, as in this book, all the periods in all their aspects, political, cultural, sport, and economic, without ignoring furthermore the sad period that seems to pose problems for the planners: one can speak of it objectively, as in this book, by a simple recall of the plain facts. When, despite the maximum of precautions taken, the manner in which this period is treated is contested by a few obstinate [people] too oriented toward the past, or political exploiters, there would result free publicity that could only favor visits![118]

In a second book, published two years later, he added:

> Many Vichy residents think today that the best way to avoid confusion between the city and the regime of Marshal Pétain is to open a museum of the period 1940–1944. This would be the occasion to show the historical reality and thus the distinction between the regime that was implanted in Vichy and its inhabitants who submitted to it. In addition, this idea responds to a strong tourism demand, as passions have attenuated sixty years after the facts.[119]

Carteret noted on his website that "this suggestion has not yet met with the slightest echo."[120] John Campbell suggested that the denial of history becomes part of that history and that the town of Vichy might do better to actively cultivate rather than attempt to hide the memory of its function during the war. This, he thought, might enable the people of Vichy to distance themselves from identification with the war, but he, no more than Carteret, saw any move in this direction on the horizon.[121] *L'année dernière à Vichy,* a film produced by Bertrand de Solliers and Paule Muxel in 2008, focused on memories of the war years, continuing to address the conflicted memory of the city.[122]

That curiosity about the 1940–1944 years enhances Vichy's role as a tourist attraction—or, in other words, that even bad publicity is good publicity—is difficult to establish. A lack of reliable statistics and related uncertainties in assessing interest in the war-related sites, the problem with this kind of tourism, sometimes categorized under the relatively new term "thanatourism," is of interest as part of the developing genre of regional French history but is very difficult to quantify. The "Vichy Sites of the Pétain Regime" tour, begun in 1987, continued thirty years later. As of 2017, the same tour with a slightly different name, "Vichy, capitale de l'État français 40–44," was offered twice weekly in July and August and once a week in June and September. A walking tour, it lasted an hour and a half, with a tour guide employed by the tourist office.[123] The itinerary includes the major hotels and related buildings used by the government during its residence there, although they must be viewed from the outside, as almost all have since been taken over for private use. Visitors are shown the Hôtel du Parc, which had central heating, a rarity in 1940, and where Pétain had his offices, now the property of the ADMP. The rest of the Hôtel du Parc has been converted into apartments. A passageway connects the Hôtel du Parc to the Hôtel Majestic, which was not appropriated for state use during the war and was used privately by Pétain.[124] The walking tour passes the Grand Casino, where Pétain was voted plenary powers by the French parliament in July 1940; the Petit Casino, which housed

Joseph Darnand's paramilitary Milice, which in 1944 fought a virtual civil war against the Resistance; the Hôtel Carlton, which housed several ministries between 1940 and 1944; the Sévigné pavilion, where Madame de Sévigné took her spa cures during the seventeenth century and which later served as Pétain's private residence; and nearby sites including the house used as the American embassy from 1940 through 1942, all of "which invite us to rediscover this troubled period in the history of France."[125] One of the tour guides in June 2010 indicated that they average some thirty visitors for each tour, which would yield an estimated 780 tourists per year.[126]

Marshal Pétain in Memory and Tourism

Connected to Vichy tourism are the sites other than the Hôtel du Parc related to Marshal Pétain, which form a real, if limited, tourist circuit for those faithful to his memory. The tensions in Pétain's imagery that stem from perceptions of his role as a hero in the First World War and a collaborator in the second result in conflicted memory and, accordingly, conflicted tourism symbolism. Pétain is mentioned several times in the 1921 Michelin guidebook to the Verdun battlefield, which includes a picture of him together with his letter congratulating the French troops for holding off the Germans on 9 April 1916. The letter encouraged them in the fighting still to come and concluded with a phrase that became famous: "Courage . . . on les aura!" (Courage, we'll get them!).[127] To some extent, he has been excused for his Second World War role. A 1993 poll found 38 percent of the people surveyed in France thought he had betrayed the country during the Second World War, while 28 percent believed he had been misled but had acted in good faith, with an additional 30 percent of the opinion that he had "sought to protect the interests of France." This means that 58 percent of those queried believed his role in the war to have been mitigated by "attenuating circumstances."[128] French book publication listings show the first reference to Pétain in 1919, when he was seen as the hero of Verdun, with the highest percentage of mentions among the books published during the Second World War—hardly surprising, as he was then head of state. There were secondary rises in the 1960s and 1990s, followed by a decline up to the present.[129] Articles published on Pétain in France and tracked from 1953 in the *Bibliothèque annuelle de l'histoire de France* also show relative increases in the 1960s and 1990s.[130] The Google website for books digitized by the company shows a similar rise for Pétain references in French and English in the mid-1990s with gradual declines into the first decade of the twenty-first century.[131]

Taken together, these series indicate a peak of interest in Pétain during his years in power and just after, when he was on trial for his wartime activities. There was a renewal of interest in him with the Algerian crisis and the return of General de Gaulle to power in the early 1960s. A second increase, though less pronounced, followed the election of François Mitterrand, a socialist with his own ties to the Vichy government, to the French presidency and the end of the Cold War, evidenced also by the making of the film *Pétain* by Jean Marbœuf in 1993.[132] Meanwhile, streets named for Pétain have been progressively renamed in France. The final such street de-baptizing, as it were, occurred in December 2010, when the Tremblois-lès-Carignan commune in the Ardennes renamed a street that had borne the marshal's name, the last one remaining.[133]

Since the war, however, a certain memory of Vichy, and especially of the marshal, has been kept alive and burnished by a small group of supporters through a variety of activities including the creation of a quasi-religious pilgrimage tourist circuit to sites associated with his life. Convicted of treason in his postwar trial at age eighty-eight, he died at age ninety-five on 23 July 1951, a prisoner on the Île d'Yeu, described in a 1954 guidebook, *Les îsles d'ouest,* as an isolated island "lost off the Vendée coast," with "wild rocks," well suited for a prison. In a move designed to thwart tourism to the gravesite, the marshal was buried at Port-Joinville on the relatively inaccessible island. Nonetheless, the interment proceedings brought out General Maxime Weygand and several other prominent personalities, themselves the objects of considerable curiosity among the small number of tourists spending their summer holidays on the tiny island.[134]

It had, indeed, briefly housed the imprisoned Comte d'Artois after the counterrevolutionary Quiberon affair of 2 October 1795. The prison had remained idle until the arrival on 16 November 1945, in the words of the guidebook, of "an old man of 90 years, supported by a cane."[135] Marshal Pétain had arrived to spend his last years on the island. When he died, according to *Les îsles d'ouest,* several veterans of Verdun attended a simple funeral ceremony. Nothing was said of the visit of Weygand and the other Pétainist luminaries who had attended the ceremony.[136] The creation of tourist sites related to the life of Marshal Pétain is discussed at length in the ADMP's organ *Le Maréchal*. Initially the ADMP included mainly Pétain's former colleagues from the Occupation years, namely, ex–cabinet ministers, prefects, army officers, and academics. From 1951 through his death in 1965, its honorary president was General Weygand. In a first step toward consecration of a pilgrimage site, in 1954 the ADMP created an organization to preserve the house where Pétain was born, in Cauchy-à-la-Tour in the Pas de Calais.[137]

One of the early and continuing goals of the association has been the reburial of Pétain's remains at Douaumont, discussed in the first issue of *Le Maréchal*, dated 23 July 1957, the sixth anniversary of Pétain's death.[138] In its second issue, published on Armistice Day, 11 November 1957, continuing its campaign to have Pétain's remains transferred to Douaumont, *Le Maréchal* included photographs of his tomb on the Île d'Yeu and the ossuary at Verdun.[139] By 1959, *Le Maréchal* had added Pétain's birthplace to the list of photographs of tourist sites it associated with his career.[140]

In its issue taking up General de Gaulle's 1959 message of reconciliation to call for a reburial of Pétain's remains at Douaumont, *Le Maréchal* included another touristic reference, this time under the title "Une visite à faire" (A Visit to Make). The recommended site was the Musée de la guerre Berrichon, established by Comte de Gontaut-Biron at the Château de Diors, ten kilometers from Châteauroux in the Indre. This museum, which contained artifacts from the wars of 1870, 1914, and 1939, devoted an entire room to Pétain, according to *Le Maréchal*, which noted that this was "how it should be in any museum devoted to the military deeds of our fatherland."[141]

In a 1959 issue of *Le Maréchal*, Pierre Henry described a cluster of buildings that could be visited on the Île d'Yeu, including the Port-Joinville house in which Pétain had died, the local church, and the "provisional tomb" where his remains awaited the anticipated transfer to Douaumont, all of which, he wrote, had become pilgrimage shrines to the memory of the marshal. Warning that the period around 23 July, the anniversary of Pétain's death, could be overcrowded, Henry advised his readers to schedule their visits at times other than the summer months and to write to the guardian of the tomb for help in finding accommodations on the small island.[142] During the annual Joan of Arc Day "pilgrimage"—the term used by the periodical—to the shrine of the Virgin Mary at Verdelais in 1959, the Bordeaux section of the Fraternité de Notre-Dame de la Merci identified Pétain and Vichy with Joan and called upon pilgrims to remember "the victims of the 1944 Revolution and especially Marshal Pétain." A mass was held at the basilica, followed by a pilgrimage of the stations of the cross to the shrine of Verdelais. All this was followed by a meal with a speaker who addressed the "misery of the freed political prisoners" and those still awaiting their freedom.[143] On the fiftieth anniversary of the Battle of Verdun, in 1966, Jacques Isorni, one of Pétain's defense attorneys, who spent much of his life subsequently trying to rehabilitate the memory of the marshal, again argued for reburial at Douaumont. His own presence, he wrote, at the cemetery in the Île d'Yeu would be a sign of respect for Pétain, who, according to Isorni, deserved better than to be buried on a small island, accessible by only a single boat, where not many people would be able to honor him.[144]

Together with several other prominent Vichy and collaboration leaders, Pétain had spent the period from the liberation of France through the fall of Nazi Germany at the Hohenzollern castle of Sigmaringen on the Danube River in Swabia in southern Germany, where he refused to have anything to do with a French government in exile set up there by the Germans. The immense and rather dour Hohenzollern castle attracted only limited tourist interest in France, but in 1969 it acquired increased notoriety as the site for the interview with Christian de la Mazière, a veteran of the Charlemagne Division of the Waffen-SS, in the film *Le chagrin et la pitié* (*The Sorrow and the Pity*). The limited but continued evocation of the sites associated with Pétain may have helped inspire the kidnapping of his remains in 1973, when supporters removed them from the Île d'Yeu and tried to transfer them to Douaumont.[145] The body-snatching "caper," to use *Time* magazine's description, occurred two weeks prior to French parliamentary elections, with potential political consequences. A public opinion poll taken in 1971 had shown 72 percent of the French people favoring a transfer of Pétain's remains to Douaumont.[146] The government, seeking to resolve the kidnapping quickly to avoid its becoming a distraction just before the elections, engaged half of France's 94,000 police in what, according to *Time*, "must have been the most intensive corpse hunt in history." The police patrolled the roads to Verdun and quickly arrested a woman involved in the renting of the van used for the theft. As the attempt to rebury the marshal's remains was in danger of failing, Hubert Massol, who in 2009 would become president of the ADMP, informed the police that the body was in a garage in Saint-Ouen and demanded it be reburied at Douaumont. President Georges Pompidou ordered it returned to the Île d'Yeu, where a beefed-up guard was installed to prevent both demonstrations and further body snatchings.[147] Massol was the founder of a second Pétainist organization in 1972, the Association nationale Pétain-Verdun (ANPV), which shared with the ADMP the goal of rehabilitating the marshal but was less overtly Catholic in its outlook.[148] Both organizations arranged annual pilgrimages to Pétain's tomb on the Île d'Yeu, and the island's name was used as the title of the ANPV's periodical.[149] The ANPV also organized annual pilgrimages to the tomb of the pro-German writer Robert Brasillach, who had been executed after the war.[150]

Despite the fiasco of the 1973 "caper," the ADMP continued its campaign to have Pétain's remains transferred to Douaumont. The cover of its first issue for 1978 showed a drawing of the quarters in which the marshal had been held in the Fort de la Pierre Levée on the Île d'Yeu.[151] In 1978 the

ADMP organized pilgrimages to the Île d'Yeu and Douaumont, at the latter joined by the ANPV, as well as another to the Fort du Portalet, where Pétain had been imprisoned briefly following his conviction in 1945. A wreath was placed in the cell in which the marshal had been incarcerated, and the visitors sang the Vichy anthem "Maréchal nous voilà."[152]

Tours to celebrate his birth, the 1 May holiday of Saint-Philippe, the anniversary of his death, and that of the armistice that ended World War I together constituted a tourist circuit of memory.[153] By the late 1980s, the ADMP was soliciting funds to convert the newly restored Cauchy-à-la-Tour house into a museum of Pétain memorabilia with a conservator to "guide visitors and answer their questions."[154] An article in the 10–11 September 1989 issue of *Le Monde* reported that a small historical museum being set up on the Île d'Yeu would not be allowed to bear the name Pétain. "Le Maréchal y est bien caché" (the marshal is well hidden there), were the newspaper's words.[155] The ANPV's *L'Île d'Yeu* commented angrily that the generically named "Musée historial de l'Île d'Yeu" did everything but name Pétain, portraying his last days so obviously that even children would understand who was being referenced.[156] Controversy over war-related tourist sites continued into the 1990s, swirling around François Mitterrand, who, as recently as 1992, had followed previous presidents in having wreaths placed at Pétain's grave in Port-Joinville.[157]

Pétain pilgrimages continued to take place. On 21 February 2006, the ADMP organized a trip to the Île d'Yeu to honor the "victor of Verdun" on the occasion of the ninetieth anniversary of the 1916 battle, and on 22 April 2006 it again sponsored a pilgrimage, this time to Cauchy-à-la-Tour, to commemorate the 150th anniversary of the marshal's birth there.[158] Another pilgrimage to the Île d'Yeu was organized in September 2007, led by the Abbé Regis de Cacqueray, a follower of the late Archbishop Marcel Lefebvre, the founder of the Society of Saint Pius X, which opposes the reforms of the Second Vatican Council.[159] The ADMP organized a trip to honor Pétain at Verdun on Armistice Day in November 2007.[160] Pilgrimages organized by the ADMP continued to visit the sites on the Pétain tourist circuit, over fifty years old by the early twenty-first century.[161]

France's Caisse nationale des monuments historiques et des sites (CNMHS, National Fund for Historical Monuments and Sites) in 1994 counted some fourteen thousand buildings and sites as historical monuments.[162] With the exception of Verdun, none of the ADMP sites was on the list. The popularity of the circuit constructed by the ADMP and its fellow Pétain *nostalgiques* was clearly limited to what might be called a "micro-niche" within the larger realm of battlefield tourism, although more research remains to be done with regard to the numbers of visits to these sites.[163]

Minoritarian Tourism: Sigmaringen and "Paris by Right"

Not all French wartime tourism sites are in France. Sigmaringen Castle, mentioned earlier, which served as the site of the then phantom Vichy government from September 1944 through the German collapse in May 1945, was the enforced residence of Marshal Pétain, Pierre Laval, and others who had fled liberated France. Largely ignored after the war, it featured prominently in the interview of Christian de la Mazière in *The Sorrow and the Pity*, during which two interruptions of the film sequence show a guide leading tour groups of Germans through the castle, helping to make this site on the Rhine a tourist spot for at least some interested in Second World War France. In an article about the castle, Andrea Loselle pointed out in 2001 that while the small town of Sigmaringen advertised the castle, with its impressive collection of antique weapons and armor, in the hope of boosting its tourist trade, no mention was made either in its publicity or in the souvenirs on sale in the castle's shop of the French collaborators who resided there in 1944–45. Only a brief mention was made of the collaborators on Loselle's tour.[164] The ambivalence toward the French collaboration story in the town of Sigmaringen, signaled by a reference to it in the tours through the castle while at the same time refraining from publicizing it in the site's advertising and souvenirs, echoes in a muted way the touristic ambivalence in the town of Vichy over its past. Sigmaringen is, of course, a German site, whereas Vichy is French, but the sense of embarrassment, of having to explain after the fact, described in Loselle's account is common to both.

Yet another example of a tourist gaze in a more metaphorical sense can be seen in the tribute paid in 1963 to the memory of Pierre Drieu la Rochelle, a fallen collaborator, by Jean Mabire in his elegiac book *Drieu parmi nous* (Drieu among Us). Drieu had committed suicide in 1945 rather than face judgment at the hands of the provisional government. Largely a collection of Drieu's comments arranged thematically, the book closed with an appeal to the spirit of Drieu. It was on an island, said Mabire, that he had wished to write his book on Drieu. And indeed, he wrote the book's conclusion on the island of Guernsey, which he felt Drieu would have liked, for Guernsey, according to Mabire, was a place where Nordics still ruled: the Union Jack floated from the top of the fort, the cliffs were encircled with bunkers built by the Germans, and all the villages had French names. On the north side of the island there was even a place called La Rochelle, which Mabire had visited. "Strange encounter with your name," he wrote. "On the entrance door to a cottage, 'La Rochelle Farm,' a window with a Scandinavian dragon represented fidelity." To Mabire, Drieu symbolized fidelity to a youth of grandeur.[165]

Given the shift in power relationships after 1944 and especially after 1945, touristic interest in Vichy remained limited in contrast to the appeal of those sites that heralded the activities of the Resistance and warrior France in tandem with the Allies. Reviewing a memoir by Jacques Chaban-Delmas in 1984, Jean-Didier Wolfromm noted that nothing was more human than a selective memory that focused on "the amiable Americans having come to die for France," as opposed to the sinister parades of the Milice—or General de Gaulle's descent down the Champs-Elysées of 26 August 1944, in contrast to the raising of the colors at the Hôtel du Parc in Vichy.[166] One must wait until the year 1987 to see the publication of Francis Bergeron's and Philippe Vilgier's *Guide de l'homme de droite à Paris (Paris by Right)*. Even in this book, which contained some two hundred references to libraries, cemeteries, museums, and restaurants, among other sites presumably dear to the political right in France, only fifteen referred specifically to a Vichyite circuit of the war years. There were two mentions of Marshal Pétain, one referring the reader to the Salon du vieux papier de collection, a book and magazine fair held each September in Paris, where for seven hundred francs in 1986 one could purchase a street marker plaque with the inscription "Place du maréchal Pétain," the other a reference to annual masses said in Pétain's honor at an unspecified location on the anniversary of his death each 23 July.[167] In its section on cemeteries, the guidebook described the burial spot of Drieu la Rochelle. After he committed suicide to avoid falling into the hands of "stupid" and "ferocious" judges, Drieu was buried in the Neuilly cemetery outside Paris on the rue Victor-Noir. A plain gray stone marks his grave with the inscription "Pierre Drieu la Rochelle, 1893–1945."[168] Bergeron and Vilgier noted that Robert Brasillach, shot at the Fort de Montrouge "for his ideas" in 1945, was buried at the Charonne cemetery, adjoining the Saint-Germain de Charonne church in the twentieth arrondissement of Paris. There follows an extract relating to the cemetery and the church from Brasillach's novel *Les sept couleurs*, published in 1939.[169]

Paris by Right also mentioned bookstores, shops, and museums in which one could acquire or pore over Vichy-related objects. These included Ogmios, a Paris bookstore, since closed, which was located in the building that had once housed the offices of Jacques Doriot's Parti Populaire Français (PPF), which had been formed in 1936 and had supported collaboration with Germany during the war. Ogmios took its name from the Celtic god of war, and the bookstore, the reader is told, was a place specializing in cultural warfare, a "Gramscism of the right," in reference to Antonio Gramsci, the Italian Marxist theorist who emphasized the role of culture in political life. The location of the shop in the former home of the PPF "proves that in this bookstore history is appreciated," wrote Bergeron and Vilgier.[170] The Librairie Française had on sale the *Documents maçonniques* of the years 1941–1944; at the Louvre des Antiquaires one might buy flags and insignia of the État français; and the military clothing store Optas offered a variety of Second World War–era items including a 1940 French pilot's leather jacket.[171]

Not surprisingly, there are gaps in the tourist circuit presented in the *Guide de l'homme de droite*. It makes no mention, for example, of the office at 93 rue Lauriston where the Bonny-Lafont clique collaborated with the German police in the often brutal inquisition of resisters and other enemies of the government. Nonetheless, the appearance of such a guidebook in the late 1980s was a sign of the historicization of Vichy and the collaboration. It is difficult to imagine such a book having been published in the years immediately after the Liberation. Because tourism imaginaries and behavior reflect the values and perspectives of their time, it is not surprising that the various sites promoted by the Vichy *nostalgiques* attract far fewer visitors and less attention than those related to General de Gaulle and the Resistance. As the years go by and eyewitnesses of the wartime period pass away, the Vichy and collaboration sites are likely to merge into the larger narrative of French history, where they will assume their place as curiosities representing lost and largely discredited causes.

The evolution of tourism to Vichy and the Resistance sites has taken place in the framework of the evolution of political and cultural norms reflecting the changed power balances that have impacted the aesthetic judgments of war and memory in the years since 1945. Narratives changed, but many of the characteristics of war-related tourism remained. Allied forces had barely liberated Normandy and freed Paris from its German occupants when new sites of memory were established and new narratives unfolded.

CHAPTER 7

Tourism, War, and Memory in Postwar France

The often imperfect and multiform methods of gathering tourism statistics render difficult any attempt to quantify tourism whether during the war or to the war sites thereafter. It has yet to be established that any collected statistics can really measure where people spend their tourism time. In general, French statistics gathered over the years were based on paid admissions to sites defined as forms of "cultural tourism," such as museums and monuments. In addition, the quantification of tourism receipts, while providing some direction for analysis, cannot assess the impact of a site on specific tourists, who, it should be noted, travel as individuals rather than hordes.[1] Any assessment must be regarded as provisional. How does one measure the numbers of the curious or, more specifically, the tourist imaginaries of the thousands who came from both near and far, lining the Champs-Élysées in August 1944, to watch the Allied forces make their descent down the famous avenue? Here one is reminded of Walter Benjamin's *flâneur* "seeing" as he strolled the arcades of Paris and of de Botton's linking of travel to "receptivity" together with curiosity and seeing rather than distance covered in touring.

The same question might be asked about those who gazed out at the Normandy coastline in the years since 1944, whatever their thoughts might have been, in retrospective contemplation of the Allied landings, or who walked along the avenue du Parc in Vichy as they looked across the way at the hotel where Pétain and the leaders of the État français had their offices. It is easier to document the development of *tourisme de mémoire* to postwar battlefield sites such as those relating to Normandy and the liberation of Paris than to document the real-time gazes of those who came from near and far to watch the Germans parade down the Champs-Élysées during the Occupation or General de Gaulle march into Paris in June 1944.

Seeing, Spectacle, and Paris: 1944 and New Tourism Narratives

Most of the thousands who turned out along the Champs-Élysées in August 1944 to watch the victory parade did not travel far, nor were they necessarily vacationers, but theirs was a tourist gaze of rapt curiosity at what Rosemary Wakeman termed "the ultimate urban spectacle."[2] The Free French forces of General Leclerc, together with the armed uprising of local *résistants*, had chased the Germans from Paris during the "heroic week" of 19 through 25 August, creating a narrative of liberation with its own tourism circuit, represented in a film made at the time, *La libération de Paris*. It was the city and its monuments more than the Parisians themselves that emerged as the heroic focus of the film. The Notre-Dame cathedral, the Madeleine, and the Arc de Triomphe figured prominently, as they had in the film of Hitler on tour four years earlier. Added to the itinerary, however, were the Police Prefecture and the Hôtel de Ville, pictured as centers of the insurrection against the occupation forces. The fighting was followed by the celebration of General de Gaulle descending the Champ-Élysées from the Arc de Triomphe, his stop at the Hôtel de Ville, where he proclaimed the continuity of the Republic, and celebrated a mass at Notre-Dame.[3] Of the thousands who watched de Gaulle walk down the Champs-Élysées, presumably many, if not most, were from Paris. If not "tourists" in the organized and formal sense of the term, coming to watch tourist spectacles such as the Parisian burlesque, to use Dean MacCannell's phrase, they nonetheless cast gazes similar to that of the tourist on the proceedings along the Champs.[4] Paid admissions to museums and monuments may be tracked and tabulated, but they tell only part of the story of tourism. Estimating the numbers of the curious who gaze at a parade in Paris or a landing beach in Normandy is arguably impossible, but they too are a part of wartime tourism.[5]

In answer to the question "What is tourism?," Alexandre Panossi Netto concluded that no one researcher is able to "construct a theoretical complete model that is able to explain the innumerous [sic] facets of tourism." Key to his definition is the impossibility of drawing a quantitative distance that must be traveled if one is to be considered a tourist. Here again, a distinction must be made between the tourism imaginary or aesthetic, in the sense of Salazar and others, and the tourist industry. Panossi Netto adds: "In a trip, there are elements involved that at the first moment do not show up, like the wishes and longings of the tourist, the search for the new, the necessity of new experiences."[6]

Postwar: Continuity and Change

With the German defeat in 1945, tourist iconography shifted once more. Much, however, remained unchanged. In 1950 the writer Ernst von Salomon, known for his depictions of the post–First World War freebooters and the post–Second World War questionnaires about the possible Nazi past of millions of Germans, published a novel, *Boche in Frankreich,* the story of a young German sent in 1931 to Saint Jean de Luz in southwestern France, where he falls in love with a local woman. As in the case of Friedrich Sieburg before the war, France was again depicted as a land of wine, women, and song, with nostalgic retrospection on the tourist adventures of a youthful protagonist.[7] A German visitor to Paris in the late 1980s listed Notre-Dame, the Invalides dome, the Louvre, and the Tuileries as the key places to see in Paris, and the sketches of Montmartre that appeared in her book recalled the images of the 1930s.[8] A continuity in the Germans' choice of sites persisted long after the war when, in 1994, German soldiers from the Federal Republic, invited to help celebrate the 14 July festival in Paris, indicated a desire to see the Eiffel Tower, the Champs-Élysées, and the Arc de Triomphe.[9] These sites continue to hold high places in the imagery of tourist Paris not only for Germans but also for many others, both French and international, up to the present.

Nevertheless, some iconic representations did change. Strasbourg, the symbol for Hitler in 1940 and Leclerc and the Free French thereafter, acquired a different kind of image, touted as one of the capital cities of a united Europe. Tourist literature in Strasbourg focused on the city's dual French and German heritage, together with the shift from Franco-German warfare for control of the city to its postwar mission of nurturing Franco-German and, by extension, European reconciliation.[10] The Compiègne railway car, or more accurately its replica, is back, and it now has a triply symbolic value, representing the Germans' defeat of 1918, their victory of 1940, of which they proved unable to reap the consequences, and another defeat in 1945, all resulting from their inability to make peace with France. Even before German reunification in 1990, while French economic influence was limited to western Europe, that of Germany had already extended to the entire continent. In other words, Germans could once again see France as a place to tour and party while they sold to the rest of Europe in the sense of Sieburg.[11]

Learning to Tour as a Soldier in France

Postwar economic expansion made tourism more accessible to larger numbers of Germans, as well as other Europeans and Americans. Indeed, the exposure of many Germans during the war to France may have contributed, as did the subsequent tourist experiences of American GIs in Europe, such as Arthur Frommer, the creator of the *Europe on 5 Dollars a Day* series, to the tourism takeoff, albeit under very different circumstances after the war.[12] Many young Americans, British, Canadians, Australians, and New Zealanders first saw France as soldiers in uniform, as had so many of the Germans between 1940 and 1944. The arrival of large numbers of American soldiers during the second half of 1944 produced sexual tensions reminiscent of the recently ended German occupation. In a 2013 study, Mary Louise Roberts argued that the liberation of France was promoted to American soldiers as an erotic adventure among oversexed Frenchwomen, "stirring up a 'tsunami of male lust' that a battered and mistrustful population often saw as a second assault on its sovereignty and dignity."[13] The mayor of Le Havre complained of "scenes contrary to decency" in the streets of his city and asked the Americans to establish brothels outside town. There was also a racial dimension, as African American soldiers received very different treatment than did whites from the American military authorities. In Le Havre, in Normandy, "some colored soldiers" were said to have created enough trouble to cause the city to be declared off-limits to American troops. American soldiers, black and white, according to eyewitness L. R. Blanchard, suffered for the transgressions of a few.[14] They seem to have been subjected to more severe complaints by the French as well.[15] Reviewing Ian Buruma's book on the year 1945, Charles Simic noted that five times more women were hospitalized in Paris for sexually transmitted diseases in 1945 than in 1939. "Allied soldiers," he wrote, "were greeted by young girls and some older women the way the Beatles, as Buruma says, were treated twenty years later when they first became popular."[16]

The excitement described by Arthur Frommer upon seeing Europe for the first time from the confines of a military transport plane was by no means unusual, and the many Allied soldiers who came to France to fight in 1944 and in peacetime during the years that followed contributed to the surge in tourism that characterized the postwar landscape and played such a large role in European prosperity. The 1951 film *An American in Paris*, with music by George

Gershwin and scenes of Paris taxis, the Eiffel Tower, Montmartre, Notre-Dame, the Folies-Bergère, and 1890s Montmartre cancans, laid out the popular itinerary for the growing numbers of Americans visiting Paris. For France, one may speculate as to the numbers and types of war souvenirs brought home by returning soldiers from the 1944–45 campaigns in Alsace and Germany, but the brisk trade in wartime memorabilia at the Marché aux Puces at Saint-Ouen and elsewhere in France attests to the continuing interest in war tourism there.[17]

Guidebooks: From German to English

Just as the appearance of German soldiers in France resulted in tour books in their language written for them, English-language guidebooks began appearing in mid-1944. Local people in France published the guidebook *For You*, oriented toward English-speaking soldiers, in 1945, just as the *Wegleiter* had been directed toward the Germans. *For You* was produced by the French American Welcome Committee, a nonprofit private group wishing "to show real France to the Allies" by arranging for Allied soldiers on leave in Paris to visit the homes of local French people, something unseen in the previous German guidebooks.[18] *For You* had a brief life, appearing in 1945 only. As did the *Paris Programmes* and the *Wegleiter*, *For You* listed a panoply of tourist activities, including music halls, concerts, dance programs, art galleries, and monuments, in an apparently seamless transition following the liberation of the city. A page devoted to Paris fashion in the first issue of *For You*, dated 1 March 1945, eagerly anticipated the new fashion season of spring 1945.[19] A French Welcome Committee office on the place de la Madeleine offered visiting Allied military personnel information about Paris as well as guided tours.[20] A *For You* issue in mid-April 1945 welcomed Allied soldiers who spent money gambling in Paris and happily reported the supplanting of the "gray mice," the German military women's auxiliaries, by the Allied women's services: "The grey uniforms of the german [*sic*] feminine units are advantageously replaced by Anglo-French-American feminine corps who have a much less harsh smile and soldiers in *kaki* [*sic*] are gambling and forecasting gladly and also may be at times loosing [*sic*] some money."[21]

Paris Leave Booklet, a similar Canadian publication, undated but appearing shortly after the war, described sites in Paris and also urged visiting soldiers to go beyond tourism and meet local civilians in their homes. Canadian military personnel were advised to retain the guidebook as a souvenir to show family and friends back home, as well as to use in subsequent visits to Paris. "The charm of Paris," according to the *Booklet*, "resides both in her streets and monuments replete with present life and past history and also in her mellow

June 1945

For you

OFFICIAL
GUIDE-BOOK

OFFERED AND
DISTRIBUTED
by the
FRENCH WELCOME
COMMITTEE

NOT TO BE SOLD

FIGURE 18.   *For You* (June 1945), cover. Author's personal collection.

atmosphere and the elegance of her construction and appearance." The guidebook focused on the historic architecture of the different areas within Paris, even offering a brief description of the city's mosque, which it referred to as a "Moslem city (1923–1927)," which included a hammam, restaurant, café, and souk.[22] It concluded with a small section devoted to living in Paris, in which it pointed out that residing in the city was very different from being a tourist there. "To see Paris really," it concluded, "its [*sic*] to stroll at leisure, having the past in mind." For entertainment, it mentioned the Opéra-Comique, Théâtre-Français or Comédie-Française, and the Odéon. In a comment that illustrated both continuity and a break with the recent German occupation, the *Paris Leave Booklet* indicated that the two most important "Music Halls" were the Folies-Bergère and the Casino de Paris, the scenes of revues with international *vedettes* including Mistinguett, Maurice Chevalier, and Josephine Baker, the last of whom had been persona non grata under the Germans. "Night haunts" (*boîtes de nuit,* or artistic cabarets), it claimed, were "only occasionally frequented by the denizens of Paris, but mostly by tourists." Horseracing events and shopping were little different from the days of the German occupation, but the dining scene had changed. "Restaurants of good standing" and "exquisite cooking" were not necessarily the same as before. Establishments were not mentioned by name, but the reader in search of fine dining was advised that such an experience would need to be "acquired anew and is sometimes costly." Canadians in Paris were well lodged and fed in hotels, "like tourists," but were encouraged to visit local people at home, even under trying conditions, so as to "taste of French hospitality."[23]

French-language guidebooks that had been translated into German during the Occupation were quickly translated into English and readapted for the Americans and the British after the Liberation of 1944.[24] Writing in *For You,* Lysiane Bernhardt commented: "Gone is the time when the Nazies [sic] whistled LILY MARLENE . . . gone too, is the time when the poet Jean COCTEAU returning from a walk to the Etoile overrun with German uniforms, catching hold of his head cried: 'Oh, what a pain I've got in my poor Champs-Elysées.' "[25]

Brochures such as "Paris*Spectacles," subtitled "What's On in Paris: Free Guide," and designated "for Allied forces," appeared in 1945 and listed stage shows, movies, and concerts for Allied personnel.[26] *See France,* by L. R. Blanchard, the 1946 American journalists' travel account referred to in chapter 5, included a large section on Paris, described as "shabby" but carrying on, "an aristocrat in hand-me-downs."[27] Wrapping up his visit after having toured much of France, Blanchard wrote that the marks of war were present everywhere. He had seen bridges knocked down and villages in ruins. Nevertheless, he also brought home more pleasant memories of

> the cider and cheese in Normandy; the gay and hopeful people of Touraine together with their castles; the friendly people at Bordeaux; the unwavering people of Marseilles and their determination to rebuild; the gaiety and beauty, the soft climate of the Riviera, the great hills and the blue waters; the hard working people of Limoges and Lyon; the historic spots in Paris and the unforgettable beauty of the

FIGURE 19. "What's On in Paris: Free Guide for Allied Forces," with illustration from *Wait for Me*, a Soviet war drama made in 1943, *Paris*Spectacles* (25 April–1 May 1945), cover. Author's personal collection.

Champs Élysées; the strange beauty of Mont St. Michel which, sadly, is only a factory in a new form since its old abbey no longer functions; the crepes suzettes at Granville; the wide beach at Deauville and the historic atmosphere of St. Malo and its sister city of Dinard across the harbor.

He wrote of the salmon of the Loire, Concale oysters, turbot from the sea, brown bread with marmalade and coffee served in bed, sole fried in butter, and fritters light as Ping-Pong balls. France, he concluded, would overcome this difficult period in its history as it had in the past. "The world needs France. She is worth preserving."[28]

Postwar Tourism Planning

The purview of the French governmental agency responsible for tourism immediately after the 1944 Liberation included tourism associations, as well as airborne, sea and lake, bicycle, university-sponsored, and colonial tourism. Already in 1943 Pierre Ollier de Marichard, commander of the armed Resistance group Francs-Tireurs et partisans (FTP) in the Ardèche, had founded with other Resistance leaders the organization Tourisme et travail (Tourism and Work), which was to supervise leisure and sports activities for a democratic state.[29] Following in the spirit of the Popular Front reforms of 1936, Tourisme et travail coordinated activities with trade unions, gymnastics and sports groups, and the youth hostel movement. Peuple et culture (People and Culture), which evolved from Vichy's Uriage School for Cadres, emerged almost immediately upon the Liberation and worked in a vein similar to Tourisme et travail to promote a "peoples' tourism considered as a factor for health and an instrument for culture. By 1946, the association numbered 450,000 members spread among seventeen delegations in France and four in Africa."[30]

Plans for the expansion of postwar tourism were under way even before the end of hostilities, as seen in a request for increased funding of the Tourism Service within the Ministry of Public Works. A memo asking for money to support expanded advertising abroad for tourism to France stated, "Thus, the end of hostilities, even if it does not allow for a resumption of tourism for the end of this year [presumably 1944] offers, however, the possibility to envision putting into effect the advertising program for 1945 in relation to the policy of expansion abroad."[31]

As a first step, the government Tourism Office requested that hotels, travel agencies, and other facilities requisitioned by military or civil governmental departments during the war be returned to their previous functions to promote tourism.[32] Advertising brochures encouraging foreign tourists to visit France focused on France itself: Paris, the Île-de-France, hotel prices, winter sports, mountains, beaches, spas, golfing, châteaux, cathedrals and abbeys, gastronomy, fishing, hunting, festivals, pilgrimages, and other attractions.[33] Although wartime sites were not mentioned, not surprising so soon after the war, a separate report focused on the need to allot funds, in short supply since 1939, for the preservation and restoration of châteaux as part of France's national heritage. Funds for preserving historic monuments and artistic heritage were to be sought from tourism revenues. In return for state support, private owners of historic properties would be asked to open them for public view.[34]

Louis Richerot, president of the Hotel Association for the Isère department, wrote to the Ministry of Public Works in February 1946 to say that the income from foreign tourism would more than compensate the 43 billion franc national budget shortfall following a recent currency devaluation. Other countries were actively promoting tourism and so, he argued, should France. Even Germany, so recently defeated in the war, was secretly (sous manteau) promoting its tourist trade.[35] The Commissariat au tourisme, in its budget planning for French tourism offices abroad for 1946, envisioned its largest expenditures for missions in the United States, Great Britain, Argentina, and Brazil, in that order.[36] In the words of one official who was requesting funds to help modernize and restore France's tourism infrastructure: "If we wish to enter honorably into conflict with our competing countries, let us at least have means equal to theirs. The attraction of France, its past, its culture, its art industries, will do the rest."[37] Clearly, the era of postwar tourism to France was at hand.

Clientele for Battlefield and War Tourism

A continuing clientele for war-related tourism in general may be seen in the numbers of battlefields and war sites listed in the guidebooks such as the Michelin series and the success of the British magazine *After the Battle*, with its articles devoted to battlefield tours throughout the world. The British Holt travel agency, established in the 1970s by Major Toni and Mrs. Valmai Holt's Battlefield Tours, offers dozens of tours annually, described in seven guidebooks devoted to sites from the two world wars of the twentieth century. The Holts, who sold their company in the 1990s and subsequently concentrated on writing battlefield guidebooks, offer the following advice to prospective tourists:

> Visiting battlefields in Europe generally involves more than going to one preserved site. American travellers who have visited their own Civil War Battlefields, marvellously preserved by the National Parks Service, may imagine that visiting European sites will be a similar experience. Not necessarily so. Where each American site seems able

to stand alone with its own reception centre, Park Rangers and book-stall, many European sites are dotted piecemeal along an old front line or along miles of beaches and often maintained by local enthusiasts in their spare time. Thus it is possible to turn up at a battlefield area to find that any museum there is closed and that there is no-one there to explain things though that is less likely in Normandy and Holland.[38]

As of 2010, the War Research Society was another British organization specializing in battlefield tourism.[39]

In 1997 the French military wrestled with the problem of decommissioning Second World War facilities beyond the Maginot forts, for example, the Keroman submarine base near Lorient, in Brittany, built by the Germans for their U-boats and tied into their defenses along the Atlantic Wall. Scheduled for closure at the end of 1997, the Keroman base, described in *Le Monde* as "monstrous but fascinating," was visited by fifteen thousand tourists each year, the majority of them German.[40] The site, described by the Lorient tourist office in 2010 as "a major piece of human heritage [*patrimoine de l'humanité*]," remains open to visitors. Guided tours in 2015 promised to "open to you the doors of one of the blockhouses for an impressive discovery of this major site of the Second World War."[41]

Although the French tourism industry had been heavily developed before the Second World War, battlefield tourism transformed the economy of Normandy in the years after 1944. Given the difficulties of assessing tourism statistics, a sense of shifting interest may nevertheless be seen in guidebook listings, such as those published by Michelin over the years, offering a retrospective on changing tourism motifs of France and its history. Designed to be used in tandem with the red Michelin guides, which focused on hotels and restaurants, and the Michelin maps, the regional guides, which later evolved into the *Green Guides*, were oriented toward the cultural heritage of France, as were the earlier battlefield guidebooks. The first regional guidebook, in 1926, covered Brittany, and with the publication of *Châteaux de la Loire* in 1938, the *Green Guides* assumed their present format, promoting, in Marc Francon's words, a *tourisme culturel populaire* (popular cultural tourism).[42]

The Michelin *Green Guides* and the War

It is of interest to follow the Michelin *Green Guides* for France as a whole, although it could be expected that attention devoted to wartime tourism would vary according to region, with areas such as Normandy having a higher degree. Echoing his earlier comments about the *Guides bleus* privileging the speed of automobile touring over the joys of more random wandering less constrained by modern efficiency, André Rauch described the new *Green Guide* aficionados as more interested in the route than in the local churches and museums. Less erudite and more affordable, the *Green Guides* "codified the supposed curiosities offering 'a real interest and meriting a stop or detour for the driver.'" These guides also focused on local culinary specialties and restaurants.[43] The first *Green Guide* for France as a whole was published in French in 1989 and in English in 1991.[44] It began with introductory sections on the French countryside followed by the history of France. The history chapter included a brief section on the Second World War, in contrast to a larger, more detailed discussion of World War I. The guidebook noted that the military defeat of June 1940 forced the government to request an armistice but that by the summer of that year, Free French forces had rallied behind General de Gaulle. The remainder of the history section focuses on the Gaullist resistance narrative.

> From the call of General de Gaulle (18 June 1940) and during the entire Occupation, the Resistance was developed and organized throughout the entire country [*toute le territoire national*]. By means of the moral force of its heroes, the martyrdom of its 20,000 executed and 115,000 deported, the courage of its fighters, it facilitated the Liberation and gave France hope and pride.[45]

By 1994, the introductory history section in the Michelin English-language *Green Guide* to France, published on the fiftieth anniversary of the Liberation, included a reference to the "French State," in quotation marks, with its slogan of "Work, Family, Fatherland," established at Vichy. In the sole mention of pro-Axis collaboration in the entire book, the introduction goes on to say that the Vichy government "collaborates closely with the Germans. France's honour," however, it continues, "is saved by General de Gaulle's Free French forces, active in many theatres of the war, and by the courage of the men and women in the Resistance." The lines devoted to the war conclude, "This major conflict [the Second World War], which inflamed all continents, is detailed in this guide under the places which it affected most in France."[46]

Of the approximately 1,320 sites listed and discussed in the 1994 guidebook, there are thirty-two references specifically to Second World War events. Of these references, twenty, or 63 percent, are to battle sites, mainly from the 1940 and 1944 campaigns, and destruction, largely during the latter. There are four references to the Resistance: in the descriptions of Ajaccio, Lille, Lyon, and Paris. Ajaccio is noted as the site of the landings of the first Free French forces on "the territory of France itself." They disembarked from the submarine *Casablanca* under Commander Jean L'Herminier at 1 a.m., 13 September 1943. In Lille, the book observes, many "patriotic French people" were killed in the Turenne bastion, a part of the citadel, which was used as a place of execution in both world wars. The *Green Guide* also describes the Traboules network of covered passageways in the Croix-Rousse hill above the Rhône River in Lyon as having proved its worth during the French Revolution and again when "much used by the Resistance in the Second World War." Lastly, the historical descriptions of Paris include references to the Resistance fighters killed in the clearing on Mont-Valérien and the "many victims of the Nazi racial myth" rounded up at the Vélodrome d'Hiver in 1942, "prior to their deportation eastward." In neither the reference to the Vélodrome d'Hiver roundup nor that to Vichy is there any mention of collaboration. On several occasions German brutality is highlighted, notably in the description of the 10 June 1944 massacre at Oradour-sur-Glane, which states that as a reminder of the "horrors of war," the stark walls of the burned-out village have been preserved.[47]

In addition to being mentioned in the historical introduction, General de Gaulle appears at three sites: Bayeux, where he was "visibly moved" in first setting foot on French soil after the Liberation, and where he laid out the principles for a new constitution in June 1944; in Colombey-les-deux-Églises, and in Abbeville.[48] In Colombey, La Boisserie, which served as the country house of "this great Frenchman" from its purchase in 1933 through his death in 1970, is now a museum. Two local sites of pilgrimage are the memorial, a giant Cross of Lorraine, and the general's tomb in the village churchyard.[49] The guidebook's description of Abbeville includes an account of the Battle of the Somme in May 1940, when General de Gaulle's Fourth Armored Division, hurriedly assembled, counterattacked on 27–29 May, driving deep into the enemy's lines, without, however, "dislodging him completely." By the beginning of June, the account continues, overwhelming German superiority in mechanized forces together with the "pusillanimous French leadership and growing general panic turned the Battle of France into a rout."[50]

The 2011 edition of the *Guide vert* in most ways followed the pattern of the 1994 version. Of some 1,500 sites mentioned, twenty-seven relate to the Second World War, a decline in percentage from the 1994 guide. Military museums are mentioned in the Paris area with notes about the Musée de l'armée, the Historial Charles-de-Gaulle, and the Musée de l'air at Le Bourget, which also exhibited warplanes.[51] A relatively new entry is the Coupole d'Helfaut-Wizernes in Saint-Omer, the site of German V2 rocket launches during the war, now converted into a museum of the history of war and rockets, "a place of memory and education." With two exhibitions, one showing the German secret arms and the other the life of the population in northern France from 1940 through 1944, the museum highlights "Nazi madness and excessiveness."[52] Many of the sites listed in the *Guide* focus on the Resistance and General de Gaulle. Not surprisingly, eleven, including the Caen Mémorial and the Musée-mémorial de la Bataille de Normandie in Bayeux, are in Normandy. A "Battle of Normandy historic space" itinerary guides the visitor through the landing beaches.[53] Mention is made of the heavy destruction caused by German and Allied bombing in Le Havre and the Allied bombing in Royan.[54] Interestingly, the *Guide vert* also refers to the bombings of 1940 in Orléans and the destruction of the old port in Marseille in 1943 but without stating by whom.[55] The Île d'Yeu is mentioned briefly but without reference to Marshal Pétain, and a two-page discussion of Vichy, including a brief history, makes no mention of the État français government there during the war years.[56]

Statistics and War Tourism

Another, arguably more direct way to assess interest in the tourist sites of the Second World War in France is to analyze the official statistics prepared by agencies of the French government over time with the caveats mentioned earlier about the fragmentary and hypothetical nature of the statistical picture. Assessing tourism statistics is, as Pierre Py wrote, a difficult and complex task. Statistics collections in France and elsewhere for international tourism are invariably partial and often are not collected in the same ways, making comparative study difficult. Py noted that tourism as an economic sector encompasses exchanges that extend into the areas of food, clothing, transportation, hospitality, and other leisure industries.[57] The tourist revenue potential of *lieux de mémoire* in France, however, is significant, especially in battlefield areas such as Normandy. In one estimate, some 3 million visitors toured the battle sites of Normandy in 2003, possibly placing them among the top twenty-five most-frequented tourist sites in France.[58] These figures bring to mind Marc Pottier's comment that because the Caen Mémorial is situated on a tourist access route to Mont Saint-Michel, it also attracts a certain "tourisme d'autoroute, de passage."[59] In anticipation of the seventieth anniversary of the Normandy landings in 2014, Michelin published a *Green Guide* specific to the landing beaches there, with sections on the history of the battles and an extensive bibliography of books and videos related to them.[60]

Imperfect as they may be, the statistics that are available enable a preliminary assessment of war-related tourism in France. Emphasizing the importance of international visitors and tourism in general for the French economy, in 1996 the general secretary of the Conseil national du tourisme,

Alain Monferrand, argued that with some 60 million international visitors per year, France was dependent on the economic revenue from tourism, which employed a million persons and constituted one of the last forms of economic development still possible for the then coming millennium. He estimated that some 15 million visitors were drawn to fortifications, battlegrounds, and military or historical museums of various kinds in France annually, but it is not clear how he derived his numbers.[61] These tourists, Monferrand emphasized, visited "spontaneously," without an organized advertising campaign, which, he believed, might have doubled the numbers of visitors.[62]

With all caveats in mind, an examination of the statistics collected in the *Annuaire statistique de la France,* which has been published in various forms since the late nineteenth century, provides a guide to the relative statistical importance of war-related tourism in France. In its various forms over the years, the *Annuaire*'s tourism statistics, gathered by INSEE, are based on paid admissions into museums and other sites, as well as on surveys sent to them. The Arc de Triomphe, one of the more popular tourist sites in France, is a memorial to Napoleon's military victories, although not everyone who visits the Arc does so from interest in military affairs, nor do the figures, based on paid entry fees, include those who come simply to gaze. Nonetheless, the statistics available do offer a picture of war sites as constituting a significant portion of tourist spots in France. Figure A1 in the appendix shows a fluctuation of between 5.9 percent of tourist visits to wartime sites in 1952, the first year for which such statistics were available, to a high of 19.8 percent in 1970.[63] From 1952 through 1977, differing categories such as "principal" monuments and museums, "diverse local curiosities," and "cultural" and "non-cultural" sites were used, with the last two sometimes combined. Indeed, the definition of the term "cultural" changes over time and must be analyzed rather than assumed.[64] In addition, statistics were unavailable for the years between 1977 and 1996, but the *Mémento du tourisme* series, beginning online dating back to 1997, offers a measure of continuity, showing paid admissions to war sites at roughly 10 percent of the most-visited "cultural sites" over the years since then. Assignment of the different sites to various categories may also be problematized as Marc Boyer did in questioning the wisdom of the *Memento*'s listing the Eiffel Tower as a cultural attraction.[65]

More striking than the ups and downs in the sequence in figure A1 is the relative consistency in visits to war sites as percentages of the totals for the most popular "cultural" sites in France. Sites related to sex, gastronomy, sports, and children do not show up on the "cultural" list, nor do convention or business tourist spots as such. While the numbers of paid visitors to "cultural" sites are significantly lower than for some of the "non-cultural" locales such as Euro Disney, they are significant, especially in regions such as Normandy, with the many visitors to the American military cemetery at Colleville-sur-Mer referenced earlier.[66] Among the most-visited military sites over the period at different times since the 1950s, in addition to the Arc de Triomphe, are the Musée de l'armée, the Château de Haut-Koenigsberg, the Château et musée des Ducs de Bretagne, the Mémorial de la paix in Caen, and, more recently, the American military cemetery at Colleville. The Château de Haut-Koenigsberg and the Château et musée des Ducs de Bretagne are included in this study as war sites, as they were militarized fortresses, whereas the châteaux at Versailles and Chambord, which never functioned as military fortresses, are excluded from the war count. Changes in the tabulation methods between 1972 and 1994 resulted in the failure to count the tourism destinations in much of the 1980s and 1990s.[67] The *Mémento*'s "cultural" tourism figures for 2014, in addition to showing the American Military Cemetery at Colleville-sur-Mer as the leading war site and eighth on the entire "cultural" list, include the Arc de Triomphe, the Musée de l'armée in Paris, and the Château et musée des Ducs de Bretagne. Together, the four war sites attracted 6,851,228 visitors of a total 60,980,980, or 11 percent.[68]

A few tentative hypotheses may be drawn from the figures studied for the period 1952 through 2014. The figures show a minority but relatively consistent market for war tourism in France. War and military sites increase from 5.9 percent in 1952 to 11.2 percent in 2014, if one looks only at the cultural lists, but are 7 percent if one takes the total 2014 listings into account. A relative high in 1996 may have reflected interest in the investigations of complicity by Vichy French officials René Bousquet, Paul Touvier, and Maurice Papon in the Holocaust and revelations about President Mitterrand's involvement in the Vichy government, all of which drew popular attention to the war years. The lower figures in the more recent surveys might reflect a growing cultural distance from the two world wars of the previous century. Frédéric Sommier indicated in 2009 that the 300,000 visitors drawn annually to the Musée du débarquement in Arromanches included forty thousand students split roughly half and half between France and the United Kingdom. Approximately one-third of the annual visitors to the Mémorial at Caen were also students, according to Marc Pottier.[69]

Measuring Tourism Interest: Publications, Films, and Museums

One way to measure cultural interest in a topic, and by extension tourism to a site, is by sampling the percentages of publications in the relevant bibliographic indexes over time. Summarizing by five-year periods from 1939 through 2008 the percentages of Second World War–related books published in France and listed in the annual bibliographical indexes prepared by the Bibliothèque nationale staff—the *Biblio, Bibliographie de la France,* and *Bibliographie nationale française* series—figure A2 in the appendix offers a sampling of the rise and fall of interest in the war there. Highs in interest may be established by examining the publication peaks of documents related to the Second World War, where one sees a peak during the war years and again in the mid-1990s, reflecting the fiftieth anniversary of the Liberation, some of the last trials of those involved in the war, and in general a higher ratio of Second World War themes in the more recent years.[70] A decrease in Second World War–related publications since the 1990s may indicate a decline in tourist interest as well and seems to be in a rough parallel with the tourism figures from the *Annuaires.*

Finally, cinema offers helpful insights into tourism values, as film may be the best single tool for the historian to measure the development of tourism imageries and the shifting cultural value of tourist sites. As has been shown, cinema imagery of French sites was well established both in France and elsewhere before the war. The use of films to illustrate tourist motifs reveals how social images are manufactured and maintained. Because directors must show the object they have in mind in films, they become very specific in time and complement the history that may be constructed from written sources. Studying films is different from charting books and articles because the audience is much broader and the details are very precise. A book such as *The Longest Day* (1959) may mention a hill or a village, and this is sufficient to the telling of the story. The reader may never learn about the vegetation on the hill or the town hall square in the village; but in the 1962 film version, entire scenes become visually iconic as images of the time and place, whether or not they are accurate representations of the period. Cinematic scenes offer the historian powerful ideas of the kinds of values and perceptions that shape the consciousness of the traveling or touring community, as expressed by Adorno among others.[71]

Just as the guides to print media allow the historian to track the listings of articles in the American popular press, the Internet Movie Database, as mentioned in the pre-1940 chapters, offers the ability to formulate models of evolving cultural imagery through film. Although the total continually changes, the numbers are now sufficiently large that the changes are statistically insignificant.[72] The IMDb series probably lists over half the meaningful films ever made, including the longer-running ones. Not surprisingly, the total number of films in all the IMDb series drops during the Second World War occupation years, but the relative importance of Paris is significant.[73] For Anglophones, Paris represented nostalgia for a place now unattainable. Some of the films produced in France were underground Resistance films, centered on Paris as the focal point of the liberation struggle.[74]

Well-known and widely viewed films mentioned earlier publicized Normandy and Paris as tourist sites. Marcel Ophuls's film *The Sorrow and the Pity* (*Le chagrin et la pitié*) in 1971 focused on the experience of Clermont-Ferrand and may have helped put the German castle at Sigmaringen on the tourist map. Lyon's Hôtel Terminus, where Klaus Barbie had headed the local Gestapo, was put on the tourist circuit by Barbie's trial in 1987, helped along by Ophuls's *Hôtel Terminus*. Interviewed about the making of *Hôtel Terminus*, Ophuls recalled that he had been criticized for making *The Sorrow and the Pity*, which had questioned the narrative of near-unanimous French resistance in 1940–1944. Claude Lanzmann, who had made the film *Shoah*, asked Ophuls with apparent sarcasm if he would "do for Lyon what you have done for Clermont-Ferrand?"[75] *The Sorrow and the Pity*, like other postwar films, showed footage of soldiers bunkered down in the Maginot fortresses in 1939 and 1940, contributing to tourism there as well. Henry Rousso provides a list of French films from 1944 through 1989 that deal with the Second World War, which, with a high of fourteen films in 1946, exhibits a pattern similar to the book publication sequence. Rousso's figures show relative highs for war-related films in 1961, when ten films appeared, and the mid-1970s, with ten premiering during the 1973–74 season and eleven in 1975–76.[76] Films addressing the role of the city of Vichy during the Occupation undoubtedly enhanced its tourism interest. Pierre Beuchot's *Hôtel du Parc*, released in 1992, focused on the hotel in which Pétain, Laval, and others had their offices. *L'année dernière à Vichy* highlighted the conflicted memory of the city and may have attracted some visitors to Vichy.[77]

In addition to the publications, films, plaques, steles, and monuments that serve as tourist sites commemorating the war, museums also play key roles in the touristic memory circuit. A guidebook to military history museums in France, published in 1982, listed and described some 433 sites covering the French past from "prehistory" to "after 1945." Because the guidebook divided its listings into several categories, its chronological index made repeated mention of specific museums, meaning that with duplications included, it offered 813 entries. The largest single time period identified in the chronological index was the Second World War (*Guerre de 1939–45*), with 116 listings, or 14.3 percent, followed by "ancien régime," or the sixteenth century through 1789, with 111 entries, or 13.6 percent. Napoleon's Consulat and First Empire period accounted for 101 museums, or 12.4 percent, for third place, followed by the 1914–1918 war, with eighty-four listings, or 10.3 percent.[78] Within the Second World War listings, there were twenty-one for the Resistance and eleven for the Maginot Line. Three museums each were listed for General de Gaulle, Jean Moulin, and Marshal Pétain; two for Marshal Jean Lattre de Tassigny; and one each for General Diego Charles Brosset, who joined de Gaulle in 1940, led the liberation of Lyon in 1944, and died during the Vosges campaign later that year, as well as for General Maxime Weygand.[79]

Assessing the Statistics

How the many statistics are seen varies with the observer. To quote the words of the European Institute of Cultural Routes portal, taken from a seminar sponsored by the organization and mentioned earlier, "If one refers to statistics, tourism related to military heritage is in full expansion. In France, for example, visits to places of military memory come second, after visits to religious buildings: fortress of Besançon and citadel of Bonifacio in Corsica (500,000 visitors per year), Maginot Line (300,000 visitors per year)."[80] What emerges from the statistics regarding war tourism is the picture of perhaps a secondary tier of destinations by popularity, but one that continues to generate significant revenue not only for the sites themselves but also for the related tourism services of hotels and restaurants around them. The hundreds of thousands of visitors to the Atlantic Wall and the Normandy battlefields, as well as the Maginot sites, reflect an interest in and passion for the battlefield *lieux de mémoire* whose history decisively affected the outcome of the war.

Other variables in war tourism, as in all tourism, are gender and age, but sorting these out is also difficult. A breakdown of tourist numbers by age and gender would help us analyze tourism in general and, for example, the place of war tourism in particular. The tourism of these visitors would differ in age and most likely social composition from that of wartime soldiers, such as by the Germans from 1940 through 1944 or the Allied forces subsequently, most of whom were relatively young men, whose subsequent tourism patterns may have been influenced by their wartime experiences. Many of the later visitors to the war sites, as their directors indicated, are children brought in school groups, raising yet another variable in assessing the quantitative or economic impact of war-related tourism.

Nothing in the sites themselves predicts what the gender breakdown will be unless there is something specific related to the site that is tied to an interest of a given visitor.[81] For example, if most professors of history are men, the historical sites are likely to attract more men than women, but if the gender balance among history professors shifts, the numbers of visitors to the historic sites will as well. If there is no special interest in a site for a specific visitor, prediction is extremely difficult. Factors of gender and age combine in the growing elderly French and international population on tour in France and elsewhere.[82] As of 1978, more than 60 percent of France's 7.3 million retirees over age sixty-five were women.[83] French legislation passed in 1990 allowed people to retire with partial benefits at age sixty and with full benefits at age sixty-five. These ages were moved up to sixty-two and sixty-seven, respectively, in 2010.[84] How the growing numbers of older tourists will affect France's wartime sites remains to be seen.

Today's war tourism appears to be largely oriented toward the historic battlefields, and as has been shown, there are timelines for meaningful attention to a tourist site, whether for a specific purpose or for incidental curiosity, in other words, paradigm shifts in how the sites are imagined. As the decades elapse since the Second World War, it may be anticipated that its history, as well as the tourist sites associated with it, will lose their immediacy and pass into general history in France. History will determine which persons and sites are worth a detour, and how many stars will be awarded the various persons associated with the French experience of the war. After his execution in 1945, for example, Pierre Laval's remains were buried first in the cemetery at Thiais, then, at the request of his daughter Josée de Chambrun, transferred to the Chambrun family plot in the Montparnasse cemetery in Paris. There he lies under a gray marble slab together with his wife, Jeanne, who died in 1959. Each year, on 15 October, the anniversary of the date of his execution in 1945, and on Toussaint, All Saints' Day, the anonymous faithful leave bouquets on the tomb.[85] In contrast, in December 2009, for example, a directive from the French Education Ministry listed volume three of General de Gaulle's war memoirs, which cover the period from the Liberation of 1944 through the end of de Gaulle's first term in power, in 1946, as required reading in the *classe terminale,* the last year of secondary school, along with authors such as Homer and Samuel Beckett.[86]

As time passes and those who lived through the war die, we are likely to see the Second World War sites of memory acquire the patina of another in the series of battles mentioned earlier, some of which were defeats at the time but later turned into victories, such as Waterloo as well as those associated with Joan of Arc, at least from the standpoint of tourism. The wartime sites will become, as with those related to Caesar's Gallic Wars, Joan of Arc, Napoleon, and World War I, a part of the battlefield tourism *lieux de mémoire.* These sites, if not the leading tourism destinations such as Euro Disney and the Eiffel Tower, nonetheless play important roles in the economic development of the tourism industry in France, as elsewhere, and in tourism imaginaries of France in the minds of domestic and international cultural constructions. In this way they are critical in the formation of historical memory in the imaginaries of individuals and in the creation of heritage, all, once again, tied into economic development.

Conclusion

Tourism and Appropriate Remembrance

The many linkages between war and tourism explored in this book should help lead to further exploration not only in the case of Second World War France but also of other times and other places around the globe. Battlefield and monument tourism, or *tourisme de mémoire*, although hardly new in the twentieth and twenty-first centuries, is part of the burgeoning tourism industry around the world and should be studied in this context. The exploration of memory tourism, however, should not lead to the exclusion of tourism during wartime, arguably a more difficult phenomenon to analyze. Both are components of war tourism, both play roles in humanizing and normalizing the experience of war and making it meaningful, and both are important in the study of the construction of France as a leading tourism destination, together with the images and narratives that inform it. Both reflect the aesthetics or cultural perspectives of their eras, whether through the imaginaries and gazes of the curious individual or the political and economic configurations sustaining the tourism industry.

The economics of tourism in occupied France meant that some of the French prospered by catering to German tourists, as did those who were able to take vacations and travel, if in a more limited way than before. Wartime stimulation of tourist imaginaries in both Germany and France contributed to the increase in tourism after the war in both countries and through it the European economic surge in general. As more private letters and diaries are explored by future researchers, we will learn more about how individual tourists were affected by their experiences, whether German soldiers touring in France, French vacationers in their occupied country, or *touristes de mémoire*, as battlefield sites and monuments are created and shift in meaning in the years since the war. Secondary school students in a group visiting the Musée départemental de la Résistance et de la déportation (Departmental Museum of the Resistance and Deportation) in Toulouse were seen chattering with one another as they arrived, happy to be away from school for part of the day. They were introduced to Robert Carrière, an escapee from the death camps. His story of death and dehumanization and of his own escape left "a leaden silence." The students respectfully thanked him as he explained that he had recently decided to tell his story because soon there would be no one left alive to recall the camps.[1] People are influenced by what they see as tourists, as the many accounts from Hitler in Paris to the students in Toulouse attest. The experiences of these secondary school students and other war tourists, however, come with a long history, whose context must be understood if we are to more fully understand Second World War tourism in France, as elsewhere.

Tourism and the War in France Revisited

The interconnections between tourism as the expression of aesthetic curiosity in France extend back to the first wanderers who visited Lascaux and other caves, through the printing of Estienne's sixteenth-century *Guide,* to the emergence of France as a tourism icon during the Belle Époque, when Paris became, again to quote Walter Benjamin, "the capital of the nineteenth century." The Belle Époque tourism model in France was democratized *entre les guerres,* or between the wars, with the Popular Front's legislating paid holidays and the expansion of vacation colonies, even if more in the tourism imaginaries, expressed in the Touring club de France's publications, than in actual travel. By the interwar years France had come to be seen as a land of charm, romance, and good food, as represented in Sieburg's *Gott in Frankreich.* The *Guides bleus* and Michelin guidebooks, among others, solidified tourism imaginaries of France both inside and outside the country.

As the war unfolded, the tourism motifs surrounding the events in Compiègne and along the Maginot Line in 1940 and after, and in Normandy and Paris in 1944 and after, shifted in response to the changing military situation. Paradigm shifts following the war are evident in the emergence of the 1944 Normandy landing beaches as a major tourism attraction and the Paris itineraries that included sites of Resistance activity in the city and the narrative of the failure to destroy it during the German retreat in August 1944.

Museums and monuments related to General de Gaulle, General Leclerc, and Jean Moulin, among others, exemplified Free French and Resistance sites, which coexisted, sometimes uneasily, with the communist narratives at Mont-Valérien, while the Mémorial de la Shoah and Rivesaltes became pilgrimage sites related to the Holocaust. On the other side, Vichy continues to struggle with how to incorporate its wartime role into its tourism itineraries, and Pétainist groups work to establish tourism sites with narratives reflecting their perspectives on the Second World War.

The tourism that occurred during the war in France included both French and Germans. There were reports of those who looked upon even the May–June 1940 flight of thousands of French seeking to escape the invading German forces as something of an impromptu camping trip. Tourism by the French in their occupied country included those who took vacations in areas not closed off by the Germans and those who followed the tips of publications such as the weekly *Paris Programmes,* and articles such as "Où aller en vacances?" (Where to Go on Vacation?), which stimulated tourism imaginaries and behavior. French tourism officials and promoters hoped and planned for better days, which indeed materialized in the years that followed the end of the war. The Vichy government's promotion of regional tourism in support of its "return to the soil" policies and its regulations organizing France's tourism infrastructure in 1942 and 1943 exemplified the continuing interest in and practice of tourism during the war, as of course did German tourism in occupied France.

While the French struggled with wartime and occupation privation, the victorious Germans after 1940 continued to see France, and especially Paris, as a *lieu de tourisme,* if not *de mémoire,* as the extensive archives relating to their military presence there make clear. Hitler set the tone with his tour of Paris in June 1940. Thousands of German military and civilian personnel, described as "tourists in uniform," followed suit in occupied France, courtesy of the Wehrmacht and organizations such as "Jeder einmal in Paris," guided by the *Wegleiter,* among others. Not only did tourism function as a means to normalize war and as an expression of German tourism imaginaries about France. It was used also in attempts to foster the self-identification of the Germans as a superior *Kulturvolk.* Germans who toured occupied France and then wrote about how their experiences had given them all the greater an appreciation of their homeland illustrate how the tourism imaginary may work in two directions, focusing not only on the sites to be visited but also on the self-image of the tourist during sightseeing travel and subsequently back at home afterward, in other words, the emitting culture as well as the receivers of tourism.

The departure of the Germans in 1944 occasioned both continuities and changes. Sites such as the Eiffel Tower, Champs-Élysées, and Côte d'Azur retained their prewar and wartime allure, entrancing the many young Americans, British, Canadians, Australians, and New Zealanders who first saw France as soldiers in uniform, as had so many Germans in 1940. After 1945, however, with the Allied victory, the replacement of the German by the Gaullist model also produced a refashioning of tourist sites. Arromanches-les-Bains in Normandy shifted from a spa town to a site of memory and saw its economic base change as a result of a new narrative in battlefield tourism. Strasbourg, the symbol for both Hitler in 1940 and the Free French thereafter, acquired a new meaning too, touted as one of the capital cities of a united Europe. Changes in the tourism iconography of Compiègne, the Maginot Line fortresses, and Vichy have been mentioned, as have the significant shifts in both the tourist imagery and economics in Lower Normandy.

By the early twenty-first century, southern France drew more than half its income from the holiday trade.[2] France, according to UNWTO (United Nations World Tourism Organization) statistics, was the most visited country in the world, and Americans alone accounted for more than 4 million nights at hotels in Paris in 2007, according to the French Direction du tourisme office.[3] As we move deeper into the twenty-first century, the sites connected to the Second World War increasingly assume their historicity in the long line of France's wars and war-related tourist culture and continue to form a significant part of the French tourism economy.

In their article, cited in this book's first chapter, addressing the transformation of memory into a tourist itinerary in Normandy and Lorraine, in which they wrote, "Until now, one spoke not of tourism, only of memory," Pierre Gastineau and Romain Rosso noted that monuments to the dead, battlefields, and other war-related sites had attracted tourists for a long time. Local governments, however, were now taking over the histories of their regions and putting together équipements de mémoire (memory facilities) reaching out to a larger public. The Caen Mémorial, they added, had 372,000 visitors in 2009. Tourism, they maintained, had never done so well as now.[4] Joseph Zimet, the adjunct director of the Direction de la mémoire, du patrimoine et des archives at the Ministry of Defense (DMPA), was quoted as saying, "We are seeing with the multiplication of these facilities a phenomenon of 'historicization' of memory, which marks a progress of knowledge to the detriment of [recalled] traditions."[5] Today the First World War Douaumont ossuary speaks to the Pétain of that war but is also likely to evoke in the visitor's mind his role during the Second World War. Latter-day supporters of the lost cause in that war have turned places related to Pétain, such as his office in Vichy, into sites of pilgrimage and tourist curiosity.

In addition to the role of tourism and its relationships to politics and culture during wartime, the preservation, restoration, and memorialization of wartime sites following the conflict speak eloquently not only to their signification but to larger issues of meanings given to the war in its entirety. Jean-Pierre Bady emphasized tourism as one of the most important reasons for the designation of historical monuments. The point of creating monuments was that they might be visited, and Bady urged that the French monuments be made as accessible as possible to tourists.[6] Many of the kinds of physical mementos, such as books, reproductions, maps, and artwork that, in the words of Jennifer Craik, help "translate" or give meaning to a site, were made available at places such as the Maginot Line forts.[7]

The configuration and reconfiguration of war-related tourist sites in France has formed a continual process of "revisionism," subject to contested political interpretation, reflecting the continually shifting retrospective views of the war itself.[8] Although distinctions have been made between cultural tourism, defined as the specific orientation toward interest in history and "tradition," including the picturesque and "local color," on the one hand, and pilgrimages, on the other, it is not always easy to separate the presumably sincere religious "pilgrim" from the more casual "tourist," whether among those participating in medieval religious treks to Canterbury and Santiago de Compostela or among visitors to the more recent shrines depicted in the film *Schindler's List*.[9] Indeed, a certain presumptuousness is involved in making such post facto evaluations of visitors to any site.

Creating Sites: Heritage and Tourism

Sites are "marked," or designated, as Dean MacCannell suggested, and often acquire a sacred quality, forming part of a pilgrimage route, sometimes called "heritage," or in French *patrimoine*, which David Lowenthal defined as "the chief focus of patriotism and a prime lure of tourism."[10] As Chris Rojek and John Urry noted, understanding "how people come to know and experience 'their culture' is an obviously huge and daunting issue."[11] Many factors contribute to the formation of tourist sites, including culture, politics, religion, and commerce, and these are often linked together in the creation of the sites.[12] The reasons for visiting wartime monuments may range from religious sentiments of devotion to "morbid curiosity."[13]

Debates in France over the construction of tourist sites with regard to the Second World War have often taken place in the context of disputes over the meaning of and control over France's heritage.[14] Since the war, groups contesting the significance of France's heritage and attempting to build competing configurations of identity through the use of sites of memory have included Gaullist and communist Resistance veterans, Jewish and other victims of Nazi and Vichy persecution in France, as well as Vichyites, Pétainists, and pro-German collaborators of varying political tendencies. Tourist symbols and circuits help form political culture and play important roles in the ways in which history is remembered in different nations.[15] The work of Serge Barcellini and Annette Wieviorka, previously mentioned, and other recent studies have addressed the cultural significance of war memorials and monuments in fashioning memory.

Within the context of a growing attention to what is sometimes called "niche tourism," historians have addressed heritage tourism, thanatourism—literally tourism of death—or "dark" tourism, related to death and sometimes war, battlefield tourism, and other variations of this theme. Although thanatourism and war tourism may overlap, not all war tourism is by any means a tourism of death. Thanatourism might apply to Mont-Valérien, as well as battlefields and concentration camps, but not necessarily to all sites related to General de Gaulle or, for that matter, Marshal Pétain. It also implies an awareness of the motives of the visitor, and this, as has been mentioned, is often multiple and at best difficult to discern. In addition, French vacationers in rural pensions and German personnel enjoying tours around Paris and the French countryside during the Occupation cannot be linked to any form of "dark" tourism. The same might be said of war veterans returning to the battlefields where they fought, often perceived as scenes of their youth, a happy time of camaraderie. How one classifies the tourism imaginaries and experiences depends in part on the mentality of the tourist, which is again often difficult if not impossible to ascertain. There is, however, a thanatourism linked to death, atrocity, or disaster, with visits to battlefields, cemeteries, and memorials, or notably to the Holocaust, specifically referred to as "Holocaust tourism."[16] Describing "dark tourism," Peter Tarlow writes: "Europe may be a model for dark tourism. It is a continent filled with bloody wars, and celebrations of the dead in pantheons and cathedrals. Death dominates much of European tourism, from visits to the graves of poets and kings, to the mass graves of soldiers who died in Europe's many wars."[17]

The kind of tourism described by Tarlow raises questions of how the sites are to be presented as well as the fact that not all tourism to wartime sites necessarily commemorates death. When the Wolf's Lair, then on the Second World War eastern front, and now in Poland, was converted into a theme resort, with staff members dressing in Wehrmacht and Luftwaffe uniforms, and nightly dancing at "Hitler's Bunker Disco," *New York Times* columnist Gary Krist wrote that "history is being reshaped into a tourist attraction," and added that unfortunately nothing in the past was too tragic, appalling, or shameful "to escape the ingenuity of the tourism industry."[18] Krist also criticized American moves to create a "Gone with the Wind Country" theme park in Georgia, transforming a society based on slavery into an amusement center, and the Walt Disney Company's move to create a "Civil War Experience" near Manassas, Virginia, where 4,200 soldiers were killed. He asked, "Can we really learn anything from history when its most sobering lessons are defanged and turned into vacation amusements?," concluding, "And how do I explain to my 2-year-old daughter the difference between the Third Reich and the Magic Kingdom?"[19]

Thanatourism, heritage, and *patrimoine* necessarily refer to postwar tourism at wartime sites, and while it may be debated whether there are more death sites in Europe than in other parts of the world, these terms do not fit much of the tourism during wartime, while the battles were actually occurring. In the case of Second World War France, people often think of sites such as the Moulin Rouge and Maxim's restaurant in Paris, both open during the Occupation, or the large hotels in the Alps and beach resorts near Nice, many of which also remained open during the war years, although the Moulin Rouge and Maxim's were hardly heritage or "dark" sites. As Wiebke Kolbe notes in her study of postwar German battlefield tourism, distinctions among pilgrimages, battlefield tourism, and tourism in general are difficult, if not impossible, to draw as reactions of visitors to *lieux de mémoire* vary. The same visitor to a battlefield or war cemetery might also visit other nearby sites.[20]

The expressions by the various personalities involved in the liberation of Paris in August 1944 all spoke to the continuing centrality of Paris in French life. French and foreign tourists were expected to feel the weight of "eternal France" in their visits to its capital. How this was expressed differed in the construction of sites of memory and, consequently, tourism circuits by various groups emerging from the war, including the differing Gaullist and communist narratives of the Resistance, which often focused on victims of German and Vichy rule, and the sites specific to anti-Semitism and the Holocaust. Sites created in the immediate aftermath of the war, such as those honoring de Gaulle, Jean Moulin, and the communists, before the reconciliation with the new Federal Republic of Germany, were often celebrated with admonitions against future German aggression.

In France, the opening of a military cemetery in the northern town of Fromelles in July 2010 for British and Australian soldiers who died in the First World War was a step in what Gastineau and Rosso described in a 2011 *L'Express* magazine article as

> transforming the work of memory into a military-touristic journey. Monuments to the dead, fortifications, battlefields, and other places have for a long time attracted numbers of visitors. But until now, one spoke not of tourism but only of memory. Today, a change is in process led in particular by territorial administrations who take over the history of their territories, in the model of Normandy—the Caen Memorial welcomed 372,000 visitors in 2009—or of Lorraine, who have been pioneers in this endeavor. Communes, departments, regions, and even [private] associations are developing "memory facilities" destined for a large public. "This is memorial fever!" a specialist charged.[21]

A Boom in War Memory Tourism

In 2011 wartime tourism was booming, as Gastineau and Rosso noted. Giant interactive screens had been set up at Valmy, recalling the battle that helped save the Republic during the French revolutionary wars; construction had begun on a new museum commemorating the First World War at Meaux; and the Memorial to the Fighting France of the Second World War at Mont-Valérien was inaugurating its two interpretive pavilions along with a permanent exposition dedicated to the Resistance prisoners who had been executed there. The posts at which prisoners had been executed were also being restored. Transformation of the Rivesaltes and Les Milles concentration camps into sites of memory contributed to the increase in wartime tourism.

New technology and multimedia were to help tell the stories of these sites without boring the public. A brochure titled "Le tourisme de mémoire," produced in April 2011 by the DMPA, addressed a partnering of the Defense Ministry with the Secrétariat d'état in charge of commerce, artisan affairs, small business and consumer affairs, tourism, and liberal professions at what it termed the first "Assises du tourisme" (Tourism Roundtable) to promote a tourism *du sens* (of meaning). As an example of using the latest technology to promote such tourism, the ministry noted a smartphone application developed in coordination with the Conseil général de la Meuse that would help guide visitors through the most salient sites of the Battle of Verdun.[22]

Memory tourism, the brochure continued, played an important role in the development of societies and territories for two fundamental reasons:

- Because it enables a better understanding of the past, it contributes to the formation of citizen awareness;
- Because it sparks tourist flows, it contributes to the economic and cultural vitality of the territories.[23]

On its web page titled "Tourisme et mémoire," in July 2012 the Defense Ministry noted that memory tourism had the support of a large public and the notion of shared memory was developing in other countries as well. The web page continued:

> The Defense Ministry assures the management and promotion of many sites. An incontestable actor in memory tourism, it is, with many partners (territorial bodies, museums, nations sharing a common memory with France) the bearer of the politics of memory. The sites of memory today are places of exchanges but also of reflection upon history. Since 2004, the Internet site "Chemins de mémoire" [Paths of Memory] invites the public to begin the discovery of a very large diversity by means of an interactive map and detailed historical notes.[24]

By 2015, the website had added an online atlas of cemeteries related to France's civil and military heritage.[25] Continuing struggles over Rivesaltes, Keroman, the Maginot fortresses, Oradour, and other sites show not only the multiplicity of voices contending for influence over time but also the powerful hold of the Second World War on the imagination in France and among visiting tourists.[26]

Holocaust sites in France also draw an international tourism clientele, for example, as part of a course titled "Representations of the Holocaust in French Film and Literature" offered at Penn State University. In this class, first offered in 2007, twelve undergraduate students, alumni, and faculty traveled to France, where they visited the site of a concentration camp near Paris and met with survivors. During a walking tour of Paris, they visited the Mémorial de la Shoah and the Monument to the Deportation, in addition to touring the Marais, the old Jewish neighborhood in Paris.[27]

As tourist sites, *lieux de mémoire* related to the traumatic effects of war and genocide may bring a heightened awareness to visitors, often schoolchildren, but may also become banal products, to use Debord's term, of commercialization and kitsch. Addressing Holocaust tourism to Kraków-Kazimierz, the

former Jewish district in Cracow, in terms also applicable to France, G. J. Ashworth writes that the popularity of Steven Spielberg's 1993 movie *Schindler's
List*, which was filmed in Kazimierz, contributed to an expansion of tourism
to Cracow and the nearby Auschwitz camp, combined into the "Auschwitzland" package.[28] Similarly, the role of tourism in regard to the preservation
and restoration of the Auschwitz camp continues to be manifested in films
such as *Am Ende kommen Touristen* (At the End Come Tourists) in 2007 and
books such as the *Guide historique d'Auschwitz* (Historical Guide to Auschwitz), published in France in 2011. Both the film, which also appeared in a
French version, and the book speak as well to an interest in Holocaust tourism in France. Filmed on location at Auschwitz, *Am Ende kommen Touristen*
tells the story of a young man from Berlin who is posted to a youth camp
near the former concentration camp. There he learns about its history from a
survivor and a young woman guide. The film was shown at the 2007 Cannes
Film Festival and won the prize for best fiction film at the Pessac Historical
Film Festival.[29]

The Auschwitz historical guidebook, published by Autrement in France in
2011, has been described by Bruno Modica, for La Cliothèque, an Internet
service largely for French secondary school instructors, as a "tourist guide,
illustrated richly with itineraries that can be adjusted according to the time
available to the visitors."[30] Organized as a tourist guidebook, the *Guide historique* indicates the highlights of the visit and offers directions for accessing
them. Specific mention was made of photographs exhibited there that had
been colorized, thus, in the opinion of the authors, "trivializing" the death
camps.[31] Nonetheless, Modica emphasized the utility of the guidebook for
teachers taking groups of students to tour Auschwitz or, for those unable to
afford the trip, as a kind of virtual visit to the camp.[32] The discussion of Auschwitz highlights the development of war tourism with its ethical dilemmas in
general but relates to France in that the organization of the tourist trips there
involved French *lycées* and their instructors, serving as a reminder that tourism
studies includes the emitting as well as the receiving destinations. Some of the
growth in war memory tourism had been foreseen long before. In her *New York
Times* article covering the expansion of tourism for the fiftieth anniversary of
the Allied landings in Normandy in 1994, Mary Blume cited Philip Johnstone,
a World War I poet envisioning subsequent tourism to High Wood, site of a
three-month battle in 1916.[33] The full poem, composed in 1918, is as follows:

Ladies and gentlemen, this is High Wood,
Called by the French, Bois des Fourneaux,
The famous spot which in Nineteen-Sixteen,

July, August and September was the scene
Of long and bitterly contested strife,
By reason of its High commanding site.
Observe the effect of shell-fire in the trees
Standing and fallen; here is wire; this trench
For months inhabited, twelve times changed hands;
(They soon fall in), used later as a grave.
It has been said on good authority
That in the fighting for this patch of wood
Were killed somewhere above eight thousand men,
Of whom the greater part were buried here,
This mound on which you stand being . . .
Madame, please,
You are requested kindly not to touch
Or take away the Company's property
As souvenirs; you'll find we have on sale
A large variety, all guaranteed.
As I was saying, all is as it was,
This is an unknown British officer,
The tunic having lately rotted off.
Please follow me—this way . . .
the path, sir, please
The ground which was secured at great expense
The Company keeps absolutely untouched,
And in that dug-out (genuine) we provide
Refreshments at a reasonable rate.
You are requested not to leave about
Paper, or ginger-beer bottles, or orange-peel,
There are waste-paper-baskets at the gate.[34]

Because of its role in history, Auschwitz might represent a more widely publicized discussion over issues of remembrance and tourism, but they arose in France as well. The courtroom trials of Nazis and their collaborators themselves became tourism sites for curious onlookers, as in the highly publicized trial of Klaus Barbie in Lyon in 1987, when additional seating was added to the Rhône Cour d'assises to allow for more spectators.[35] Indeed, Lyon city officials welcomed the trial as a means of publicizing their city with gastronomic guides and touring kits but were disappointed when most of the foreign journalists left after Barbie ceased to appear at the trial during its first week.[36]

The Lyon Palais de Justice, scene of the trial, became part of the war-remembrance tourism circuit. Marcel Ophuls's film *Hôtel Terminus*, about the building that housed the wartime Gestapo offices in Lyon, helped put it on the tourist map, as witnessed in Claude Lanzmann's sarcastic comment, quoted earlier.[37] The École du Service de Santé Militaire, Gestapo headquarters from March 1943 until the Liberation, had been converted into a natural history museum after the war. In 1965 a museum dedicated to the Resistance in Lyon had been created by a private association in another part of the city. Publicity around the events leading up to the Barbie trial led to a move to turn the private museum into a public institution, with the result that in 1985 the private organization was made public, and in 1992 it moved into the former Gestapo headquarters.[38] From its opening in 1992 through 1996, 230,000 visitors registered at Lyon's Centre d'histoire de la Résistance et de la déportation (CHRD, Center for the History of the Resistance and Deportation), at least half of them "young," many having been brought on school excursions.[39] It was the shock of the Barbie trial, the first in France for Nazis charged with crimes against humanity, that had led to the creation of the CHRD. The historian Laurent Douzou wrote that a municipal museum such as the CHRD would never have been established in Lyon in the 1960s, when the political mood was to forget the war years. "Today, the bridge between all this past and the present has been established."[40] In another gesture stimulated by the legacy of the Barbie trial, President Mitterrand also participated in the inauguration in 1994 of a museum-memorial at Izieu, where forty-four Jewish pupils and their teachers had been rounded up by Barbie on 6 April 1944 for ultimate deportation to Auschwitz.[41]

In France itself, problems arose when efforts to retain what were considered proper aesthetic standards for public monuments came into conflict with the interests of the tourist trade. In one compromise in 1948, to meet the advertising needs of local tourist interests, the Education Ministry, under whose jurisdiction the erection of commemorative monuments fell, proposed a law authorizing local prefects to allow tourist advertisements to be posted at classified sites. Commercial signs indicating the directions to various tourist attractions could thereby be displayed at the monuments.[42]

The relationships among tourism, memory, and the war, involving politics and the establishment of heritage, or, in the French case, *patrimoine*, with its legal definitions, together with the economic interests of those who stand to gain from war-related tourism, including hawkers of souvenirs at Auschwitz and elsewhere, illustrate the complexities in the creation of tourism imaginaries and behavior. Many of the narratives changed after the 1940–1944 years, and in many ways, French wartime tourist imaginaries have become international. References to "the potted guide one might buy at the entrance to any of the Second World War museums that dot the Normandy region" and Friedhelm Boll's critique of Normandy war tourist sites suggest parallel discussions regarding the tensions between heritage and kitsch surrounding French wartime sites as well.[43]

The confluence of memory and tourism has led to many questions of pedagogy and propriety, some involved in the discussions of thanatourism at Auschwitz and elsewhere. To Gastineau and Ross, the key issue was being faithful to the complexities of history without boring the public. Marianne Petit, director of the Rivesaltes project, argued for a multidisciplinary approach with conferences, lectures, and film. Dance could be used to open discussion of historical issues. "People don't want a history course," she added.[44]

The Rivesaltes project is but one example of the continuing impact of Second World War tourism in France. It is one way of remembering and understanding, in a certain sense, humanizing the war. The tourist imaginary or the tourist gaze, the expression of curiosity, helps impart meaning to war for both victors and vanquished, whether for the soldier from afar, the local civilian watching events unfold, the pilgrim, or merely the curious traveler to a site of memory. This is not to argue that people go to war to extend tourism, although the phrase "join the army and see the world" has appeared at times in history.[45] Not surprisingly, France, a country that inspired the tourist imaginary long before the Second World War and has continued to do so since, did so during the war as well, which itself became an object of the postwar tourist gaze often referenced today as memory. German soldiers toured occupied France, as did their Allied successors following the Liberation. Places related to battles, concentration camps, and larger-than-life figures such as General de Gaulle became tourism sites for cultural and economic reasons, manifestly clear at the time and later.

Looking to the Future

The future of Second World War tourism in France remains, of course, to be seen. On the one hand, Resistance organizations' efforts to block retrospective tours of sites related to the Pétain government in the city of Vichy may help perpetuate their obscurity until they pass into the dimmer recesses of history's lost causes. On the other hand, the curiosity that Eric Conan found among the tourists to the wartime sites in Vichy, even if primarily among visiting Germans and Americans, might force or otherwise nudge the various French authorities into opening more tourist circuits relating to the "other side" in the Second World War.[46] The tourism industry with its commercial interests reflects an evolving cultural aesthetic and may play a role should demand be perceived as sufficient. Arguments for this are already evident in the topology of the Vichy tourist circuit today. Resistance sites also shift in their meanings and tourism potential. As cultural values change over time, so do historical sites such as Mont-Valérien and Rivesaltes, despite the best efforts to keep some of them preserved, as Sarah Farmer's study of the Oradour ruins shows.[47] With Vichy and the collaboration as well as the Gaullist and communist Resistance becoming more historical, or perhaps historicized, future generations are likely to be curious about them. Their evolving views of the wartime tourist circuit will help determine where and how the different sides will be understood.

While the future will most likely see France's Second World War tourist sites integrated into the long list of France's war and military *lieux de mémoire*, which will continue to attract tourist curiosity as do the sites related to the Roman occupation, the Hundred Years' War, and Joan of Arc, as well as the more recent conflicts in which France was engaged, specific changes in French tourism may be explained as resulting from the Second World War. During the 1950s, nonprofit vacation villages were organized by *comités d'entreprise* (work councils), which had been created under Vichy, in collaboration with labor unions. The Villages vacances familiales program established rural villages where families could vacation together, an idea that came out of the war years.[48] From 1945 to 1955, French soldiers occupied parts of Germany and Austria. With roles reversed, the French authorities began the work of collaboration with a new German leadership, encouraging reciprocal Franco-German exchanges that helped set the stage for the European Union. Although the French soldiers were on a military mission, as had been the German soldiers with their cameras in France noted by Shirer in 1940, tourism was not far removed from their preoccupations, as evidenced in the French Foreign Ministry archives in Colmar.[49] The tourist activities of the French soldiers stationed in Germany, however, remain to be examined.[50]

Appendix

References and Sites

1952: Institut National de la Statistique et des Études Économiques, Ministère des Finances et des Affaires Économiques, *Annuaire Statistique de la France 1952* (Paris: Imprimerie Nationale and Presses Universitaires de France, 1953), n.s., 1, table 17, p. 206.

1957: Institut National de la Statistique et des Études Économiques, Ministère des Finances et des Affaires Économiques, *Annuaire Statistique de la France 1957* (Paris: Imprimerie Nationale and Presses Universitaires de France, 1958), n.s., 6, table 12, p. 250.

1960: Institut National de la Statistique et des Études Économiques, Ministère des Finances et des Affaires Économiques, *Annuaire Statistique de la France 1962* (Paris: Imprimerie Nationale and Presses Universitaires de France, 1962), pp. 291–92.

1966: Institut National de la Statistique et des Études Économiques, Ministère des Finances et des Affaires Économiques, *Annuaire Statistique de la France 1967, Résultats de 1965 et de 1966*, vol. 73, n.s., 15 (Paris: Imprimerie Nationale and Presses Universitaires de France, 1967), pp. 560–61.

1970: République Française, Ministère de l'Économie, *Annuaire Statistique de la France 1972*, vol. 77, n.s., 19 (Paris: Imprimerie Nationale and Presses Universitaires de France, 1972), results for 1970, pp. 442–43.

1977: République Française, Ministère de l'Économie, *Annuaire Statistique de la France 1978* (Paris: Ministère de l'Économie/INSEE, 1978), pp. 472–73, table 13: Entrées payantes dans quelques musées nationaux, p. 472, and table 14: Entrées payantes dans les principaux monuments et musées (autre que musées nationaux), p. 473. The two tables are combined.

1996: "Pastoral du tourisme et Rapport ONT, La frequentation des lieux culturels et non culturels en France métropolitaine en 1991 et 1996, mars 1998 (plus de 20 000 visiteurs annuels)," in Claude Origet du Cluzeau, *Le tourisme culturel/Que sais-je?* (1998; Paris: Presses Universitaires de France, 2000), p. 33, paid entrances.

1997: "Memento du Tourisme," 2005 ed., "Les 22 sites culturels payants les plus fréquents," p. 67, http://www.insee.fr/fr/ppp/sommaire/FRATOUR05.PDF (accessed 26 July 2016).

2002: "Memento du Tourisme," 2005 ed., "Les 22 sites culturels payants les plus fréquents," p. 67, http://www.insee.fr/fr/ppp/sommaire/FRATOUR05.PDF (accessed 26 July 2016).

2007: "Memento du Tourisme," 2009 ed., "Sites Culturels," http://archives.entreprises.gouv.fr/2012/www.tourisme.gouv.fr/stat_etudes/memento/memento_2009.html (accessed 26 July 2016).

2014: "Memento du Tourisme," 2015 ed., (top 30), "Sites Culturels." http://www.entreprises.gouv.fr/etudes-et-statistiques/memento-du-tourisme-edition-2015 (accessed 26 July 2016).

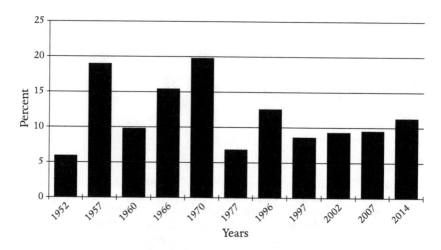

FIGURE A1. War sites as percentages of the most visited sites in France in the listings at five-year intervals, or as close as possible, from the first publication of the official *Annuaire statistique de la France* in 1952 through 2014. The methods of collecting these figures varied over time, and changes in the tabulation methods between 1972 and 1994 resulted in the failure to count the tourism destinations in much of the 1980s and 1990s. (See my article "The Evolving Popularity of Tourist Sites in France: What Can Be Learned from French Statistical Publications?," *Journal of Tourism History* 3, no. 2 (August 2011): 99–100.) Nevertheless, the proportions give an approximate sense of the ups and downs of the relative interest in tourism to war sites in France.

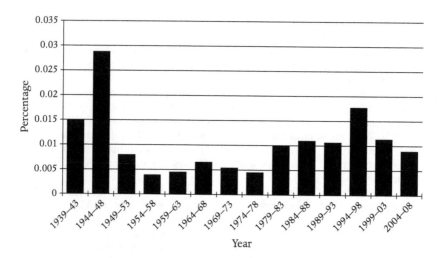

FIGURE A2. World War II entries by percent in French published bibliographical listings (*Biblio, Bibliographie de la France,* and *Bibliographie nationale française* for five-year periods from 1939 through 2008. The numbers in both figures A1 and A2 tend to be higher in the years closer to the war, with an increase possibly reflecting renewed discussion of the Occupation years with the trials in the 1990s, though it should be noted that the figures for both charts reflect all war references, not only those relating to the Second World War.

Notes

Preface

1. Bertram M. Gordon, *Collaborationism in France during the Second World War* (Ithaca: Cornell University Press, 1980).
2. Robert Tombs, "The Dark Years," *Times Literary Supplement*, 28 January 1994, p. 9.
3. Bertram M. Gordon, "Touring the Field: The Infrastructure of Tourism History Scholarship," *Journal of Tourism History* 7, no. 1–2 (September 2015): 135–56.

Introduction

1. William L. Shirer, *Berlin Diary: The Journal of a Foreign Correspondent, 1934–1941* (New York: Alfred A. Knopf, 1941), p. 413.
2. Pierre Audiat, *Paris pendant la guerre* (Paris: Hachette, 1946), pp. 240–41.
3. P. Bouis, "Le bureau de renseignements de l'hôtellerie: Plus de 500.000 Parisiens ont déjà été aiguillés vers d'agréables 'séjours de remplacement,'" *Paris-Midi*, 29 August 1942, Archives nationales, Paris (hereafter AN), AJ/40/784, folder 4.
4. Author's interview with Frédéric Sommier, director of the Musée du débarquement, Arromanches les Bains, 18 May 2009.
5. Jean Plumyène and Raymond Lasierra, *Les fascismes français, 1923–1963* (Paris: Seuil, 1963), p. 9. The historical context of my own study of the Second World War and France is told in my chapter "The Other Side: Investigating the Collaborationists in World War II France," in *Ego-histories of France and the Second World War: Writing Vichy*, ed. Manu Braganca and Fransiska Louwagie (Basingstoke, U.K.: Palgrave Macmillan, 2018), pp. 219–41.
6. Bertram M. Gordon, *Collaborationism in France during the Second World War* (Ithaca: Cornell University Press, 1980). See also Bertram M. Gordon, ed., *Historical Dictionary of World War II France: The Occupation, Vichy, and the Resistance, 1938–1946* (Westport, Conn.: Greenwood Press, 1998).
7. My two interviews of Marc Augier took place on 4 July 1974 and 19 July 1976 in Paris. His discussion of the periodicals for which he wrote in the 1930s occurred during the latter interview.
8. See Marc Augier, *Les jeunes devant l'aventure européene* (Paris: Les Conférences du Groupe "Collaboration," 1941), p. 20.
9. Ibid., p. 24.

10. For the analogy with the more recent French magazines, see Laurent Lamire, ed., *Où sortir à Paris? Le guide du soldat allemand, 1940–1944* (Paris: Alma, 2013), p. 9.

11. My original research was the basis for two journal articles, Bertram M. Gordon, "Ist Gott Französisch? Germans, Tourism, and Occupied France, 1940–1944," *Modern and Contemporary France*, n.s., 4, no. 3 (1996): 287–98; and "Warfare and Tourism: Paris in World War II," *Annals of Tourism Research* 25, no. 3 (July 1998): 616–38, and a book chapter, "French Cultural Tourism and the Vichy Problem," in *Being Elsewhere: Tourism, Consumer Culture, and Identity in Modern Europe and North America,* ed. Shelley Baranowski and Ellen Furlough (Ann Arbor: University of Michigan Press, 2001), pp. 239–72.

12. Examples for France include Louis-Michel Jocard, *Le tourisme et l'action de l'état* (Paris: Berger Levrault, 1966); Marc Boyer, *Le tourisme* (1972; Paris: Seuil, 1982); André Rauch, *Vacances en France de 1830 à nos jours* (Paris: Hachette, 1996); and Catherine Bertho Lavenir, *La roue et le stylo: Comment nous sommes devenus touristes* (Paris: Odile Jacob, 1999). All are excellent studies of tourism but all pass over the war years.

13. Bertram M. Gordon, "World War II," in *France and the Americas: Culture, History, Politics,* ed. Bill Marshall, vol. 3 (Santa Barbara: ABC-Clio Press, 2005), pp. 1229–33.

14. Julian Jackson, *France: The Dark Years, 1940–1944* (Oxford: Oxford University Press, 2001), pp. 131–32.

15. Susan K. Foley, *Women in France since 1789* (Houndsmill: Palgrave Macmillan, 2004), p. 214.

16. Jackson, *France: The Dark Years,* p. 150.

17. Shannon L. Fogg, *The Politics of Everyday Life in Vichy France: Foreigners, Undesirables, and Strangers* (Cambridge: Cambridge University Press, 2009), 4. See also Sarah Fishman, *The Battle for Children: World War II, Youth Crime, and Juvenile Justice in Twentieth-Century France* (Cambridge: Harvard University Press, 2002), p. 54.

18. Fogg, *The Politics of Everyday Life in Vichy France,* 5–6. In the Loiret, for example, the Services du contrôle mobile du ravitaillement général, the French agency that checked local food supplies, reported in 1942 that almost 30 percent of the potato crop was sold on the black market. "Note sur la répression du marché noir," annex 2, attached to "Rapport sur la possibilité d'augmenter la commercialisation des produits agricoles," to Directeur Régional de la Production Agricole, Clermont-Ferrand, 19 January 1942, AN, F^{10} 2184, folder: Commercialisation des Produits Agricoles.

19. "Bulletin d'Information," no. 83, 3 July 1941, pp. 3–5, AN, F/60/1012. The use of private automobiles was allowed at night in the event of alerts, in which case they were to be used to reach shelters and with their headlights camouflaged. See Police Report, 28 October 1940, Archives de la Préfecture de Police, Paris, APP-220-W-1.

20. Rosemary Wakeman, *The Heroic City: Paris, 1945–1958* (Chicago: University of Chicago Press, 2009), p. 22.

21. A formative history of Vichy France, arguing that collaboration with the Germans had been far more extensive than recalled in the immediate postwar government narratives, is Robert O. Paxton, *Vichy France: Old Guard and New Order, 1940–1944* (New York: Alfred A. Knopf, 1972).

22. Referenced from Jean-Didier Urbain, *Sur la plage* (Paris: Petit Bibliothèque Payot, 1996), cited in Jean-Michel Hoerner and Catherine Sicart, *The Science of Tourism: An Anglo-French Précis on Tourismology* (Baixas: Balzac, 2003), p. 17. The quotation

is originally from Hippolyte Taine, *Voyage aux Pyrénées* (Paris: Hachette, 1872). See "Homo turisticus selon Taine," *Revue de géographie alpine* 79, no. 4 (1991): 40.

23. Noel B. Salazar, "Tourism Imaginaries: A Conceptual Approach," *Annals of Tourism Research* 39, no. 2 (2012): 865.

24. For an earlier foray into this subject, specific to the Germans in occupied Paris, see my article "Warfare and Tourism.

25. Hannah Arendt, *Eichmann in Jerusalem: A Report on the Banality of Evil* (1963; New York: Penguin Books, 1977), p. 252. See also Christopher R. Browning, *Ordinary Men: Reserve Police Battalion 101 and the Final Solution in Poland* (New York: Harper-Collins, 1992), pp. 159–63 and 188–89; and Daniel Jonah Goldhagen, *Hitler's Willing Executioners: Ordinary Germans and the Holocaust* (New York: Alfred A. Knopf, 1996), pp. 100–101, 248–50, 395, and 401–2.

26. Arendt, *Eichmann in Jerusalem*, p. 276.

27. ww2museums.com, STIWOT (Stichting Informatie Wereldoorlog Twee), http://www.ww2museums.com/article/62/Mus%E9e-M%E9morial-de-la-Bataille-de-Normandie.htm (accessed 17 July 2010 and 7 January 2016).

28. Guy Debord, *Society of the Spectacle* (first published in French in 1967), trans. Fredy Perlman et al. (Detroit: Black and Red, 1977), thesis 168; reproduced in https://www.marxists.org/reference/archive/debord/society.htm (accessed 3 February 2017).

29. Dean MacCannell, "Sights and Spectacles," in *Iconicity: Essays on the Nature of Culture, Festschrift for Thomas A. Sebeok on his 65th Birthday*, ed. Paul Bouissac, Michael Herzfeld, and Roland Posner (Tübingen: Stauffenberg Verlag, 1986), p. 424.

30. John Urry, *The Tourist Gaze: Leisure and Travel in Contemporary Societies* (1990; London: Sage, 2000), p. 3.

31. Richard Butler and Geoffrey Wall, "Introduction: Themes in Research on the Evolution of Tourism," *Annals of Tourism Research* 12, no. 3 (1985): 292–93.

32. See my article "Touring the Field: The Infrastructure of Tourism History Scholarship," *Journal of Tourism History* 7, no. 1–2 (September 2015): 135–56.

33. For Germany, see Hasso Spode, *Wie die Deutschen "Reiseweltmeister" wurden: Eine Einführung in die Tourismusgeschichte* (Erfurt: Landeszentrale für politische Bildung Thüringen, 2003).

34. Quoted in Boyer, *Le tourisme*, p. 8.

35. The UN Statistical Commission endorsed the UNWTO's definition in 1993 following an international government conference held in Ottawa, Canada, in 1991. See "An Introduction to Tourism," http://tourism.emu.edu.tr/tyt/concordances/bot/ (accessed 16 July 2008).

36. Theodor Adorno, *The Culture Industry: Selected Essays on Mass Culture*, ed. with intro. by J. M. Bernstein (1991; London: Routledge, 2001), p. 189.

37. For the "tourist gaze," see Urry, *The Tourist Gaze*, pp. 1–2; also Carol Crawshaw and John Urry, "Tourism and the Photographic Eye," in *Touring Cultures: Transformations of Travel and Theory*, ed. Chris Rojek and John Urry (London: Routledge, 1997), p. 176.

38. Rachid Amirou, *L'imaginaire touristique* (1995; Paris: CNRS Éditions, 2012), 25–26. Unless otherwise noted, all translations are my own.

39. Salazar, "Tourism Imaginaries," p. 866.

40. Morris Bishop, *Petrarch and His World* (Bloomington: Indiana University Press, 1963), p. 92.

41. Mike Robinson, foreword to *Niche Tourism: Contemporary Issues, Trends and Cases,* ed. Marina Novelli (Amsterdam: Elsevier, 2005), p. xix.

42. An example of the academic focus on tourist imaginaries was an international conference, Imaginaires Touristiques / Tourist Imaginaries, organized in February 2011 by the Tourism Studies Working Group (TSWG) of the University of California, Berkeley; the Interdisciplinary Group of Tourism Studies (EIREST); and the Institute of Advanced Studies and Research on Tourism (IREST) of the University of Paris 1 Pantheon-Sorbonne, in Berkeley, California. For a more recent study addressing this subject, see Noel B. Salazar and Nelson Graburn, eds., *Tourism Imaginaries: Anthropological Approaches* (New York: Berghahn Books, 2014).

43. Daniel C. Knudsen, Michelle M. Metro-Roland, and Jillian M. Rickly, "Tourism, Aesthetics, and Touristic Judgment," *Tourism Review International* 19, no. 4 (2015): 186.

44. Alexander Gottlieb Baumgarten, *Theoretische Ästhetik: Die grundlegenden Abschnitte aus der Aesthetica* (1750–1758), trans. and ed. Hans Rudolf Schweizer (Hamburg: Meiner, 1988). See also *Oxford English Dictionary* (hereafter *OED*), vol. 1 (Oxford: Clarendon Press, 1989), p. 206.

45. The term "landscapes" appears in English in 1598 and again in 1661. "Tour" shows up in 1643 and 1652, and "romantic" in 1659. "Picturesque" appears in 1703, with its cognates *pittoresco* in Italian in 1708 and *pittoresquement* in French in 1732. In 1780 the word "tourist" appeared in English and in 1816 *touriste* in French. See *OED* and *Trésor de la langue française* (Paris: Éditions du Centre national de la recherche scientifique, 1971–), passim.

46. Maurice Merleau-Ponty, "Eye and Mind," in *Art and Its Significance: An Anthology of Aesthetic Theory,* ed. Stephen David Ross (Albany: State University of New York Press, 1984), p. 304.

47. Hannah Arendt, intro. to Walter Benjamin, *Illuminations,* trans. Harry Zohn (New York: Schocken Books, 1969), p. 21; and Alexander Gelley, "Contexts of the Aesthetic in Walter Benjamin," *MLN (Modern Language Notes)* 114, no. 5, Comparative Literature Issue (December 1999): 952.

48. Susan Buck-Morss, *The Dialectics of Seeing: Walter Benjamin and the Arcades Project* (Cambridge: MIT Press, 1991), pp. 27 and 304.

49. Kevin Meethan, *Tourism in Global Society: Place, Culture, Consumption* (Houndmills: Palgrave, 2001), p. 81.

50. Alain de Botton, *The Art of Travel* (New York: Vintage International, 2002), p. 242. See also Cain Samuel Todd, "Nature, Beauty and Tourism," in *Philosophical Issues in Tourism,* ed. John Tribe (Bristol: Channel View Publications, 2009), pp. 167–68.

51. For paradigms and tourism, see Alexandre Panosso Netto, "What Is Tourism? Definitions, Theoretical Phrases and Principles," and Maureen Ayikoru, "Epistemology, Ontology and Tourism," in Tribe, *Philosophical Issues in Tourism,* pp. 46–48 and 65–66, respectively.

52. For UNESCO, see "World Heritage List," United Nations Educational, Scientific and Cultural Organization, http://whc.unesco.org/en/list/&order=year (accessed 22 July 2016).

53. For a good summary of some of the discussion around the issue of memory, see Elizabeth Karlsgodt, "Recycling French Heroes: The Destruction of Bronze Statues under the Vichy Regime," *French Historical Studies* 29, no. 1 (Winter 2006): 145–46. An account of an unauthorized use of the term *lieux de mémoire* in Italy is offered in Nicolas Weill, "Démarquage sauvage des 'Lieux de mémoire' en Italie," books section, *Le Monde*, January 3, 1997.

54. Hue-Tam Ho Tai, "Remembered Realms: Pierre Nora and French National Memory," *American Historical Review* 106, no. 3 (June 2001), http://www.historyco operative.org/journals/ahr/106.3/ah000906.ht (accessed 10 September 2008).

55. Rachid Amirou, *Imaginaire du tourisme culturel* (Paris: Presses Universitaires de France, 2000), p. 7. The CNMHS recorded more than 9 million paid entrances to these monuments in 1998; see Jean François Grunfeld, *Tourisme culturel: Acteurs et actions* (Paris: Association Française d'Action Artistique/Ministre des Affaires Étrangères, 1999), p. 32.

56. For discussion of the memory of the war years in France, see Henry Rousso, *The Vichy Syndrome: History and Memory in France since 1944*, trans. Arthur Goldhammer (Cambridge: Harvard University Press, 1991); Eric Conan and Henry Rousso, *Vichy: An Ever-Present Past*, trans. Nathan Bracher (Hanover: University Press of New England, 1998); and my article "The 'Vichy Syndrome' Problem in History," *French Historical Studies* 19, no. 2 (Fall 1995): 495–518. See also Susan Rubin Suleiman, *Crises of Memory and the Second World War* (Cambridge: Harvard University Press, 2006), for a study extended beyond the French experience.

57. See Robert Tombs, "The Dark Years," *Times Literary Supplement*, 28 January 1994, p. 9. For the debates about Vichy, especially in the 1980s and 1990s, see my chapter "World War II France Half a Century After: In Historical Perspective," in *Fascism's Return: Scandal, Revision, and Ideology*, ed. Richard J. Golsan (Lincoln: University of Nebraska Press, 1998), pp. 152–81. For the background leading to the Papon trial, see my chapter "Afterward: Who Are The Guilty and Should They Be Tried?" in *Memory, the Holocaust, and French Justice*, ed. Richard J. Golsan (Hanover: University Press of New England, 1996), pp. 179–98.

58. Tombs, "The Dark Years," p. 9.

59. Serge Barcellini and Annette Wieviorka, *Passant, souviens-toi: Les lieux du souvenir de la Seconde Guerre mondiale en France* (Paris: Plon, 1995), pp. 7–8. Alain Carteret would later make a similar point that the city of Vichy's wartime role was of more interest to journalists than to their readers. See Alain Carteret, *Vichy charme* (Olliergues: Éditions de la Montmarie, 2006), p. 68, cited in "Patrimoine Vichy," http://pagesperso-orange.fr/carteret/Patrimoine%20Vichy.htm (accessed 7 October 2009).

60. Olivier Wieviorka, *La mémoire désunie: Le souvenir politique des années sombres, de la Libération à nos jours* (Paris: Seuil, 2010), pp. 16–17.

61. Josette Mesplier-Pinet, "Culture et patrimoine aujourd'hui, peuvent-ils contribuer au développement touristique?" in Université Montesquieu–Bordeaux IV, I.U.T. Périgueux–Bordeaux IV, *Patrimoine et tourisme* (Bordeaux: Presses Universitaires de Bordeaux, 2009), pp. 12–13. See also Marc Chesnel, *Le tourisme culturel de type urbain: Aménagement et stratégies de mise en valeur* (2001; Paris: L'Harmattan, 2009), p. 8.

62. For an exception, see my essay "French Cultural Tourism and the Vichy Problem."

63. The archives were opened officially by a decree of 24 December 2015. See "Les archives de la Seconde Guerre mondiale sont désormais toutes ouvertes," Archives nationales, Fontainebleau–Paris–Pierrefitte-sur-Seine, http://www.archives-nationales. culture.gouv.fr/web/guest/archives-de-la-seconde-guerre-mondiale (accessed 1 January 2017).

64. "French Public Get Access to Archives of WWII Regime," New York Times, 29 December 2015, http://www.nytimes.com/aponline/2015/12/29/world/europe/ ap-eu-france-vichy-documents.html (accessed 8 January 2016).

65. For Oradour, see the work of Sarah Bennett Farmer, "Oradour-sur-Glane: Memory in a Preserved Landscape," French Historical Studies 19, no. 1 (Spring 1995): 27–48, and her more extensive study Martyred Village: Commemorating the 1944 Massacre at Oradour-sur-Glane (Berkeley: University of California Press, 1999). For the Mémorial–Musée de la Paix opened in 1988 in Caen, as well as the Mémorial de Verdun, erected in 1967, and the Péronne Historial de la Grande Guerre, which opened in 1992, see Daniel J. Sherman, "Objects of Memory: History and Narrative in French War Museums," French Historical Studies 19, no. 1 (Spring 1995): 50.

66. Jean-Louis Panicacci, L'occupation italienne, Sud-Est de la France, juin 1940–septembre 1943 (Rennes: Presses Universitaires de Rennes, 2010), pp. 58–59.

67. Ibid., p. 249.

68. See Nelson Graburn, "Tourism: The Sacred Journey," in Hosts and Guests: The Anthropology of Tourism, ed. Valene Smith (Philadelphia: University of Pennsylvania Press, 1977), pp. 17–31. In contrast, for the expression of concern that installations at trauma tourism sites might spill over into kitsch, see also Laurie Beth Clark, "Ethical Spaces: Ethics and Propriety in Trauma Tourism," in Death Tourism: Disaster Sites as Recreational Landscape, ed. Brigitte Sion (London: Seagull Books, 2014), p. 24.

69. Geoffrey M. White and Eveline Buchheim, "Introduction: Traveling War—Memory Practices in Motion," History and Memory 27, no. 2, ed. Geoffrey M. White and Eveline Buchheim (Fall–Winter 2015): 7 and 13.

70. Lionel Casson, Travel in the Ancient World (1974; Baltimore: Johns Hopkins University Press, 1994), pp. 235–36. See also Maxine Feifer, Tourism in History: From Imperial Rome to the Present (New York: Stein and Day, 1985), p. 21.

71. See Joyce Marcel, "Death Makes a Holiday," The American Reporter 9, no. 2114 (29 May 2003), cited in Peter E. Tarlow, "Dark Tourism: The Appealing 'Dark' Side of Tourism and More," in Niche Tourism, ed. Marina Novelli (Amsterdam: Elsevier, 2005), p. 48.

1. The Emergence of France as a Tourist Icon in the Belle Époque

1. As Alan Williams points out in his Republic of Images: A History of French Filmmaking (Cambridge: Harvard University Press, 1992), p. 32, the Belle Époque was less belle for workers, peasants, and servants than for the upper social strata.

2. Walter Benjamin, "Paris: Capital of the Nineteenth Century," Perspecta 12 (1969): 163–72.

3. For the Chauvet cave, see Jean Clottes, "Chauvet Cave: France's Magical Ice Age Art," National Geographic (August 2001), http://ngm.nationalgeographic.com/ ngm/data/2001/08/01/html/ft_20010801.6.html; and for Lascaux, see Marlise Simons, "Fungus Once Again Threatens French Cave Paintings," New York Times,

9 December 2007, http://www.nytimes.com/2007/12/09/world/europe/09cave.
html?_r=1&ref=world&oref=slogin (accessed 9 December 2007).

4. Norbert Ohler, *The Medieval Traveller,* trans. Caroline Hiller (Woodbridge,
Suffolk: Boydell Press, 1989), pp. 108 and 221–22.

5. Noël Coulet, intro. to Société des historiens médiévistes de l'enseignement
supérieur public, *Voyages et voyageurs au Moyen Âge* (Paris: Publications de la Sor-
bonne, 1996), pp. 25–26.

6. Jean Bonnerot, *La guide des chemins de France de 1553 par Charles Estienne,* vol. 1
(Paris: Librairie Ancienne Honoré Champion, 1936), p. 59.

7. Ibid., pp. 79–80.

8. "Le Musée Jeanne d'Arc ferme à Rouen," *La Croix,* 27 October 2012, http://
www.la-croix.com/Culture/Actualite/Le-musee-Jeanne-d-Arc-ferme-a-Rouen-
_NG_-2012-10-27–869504 (accessed 8 November 2015); and Historial Jeanne d'Arc,
http://www.historial-jeannedarc.fr/en (accessed 8 November 2015).

9. "L'historial Jeanne d'Arc à Rouen ouvert au public samedi," Culturebox/
Francetvinfo, 21 March 2015, http://culturebox.francetvinfo.fr/expositions/patri
moine/lhistorial-jeanne-darc-a-rouen-ouvert-au-public-samedi-214541 (accessed 8
November 2015).

10. "L'épopée de Jeanne d'Arc," Historial Jeanne d'Arc, http://www.historial-
jeannedarc.fr/fr/qu-est-ce-que-l-historial (accessed 21 December 2015).

11. "Le Centre historique médiéval d'Azincourt," www.France-Insolite.fr,
http://www.france-insolite.fr/le-centre-historique-medieval-d-azincourt-a123.html
(accessed 5 January 2010).

12. Cl. Couillez-Brouet, "La fréquentation du Centre historique médiéval
d'Azincourt stable avec 35 000 visites en 2008," *La Voix du Nord,* Saint Pol sur Ter-
noise, Presse regionale, 10 January 2009, http://www.lavoixdunord.fr/Locales/
Saint_Pol_sur_Ternoise/actualite/Saint_Pol_sur_Ternoise/2009/01/10/
article_la-frequentation-du-centre-historique-me.shtml (accessed 5 January 2010).

13. Thibault Camus, "French Host Reenactment of 1415 Battle of Agincourt,"
Associated Press, 25 July 2015, http://www.nytimes.com/aponline/2015/07/25/
world/europe/ap-eu-france-britain-battle-of-agincourt.html (accessed 26 July 2015).

14. Antoni Maczak, *Travel in Early Modern Europe* (Cambridge: Polity Press,
1995), p. 25; and Marc Boyer, "Les séries des guides imprimés portatifs, de Charles
Étienne aux XIXe et XXe siècles," in *Les guides imprimés du XVIe au XXe siècle: Villes,
paysages, voyages.* ed. Gilles Chabaud et al. (Paris: Belin, 2000), p. 339; also Marc
Boyer, *L'invention du tourisme* (Paris: Découvertes Gallimard/Art de Vivre, 1996),
pp. 16–17.

15. Bonnerot, *La guide des Chemins de France de 1553 par Charles Estienne,* 1:11–19.
The *Guide* fell out of use after 1707 with the publication of the *Listes générales des
postes* and the organization of postal service with coaches. Only in the middle of the
nineteenth century did interest in the Estienne book revive as interest in the old and
often lost routes grew in France. See ibid., p. 19.

16. For Calais and Champagne, see ibid., pp. 25 and 51, respectively.

17. Marc Boyer, *Histoire générale du tourisme, du XVIe au XXIe siècle* (Paris:
L'Harmattan, 2005), p. 18.

18. Michel de Montaigne, *Travel Journal* (1580–1581), trans. Donald M. Frame
(San Francisco: North Point Press, 1983).

19. Paul Gerbod, *Voyager en Europe (du Moyen Âge au IIIe millénaire)* (Paris: L'Harmattan, 2002), p. 22.

20. Russell Goulbourne, "Mail in the Time of Madame de Sevigne," email to H-NET French History discussion group, h-france@lists.uakron.edu," 15 February 2002. See also Gerbod, *Voyager en Europe*, pp. 22–23.

21. Boyer, *L'invention du tourisme*, p. 20.

22. The term Grand Tour first appeared in travel literature in Richard Lassels, *The voyage of Italy, or, A compleat journey through Italy in two parts,* in 1670, although it had probably been in use for some time before then. In Lassels's words, "No man vnderstands *Livy* and *Caesar, Guicciardini* and *Monluc,* like him, *who* hath made exactly the *Grand Tour* of France, and the *Giro of Italy.*" Richard Lassels, *The voyage of Italy, or, A compleat journey through Italy in two parts: with the characters of the people, and the description of the chief towns, churches, monasteries, tombs, libraries, pallaces, villas, gardens, pictures, statues, and antiquities: as also of the interest, government, riches, force, &c. of all the princes: with instructions concerning travel* (Newly printed at Paris: [s.n.], and are to be sold in London, by John Starkey, 1670), http://quod.lib.umich.edu/e/eebo/A49620.0001.001/1:5?rgn=div1;view=fulltext (accessed 24 July 2015).

23. Le sieur Berthod, *Paris burlesque* (Paris: Veuve Loyson, 1652), title page.

24. Ueli Gyr, "The History of Tourism: Structures on the Path to Modernity," EGO European History Online, http://www.ieg-ego.eu/en/threads/europe-on-the-road/the-history-of-tourism/ueli-gyr-the-history-of-tourism (accessed 20 September 2015).

25. Bertram M. Gordon, "Reinventions of a Spa Town: The Unique Case of Vichy," *Journal of Tourism History* 4, no. 1 (April 2012): 39. For spas, see also Boyer, *L'invention du tourisme*, p. 25; and Boyer, *Histoire générale du tourisme*, pp. 34–36 and 57–66. For the difficulties accessing and climbing mountains prior to the development of alpinism (mountain climbing) in the nineteenth century, see Boyer, *Histoire générale du tourisme*, pp. 119–61.

26. Quoted in Boyer, *Histoire générale du tourisme*, p. 31. See also Thomas Parker, *Tasting French Terroir: The History of an Idea* (Oakland: University of California Press, 2015), p. 91.

27. "Fortifications of Vauban," UNESCO World Heritage Centre, World Heritage List, http://whc.unesco.org/en/list/1283 (accessed 4 December 2012 and 10 November 2015).

28. "History of the Louvre, from Château to Museum," http://www.louvre.fr/en/history-louvre (accessed 28 September 2015).

29. "Les sites touristiques en France: Les 30 sites culturels les plus fréquentés (entrées totales)," in Ministère de l'économie de l'industrie et du numérique, *Memento du tourisme*, 2015 ed. (Ivry-sur-Seine: Direction Générale des Entreprises, 2015), p. 132.

30. Jan Mieszkowski, "War, with Popcorn," *Chronicle of Higher Education*, 18 July 2014, http://chronicle.com/blogs/conversation/2014/07/18/watching-war/?cid=wb&utm_source=wb&utm (accessed 9 November 2015).

31. Luke Reynolds, "Re: War as a Spectator Sport," H-War, 23 July 2014, https://networks.h-net.org/node/12840/discussions/35614/war-spectator-sport#reply-35826 (accessed 24 July 2014).

32. Trésor de la langue française, http://atilf.atilf.fr/dendien/scripts/tlfiv5/advanced.exe?8;s=401128260 (accessed 20 December 2015).

33. André Rauch, *Vacances en France de 1830 à nos jours* (Paris: Hachette, 1996), p. 20. See also my article "The Mediterranean as a Tourist Destination, from Classical Antiquity to Club Med," *Mediterranean Studies* 12 (2003): 207 and 209.

34. H. Hazel Hahn, *Scenes of Parisian Modernity: Culture and Consumption in the Nineteenth Century* (New York: Palgrave Macmillan, 2009), pp. 46–47.

35. "La Grande ville, nouveau tableau de Paris, comique, critique, et philosophique (Paris: Publications Nouvelles 1842–1843)," cited in Hahn, *Scenes of Parisian Modernity*, p. 51.

36. Julia Csergo, "Extension et mutation du loisir citadin: Paris XIXe siècle–début XXe siècle," in *L'avènement des loisirs, 1850–1960,* ed. Alain Corbin (Paris: Aubier, 1995), p. 143.

37. Alan Williams, *Republic of Images: A History of French Filmmaking* (Cambridge: Harvard University Press, 1992), p. 32. The Châtelet Theater, near the Seine, has been used over the years for dramatic and musical performances.

38. Eva Barlösius, "France," in *The Cambridge World History of Food,* ed. Kenneth F. Kiple and Kriemhild Coneè Ornelas, vol. 2 (Cambridge: Cambridge University Press, 2000), p. 1213. See also Jean-Robert Pitte, "Naissance et expansion des restaurants," in *Histoire de l'alimentation,* ed. Jean-Louis Flandrin and Massimo Montanari (Paris: Fayard, 1996), p. 771. Rebecca L. Spang, *The Invention of the Restaurant: Paris and Modern Gastronomic Culture* (Cambridge: Harvard University Press, 2000), holds that the often repeated claim that the first restaurant opened was that of a Monsieur Boulanger in Paris in 1765 is a myth not supported by French archival documents. For the controversy that ensued, see Edward Rothstein, "Shelf Life: Dine Like Rabelais (Till the Bill Comes)," *New York Times,* 7 October 2000. See also Thomas B. Preston, "French Cooks and Cooking," *Chautauquan* 25 (1897): 34.

39. The range of Paris restaurants in the early nineteenth century is surveyed by Jean-Paul Aron, *The Art of Eating in France* (first published in French in 1973), trans. Nina Rootes (London: Peter Owen, 1975). For the restaurant as a marker of social prestige, see Christian Drummer, "Das sich ausbreitende Restaurant in deutschen Großstädten als Ausdruck bürgerlichen Repräsentationsstrebens 1870–1930," in *Essen und kulturelle Identität: Europäische Perspektiven,* ed. Hans-Jürgen Teuteberg, Gerhard Neumann, and Alois Wierlacher (Berlin: Akademie Verlag, 1997), p. 319.

40. Amy B. Trubek, *Haute Cuisine: How the French Invented the Culinary Profession* (Philadelphia: University of Pennsylvania Press, 2000), p. 46.

41. Eric Hobsbawm, *The Invention of Tradition* (Cambridge: Cambridge University Press, 1983).

42. Catherine Bertho-Lavenir, *La roue et le stylo: Comment nous sommes devenus touristes* (Paris: Odile Jacob, 1999), p. 233 and n. 15.

43. Félix Urbain-Dubois, *La cuisine de tous les pays* (1856; Paris: Flammarion, 1926).

44. Bertram M. Gordon, "Going Abroad to Taste: North Americans, France and the Continental Tour from the Late Nineteenth Century to the Present," *Proceedings of the Western Society for French History; Selected Papers of the Annual Meeting* (Greeley, Colo.: University Press of Colorado, 1998), p. 166.

45. Thomas B. Preston, "French Cooks and Cooking," *Chautauquan* 25 (1897): 32–33.

46. *Paris Pages/Paris Train Stations,* http://www.paris.org:80/Gares/ (accessed 17 January 2002).

47. "French Home Life, No. IV. Food," *Blackwood's Edinburgh Magazine* 111, no. 626 (February 1872): 128.

48. Bertram M. Gordon, "El turismo de masas: Un concepto problématico en la historia del siglo XX," *Turismo y nueva sociedad: Historia contemporánea* 25 (2002): 129.

49. See Jean-Robert Pitte, "Naissance et expansion des restaurants," in Flandrin and Montanari, *Histoire de l'alimentation,* pp. 774–75.

50. Rauch, *Vacances en France de 1830 à nos jours,* p. 46.

51. "The Man in Seat 61 . . . The Truth behind the Legend . . . The Orient Express," http://www.seat61.com/OrientExpress.htm#.VgzWDb4mTww (accessed 30 September 2015).

52. *Les guides bleus Paris* (Paris: Hachette, 1937), pp. xc–xci. The 1856 Congress of Paris fashioned the peace settlement that followed the Crimean War.

53. Ibid., p. xcii.

54. See Pitte, "Naissance et expansion des restaurants," pp. 774–75.

55. Eugen Weber, *Peasants into Frenchmen: The Modernization of Rural France, 1870–1914* (Stanford: Stanford University Press, 1976), p. 210. See also Annie Moulin, *Peasantry and Society in France since 1789,* trans. M. C. and M. F. Cleary (Cambridge: Cambridge University Press, and Paris: Éditions de la Maison des Sciences de l'Homme, 1991), pp. 116–18.

56. Harvey Levenstein, *Seductive Journey: American Tourists in France from Jefferson to the Jazz Age* (Chicago: University of Chicago Press, 1998), p. 125.

57. Marcel Aymard, "Toward the History of Nutrition: Some Methodological Remarks," in *Food and Drink in History,* ed. Robert Forster and Orest Ranum (Baltimore: Johns Hopkins University Press, 1979), pp. 5–6.

58. For a measure of French cultural iconicity in the American popular press, see my article "The Decline of a Cultural Icon: France in American Perspective," *French Historical Studies* 22, no. 4 (Fall 1999): 629–30.

59. Dean MacCannell, *The Tourist: A New Theory of the Leisure Class* (New York: Schocken Books, 1976), p. 43.

60. Alden Hatch, *American Express: A Century of Service* (Garden City, N.Y.: Doubleday, 1950), pp. 109–10, quoted in MacCannell, *The Tourist,* pp. 59 and 194.

61. See the series of paintings of the Normandy beaches by Eugène Boudin, 1863–1865.

62. Gordon, "The Decline of a Cultural Icon," p. 632.

63. See Andrea Loselle, *History's Double: Cultural Tourism in Twentieth-Century French Writing* (New York: St. Martin's Press, 1997), pp. 14 and 33.

64. Minnie Buchanan Goodman, "Americans on the Eiffel Tower," *Harper's Weekly* 34 (1 November 1890): 851.

65. Gordon, "The Decline of a Cultural Icon," p. 650.

66. Anne Jeanblanc, "Tourisme: Gare au "syndrome du voyageur; Des émotions intenses ressenties à l'étranger peuvent entraîner des troubles psychosomatiques, voire psychiatriques, parfois sévères," *Le Point,* 25 December 2012, http://www.lepoint.fr/chroniqueurs-du-point/anne-jeanblanc/tourisme-gare-au-syndrome-du-voyageur-25-12-2012-1605895_57.php?xtor=EPR-6-[Newsletter-Quotidienne]-20121226 (accessed 26 December 2012). For the original Stendhal syndrome, see Stendhal, *Naples and Florence: A Journey from Milan to Reggio* (1817). Both Stendhal's passion for Florence and its antiquities and the Stendhal syndrome are addressed by Graziella Magherini, *La sindrome di Stendhal* (Florence: Ponte Alle Grazie, 1989).

67. Lecture by Annie Cohen-Solal, France-Amérique Conference, Institute for Cultural Diplomacy, Paris, 21 June 2002.

68. Nancy Mowll Mathews, *Mary Cassatt: A Life* (New York: Villard Books, 1994), p. 11.

69. Marc Francon, "L'univers touristique Michelin," in Chabaud et al., *Les guides imprimés du XVIe au XXe siècle*, p. 114.

70. Cédric Gruat, *Hitler à Paris juin 1940* (Paris: Éditions Tirésias, 2010), p. 113.

71. These and other films are documented in the IMDb, http://www.imdb.com.

72. For a fuller discussion, see my paper "'La Grande France': The Rise and Decline of a Filmic Icon," presented to the Western Society for French History, Los Angeles, 11 November 2000.

73. IMDb, http://www.imdb.com/title/tt0225802/ (accessed 30 September 2015).

74. For the Château fort, see http://www.tourisme-sedan.fr/chateau-fort-de-sedan/sedan/tabid/38983/offreid/906195e1-8f9f-40ff-afa8-293023533162/detail. aspx. The mural depicting the 1870 battle may be seen on the website http://www. cheminsdememoire.gouv.fr/en/sedan-0. (Both accessed 31 March 2018).

75. "Les guides des champs de bataille 1914–1918 de Michelin," *14–18 Mission centenaire, en France, République française;* http://centenaire.org/fr/en-france/les-guides-des-champs-de-bataille-1914-1918-de-michelin (accessed 25 November 2015). See also Sandie Holguín, "'National Spain Invites You': Battlefield Tourism during the Spanish Civil War," *American Historical Review* 110, no. 5 (December 2005): 1403.

76. "L'œuvre du souvenir des défenseurs de Verdun: Ossuaire de Douaumont," in *Les batailles de Verdun (1914–1918)* (Clermont-Ferrand: Michelin, 1921), p. 1; see also p. 77.

77. Ibid., p. 129.

78. *Compiègne Pierrefonds: Un guide, un panaroma, une histoire* (Clermont-Ferrand: Michelin, 1921), pp. 3–5.

79. Béatrice Pujebet, "Mémoire: Un parcours sur les champs de bataille à découvrir en famille; Somme: L'histoire sur le terrain," *Le Figaro*, 11 November 2001.

80. See Friedhelm Boll, "'Vous n'avez pas honte de venire ici?' Widerpsrüche in der Erinnerungskultur der Normandie," in *Médiation et conviction: Mélanges offerts à Michel Grunewald*, ed. Pierre Béhar, Françoise Lartillot, and Uwe Puschner (Paris: L'Harmattan, 2007), pp. 139–40.

81. "Les premiers sites touristiques fréquentés de Picardie, Palmarès 2008," Picardie Comité régional du tourisme, la salle de presse des professionels du tourisme en Picardie, http://www.picardietourisme-presse.com/var/picardie/storage/original/application/2980724eb6a52386a6680f417320b796.pdf (accessed 7 January 2010). This source is otherwise unidentified but appears to be a compilation by the regional tourism office.

82. Camille Dicrescenzo, "Péronne (80): L'Historial bat son record de fréquentation," *Franceinfo 3 Picardie*, 15 December 2014, updated 27 July 2017, http://france3-regions.francetvinfo.fr/picardie/aisne/peronne-80-l-historial-bat-son-record-de-frequentation-613510.html (accessed 31 March 2018).

83. "Fréquentation exceptionnelle du musée en 2014," Le portail la Seine et Marne, http://www.la-seine-et-marne.com/actualites/frequentation-exceptionnelle-du-musee-en-2014/ (accessed 22 December 2015).

84. "La première pierre du musée de la Grande Guerre à Meaux," Ministry of Culture and Communication website, 19 April 2010, http://www.culture.gouv.fr/mcc/Actualites/A-la-une/La-premiere-pierre-du-musee-de-la-Grande-Guerre-a-Meaux (accessed 16 June 2011). See also Pierre Gastineau, "Meaux-Péronne: La bataille,"

L'Express 3084 (11 August 2010): 14 (my thanks to Kathy Dodge for finding this reference); Pierre Gastineau and Romain Rosso, "La mémoire de nos terres," *L'Express* 3084 (11 August 2010): 14–15; and Edward Rothstein, "Bringing the War Home," *New York Times,* 11 November 2011, http://www.nytimes.com/2011/11/12/arts/design/museum-of-the-great-war-opens-in-meaux-france.html?scp=2&sq=edward+rothstein&st=nyt (accessed 25 December 2011).

85. Dicrescenzo, "Péronne (80): L'Historial bat son record de fréquentation."

86. Arthur Joseph Norval, *The Tourist Industry. A National and International Survey* (London: Sir Isaac Pitman and Sons, 1936), p. 279.

87. Rauch, *Vacances en France de 1830 à nos jours,* p. 85.

88. Ibid., pp. 82–83 and 86–88.

89. Florence Deprest, *Enquête sur le tourisme de masse: L'écologie face au territoire* (Paris: Belin, 1997), p. 13.

90. *Quand viendras-tu en Italie* (Milan: Ministero per la Stampa e la Propaganda, Direzione Generale per il Turismo, ENIT, Ferrovie dello Stato, 1936), unpaginated.

91. Shelley Baranowski, "Strength through Joy: Tourism and National Integration in the Third Reich," in *Being Elsewhere: Tourism, Consumer Culture, and Identity in Modern Europe and North America,* ed. Shelley Baranowski and Ellen Furlough (Ann Arbor: University of Michigan Press, 2001), p. 216. See also Shelley Baranowski, "Radical Nationalism in an International Context: Strength through Joy and the Paradoxes of Nazi Tourism," in *Histories of Tourism: Representation, Identity and Conflict,* ed. John K. Walton (Clevedon: Channel View Publications, 2005), pp. 127–28.

92. The story of SITA, the Student International Travel Association, begun in the 1930s, is told in Helen Dengler, *Travels with Bicycle and Accordion* (Baltimore: Gateway, 1997).

93. Alfred Sauvy, with the help of Anita Hirsch, *Histoire économique de la France entre les deux guerres,* 3 vols. (Paris: Economica, 1984), 3:222.

94. Julian Jackson, *The Popular Front in France: Defending Democracy, 1934–38* (Cambridge: Cambridge University Press, 1988), p. 136. See also Alain Mesplier, *Le tourisme en France: Étude régional,* 2nd ed. (Montreuil: Bréal, 1986), pp. 41–43.

95. Bertram M. Gordon, "Colonies de Vacances," in *French Culture and Society: A Glossary,* ed. Michael Kelly (London: Arnold Publishers, 2001), p. 59. To guarantee the financial solvency of travel agents arranging the visits of tourists to the 1937 Paris Exposition, the French government began licensing them; see Robert Lanquar, *Agences et industrie du voyage: Que sais-je?* (Paris: Presses Universitaires de France, 1995), p. 8.

96. Michael Wala, "'Gegen eine Vereinzelung Deutschlands': Deutsche Kulturpolitik und akademischer Austausch mit den Vereinigten Staaten von Amerika in der Zwischenkriegszeit," in *Deutschland und die USA in der Internationalen Geschichte des 20 Jahrhunderts,* ed. Manfred Berg and Philipp Gassert, Transatlantische Historische Studien 19 (Wiesbaden: Franz Steiner Verlag, 2004), p. 313.

97. IMDb, http://www.imdb.com/title/tt0020129/?ref_=fn_al_tt_2. Another film with the same title was released in 1955; see http://www.imdb.com/title/tt0143549/ (both accessed 4 October 2015).

98. George Behrend, *Histoire des trains de luxe: De l'Orient-Express au Tee* (Fribourg: Office du Livre, 1977), pp. 88–90.

99. See Richard Aldrich, "Le guide de l'Exposition coloniale et l'idéologie colo-niale dans l'entre-deux-guerres," in Chabaud et. al., *Les guides imprimés du XVIe au XXe siècle*, pp. 607–8. For the promotion of colonial tourism in the 1930s, see Ossip Pernikoff, *La France, pays du tourisme* (Paris: Plon, 1938), pp. 657–58.

100. Claude Fischler, "La cuisine selon Michelin," in *Nourritures: Plaisirs et ango-isses de la fourchette*, Autrement Série Mutations 108 (Paris: Autremont Revue, 1989), p. 42. For the beginnings of a systematic study of food preferences as expressed in the *Guides Michelin*, see also Claude Fischler, *L'homnivore: Le goût, la cuisine et le corps* (Paris: Odile Jacob, 1990), pp. 243–44. Characteristic of the way in which the *Guides Michelin* have set the standard and the vocabulary in the Anglophone world are dis-cussions of chefs in terms of the three-star rating system; see, for example, Rudolph Chelminski, "A French Chef's Long, Hard Ascent to a Third Star," *Smithsonian*, 1 May 1992, p. 45.

101. Bertho-Lavenir, *La roue et la stylo*, p. 238. See also Stephen Mennell, *All Manners of Food: Eating and Taste in England and France from the Middle Ages to the Present* (1985; Urbana: University of Illinois Press, 1996), pp. 276–77.

102. Bertho-Lavenir, *La Roue et la stylo*, p. 237. See also Philip Whalen, "The Gas-tronomical Fair of Dijon: 'Food Palaces Built of Sausages [and] Great Ships of Lamb Chops,' " Coastal Carolina University, http://ww2.coastal.edu/pwhalen, 2006.

103. Rauch, *Vacances en France de 1830 à nos jours*, p. 91.

104. IMDb, http://www.imdb.com/title/tt0160636/ (accessed 3 October 2015).

105. Boyer, *L'invention du tourisme*, pp. 116–17. See also Sauvy, *Histoire économique de la France entre les deux guerres*, 3:222.

106. IMDb, http://www.imdb.com, passim.

107. IMDb, http://www.imdb.com/find?ref_=nv_sr_fn&q=follies+bergère&s=all.

108. IMDb, passim. *À propos de Nice* focuses on the bourgeois tourists in that city; see Williams, *Republic of Images*, p. 217.

109. For the comment about Stein, see Shari Benstock, *Women of the Left Bank: Paris, 1900–1940* (1986; Austin: University of Texas Press, 1988), p. 13. The years described by Hemingway were 1921 through 1926; see M. H., "Note," in Ernest Hemingway, *A Moveable Feast* (New York: Charles Scribner's Sons, 1964), unpaginated. Much of the life of this community was chronicled by the *New Yorker* columnist Janet Flanner; see Olivier Bernier, *Fireworks at Dusk: Paris in the Thirties* (Boston: Little, Brown and Co., 1993), pp. 39–41.

110. Brooke Lindy Blower, *Becoming Americans in Paris: Transatlantic Politics and Culture between the World Wars* (New York: Oxford University Press, 2011), p. 19.

111. Rauch, *Vacances en France de 1830 à nos jours*, pp. 80–81.

112. Boyer, *L'invention du tourisme*, pp. 118–19.

113. Frederic Spotts, *The Shameful Peace: How French Artists and Intellectuals Survived the Nazi Occupation* (New Haven: Yale University Press, 2009), p. 20.

114. MacCannell, *The Tourist*, p. 76.

115. Friedrich Sieburg, *Gott in Frankreich? Ein Versuch* (Frankfurt am Main: Societäts-Verlag, 1929), translated into French as *Dieu est-il français?* (Paris: Bernard Grasset, 1930), and into English as *Is God a Frenchman? or, The Gospel of St. Joan, by Friedrich Sieburg: A German Study of France in the Modern World*, by Alan Harris (Lon-don: Jonathan Cape, 1931).

116. Stéphane Baumont, "Fête nationale: Le dernier 14-Juillet?" *Le Monde,* 13 July 2001; and François Lenglet, "Dieu est-il français?" *La Tribune,* 15 May 2009, http://www.latribune.fr/opinions/20090515trib000376664/dieu-est-il-francais-.html (accessed 10 October 2015). In the latter instance, the author referred to the French economic model protecting the country from the severe unemployment experienced elsewhere in the 2008 economic downturn metaphorically as God being French.

117. Cecilia von Buddenbrock, *Friedrich Sieburg (1893–1964): Ein deutscher Journalist vor der Herausforderung eines Jahrhunderts* (Frankfurt: Societäts-Verlag, 2007), p. 58, a translation of Cecilia von Buddenbrock, *Friedrich Sieburg, 1893–1964: Un journaliste allemand à l'épreuve du siècle* (Paris: Éditions de Paris, 1999).

118. Geiger made his comments in an address on national stereotypes presented in Frankfurt at the Johann-Wolfgang-Goethe-Universität in 2000 that summarized his dissertation, written in 1996; see http://www.historia-interculturalis.de/histo ria_interculturalis/Fremde%20Nachbarn.htm (accessed 16 February 2014).

119. Julia S. Torrie, "'Our Rear Area Probably Lived Too Well': Tourism and the German Occupation of France, 1940–1944," *Journal of Tourism History* 3, no. 3 (November 2011): 316.

120. Friedrich Sieburg, *Geliebte Ferne* (Tübingen: Wunderlich, 1952), p. 14, cited in Monika Miehlnickel, *Feuilletonistische Sprache und Haltung bei Friedrich Sieburg und Sigismund von Radecki. Inaugural-S=Dissertation zur Erlangung des Doktorgrades der Philosophischen Fakultät der Freien Universität Berlin* (Berlin: Philosophischen Fakultät der Freien Universität Berlin, 1962), p. 7, n. 26. In a history of France published in 1960, he reiterated that his long relationship with France would have to suffice in place of scientific (*wissenschaftliche*) knowledge, "for which I do not raise the slightest claim." See Friedrich Sieburg, *Kleine Geschichte Frankreichs* (1953; Frankfurt am Main: Verlag Heinrich Scheffler, 1960), p. 191.

121. Gunther Nickel, "Sieburg, Friedrich Karl Maria," in *Neue deutsche Biographie,* ed. Otto zu Stolberg-Wernigerode, vol. 24 (Berlin: Schwarz-Stader, 2010), pp. 332–33, http://daten.digitale-sammlungen.de/~db/0008/bsb00085893/images/index.html?id=00085893&nativeno=332 and http://daten.digitale-sammlungen.de/~db/0008/bsb00085893/images/index.html?id=00085893&nativeno=333 (accessed 14 February 2014).

122. It was, according to von Buddenbrock, "the most important post that the largest newspaper in Germany had to offer." See von Buddenbrock, *Friedrich Sieburg (1893–1964),* p. 38.

123. Friedrich Sieburg, *Germany: My Country,* trans. Winifred Ray (London: Jonathan Cape, 1933). See also Margot Taureck, *Friedrich Sieburg in Frankreich: Seine literarisch-publizistichen Stellungnahmen zwischen den Weltkriegen in Vergleich mit Positionen Ernst Jüngers* (Heidelberg: Carl Winter–Universitätsverlag, 1987), pp. 70–72 and 99. "Es werde Deutschland" was published in French as *Défense du nationalisme allemand,* trans. Pierre Klossowski (Paris: Grasset, 1933). For a review in France of this book as "heavy and indigestible," in which the author posits a petit-bourgeois French penchant for owning landed property against a German "idealism," see *Crapouillot* (July 1933): 48–52, http://jfbradu.free.fr/crapouillot/p48-52.html (accessed 5 April 2014).

124. Friedrich Sieburg, *Visage de la France en Afrique,* translated from German by Mauritz Betz (Paris: Les Éditions de France, 1938), p. vi.

125. Fritz J. Raddatz, "Schreiben ist Leben," in *Friedrich Sieburg zur Literatur,* ed. Fritz J. Raddatz, vol. 1 (Stuttgart: Deutsche Verlags-Anstalt, 1981), p. 4.

126. Friedrich Sieburg, *Blick durchs Fenster: Aus zehn Jahren Frankreich und England* (Frankfurt: Societäts-Verlag, 1939), pp. 158–59.

127. In "Geflügelten Worten" (1864), Georg Büchmann references Zincgref-Weidners "Apophtegmata" of 1693, according to which Maximilian I stated, "Wenn es möglich wäre, dass ich Gott sein könnte und zwei Söhne hätte, so müsste mir der älteste nah mir und der andere König in Frankreich sein" (Were it possible that I might be God and have two sons, then I would want the elder close to me and the other King of France). Cited in "Paris Leben wie Gott Frankreich," Reise-Travel, http://reisetravel.eu/lifestyle/news/leben-wie-gott-frankreich/ (accessed 29 December 2010). See also "Suchergebnis für 'leben wie Gott in Frankreich,'" Redensarten-Index, http://www.redensarten-index.de/suche. php?suchbegriff=~~leben%20wie%20Gott%20in%20Frankreich&suchspalte[]=rart_ ou (accessed 26 March 2014). For variations of this expression, including its use in Yiddish, see Robert Michael, post to H-Judaic, 15 December 1999, http://h-net.msu.edu/ cgi-bin/logbrowse.pl?trx=vx&list=h-judaic&month=9912&week=c&msg=6auNrysl3 YBD1JcXY265IQ&user=&pw= (accessed 26 March 2014). The title *Heureux comme Dieu en France* was used for an account of Jewish narratives during the 1940–1944 Occupation by Gérard Israël, *Heureux comme Dieu en France, 1940–1944* (Paris: Laffont, 1975), and for a novel about a young communist *résistant* during the war by Marc Dugain, *Heureux comme Dieu en France* (Paris: Gallimard, 2002).

128. Taureck, *Friedrich Sieburg in Frankreich,* p. 119.

129. Friedrich Sieburg, *Dieu est-il français?,* trans. Mauritz Betz (Paris: Bernard Grasset, 1942), p. 15.

130. Ibid., p. 89.

131. Ibid. Over time the image of the Genesis story of the Tower of Babel has been used to explain the origin of the multiplicity of human languages. Whether Sieburg had in mind the Tower of Babel or the sexualized images of Babylon is unclear. There was a Babylonian tower temple north of the Marduk temple called Bab-ilu (Gate of God), according to the *Encyclopedia Britannica;* see http://www.britannica. com/topic/Tower-of-Babel (accessed 25 October 2015).

132. Sieburg, *Dieu est-il Français?* (1942), p. 89.

133. André Rousseaux, "Gott mit uns," *Le Figaro,* 27 November 1930; and Paul Distelbarth, *Lebendiges Frankreich* (Berlin: Rowohlt, 1936), p. 105, both cited in Taureck, *Friedrich Sieburg in Frankreich,* p. 115.

134. Charlotte Heymel, *Touristen an der Front: Das Kriegserlebnis 1914–1918 als Reiseerfahrung in zeitgenössischen Reiseberichten* (Münster: Lit Verlag, 2007), pp. 11–12.

135. Taureck, *Friedrich Sieburg in Frankreich,* pp. 99 and 121.

136. Rauch, *Vacances en France de 1830 à nos jours,* p. 59.

137. MacCannell, *The Tourist,* p. 43.

138. *Les guides bleus: France automobile en un volume* (Paris: Hachette, 1938), title page and pp. v–ix. For the history of the *Guides bleus,* which first appeared in conjunction with the British *Blue Guides* in 1918, see "History of the Blue Guides," http://www. blueguides.com/our-titles/history-of-the-blue-guides/ (accessed 11 October 2015).

139. *Les guides bleus,* title page and pp. xi–xxi.

140. Ibid., pp. 1–16.

141. Ibid., p. 16.

142. Raymond A. Jonas, "Sacred Tourism and Secular Pilgrimage: Montmartre and the Basilica of Sacré-Cœur," in *Montmartre and the Making of Mass Culture,* ed. Gabriel P. Weisberg (New Brunswick: Rutgers University Press, 2001), pp. 108–9.

143. "Babylone," in the Trésor de la langue française, http://atilf.atilf.fr/dendien/scripts/tlfiv5/advanced.exe?8;s=4077673380 (accessed October 25, 2015).

144. I am indebted for this reference to Robin Walz, of the University of Alaska Southeast, who responded to my query in "Rupert Christiansen's Paris Babylon," email to French History discussion group H-FRANCE@LISTS.UAKRON.EDU 25 February 2005. The back cover of Rupert Christiansen, *Paris Babylon: The Story of the Paris Commune* (1994; New York: Penguin Books, 1996), maintains that Paris was known as "the new Babylon, . . . obsessed with sex and money" in the latter years of the Second Empire. *Le club des valets de cœur* ponson_du_terrail_rocambole_club_des_valets_de_coeur_1.pdf (accessed 25 October 2015).

145. Pierre-Joseph Proudhon, "Élections de 1863: Les Démocrates Assermentés et les Réfractaires," pp. 261–324, in *Œuvres complètes de P.-J. Proudhon,* vol. 16 (Paris: Librairie Internationale; Brussels, Leipzig, and Livorno: A. Lacroix, Verboeckhoven, and Co., 1868), p. 291.

146. Jonas, "Sacred Tourism and Secular Pilgrimage," pp. 108–9. For the role of the sacred in modern tourism, see Nelson Graburn, "Tourism: The Sacred Journey," in *Hosts and Guests: The Anthropology of Tourism,* ed. Valene Smith (Philadelphia: University of Pennsylvania Press, 1977), pp. 20–21.

147. *Les guides bleus,* pp. 10–11.

148. Ibid., p. 8.

149. Ibid., pp. 18, 76–77, 80–83, 217–18 (Vichy), 241–42 (La Bourboule and Le Mont-Dore), 351, and 354.

150. Ibid., pp. 418–20, 437, 643, 689, and 704–5.

151. Marcel Monmarché, preface to *Les guides bleus Paris,* p. v.

152. G. Lenôtre, "Avant de visiter Paris," in *Les guides bleus Paris,* pp. xv–xvii. Jean de Garlande's dates are given as 1195–1272 by the Bibliothèque national de France, http://data.bnf.fr/12142193/jean_de_garlande/ (accessed 15 October 2015). The *Guides bleus Paris* does not identify an author for *L'Ulysse français,* but it appears to have been translated from a Latin text by Louis Coulon; see *Publications de la Société des Bibliophiles de Guyenne,* vol. 3 (Bordeaux: G. Gounouilhou, 1882), p. xvi. The original Latin edition is Abraham Golnitz, *Ulysses Belgico-Gallicus* (1631).

153. Lenôtre, "Avant de visiter Paris," pp. xix–xx.

154. Ibid., p. xxi.

155. *Les guides bleus Paris,* pp. lvii and lix.

156. Ibid., pp. lx–lxi. France had definitively recognized the Greenwich meridian in 1911.

157. Ibid., pp. lxv–lxvi.

158. Ibid., pp. 55, 26–29, 32, 110, 115, and 120.

159. Ibid., pp. 142, 158–59, 183–84, and 211–14.

160. Ibid., pp. 189 and 191.

161. Ibid., pp. 415 and 478.

162. G. Bn [Georges Bourgin?], "Notes bibliographiques," *Revue historique* 66, no. 191 (April–June 1941): 357.

163. Ossip Pernikoff, *La France, pays du tourisme* (Paris: Plon, 1938).

2. Two 1940 Sites as Symbols

1. Bitterly described as a "useless bastion" by one of its French defenders, the fortifications had cost an estimated 5 billion francs in the 1930s; see Claude-Armand Masson, *La veille inutile* (Paris: Sercap, 1985), title page.

2. W. Somerset Maugham, *France at War* (New York: Doubleday, Doran and Co., 1940), p. 15.

3. Ibid., pp. 17–18.

4. Anthony Kemp, *The Maginot Line: Myth and Reality* (London: Frederick Warne, 1981), p. 101. See also Cédric Gruat, *Hitler à Paris juin 1940* (Paris: Éditions Tirésias, 2010), p. 47.

5. Kemp, *The Maginot Line*, p. 106; and Wolf von Bleichert, *Als Artillerie-Beobachter durch das Maginot-Linie* (Reutlingen: Ensslin and Laiblin, 1942).

6. Vivian Rowe, *The Great Wall of France: The Triumph of the Maginot Line* (London: Putnam, 1959), pp. 14–15. See also Francis Deron, "La Grande Muraille, du Maginot imaginaire," *Le Monde*, 28 December 1996.

7. *The Economist*, 13 July 1940, cited in *The Oxford English Dictionary*, http://www.oed.com.www.mills.edu:2048/viewdictionaryentry/Entry/112201 (accessed 5 June 2011).

8. Kemp, *The Maginot Line*, p. 9.

9. Claude Imbert, "La France Maginot," *Le Point*, 22 March 2011, http://www.lepoint.fr/editos-du-point/claude-imbert/la-france-maginot-31-03-2011-1313672_68.php?xtor=EPR-6-[Newsletter-Quotidienne]-20110331 (accessed 31 March 2011); and Alain Faujas, "Le protectionnisme, nouvelle Ligne Maginot," *Le Monde*, 25 June 2011, http://www.lemonde.fr/idees/article/2011/06/25/le-protectionnisme-nouvelle-ligne-maginot_1540963_3232.html (accessed 26 June 2011).

10. Vladimir de Gmeline, "Alain Bauer: 'Nous sommes dans un cycle de Ligne Maginot,'" *Marianne*, 18 November 2015, http://www.marianne.net/alain-bauer-nous-sommes-cycle-ligne-maginot-100238095.html (accessed 23 December 2015).

11. Michaël Seramour, "Histoire de la Ligne Maginot de 1945 à nos jours," *Revue historique des armées* 247 (2007): 86–97, http://rha.revues.org/index1933.html (accessed 18 April 2009). See also European Institute of Cultural Routes, "Fortified Military Architectures in Europe: Conflicts and Reconciliations," a portal prepared in the framework of the Luxembourg chairmanship of the Council of Europe, http://www.culture-routes.lu/php/fo_index.php?lng=en&dest=bd_pa_det&rub=57 (accessed 24 June 2009).

12. European Institute of Cultural Routes, "Fortified Military Architectures in Europe."

13. "Visites virtuelles," http://www.lignemaginot.com/ligne/visite.htm (accessed 24 December 2015).

14. Seramour, "Histoire de la Ligne Maginot de 1945 à nos jours," pp. 86–97.

15. Kemp, *The Maginot Line*, p. 106.

16. Seramour, "Histoire de la Ligne Maginot de 1945 à nos jours," pp. 86–97.

17. Jean-Paul Pallud, "The Maginot Line," *After the Battle*, no. 60 (1988): 19.

18. Ibid., p. 35.

19. See, for example, Paul Gamelin, *La Ligne Maginot Hackenberg ouvrage A19: Die Maginot-Linie Besichtigung des Werkes Hackenberg im Bezirk Thionville* (Nantes: published by the Author, 1976).

20. Alain Hohnadel and Michel Truttmann, *Guide de la Ligne Maginot*, published as *39/45 Guerres contemporaines magazine*, special issue, no. 6 (August–September 1988): 29–30.

21. The Marckolsheim fortress was opened to tourism in 1972. See Jean Pascal Soudagne, *L'histoire de la Ligne Maginot* (Rennes: Éditions Ouest-France, 2006), pp. 117–18.

22. Pallud, "The Maginot Line," pp. 15–16. As early as in 1941, French prisoners removing mines from the La Ferté area discovered the remains of soldiers there who had been summarily buried by the Germans. They received German permission to identify and rebury their fallen comrades in local cemeteries. See Serge Barcellini and Annette Wieviorka, *Passant, souviens-toi: Les lieux du souvenir de la Seconde Guerre mondiale en France* (Paris: Plon, 1995), p. 42.

23. Gamelin, *La Ligne Maginot Hackenberg*, p. 14.

24. Hohnadel and Truttmann, *Guide de la Ligne Maginot*, p. 40.

25. Pallud, "The Maginot Line," p. 19. See also Hohnadel and Truttmann, *Guide de la Ligne Maginot*, p. 30.

26. Paul Gamelin, ed., *La Ligne Maginot: Images d'hier et d'aujourd'hui*, published as *Gazette des armes*, special issue, no. 9 (1979): 68.

27. Elisabeth Raffray, "La protection du patrimoine militaire de la Seconde Guerre mondiale en Basse-Normandie: Le Mur de l'Atlantique et le port artificiel d'Arromanches" (thesis, École du Louvre/Muséologie, 1998–99), p. 7.

28. Seramour, "Histoire de la Ligne Maginot de 1945 à nos jours," pp. 86–97. Seramour's figures of 250,000 visitors in Lorraine in 2003 and 300,000 for the total fortifications in 2007 imply that Lorraine draws the most tourism, more than Alsace, to the forts.

29. Hohnadel and Truttmann, *Guide de la Ligne Maginot*, p. 40.

30. Pallud, "The Maginot Line," p. 35. See also N. Smart, "The Maginot Line: An Indestructible Inheritance," *International Journal of Heritage Studies* 2:4 (1996): 222–33.

31. Kemp, *The Maginot Line*, p. 106.

32. Pallud, "The Maginot Line," inside front cover. Twelve fortifications were open to the public at the end of 1987, according to Hohnadel and Truttmann, *Guide de la Ligne Maginot*, p. 30.

33. For estimates of visitors to the Maginot Line sites, see European Institute of Cultural Routes, "Fortified Military Architectures in Europe." See also Seramour, "Histoire de la Ligne Maginot de 1945 à nos jours," pp. 86–97.

34. "Annexe 2: Fréquentation des sites de défense en nombre d'entrées totales; 554,000 entrées," in "Le Tourisme de Mémoire en Lorraine, *La Lorraine*, p. 25, http://www.observatoire-lorraine.fr/publications/le-tourisme-de-memoire-militaire-en-lorraine-2 (accessed 22 August 2016).

35. "Fréquentation détaillée des 20 sites de 2010 à 2014," in Agence Attractivité Alsace/Observatoire Régional Tourisme, clicalsace.com, *Lieux de Mémoire en Alsace 2014* (September 2015): 6, http://www.clicalsace.com/sites/clicalsace.com/files/article/pdf/lieux_de_memoire_en_alsace_en_2014.pdf (accessed 22 August 2106).

36. My observation during a visit to the Fermont fortification, June 1993.

37. Curt Riess, *Joseph Goebbels* (Garden City, N.Y.: Doubleday, 1948), pp. 185–86. See also Roger Manvell and Heinrich Fraenkel, *Dr. Goebbels: His Life and Death* (1960; New York: Pyramid Books, 1961), p. 164; and Claude Paillat, *Dossiers secrets de la*

France contemporaine, vol. 5, *Le désastre de 1940 La guerre éclair 10 mai–24 juin 1940* (Paris: Robert Laffont, 1985), p. 587. The first mention of a decision for signing the armistice at Compiègne, in General Alfred Jodl's diary, dates to 20 May, when Hitler instructed his high command to prepare an armistice following the model of that of November 1918, to be signed in the railway car used by Marshal Foch at Compiègne. See Eberhard Jäckel, *Frankreich in Hitlers Europa: Die deutsche Frankreichpolitik im zweiten Weltkrieg* (Stuttgart: Deutsche Verlags-Anstalt, 1966), p. 37.

38. *Die Tagebücher von Joseph Goebbels: Sämtliche Fragmente,* ed. Elke Fröhlich, pt. 1, *Aufzeichnungen 1924–1941,* vol. 4, 1 January 1940–8 July 1941 (Munich: H. Saur, 1987), entry of 26 May 1940, p. 176.

39. For the use of diaries in tourism history research, see John Towner, "Approaches to Tourism History," *Annals of Tourism Research* 15 (1988): 56.

40. The words are from a plaque that read, "Here on 11 November 1918 the criminal pride of the German Empire was brought low, vanquished by the free peoples whom it had sought to enslave." Following the 1918 armistice signing, the railway car, Wagon-Lits Company car number 2419D, was restored to its previous use as a restaurant car but later placed in the courtyard of the Invalides in Paris. Arthur Fleming, an American, paid for its restoration. The car was brought back to Compiègne in 1927, where it remained until the June 1940 defeat. See "Armistice—The First World War," http://www.webmatters.net/france/ww1_rethondes_2.htm (accessed 30 June 2010).

41. Goebbels, *Die Tagebücher,* p. 224. An account of the negotiations between the French and German representatives that led to the signing of the armistice in the railway car at Compiègne is given in the post–World War I Michelin guidebook *Compiègne Pierrefonds: Un guide, un panaroma, une histoire* (Clermont-Ferrand: Michelin, 1921), p. 61.

42. Goebbels, *Die Tagebücher,* entry of 22 June 1940, p. 213.

43. Ibid., entry of 24 June 1940, p. 217.

44. William L. Shirer, *Berlin Diary: The Journal of a Foreign Correspondent, 1934–1941* (New York: Alfred A. Knopf, 1941), pp. 428–29.

45. Robert Aron, "Rethondes, le Diktat," in *1940: La défaite* (Paris: Tallandier, 1978), pp. 367, 370, and 376.

46. Heinrich Hoffmann, *Mit Hitler im Westen* (Munich: Verlag Heinrich Hoffmann, 1940), pp. 125–27.

47. Paillat, *Dossiers secrets de la France contemporaine,* 5:598–602.

48. Bertram M. Gordon, "World War II," in *France and the Americas: Culture, History, Politics,* ed. Bill Marshall, vol. 3 (Santa Barbara: ABC-Clio Press, 2005), pp. 1229–33.

49. Jacques Benoist-Méchin, *Sixty Days That Shook the West* (New York: G. P. Putnam's Sons, 1963), p. 534.

50. Cited in Robert O. Paxton, *Vichy France: Old Guard and New Order, 1940–1944* (New York: Alfred A. Knopf, 1972), p. 15.

51. I made the case for Hitler's possibly having been distracted by tourism inclinations in "Compiègne," in *Historical Dictionary of World War II France: The Occupation, Vichy, and the Resistance, 1938–1946,* ed. Bertram M. Gordon (Westport, Conn.: Greenwood Press, 1998), pp. 83–84. The choices and possible errors in German military thinking are discussed in greater detail in my article "El papel de España en la derrota de la Alemania nazi durante la Segunda guerra," *Studia historica/Studia*

contemporanea 18 (2000): 249–82. A similar argument relating to Hitler's failure to engage Spain in June 1940 was made, without reference to Hitler's tourism, by Mark Grimsley, "Counterfactual History: Forays into 'What If' History; An After Action Report," in American Historical Association, *Perspectives on History* (May 2015), http://www.historians.org/publications-and-directories/perspectives-on-history/may-2015/forays-into-"what-if"-history (accessed 13 June 2015).

52. Generaloberst Franz Halder, *Kriegstagebuch*, vol. 1, *Vom Polenfeldzug bis zum Ende der Westoffensive (14.8.1939–30.6.1940)* (Stuttgart: W. Kohlhammer Verlag, 1962), entry of 19 June 1940, p. 363.

53. Walter Warlimont, *Inside Hitler's Headquarters, 1939–45*, trans. R. H. Barry (1962; London: Weidenfeld and Nicolson, 1964), p. 103.

54. For Hitler's tour of the World War I trenches, see Goebbels, *Die Tagebücher*, p. 192; and for his touristic posing in Paris, see Hoffmann, *Mit Hitler im Westen*, p. 108.

55. Philipp Blom, "At Versailles," *Times Literary Supplement*, 13 February 2009, p. 8.

56. Marie-Théophile-Armand-Théodore Codevelle, *Armistice 1918: Sa signature la clairière Compiègne* (Compiègne: Imprimerie du "Progrès de l'Oise," 1950), p. 13. For another argument that the statue of Foch was left standing "by derision," see Marc Boulanger, *Juin 1940: Trois semaines en France; Vers l'armistice de Compiègne* (Luneray, France: Éditions Bertout "La Mémoire Normande," 1992), p. 132.

57. Gérard Namer, *Batailles pour la mémoire: La commémoration en France, 1944–1982* (Paris: SPAG, 1983), p. 172. On souvenirs and symbols of the sacred in tourism, see Nelson Graburn, "Tourism: The Sacred Journey," in *Hosts and Guests: The Anthropology of Tourism*, ed. Valene Smith (Philadelphia: University of Pennsylvania Press, 1977), pp. 28–29.

58. See the folder "Voyage de journalistes à Paris et à Compiègne à l'occasion de l'arrivée du premier train de prisonniers rapatriés," 11 August 1942, AN, F41/118.

59. De Barroy, Secretary General, Union Française des Associations d'Anciens Combattants, to the Mayor of Compiègne, April 1948, AN, F21/7085A Oise/Compiègne/Monument commémoratif.

60. Codevelle, *Armistice 1918*, p. 15.

61. Inge von Wangenheim, *Der Goldene Turm: Eine Woche Paris* (Rudolstadt: Greifenverlag, 1988), p. 120. For "staged authenticity," see Dean MacCannell, *The Tourist: A New Theory of the Leisure Class* (New York: Schocken Books, 1976), pp. 98–99.

62. Barcellini and Wieviorka, *Passant, souviens-toi*, pp. 78–79.

63. Comité régional de tourisme de Picardie, http://picardietourisme.com/fr/sejour-picardie/visites/detail.aspx?id=PCUPIC1600000072 (accessed 16 July 2010).

64. Examples in French include Henry Rousso, *Les années noires: Vivre sous l'Occupation* (Paris: Gallimard, 1992); and Denis Peschanski, *Les années noires, 1938–1944* (Paris: Hermann, 2012); and in English, Julian Jackson, *France: The Dark Years, 1940–1944* (Oxford: Oxford University Press, 2001).

3. The French as Tourists in Their Occupied Country

1. Jean Berthelot, *Sur les rails du pouvoir (1938–1942)* (Paris: Robert Laffont, 1967), p. 43.

2. Eric Alary, Bénédicte Vergez-Chaignon, and Gilles Gauvin, *Les Français au quotidien 1939–1949* (2006; Paris: Perrin, 2009), p. 40.

3. Ibid., p. 42.

4. "Le Touring-club agit: L'évacuation—La carte d'identité—Les bons d'essence—Les sauf-conduits," *La revue du Touring club de France,* no. 540 (November 1939): 6.

5. Conseil d'Administration, Séance du 10 octobre 1939, Touring Club de France, AN/20000028/10, vol. 26, p. 15.

6. Conseil d'Administration, Séance du 6 février 1940, Touring Club de France, AN/20000028/10, vol. 26, p. 88.

7. Conseil d'Administration, Séance du 7 mai 1940, Touring Club de France, AN/20000028/10, vol. 26, pp. 140–41.

8. Roland Dorgelès, *La drôle de guerre: 1939–1940* (Paris: Albin Michel, 1957), p. 232.

9. Vassili Soukhomline, *Les hitlériens à Paris,* translated from Russian by Lily Denis (Paris: Les Éditeurs Français Réunis, 1967), p. 33.

10. Ibid., p. 33. See also Dorgelès, *La drôle de guerre,* p. 244.

11. Dorgelès, *La drôle de guerre,* p. 275.

12. Maurice Toesca, *Cinq ans de patience (1939–1945)* (Paris: Éditions Émile-Paul, 1975), p. 57.

13. Robert Cardinne-Petit, *Les soirées du continental: Ce que j'ai vu à la censure 1939–1940* (Paris: Jean Renard, 1942), pp. 195–96.

14. Robert O. Paxton, "Inside the Panic," *New York Review of Books,* 22 November 2007, p. 50. This article reviews Hanna Diamond, *Fleeing Hitler: France 1940* (Oxford: Oxford University Press, 2007).

15. Cardinne-Petit, *Les soirées du continental,* p. 254. Cardinne-Petit's account of the censorship office's role in the 1939–40 war was published in 1942. During the Occupation he was a journalist for *La Gerbe* and *L'Appel,* two newspapers that supported Franco-German collaboration. He served eight months in prison following the Liberation. See Andries Van den Abeele, *Louis Thomas (1885–1962) Biographie,* October 2007, chap. 9 and note 20, http://users.skynet.be/sb176943/AndriesVanden Abeele/AVDA448.htm (accessed 8 July 2012).

16. Michèle Cointet, *Vichy capitale 1940–1944: Vérités et légendes* (Paris: Perrin, 1993), pp. 18–20. Sometimes referred to as "premier" or "prime minister," Pierre Laval was formally vice president of the Council of Ministers (under Pétain, the Council's president) from July through December 1940 and again from April 1942 through the end of the Vichy government in August 1944.

17. Maurice Constantin-Weyer, *Vichy et son histoire* (Vichy: Szabo, 1947), p. 140.

18. Philippe Boegner, "Mon été 40," *Le Figaro Magazine,* 21 July 1990, p. 85.

19. Philippe Burrin, *France under the Germans: Collaboration and Compromise,* trans. Janet Lloyd (New York: New Press, 1996), pp. 460–62.

20. André Halimi, *Chantons sous l'Occupation* (Paris: Olivier Orban, 1976), released as a film the same year. See Janet Maslin, movie review of *Chantons sous l'Occupation, New York Times,* 25 November 1994, http://movies.nytimes.com/movie/review?res=9907E4D81430F936A15752C1A962958260 (accessed 30 June 2010).

21. Boegner, "Mon été 40," pp. 86–88.

22. The wartime "Paris" films were produced in a variety of countries. For Anglophones, Paris represented nostalgia for a place now unattainable. Some of the films produced in France were underground Resistance films, centered on Paris as the focal point of the liberation struggle. See Sylvie Lindeperg, *Les écrans de l'ombre: La*

Seconde Guerre mondiale dans le cinéma français (1944–1969) (Paris: CNRS Editions, 1997), pp. 29–32.

23. Police report, 29 July 1940, Archives de la Préfecture de police, Paris, APP-220-W-1.

24. "Paris veut vivre," *Paris Programmes: Guide de la vie parisienne*, no. 1 (26 September–2 October 1940): 1.

25. Pierre Andrieu, "On peut très bien manger . . . en sachant s'adapter!" *Paris Programmes: Guide de la vie parisienne*, no. 1 (26 September–2 October 1940): 14. For subsequent writings of Andrieu during the Occupation, see his praise of Parisian gastronomy in *France, Paris, and the Provinces: Text by Roger Roumagnac, Gastronomy by Pierre Andrieu*, ed. Doré Ogrizek, trans. Marguerite Bigot and Madeleine Blaess, illustrated by G. Beuville, L. Firsca, E. Grau-Sala, V. Pilon, and G. de Sainte-Croix (Paris: Odé [Impr. de Croutzer-Depost], 1944).

26. *Paris Programmes: Guide de la vie parisienne*, no. 1 (26 September–2 October 1940): 24, 31, 32, and inside back cover.

27. "Paris veut vivre—du réel au fantaisiste," *Paris Programmes; Guide de la vie parisienne*, no. 2 (3–9 October 1940): 1.

28. Police report, 28 December 1940, Archives de la Préfecture de police, Paris, APP-220-W-1.

29. Berthelot, *Sur les rails du pouvoir*, p. 99.

30. "La presentation des voitures de tourisme de 14 CV et au-dessous datant de 1938 à 1940 commençera demain à Paris," *L'Œuvre*, 25 September 1940.

31. Note, Inspection Générale des Services des Renseignements Généraux, Nr. 4804/2/Pol. Rens., a/s d'une recrudescences d'allemands et d'italiens à Marseille, Vichy, 27 June 1941, AN, F/7 14903.

32. Stéphane Nicolas, "Guider le touriste: Du guide rouge à ViaMichelin," in "Cent ans de l'administration du tourisme," *Revue du Ministère de l'écologie, du développement durable et de l'énergie*, special issue (July 2012): 51.

33. *Pneu Michelin: Atlas des routes de France* (Paris: Services de Tourisme Michelin, 1942).

34. Noël Blandin, "Guide Michelin," *La République des Lettres*, 2 March 2009, http://www.republique-des-lettres.fr/10674-guide-michelin.php (accessed 15 June 2009); and "Le Guide MICHELIN: 109 ans d'histoire d'aide à la mobilité," 2 March 2009, http://www.viamichelin.fr/viamichelin/fra/tpl/mag6/art200903/htm/tour-saga-michelin.htm (accessed 15 June 2009).

35. "Où aller en vacances?," in *Almanach François 1941* (Corbeil, France: Crété, 1941), pp. 11–12.

36. H. Cherpin, "Comment alimenter sans essence les moteurs d'automobile" *Almanach de la Bonne Presse pour 1941* (Paris: Maison de la Bonne Presse, 1941), p. 70.

37. M. Simmonet, "Les églises fortifiées," and P.-J. Bourgès, "Une visite aux Catacombes de Paris," ibid., pp. 60–62 and 86, respectively.

38. *1943 Almanach Hachette* (Paris: Librairie Hachette, 1943), pp. 81–82.

39. Von Stülpnagel, Der MBF, Kommandostab Abt. Ic, Br. B. no. 78/41, Paris, 9 January 1941, AN, AJ/40/561, folder 3, Verwaltungsstab Abt. Verwaltung Passierscheine 1941, Band 2, V kult 408.

40. Keser to Passierscheinstelle VI, Paris, 8 April 1941, AN, AJ/40/561, folder 3.

41. Police report, 9 September 1940, Archives de la Préfecture de police, Paris, APP-220-W-1.

42. P. Bouis, "Le bureau de renseignements de l'hôtellerie: Plus de 500.000 Parisiens ont déjà été aiguillés vers d'agréables 'séjours de remplacement,' " *Paris-Midi*, 29 August 1942, AN, AJ/40/784.

43. Ibid.

44. Suzanne Sauvan, "Le Haut-Bochaine (du Col de la Croix-Haute au Pont-la-Dame)," *Revue de géographie alpine* 30, no. 2 (1942): 350 and 359, http://www.per see.fr/web/revues/home/prescript/article/rga_0035-1121_1942_num_30_2_4342 (accessed 7 April 2009). I am indebted for this reference to Laurent Beauguitte, "Un champ scientifique à l'épreuve de la Seconde Guerre mondiale: Les revues de géographie françaises de 1936 à 1945" (master's thesis, Université Paris 7, 2006–7), p. 84, http://www.cybergeo.eu/index19853.html (accessed 4 April 2009).

45. Quoted in Nicolas, "Guider le touriste," pp. 50–51.

46. Police report, 16 September 1940, Archives de la Préfecture de police, Paris, APP-220-W-1.

47. Christian Faure, *Le projet culturel de Vichy: Folklore et révolution nationale 1940–1944* (Lyon: Presses Universitaires de Lyon, 1989), p. 30.

48. Marc Boyer, *Le tourisme de masse* (Paris: L'Harmattan, 2007), pp. 151–52.

49. Berthelot, *Sur les rails du pouvoir*, pp. 115–16.

50. Boyer, *Le tourisme de masse*, pp. 151–52.

51. Ibid., p. 130.

52. Ibid., p. 96.

53. Comité d'organisation professionnelle de l'industrie hôtelière: Hôtels restaurants/débits de boissons, État français, Secrétariat d'état aux communications aux PTT et au tourisme, "Organisation des congés payés: Création d'un Bureau de renseignements hôtels gratuits," 30 March 1942, AN, F14/13625. The report discusses the lodging of workers on paid vacations. See also "Cherchez-vous un hôtel où passer votre congé payé?" *Le Petit Parisien*, 3 April 1942, AN, F14/13625.

54. Lucien Serre, Secrétaire Général, État Français, Secrétariat d'État aux Communications, Comité d'organisation professionnelle de l'industrie hôtelière, Secrétariat Général, Circulaire No. 19, Paris, "À tous les Présidents des Chambres Professionnelles de la zone occupé," 30 March 1942, p. 1, AN, F14/13625.

55. Robert Kanigel, *High Season: How One French Riviera Town Has Seduced Travelers for Two Thousand Years* (New York: Viking, 2002), p. 194. Kanigel adds that the regional committee replaced a "festivals committee," judged insufficiently proper in Vichy's moralistic National Revolution.

56. T. Guedel, "Vive le Maréchal! À bas les politiciens!" *Jeunesse: Organe de la génération 40* 3 (12 January 1941). This periodical was a four-page weekly; see BNF, Gr. fol. L²c 6644.

57. *L'Œuvre*, 9 October 1940.

58. "L'importance du tourisme dans la France de demain," *Lyon-Touriste: Journal Officiel du Syndicat d'Initiative de Lyon et de ses environs* 37, no. 292 (1st half 1943): 1.

59. "Le congrès des présidents des chambres départementales de la Zone Sud des 9 et 10 mars 1943, à Brive-la-Gaillarde," *L'hôtelier alpin: Organe de la Chambre*

professionelle départementale de l'industrie hôtelière et débitants de boissons des Hautes-Alpes 3, no. 20 (March 1943): 1.

60. Conseil d'administration, Séances du 4 juin 1940 and 4 novembre 1940, Touring Club de France, AN/20000028/10, vol. 26, pp. 152 and 208–9, respectively.

61. Assemblée Générale du 21 décembre 1941, Touring Club de France, AN/20000028/10, vol. 27, p. 96.

62. President's Report to Assemblée Générale du 21 décembre 1941, Touring Club de France, AN/20000028/10, vol. 27, pp. 96–97.

63. Ibid.

64. Conseil d'Administration, Séance du 1er juin 1942, Touring Club de France, AN/20000028/10, vol. 27, pp. 158–59.

65. Conseil d'Administration, Séance du 10 mai 1943, Touring Club de France, AN/20000028/10, vol. 28, pp. 52–53.

66. For an example of the many such applications in the records of the German military authorities, see Der MBF Kommandostab Abt. Ic (III), AZ: 07a/III, Betr., Ferienreisen der Schüler der Polytechnischen Schule in Lyon under der Nationalschule für Bautechnik, an den General bevollmächtigten der französischen Regierung beim MBF, Paris, 20 February 1942, AN, AJ/40/561 (folder 1). See also P. Isoré, Chef du Service des Voyages de Vacances, Secrétariat d'État, L'Éducation Nationale et à la Jeunesse, Office du Tourisme Universitaire, "Rapport sur les convois interzones de Paques 1942," to Monsieur le Ministre de l'Éducation Nationale, undated (probably early 1942), p. 4, AN, AJ/40/561, folder 1, Verwaltigungsstab Abt. Verwaltung, betr.: Vorgänge betr. Passierscheine, Band Nr. 1, Akten Nr. V kult 408A.

67. Dr. Best, Der Chef des Verwaltungsstabes, Für den MBF, Abt. Verw. Az. V pol 256/02/2, Paris, 24 June 1941, to Chefs der Mil. Verw. Bez. A, B, C und Bordeaux—Verwaltungsstab und den Kommandanten von Gross-Paris—Verwaltungsstab, AN, AJ/40/891 (folder 3), GP VII 26. See also Der Chef des Verwaltungsstabes, "Entwurf," to Feldkommandantur (V) 748, Rennes, Paris, 9 July 1941, AN, AJ/40/891 (folder 3), GP VII 26. For the Compagnons de France and the Chantiers de la jeunesse, see "Merkblatt," Der Oberbefehlshaber des Heeres, Der Chef der Militärverwaltung in Frankreich, Kommandostab Abt. Ic., Paris, 6 October 1940; and Der Chef des Militärverwaltungsbezirks Paris, I. A., an den Herrn MBF—Verwaltungsstab—Hotel Majestic, Paris, 21 December 1940, AN, AJ/40/891 (folder 4), GP VII 25.

68. Kriegsverwaltungsrat, Feldkommandatur, Aktz I83 a/851/42/Ld, Orléans, to Monsieur l'Inspecteur d'Academie sous le couvert de M. le Préfet à Chartres, 23 January 1942, AN, AJ/40/565, Abt. Verwaltung, betr.: Angelegenheiten der Akademie Paris, Band no. II, Angelegt am 1 January 1942, Akten no. V, Kult 421 (folder 5).

69. The request for authorization originated with Mademoiselle Marcelle Le Verrier, a teacher at the Collège Octave Gréard, in a note to the Feldkommandantur—Auxerre, 17 June 1942. For its approval by the German authorities, see Major Reiprich to Feldkommandantur 745 in Auxerre (Yonne), 4 July 1942, and SS-Hauptsturmführer (name illegible), Der Befehlshaber der Sicherheitspolizei und des SD im Bereich des Militärbefehlshabers in Frankreich Sicherheitspolizei (SD)—Kommando Dijon, II Pol 214 Tgb. no. 4228/42 Me/Fe, to MBF Verwaltungsstab—Abt. V 1/2 Paris, 15 July 1942, AN, AJ/40/565 (folder 5).

70. The request was made by Sisters Conderc and Bousquet, École Notre-Dame de Paris, to the Minister des Unterrichtswesens, 10 February 1943, and denied in Major Hartmann (?), V 1/2 Tgb. no. 265/43, Führungsabtlg. Ib (1), to the Verwaltungsabteilung/Gruppe Schulwesen, 15 May 1943, AN, AJ/40/565, folder 5.

71. Henry Gal, *Un maire dans la tourmente 1941–1944* (Paris: Éditions les Neuf Muses, 1983), pp. 17–18.

72. Ibid., p. 87.

73. *Auberges françaises de la jeunesse, écoles de formation humaine* (Lyon: Les Auberges Françaises de la Jeunesse; Secrétariat Général de la Jeunesse, 1943), p. 11; and *Auberges françaises de la jeunesse* (Vichy: Secrétariat Général de la Jeunesse, 1942), p. 25.

74. *Auberges françaises de la jeunesse, écoles de formation humaine* (1943).

75. *Auberges françaises de la jeunesse* (1942), p. 58.

76. P. Isoré, Le Chef du Service des Voyages de Vacances, à Monsieur le Ministre de l'Éducation Nationale, Objet: Rapport sur les convoys interzones de Paques 1942, undated, AN, AJ/40/561 (folder 1). See also Jean Guéhenno, *Journal des années noires (1940–1944)* (Paris: Gallimard, 1947), diary entry of 17 July 1942, p. 313.

77. Fritz Gabler, Der Leiter der Wirtschaftsgruppe Beherbergungsgewerbe in der Reichsgruppe Fremdenverkehr, Heidelberg, letter to Leiter der Wirtschaftsabteilung beim MBF Herrn Kriegsverwaltungchef Dr. Michel, 10 April 1943, no. 06 661 Wi., WI. II/L3/237/63; also Michel's reply, An den Leiter der Wirtschaftsgruppe Beherbergungsgewerbe in der Reichsgruppe Fremdenverkehr, Herrn Fritz Gabler, 7 May 1943, L3/237/63, AN, AJ/40/785, MBF 38, 22119 (folder 1). By the end of the nineteenth century, the English word "tourism" had spread into nearly all the European languages, including German, which retained *Fremdenverkehr* but also had assimilated the word *Tourismus*. See Marc Boyer, *Le tourisme de masse* (Paris: L'Harmattan, 2007), p. 8.

78. Hermann Esser, Abschrift, Der Staatsekretär für Fremdenverkehr, Az.: FV 12170–22c/9.4.42/.169–2.8, Berlin, to Generaldirektor für den Tourismus Giuseppe Toffano, Ministerium für Volkskultur, Rome, 28 January 1943; and Der Staatsekretär fur Fremdenverkehr im Reichsministerium für Volksaufklärung und Propaganda, Der personliche Referat, FV 12 170–22c, Berlin, 5 April 1943, AN, AJ/40/785, MBF 38, 22119 [folder 1].

79. Kanigel, *High Season,* p. 194.

80. Jean Lacoste, Notre-Dame de Briançon, Savoie, letter to Jean Fangeat, Editor, *Petit Dauphinois,* Grenoble, 8 August 1943, intercepted 10 August 1943, AN, F/7/15299, folder "Marché Noir Case 1, no. 10.

81. M. R. 4., Vichy, 15 September 1943, AN, F/7/15299, folder "Marché Noir Case 1, no. 10.

82. "Procès-Verbal de la Réunion du Comité du 19 Juilllet 1941," République Française, Bordereau d'Envoi, Le Chef du Service du Tourisme, à Monsieur Moroni, Directeur du Cabinet du Secrétaire Général d'État aux Communications, Paris, 16 October 1941, pp. 8–9, AN, F14/13625.

83. Ibid., p. 3.

84. Liste des Agences de Voyages (20 September 1942), folder "Comité d'Organisation des Agences et Bureaux de Voyages, AN, F/14/13714.

85. Ibid.

86. Richard Vainopoulos and Sandrine Mercier, *Idées reçues: Le tourisme* (Paris: Le Cavalier Bleu, 2009), p. 10.

87. "Agences et bureaux de voyages," Extrait du *Journal officiel* du 3 janvier 1941, AN, F14/13625. For the text of the law, see "Loi portant suppression du Centre National d'Expansion du Tourisme, du Thermalisme et du Climatisme," 15 October 1940, "Projets d'articles de loi," n.d., and Comité d'Organisation Professionnelle des Agences & Bureaux de Voyages, "Création et Activité du Comité," n.d., folder "Tourisme 1946–1947," AN, F/14/13714.

88. Comité d'Organisation Professionnelle des Agences & Bureaux de Voyages, "Travaux du Comité," n.d., folder "Tourisme 1946–1947," AN, F/14/13714.

89. Comité d'Organisation Professionnelle des Agences & Bureaux de Voyages, "Procès-Verbal de la 13e Séance de 8 Octobre 1941 à 17 Heures," République Française, Bordereau d'Envoi, Le Chef du Service du Tourisme to Monsieur Moroni, Directeur du Cabinet du Secrétaire Général d'État aux Communications, Paris, 16 October 1941, pp. 8–9, AN, F14/13625.

90. "Organisation Corporative du Tourisme," Secrétariat d'État aux Communications, Service du Tourisme, 25 September 1941, pp. 1–3, AN, F14/13625.

91. "Organisation Corporative du Tourisme," Secrétariat d'État aux Communications, Service du Tourisme, 25 September 1941, pp. 4–5, AN, F14/13625.

92. Bernard Chenot, "Note pour Monsieur le Ministre," 13 May 1941, AN, F14/13625. Bernard Chenot was *commissaire du gouvernement, délégué général au tourisme.* Typewritten on the note was the agreement of the minister, Jean Bertholot.

93. Georges Mathiot, *Le tourisme réceptif français: Sa place dans l'économie nationale et internationale, sa position devant la nouvelle règlementation de 1942–1943* (Nancy: Société d'Impressions Typographiques, 1945), pp. 171–72. See also Gaston Mortier, *Le tourisme et l'économie nationale: Un passé encourageant ... Vers un meilleur avenir* (Paris: B. Arthaud, 1941), p. 172; and Chantal Henry, documentaliste, *Ministre du Tourisme. Direction du Tourisme. Mission des Archives Nationales. Les Archives du Tourisme. État des versements effectuées aux Archives nationales de 1979 à 1993,* p. 6, AN, CAC/15.

94. Alain Monferrand and Arnaud Berthonnet, "Cent ans de l'administration du Tourisme, 1920s à nos jours," Actes de la journée d'études du 12 mai 2011," *Pour mémoire: Revue du Ministère de l'écologie, du développement durable et de l'énergie,* special issue (July 2012): 20.

95. Mathiot, *Le tourisme réceptif français,* p. 174. For the Comités régionaux de tourisme, see "Futures autostrades en France: Le point de vue économique, les principaux généraux de leur établissement et de leur utilization," *Bulletin de la Chambre de commerce de Paris* 49, no. 10–13 (28 March 1942): 98, which refers to the text in the *Journal officiel,* 12 March 1942.

96. "La loi sur l'organisation du Tourisme," Touring Club de France, 5 July 1943, pp. 68–72, AN, 20000028–10.

97. Rapport de M. Poupet, Inspecteur Général des Ponts et Chaussées au Gouvernement Général de l'Algérie—Révision de l'Organisation chargée d'assurer l'action touristique en Algérie, n.d., p. 2, folder "Tourisme 1946–1947," AN, F/14/13714. Poupet recommended creating a committee in Algeria to synchronize its tourism program with the regions of metropolitan France as established by the Vichy directives.

98. Lucien Lacambre, Commissaire de la Voie Publique, Report, 17 April 1941, AN, AJ/40/890 [folder 5], pp. 43–47. This report had been demanded by the German authorities. The page numbers were apparently written in later by an archivist.

99. Service Special, Rapport, Paris, 11 January 1942, "Objet: Réunion R. N. P. Montrouge," AN, AJ/40/890 [folder 8], GP VII 8.

100. "Syndicats d'initiative," *Lyon-Touriste: Journal Officiel du Syndicat d'Initiative de Lyon et de ses environs* (2nd half 1940): 1.

101. Le Chef du Cabinet, Cabinet du Ministre du Travaux Publics, Note pour Monsieur Chenot, 11 November 1941, AN, F14/13625.

102. "Representation et action du Service du Tourisme à l'étranger," pp. 2–3, AN, F14/13625, an undated request for budgetary support for the year 1942, undoubtedly written in the second half of 1941.

103. "Futures autostrades en France: Le point de vue économique, les principaux généraux de leur établissement et de leur utilization," *Bulletin de la Chambre de commerce de Paris* 49, no. 10–13 (28 March 1942): 282–83.

104. Mortier, *Le tourisme et l'économie nationale*, p. 31.

105. Ibid., p. 9.

106. Mathiot, *Le tourisme réceptif français*, pp. 8–9. See also "Tourisme: Loi, no. 85, du 12 janvier 1942 instituant des Comités régionaux du tourisme (Journal Officiel du 12 mars)," *Bulletin de la Chambre de commerce de Paris, Année 1942*, nos. 10–13 (28 March 1942): 98.

107. Mathiot, *Le tourisme réceptif français*, p. 224.

108. Ibid., p. 226.

109. Ibid., p. 7.

110. Sebastien Cote, "1940: Le gouvernement de Vichy interdit les apéritifs," *Domitia: Revue du Centre de recherches historiques sur les sociétés méditerranéenes* 5 (2004): 128–30.

111. Ibid., pp. 132–33.

112. "Procès-Verbal de la Réunion du Comité du 19 Juilllet 1941," République Française, Bordereau d'Envoi, Le Chef du Service du Tourisme, à Monsieur Moroni, Directeur du Cabinet du Secrétaire Général d'État aux Communications, Paris, 16 October 1941, p. 6, AN, F14/13625.

113. "Procès-Verbal de la Réunion du Comité du 27 Septembre 1941," ibid., p. 4.

114. Ibid.

115. René Hure, "Message mensuel du groupement de répartition," *Bulletin d'informations de la Chambre professionnelle de l'industrie hôtelière, hôtels—restaurants— débit de boissons, Département de l'Yonne*, n.s., no. 1 (January 1942), Wi II L4/29/42, AN, AJ/40/785, MBF 38 [folder 4].

116. See the request for German authorization to publish by the Chef des Services Administratifs and the Secrétaire-Général, Adm. Administratifs, HG. TM., to Dr Gehrhardt, Conseiller Supérieur de Guerre, Paris, 2 February 1942, AN, AJ/40/784, folder 1, MBF 29B.

117. Lucien Serre, Secrétaire Général, État Français, Secrétariat d'État aux Communications aux P. T. T. et au Tourisme, Comité d'Organisation Professionnelle de l'Industrie Hôtelière, to Dr. Gerhardt, Conseiller en Chef, Hôtel Majestic, Paris, 25 August 1942, AN, AJ/40/785 [folder 4], MBF 38 22119 WiII/L4/150/42; and note to

the Comité d'Organisation Professionnelle de l'Industrie Hôtelière, 19 August 1942, AN, AJ/40/785 [folder 4], MBF 38 22119 Will/L4/116/42.

118. "Rubrique régionale," *Chambres professionnelles départementales de l'industrie hôtelière de la région de Rennes, hôtels—restaurants—débit de boissons,* (May 1942): 2, 22119, Wi II L4/150/42, AN, AJ/40/785, MBF 38 [folder 4].

119. Ibid.

120. Der Chef des Verwaltungsstabes, für den Kommandanten von Gross-Paris, "Entwurf," An die Propagandastaffel Paris, and letter of request for permission to sponsor a lecture from *Sciences et voyages* to Dr Bock, 8 November 1941, AN, AJ40/890, folder 8.

121. They are listed in Steve Wharton, *Screening Reality: French Documentary Film during the German Occupation* (Bern: Peter Lang, 2006), appendix 2, pp. 209–28. The list is taken from the *Brochure du premier congrès du Film Documentaire,* CARAN, Paris, F42/114 and F42/132, and *Le nouveau film* (January 1943).

122. Jean-Pierre Rioux, "Survivre," *L'histoire* 80 (July–August 1985): 92–93.

123. Pierre Audiat, *Paris pendant la guerre* (Paris: Hachette, 1946), pp. 240–41.

124. "Titine et Dora: Souvenirs de l'an 40," *La Bourgogne d'Or: Littérature, arts, régionalisme, histoire, archéologie, tourisme* 128 (January–February–March 1943): 24–25.

125. "Notes bourguignons," *La Bourgogne d'Or: Littérature, arts, régionalisme, histoire, archéologie, tourisme* 131 (October–November–December 1943): 150.

126. Petrus Sambardier, "Les vacances à Lyon," *Lyon-Touriste. Journal Officiel du Syndicat d'Initiative de Lyon et de ses environs* (1st half 1944): 15–17.

127. "Les bars parisiens dits . . . Américains," *L'hôtelier français: La gazette de la vie hôtelier et du tourisme* 4, no. 38 (5 June 1944): 13.

128. Conseil d'Administration, Séance du 5 juin 1944, Touring Club de France, AN/20000028/10, vol. 28, pp. 149–50.

129. Audiat, *Paris pendant la guerre*, pp. 246–47.

130. For contemporary pilgrimages to Santiago de Compostela, see Simon Winchester, "The Long, Sweet Road to Santiago de Compostela," *Smithsonian Magazine* (February 1994): 65.

131. Norbert Ohler, *The Medieval Traveller* (1986; Woodbridge, Suffolk: Boydell Press, 1989), pp. 90–91.

132. Robert Gildea, *Marianne in Chains: Daily Life in the Heart of France during the German Occupation* (New York: Picador, 2002), p. 203.

133. Ibid., pp. 205–6.

134. In Paris in 1933, the thirty-year-old Dominican Deryckère was given the task of organizing annual pilgrimages to Lourdes, a position he maintained until 1972. See "Billet de Lourdes: L'histoire du pèlerinage du rosaire dans la région de Paris," "Laïcs et Dominicains: Blog de la fraternité laïque dominicaine "Pierre Claverie" de Paris, 9 October 2007, http://ladom.typepad.fr/lacs_et_dominicains/2007/10/histoire-du-ple.html (accessed 4 July 2010).

135. For Lourdes prior to 1914, see Ruth Harris, *Lourdes: Body and Spirit in the Secular Age* (London: Allen Lane, 1999).

136. Conseil d'Administration, Séance du 6 décembre 1943, Touring Club de France, AN/20000028/10, vol. 28, pp. 110–14.

137. Author's interview with Jacques Schweizer, Paris, 28 June 1974. For another would-be pro-German view of the transfer of l'Aiglon, see the letter written to

Hitler, listed as "Uebersetzung," c/o Kommandanteur, Paris, "Personelle," posted 16 December 1940, AN, AJ/40/878 [folder 2], C. 6 4 III I c 6, nos. 451 and 452.

138. Georges Poisson, *Le retour des cendres de l'Aiglon* (Paris: Nouveau Monde, 2006), pp. 157–58.

139. Anonymous, *Vae victis, ou deux ans dans la L. V. F.* (Paris: La Jeune Parque, 1948), pp. 8–10. In an interview with the author, Paris, 8 July 1974, Patrick Humbert Droz, a volunteer with the French Sturmbrigade in the Waffen-SS, recalled his interest in joining the unit fighting in Russia to see more of the world.

140. For a discussion of the potential right-wing implications in Giono's writings, see Henri Pollès *L'opera politique* (Paris: Gallimard, 1937), p. 207; and a review of his book by André Billy, "Naturisme et 'Fascisme' de Giono," *L'Œuvre*, 29 August 1937.

141. See Marc Augier, "CLAJ 60° latitude nord," *Le cri des auberges de jeunesse* 3, no. 17 (May 1936).

142. Marc Augier, "Le Congrès mondiale de la jeunesse: New York Poughkeepsie, août 1938," *Le cri des auberges de jeunesse* 5, no. 40 (October 1938).

143. Marc Augier, *Les partisans* (Paris: Denoël, 1943), pp. 13–17. The evolution of Augier toward a pro-German position can be seen in his article "Nous sommes 'le parti de la vie,'" *Le cri des auberges de jeunesse* 7, no. 52 (February–March 1940). Augier elaborated on this account in two interviews with the author, Paris, 2 July 1974 and 19 July 1976.

144. Marc Augier, *Les jeunes devant l'aventure européene* (Paris: Les Conférences du Groupe "Collaboration," 1941), p. 24.

145. Ibid., p. 32.

146. See ibid., pp. 14–15, 20, and passim. For his views on his engagement in the Anti-Bolshevik Legion, see Augier, "Ce siècle avait deux ans . . . ," *Le combattant européen*, no. 2 (June 1943).

147. Augier, *Les partisans*, pp. 83 and 85.

148. Ibid., pp. 76–77.

149. Ibid., pp. 121–22.

150. Bertram M. Gordon, *Collaborationism in France during the Second World War* (Ithaca: Cornell University Press, 1980), p. 272.

151. Marcel Montarron, "Pour assurer les relais du dessert: Une poignée de français lutte dans le Sahara," *Jeune force de France* 1 (18 November 1942): 5.

152. Author's interview with Lucie Aubrac, Paris, October 1996.

153. See François Dufay, *Le voyage d'automne, octobre 1941, des écrivains français en Allemagne* (2000; Paris: Perrin Tempus, 2008).

154. Reichswirtschaftskammer, Erweka, Berlin, telegram to Herr Oberkriegsverwaltungsrat Dr. Gerhardt beim MBF, Verwaltungsstab, Wirthschaftsabteilung, Paris, 6 May 1943; and the transcript of a telephone call in response, MBF to Reichswirtschaftskammer, Berlin NW1, Neue Wilhelmstrasse 9–11, Spruch no. 12424, 10 May 1943, AN, AJ/40/785, MBF 38, 22105 G [folder 1].

155. Guéhenno, *Journal des années noires*, diary entry of 27 April 1943, p. 391.

156. Ibid., diary entry of 6 October 1943, p. 412.

157. Soukhomline, *Les hitlériens à Paris*, pp. 112–13.

158. Christine Levisse-Touzé, cited in Bruno D. Cot, "Paris," in Pascal Ory, *Voyage dans la France occupée* (Mayenne, France: L'Express Bibliomnibus, 2014), pp. 124 and 120.

159. Olivier Barrot and Raymond Chirat, *La vie culturelle dans la France occupée* (Paris: Découvertes Gallimard Histoire, 2009), p. 29.

160. Marc Chesnel, *Le tourisme culturel de type urbain: Aménagement et stratégies de mise en valeur* (2001; Paris: L'Harmattan, 2009), p. 51.

161. Le Préfet du Puy-de-Dôm Délégué à Monsieur le Général Commandant l'État-Major Principal de Liaison 588, Group Administration et Économie, Hôtel de l'Univers, Clermont Ferrand, Service des Requisitions Allemandes, no. 1651/RFA, 18 July 1944, AN, AJ/40/573 [folder 6], Schutzkunst.

162. Gérard Namer, *Batailles pour la mémoire: La commémoration en France, 1944–1982* (Paris: SPAG, 1983), p. 13.

163. Conseil d'Administration, Séance du 4 décembre 1944, Touring Club de France, AN/20000028/10, vol. 28, pp. 200–201.

4. German Tourism in Occupied France, 1940–1944

1. For a discussion of Benjamin on film and power, see Vanessa R. Schwartz, "Walter Benjamin for Historians," *American Historical Review* 106, no. 5 (December 2001): 1736.

2. Pierre Andrieu, "Gastronomie," in *Paris, Frankreich und Provinzen*, ed. Doré Ogrizek (Paris: Odé, 1943), p. 189.

3. "Junge deutschen lernen in diesem Kriege Länder und Völker kennen, über deren natürliches und politisches Wesen sie sich in friedlichen Zeiten nur aus Büchern unterrichtet haben könnten," *Der deutsche Wegleiter*, no. 45 (26 May–6 June 1942): 5.

4. Directive 490, 9 July 1940, cited in Jean-Pierre Azéma, "Adolf Hitler, le visiteur du matin," "1939–1940: L'Année terrible," *Le Monde*, 27 July 1989. For more on Hitler's lack of interest in a collaborationist France, see Bertram M. Gordon, *Collaborationism in France during the Second World War* (Ithaca: Cornell University Press, 1980), pp. 24 and 66, especially p. 66, footnote 4, also pp. 345–46.

5. Shelley Baranowski, "Radical Nationalism in an International Context," in *Histories of Tourism: Representation, Identity and Conflict*, ed. John K. Walton (Clevedon: Channel View Publications, 2005), p. 138.

6. Hermann Esser, "Deutschland als Reiseland/L'Allemagne pays de tourisme/Touring in Germany," in *Der Reichskommissar für die Internationale Ausstellung Paris 1937*, ed. Internationale Ausstellung Paris 1937 für Kunst und Technik, Deutsche Abteilung/Section Allemande/German Section (Berlin: Ala Anzeigen AG, 1937), pp. 55–56. For Esser, see "Hermann Esser (1900–1981)," Jewish Virtual Library, a division of the American-Israeli Cooperative Enterprise, http://www.jewishvirtual library.org/jsource/biography/Esser.html (accessed 30 July 2010).

7. Vera Lynn, *We'll Meet Again: A Personal and Social History of World War Two* (London: Sidgwick and Jackson, 1989), p. 89. See also A. C. Grayling, *Among the Dead Cities: Is the Targeting of Civilians in War Ever Justified?* (London: Bloomsbury, 2006), p. 51; and "Fact File: Baedeker Raids," WW2 People's War, an archive of World War Two memories, written by the public, gathered by the BBC, Timeline—1939–1945, BBC Home, http://www.bbc.co.uk/history/ww2peopleswar/timeline/factfiles/nonflash/a1132921.shtml (accessed 20 December 2015).

8. For his account of the interview, see Fernand de Brinon, *France Allemagne 1918–1934* (Paris: Grasset, 1934), pp. 215–22.

9. Gordon, *Collaborationism in France during the Second World War*, p. 67.

10. Count Welczeck, telegram (geh. Ch. v.), Paris, 20 July 1939, to R.A.M. (Reichsaussenministerium), 20 July, Frame 248, AN, 562/MI/1; and Chef der Sicherheitspolizei und des SD, 4 December 1940, Report to Reichsaussenminister, Anlage no. 45, 30 December 1940, captured German documents, Microfilm T-120/475/229307, Captured German and Related Records on Microfilm, National Archives, Washington, D.C.

11. Otto Abetz, Notiz für den Reichsaussenminister, 24 April 1938, Microfilm T-120/1746/403592–3; and Notiz für Parteigenosse Hewel, 30 August 1938, Microfilm T-120/1746/403579–80, Captured German Records, National Archives, Washington, D.C. See also Count Johannes von Welczeck, telegram from Paris to German Foreign Ministry, 20 July 1939, AN, Microfilm 562/MI/1, frame 248.

12. Hasso Spode, *Wie die Deutschen "Reiseweltmeister" wurden: Eine Einführung in die Tourismusgeschichte* (Erfurt: Landeszentrale für politische Bildung Thüringen, 2003), p. 130.

13. See, for example, André Halimi, *Chantons sous l'Occupation* (Paris: Olivier Orban, 1976), released as a film the same year; also Janet Maslin, movie review, *Chantons sous l'Occupation* (1976), *New York Times,* 25 November 1994, http://movies.nytimes.com/movie/review?res=9907E4D81430F936A15752C1A962958260 (accessed 30 June 2010).

14. Bertram M. Gordon, "*Ist Gott Französisch?* Germans, Tourism, and Occupied France, 1940–1944," *Modern and Contemporary France*, n.s., 4, no. 3 (1996): 292.

15. See introduction, note 1; also Olivier Barrot and Raymond Chirat, *La vie culturelle dans la France occupée* (Paris: Découvertes Gallimard Histoire, 2009), p. 34; and Ronald C. Rosbottom, *When Paris Went Dark: The City of Light under German Occupation, 1940–1944* (New York: Little, Brown, and Co., 2014), pp. 67–68.

16. Larry Collins and Dominique Lapierre, *Is Paris Burning?* (New York: Simon and Schuster, 1965).

17. There is some controversy over the timing of Hitler's visit to Paris as his companions gave different dates for it, with Speer noting it as 28 June and others among Hitler's entourage as 23 June, a Sunday. Two more recent accounts argue for 28 June. See Rosbottom, *When Paris Went Dark*, p. 72; and David Drake, *Paris at War, 1939–1944* (Cambridge: Belknap Press of Harvard University Press, 2015), pp. 76 and 438, note 63. Arno Breker, however, gave the date as 23 June; see Breker, "Hitler: Paris à la sauvette," *Historia* 319 (June 1973): 123. Speer refers to the tour as occurring "three days after the beginning of the armistice," which would place it on 28 June 1940. See Albert Speer, *Inside the Third Reich*, trans. Richard and Clara Winston (New York: Macmillan, 1970), p. 171. In his book devoted to Hitler's visit to Paris, Cédric Gruat, *Hitler à Paris, juin 1940* (Paris: Éditions Tirésias, 2010), pp. 40–44, opts for 23 June.

18. Arno Breker, *Paris, Hitler et moi* (Paris: Presses de la Cité, 1970), p. 100. Breker, one of Hitler's favorite artists, saw his work condemned after the war. André-Louis Dubois, a government official fired by Vichy in 1940 and hardly a partisan of the Nazis or their art, criticized what he believed to be an injustice in that, while many artists active under Hitler continued successful careers after the war, Breker was virtually blacklisted. See André-Louis Dubois, *À travers trois républiques: Sous le signe de l'amitié* (Paris: Plon, 1972), p. 123.

19. Breker, *Paris, Hitler et moi*, p. 107.

20. Ibid., p. 106. See also Gruat, *Hitler à Paris, juin 1940*, p. 144.

21. Breker, *Paris, Hitler et moi*, p. 110. See also David Pryce-Jones, *Paris in the Third Reich* (New York: Holt, Rinehart, and Winston, 1981), p. 13.

22. See Heinrich Hoffmann, *Mit Hitler im Westen* (Munich: Verlag Heinrich Hoffmann, 1940), cover; also Bertram M. Gordon, "Warfare and Tourism: Paris in World War II," *Annals of Tourism Research* 25, no. 3 (July 1998): 620. This frequently seen photo appeared again in a *New York Times* book review in 2010; see Brenda Wineapple, "We Love Paris," *New York Times Book Review,* 2 May 2010, p. 19.

23. Hoffmann, *Mit Hitler im Westen*, pp. 113 and 115, respectively. On Hoffmann, who grew wealthy from his monopoly on the photographs he took of Hitler, see Lynn H. Nicholas, *The Rape of Europa: The Fate of Europe's Treasures in the Third Reich and the Second World War* (New York: Alfred A. Knopf, 1994), pp. 16 and 31.

24. Pryce-Jones, *Paris in the Third Reich*, p. 13.

25. Roger Langeron, *Paris juin 40* (Paris: Flammarion, 1946), p. 92.

26. Gruat, *Hitler à Paris, juin 1940*, pp. 137–38.

27. Hoffmann, *Mit Hitler im Westen*, p. 25.

28. Ibid., pp. 109 and 116–19.

29. Pryce-Jones, *Paris in the Third Reich*, p. 88.

30. Claude Paillat, *Dossiers secrets de la France contemporaine*, vol. 5, *Le désastre de 1940 La guerre éclair 10 mai–24 juin 1940* (Paris: Robert Laffont, 1985), p. 591.

31. Gruat, *Hitler à Paris, juin 1940*, pp. 114–15.

32. *Signal*, 25 July 1940, cover.

33. *Die Tagebücher von Joseph Goebbels: Sämmtliche Fragmente*, ed. Elke Fröhlich, vol. 4 (Munich: H. Saur, 1987), pp. 224–25.

34. Boegner, "Mon été 40," p. 86. Henri Meilhac (1831–1897) and Ludovic Halévy (1834–1908) wrote the libretto for *Carmen*, based on Prosper Mérimée's eponymous novella (1845).

35. Chef der Sicherheitspolizei und des SD, 4 December 1940, Report to Reichsaussenminister, Anlage no. 45, 30 December 1940, captured German documents, Microfilm T-120/475/229307. For Sieburg's continuing influence, see Julia S. Torrie, "'Our Rear Area Probably Lived Too Well': Tourism and the German Occupation of France, 1940–1944," *Journal of Tourism History* 3, no. 3 (November 2011): 316.

36. Torrie, "'Our Rear Area Probably Lived Too Well,'" p. 316.

37. Robert Gildea, *Marianne in Chains: Daily Life in the Heart of France during the German Occupation* (New York: Picador, 2002), p. 48.

38. Von Rundstedt, Abschrift: Geheim! Der Oberbefehlshaber West/ Ia Nr. 1323/40 geh., 30 October 1940, AN, AJ/40/451 [folder 1, no. 27], AG 104. For Hitler's overestimation of the effectiveness of the Atlantic Wall fortifications, which, moreover, he had never seen, see Walter Warlimont, *Inside Hitler's Headquarters, 1939–45*, trans. R. H. Barry (1962; London: Weidenfeld and Nicolson, 1964), pp. 405–6.

39. Gérard Le Marec, *Guide des maquis et hauts-lieux de la Résistance en Bretagne/ Ille-et-Vilaine/Loire-Atlantique* (Paris: Presses de la Cité, 1987), p. 33.

40. Scott McCabe, "Who Is a Tourist? Conceptual and Theoretical Developments," in *Philosophical Issues in Tourism*, ed. John Tribe (Bristol: Channel View Publications, 2009), p. 31.

41. For Rommel on an inspection tour of the Atlantic Wall, see Photo Kurth Januar 1944, Bundesarchiv Bild 101I-295–1596–10, Frankreich, Atlantikküste, Erwin Rommel.

jpg., http://commons.wikimedia.org/wiki/File:Bundesarchiv_Bild_101I-295-1596-10,_Frankreich,_Atlantikk%C3%BCste,_Erwin_Rommel.jpg (accessed 12 June 2009). For the attention paid to the Atlantic Wall in 1943 and 1944, see Pierre Audiat, *Paris pendant la guerre* (Paris: Hachette, 1946), p. 232.

42. On aerial photography and the Atlantic Wall, see Rémy Desquesnes, *Normandy 1944: The Invasion and the Battle of Normandy*, trans. John Lee (Rennes: Éditions Ouest-France, 2009), pp. 74–75.

43. Ernst Jünger, *Journal de guerre et d'Occupation, 1939–1948*, trans. Henri Plard (Paris: René Julliard, 1965), Paris, 4 May 1944 entry, p. 315.

44. *L'Illustration*, 23 May 1943, cited in Desquesnes, *Normandy 1944*, pp. 22–23. For Rommel's repeated visits to Normandy and his urgent requests for more extensive building of the Atlantic Wall, see Toni and Valmai Holt, *The Visitor's Guide to Normandy Landing Beaches, Memorials and Museums* (Ashbourne, Derbyshire: Moorland, 1994), pp. 33–34. Named for a prominent engineer and Nazi official, the Organization Todt undertook engineering projects, including the *Autobahnen* (freeways), both before and during the war, when it frequently used forced labor.

45. "C'est tout ce qui reste du mur de l'Atlantique," cartoon, *Le Parisien Libéré*, 7 September 1944.

46. William L. Shirer, *Berlin Diary: The Journal of a Foreign Correspondent, 1934–1941* (New York: Alfred A. Knopf, 1941), p. 413.

47. Jean Berthelot, *Sur les rails du pouvoir* (1938–1942) (Paris: Robert Laffont, 1967), p. 69.

48. Audiat, *Paris pendant la guerre*, pp. 27 and 29.

49. État Français, Secrétariat d'État aux Communications et au P.T.T. et au Tourisme, Comité d'Organisation Professionnelle de l'Industrie Hôtelière/Hôtels—Restaurants—Débits de Boissons, note to Dr. Gehrhardt, Conseiller Supérieur de Guerre, Hôtel Majestic, Paris, 3 February 1942, Annexes 1 and 2, AN, AJ/40/784, folder 7, MBF 35, 22105E. For the restaurant rating system adopted 7 May 1941 by the French government, see Christian Guy, *Histoire de la gastronomie en France* (Paris: Éditions Fernand Nathan, 1985), p. 132. An otherwise unidentified German military report of 1943 stated that at least some of the twenty-one Paris nightclubs allowed to remain open until 5 a.m. should remain so, even in the face of increased Resistance activity, as German soldiers, sailors, and airmen brought from the battlefronts needed places to relax, as seen in a typewritten carbon copy of the report, Paris, 20 February 1943, AN, AJ/40/785, folder 1, MBF 38, 22105G. Gerhard Heller wondered rhetorically in his memoir how many meals he had taken with Bernard Grasset at Lipp; see Gerhard Heller, *Un Allemand à Paris, 1940–1944* (Paris: Seuil, 1981), p. 132.

50. For a list of those authorized to sell postcards and souvenirs, see Der Chef des Vorwaltungsstabes, Im Auftrag, Dr Labs, to Kommandostab I c, Paris, 28 April 1941, AN, AJ/40/890 [folder 6], GP VII 10. Collaborationist groups also tried to use their contacts with the Germans in the sale of souvenirs, as exemplified by a request that a certain Mademoiselle Mengin be allowed to sell souvenirs in the streets of Paris. See Le secrétaire-général de l'Organisation Territoriale (Province), Rassemblement National Populaire, Paris 12 July 1941, to M. le Commandant, Chef des Verwaltungsstabes, Service Interventions, N/réf. LG/MM, AN, AJ/40/890 [folder 6].

51. Vassili Soukhomline, *Les hitlériens à Paris*, translated from Russian by Lily Denis (Paris: Les Éditeurs Français Réunis, 1967), pp. 56–57. The purchasing power

of one French franc in 1943 was equal to 21.7 cents in 2015 according to Rodney Edvinsson, "Historical currency converter," http://www.historicalstatistics.org/ Currencyconverter.html (accessed 6 April 2018).

52. Soukhomline, *Les hitlériens à Paris*, pp. 28–29.

53. "Bericht vom 16. September über die Tätigkeit der General-Delegation bei der französischen Regierung in Paris," French Labor Ministry report to President of the French Delegation to the Armistice Commission, Wiesbaden, Anlage Nr. 2, from the Head of the Security Police and the *SD* to the Foreign Minister, 18 December 1940, Microfilm T120/300/228836.

54. Boegner, "Mon été 40," p. 84.

55. Emilie Brouze, "Lille," in *Voyage dans la France occupée*, ed. Pascal Ory (Mayenne: L'Express Bibliomnibus, 2014), p. 79.

56. Alfred Fabre-Luce, *Journal de la France 1939–1944* (Brussels: Cheval Ailé, 1946), p. 349.

57. Leutnant Müller, F. d. R. d. A., Kommandur 30. Division (Kommandant der Stadt Paris, 16 July 1940;, AN, AJ/40/451 [folder 5, no. 8], M. B. F. C. 59 L. Vii AG. 102, 1 Juli 1940–30 Juni 1941. The theme of Paris as an *Etappenstadt*, a rest and rehabilitation site for malingerers, is highlighted by Torrie, "'Our Rear Area Probably Lived Too Well,'" p. 316. See also August von Kageneck, *La France occupée* (Paris: Perrin, 2011), p. 71.

58. "Der Platzkommandant von Paris," *Der deutsche Wegleiter*, no. 21 (1–15 June 1941): 7.

59. Von Kageneck, *La France occupée*, pp. 70–71.

60. Für den Chef des Mil.-Verw.-Bezirks Paris, Der Chef des Kommandosstabes, note to Verwaltungsstab, Chambre des Députés, Paris, 29 September 1940, AN, AJ/40/890 [folder 4], no. 128.

61. Von Kageneck, *La France occupée*, p. 72.

62. Anti-German incidents were reported in Paris nightclubs; see Oberfeldwebel d. Feldgend., Incidents at "Au Vrai Saumur," 3 June 1941, AN, AJ/40/890 [folder 5], GP VII II, no. 11.

63. Von Kageneck, *La France occupée*, pp. 77–78.

64. Henri Amouroux, *La grande histoire des Français sous l'Occupation*, vol. 3, *Les beaux jours des collabos, juin 1941–juin 1942* (Paris: Robert Laffont, 1978), p. 14.

65. See Marc Milner, "The Battle That Had to Be Won," *Naval History Magazine* (U. S. Naval Institute) 22, no. 3 (June 2008), http://www.usni.org/magazines/ navalhistory/2008-06/battle-had-be-won (accessed 13 July 2012). See also Allan Mitchell, *Nazi Paris: The History of an Occupation, 1940–1944* (New York: Berghahn, 2010), p. 14.

66. Abschrift, from Oberbefehlshaber West, Heeresgruppe I a, no. 1547/40 geheim, to Militärbefehlshaber in Frankreich, 1 December 1940, in AN, AJ 40/451, folder M.B.F. C. 59. L. VIII A.G. 104.

67. Leutnant Dr. Roesch, Abschrift, Oberbefehlshaber West (Heeresgruppe A) Ia, Nr. 180/41 geh., to the MBF, 31 January 1941, AN, AJ/40/451 [folder 2, no. 16], MBF C. 59 L. VIII, AG, 105.

68. Christine Levisse-Touzé cited in Bruno D. Cot, "Paris," in Ory, *Voyage dans la France occupée*, p. 123.

69. Von Kageneck, *La France occupée*, pp. 72–73.

70. Ibid., pp. 74–75.

71. "Vorwart" and "Préface," in *Der deutsche Dr deutche Wegleiter für Paris*, no. 1 (15 July 1940): 3.

72. Ibid., pp. 13–15.

73. *Der deutsche Wegleiter*, no. 2 (15 August 1940): 3 and 17, respectively. *Der deutsche Wegleiter* was the new title given to *Der deutsche Wegleiter, für Paris*.

74. Deutsches Verkehrsburo, Reichsbahnzentrale für den Deutschen Reiseverkehr, Paris, 38 Avenue de l'Opéra, Paris, note, 20 September 1940, AN, AJ/40/878 [folder 2], C. 6 4III Ic 6; no. 434 in German, no. 435 in French.

75. Abteilung I c, "Entwurf," to I C (Besichtigung), Paris, 8 October 1940, AN, AJ/40/878 [folder 3], C. 6 LV Ic 17, no. 53.

76. *Deutscher Soldaten-Führer durch Paris* (Paris: M. Kenoun, 1940). For the comment about the beauty of Paris, see p. 11.

77. Dompol, letter to Major Prince Fritz von Ratibor und Corvej, Paris Command, Abteilung I c., 5 December 1940, AN, AJ/40/878 folder 1, C. 6 L. II. I c–5.

78. Propaganda-Abteilung M.B.F., Schrifttum, Daily Report, 17–23 May 1941, AN, AJ/40/1005, envelope 1.

79. *Deutscher Soldaten-Führer durch Paris*, pp. 23 and 28.

80. *Paris 1940* (Paris: Imprimerie Mouillier and Dermont, 1940), p. 6.

81. For the Louvre, see Audiat, *Paris pendant la guerre*, p. 76. The *Guide Aryen: Arischer Wegweiser* was published in 1941 and is unavailable in the BNF.

82. Interestingly, a cabaret, "L'Aiglon," was opened, with performers including Édith Piaf, in October 1940. The joke was that Napoleon's son was said not to like music. See "Les Nouveaux Programmes: L'Aiglon," in *Paris Programmes: Guide de la Vie Parisienne*, no. 2 (3–9 October 1940): 9 and 21 (an advertisement featuring Piaf).

83. Goebbels, *Die Tagebücher*, 4:434. See also H. Gz., "Auf den Spuren Napoleons in Paris, Zur Überführung der sterblichen Reste des 'Aiglons' in der Invalidendom," *Der deutsche Wegleiter*, no. 11 (1–12 January 1941): 6–7 and 77; and the guidebook *Paris und Umgebung: Odé-Buch* (Paris: Verlag Odé, 1941), pp. 11–12.

84. Eberhard Jäckel, *Frankreich in Hitlers Europa: Die deutsche Frankreichpolitik im zweiten Weltkrieg* (Stuttgart: Deutsche Verlags-Anstalt, 1966), p. 140.

85. Soukhomline, *Les hitlériens à Paris*, p. 182. See also Georges Poisson, *Le retour des cendres de l'Aiglon* (Paris: Nouveau Monde, 2006), pp. 132–33 and 142.

86. German translation of a letter written to Hitler, c/o Kommandantur, Paris, "Personelle," posted 16 December 1940, AN AJ/40/878 [folder 2], C. 6 4III I c 6, no. 452.

87. *Paris und Umgebung*, pp. 11–12.

88. "Richard Wagner in Paris," *Der deutsche Wegleiter*, no. 9 (1940): 4–5 and 60; and "Deutsche in Paris," *Pariser Zeitung* 1 (1941): 5.

89. "Vortragsnotiz," Abt. I c. 18 September 1940, AN, AJ/40/878 [folder 1], C. 6 4 II Ic. 5.

90. "Vorläufiges Programm für den Besuch der Gauleiter in Paris," angegeben durch Haupt. Froneberg—OKW—Berlin, AN AJ/40/878 [folder 3], C. 6 LV Ic 17, no. 56. This program is undated, but the dates for the visit described in the text were 3 through 6 October 1940.

91. Major Prinz von Ratibor, Kommandantur Paris, to General [unnamed], Paris, 18 October 1940 AN, AJ/40/878 [folder 3], C. [Caisse], 6, LV Ic 17, no. 28.

92. "Unterhaltungsprogramm für O. B. und Stab," H. Gr. Kdo. D, AN, AJ/40/451 [folder 2], C. 6 4III c 6, no. 393. There is no date on this report, but it is filed with material from December 1940. For the postwar Bal Tabarin, see Horace Sutton, *Footloose in France* (New York: Rinehart, 1948), p. 82.

93. Breker, *Paris, Hitler et moi*, pp. 137–38.

94. A menu from Maxim's, dated 23 June 1941, is mentioned in René Héron de Villefosse, *Histoire et géographie gourmands de Paris* (Paris: Les Éditions de Paris, 1956), p. 301.

95. Déat's unpublished "Carnet noir," his wartime diary, notes that he dined at Maxim's on 16 May 1941 with ten officers of the Propagandastaffel and on 7 July 1941 with the head of the Gestapo in Paris. See Marcel Déat, "Carnet noir," in Raymond Tournoux, *Le royaume d'Otto: France 1939–1945; Ceux qui a choisi l'Allemagne* (Paris: Flammarion, 1982), entries for 16 May and 10 July 1941, pp. 94–95.

96. "Mit den gruppen in Paris," *Der deutsche Wegleiter*, no. 19 (May 1941): 4–7.

97. Hauptmann Weiss, Den Kommandant von Paris, Abt Ic (Besichtigungen), Paris, 30 September 1940, Z. Hd, von Major Prinz Ratibor, AN, AJ/40/878 [folder 3], C. 6 LV Ic. 17, no. 60.

98. Stärkenmeldungen von I c/Bes. 1940 7, Abteilung I c, Paris Command, 9 October–29 December 1940, AN, AJ 40/878 folder 4, C. 6 L. III. I c–7.

99. "Besichtigung der Stadt Paris," Abteilung I c, Paris Command, Feldpostnummer 01468, 18 November 1940, AN, AJ 40/878 folder 4, C. 6 L. III. I c–7. See also "A Special Tour through 'Historical Paris' with the A. O. [Auslands Organisation, or Foreign Organization]," *Der deutsche Wegleiter*, no. 59 (5–19 December 1942): 43.

100. "Mit den Besichtigungsgruppen in Paris," *Der deutsche Wegleiter*, no. 19 (May 1941): 4–7.

101. Gilles Perrault and Jean-Pierre Azéma, *Paris under the Occupation*, trans. Allison Carter and Maximilian Vos (1987; New York: Vendome, 1989), p. 17. "Jeder einmal in Paris," or "J. E. I. P.," also called "Paris bei Nacht," was said to be a slogan of Werner Best, an Occupation officer, to emphasize the recreational use of the occupied French capital. See Pryce-Jones, *Paris in the Third Reich*, p. 88.

102. Auslands-Organisation der NSDAP, Landesgruppe Frankreich, Die deutsche Arbeiterfront [sic], *Tägliche Stadtbesichtigungen und Kulturfahrten durchgefuhrt vom Reichsamt Deutsches Volksbildungswerk* (Kaiserslautern: Tafels-Verlag, 1941).

103. Ibid.

104. "Paris wie es nicht im Baedeker steht," *Der deutsche Wegleiter*, no. 27 (1941): 4–9.

105. Hauptmann Weiss, Der Kommandant von Paris, Abt. Ic/Besichtigungen, Paris, note to Kommandatur von Paris, Abteilung I c, 11 September 1940, AN, AJ/40/878 [folder 4], C. 6 4III Ic. 7. A Reichsmark was valued at $2.50 in 1940. See Harold Marcuse, Historical Dollar-to-Marks Currency Conversion Page, http://www.history.ucsb.edu/faculty/marcuse/projects/currency.htm#tables (accessed 28 August 2016).

106. Abschrift, from Soldatenkaufhaus der Kommandanteur Paris, Verbindungsstelle, to Militärverwaltungsbezirk Paris, Verwaltungsstab. 30 October 1940, AN, AJ 40/878, folder 3–C. 6 LV I c 17; and Der Chef des Militärverwaltungsbezirks Paris, Verwaltungsstab, note to Platzkommandant, Paris, 12 October 1940, AN, AJ/40/878, folder 4–C. 6 LIII, I c 7.

107. Rudolf Krell, 21 rue Tronchet, Paris, 24 October 1940, letter to S. E. Herrn Major Prinz von Ratibor, Hôtel Meurice, Paris, AN, AJ/40/878 [folder 4], C. 6 4III Ic 7.

108. Der Chef des Militärverwaltungsbezirks Paris, Verwaltungsstab, An den Herrn Platzkommandant, Place de l'Opéra 2, Paris, 12 October 1940, AN, AJ/40/878 [folder 4], C. 6 LIII, Ic 7. See also Soldatenkaufhaus der Kommandantur Paris, Verbindungsstelle, "Abschrift," to Militärverwaltungsbezirk Paris, Verwaltungsstab, 30 October 1940, AN, AJ 40/878 [folder 3], C. 6 LV Ic 17.

109. Lieutenant Müller, 1940 Command Office, Thirtieth Division, Command Office of the City of Paris, flyer, 16 July 1940, AN, AJ 40/451, folder M.B.F. C. 59 L. VII. A. G. 102. See also Head Doctor (*Obersartzt*) Schreiber, 1940 Army Medical Office, High Army Command, "Prostitution und Bordelwesen im besetzten Gebiet Frankreichs, 16 July 1940, AN, AJ 40/451, folder M.B.F. C. 59 L. VIII. A. G. 104.

110. Schreiber, Oberarzt, Der Heeresarzt, Oberkommando des Heeres, Gen. St. d. H./Gen. Qu., Az. 265, Nr. 17150/40, "Betr.: Prostitution und Bordellwesen im besetzten Gebiet," 16 Juli 1940, AN, AJ/40/451 [folder 1, no. 6], AN, AJ/40/451 [folder 1, no. 5], Akte Nr. 130 geh.; also Der Generalquartiermeister Müller, Geheim. Oberkommando des Heeeres, Generalquartiermeister, Az.: 265 IVb Nr.: 11244//40 geh., "Betr.: Prostitution und Bordellwesen in Belgien und im bestzten Gebiet Frankreichs," 29 Juli 1940, AN, AJ/40/451 [folder 1, no. 5], Akte Nr. 130 geh. For German interest in clean brothels, see von Brauchitsch, Der Oberbehlshabers des Heeres, Gen. Qu. Gen St d H/Nr. 18 497/40, Anlage 1 zu Ob d H Nr. 8840/41, PA 2 (I/Ia) vom 6 September 1941, H. Qu den 31 Juli 1940, AN, AJ/40/451 (folder 2, no. 109).

111. Von Brauchitsch, Der Oberbefehlshaber des Heeres, Gen. Qu. Gen St d H/ Nr. 18 497/40, H. Qu., 31 July 1940, AN AJ/40/451 [folder 2, no. 109].

112. Insa Meinen, *Wehrmacht et prostitution sous l'Occupation (1940–1945)*, translated from German by Beate Husser (Paris: Payot, 2006), pp. 47 and 50.

113. Von Kageneck, *La France occupée*, p. 81.

114. Jean Guéhenno, *Journal des années noires (1940–1944)* (Paris: Gallimard, 1947), entry of 3 December 1941, p. 251.

115. Heinrich von Tyszka, Fregatenkapitan, Rouen, 2 July 1942, letter to MBF, transmitted to Herrn Oberst Karl-Richard Kossmann, Chef des Generalstabes beim MBF, AN AJ/40/784 [folder 8], MBF 38 22105 F.

116. Michèle Cointet, "Les cabarets parisiens doivent fermer," "100 idées reçues sur la Deuxième guerre mondiale," *Le point historia*, special issue (February–March 2012): 58.

117. Alan Riding, *And the Show Went On: Cultural Life in Occupied Paris* (New York: Alfred A. Knopf, 2010), p. 92.

118. Patrick Buisson, *1940–1945 Années érotiques: Vichy ou les infortunes de la vertu* (Paris: Albin Michel, 2008), pp. 264–65.

119. Riding, *And the Show Went On*, p. 202.

120. MBF [Militärbefehlshaber in Frankreich], Verwaltungsstab, Abteilung Wirtschaft, Entwurf, note to Secrétariat d'État au Ravitaillement, 26 May 1941, AN, AJ/40/784 [folder 3], 22105A.

121. From Herrn Leitenden Feldpolizeidirektor bei der Militärverwaltung Frankreich überrreicht, I. A., Dr. Hauke, Feldpolizeikommissar, to Geheime Feldpolizei, Sittenkommissariat Paris, Paris, 14 August 1940, AN, AJ/40/890 [folder 4], no. 150.

122. Für den Chef des Mil.=Verw.=Bezirks Paris, Der Chef des Kommandoss-tabes, note to Herrn Stadtkommandanten der Stadt Paris, pol/in Tgb. Nr. 4517/40, 21 September 1940, AN, AJ/40/890 [folder 4], no. 132. German prohibitions against dining in "Mohammedan" restaurants do not appear to have prevented Gerhard Heller from dining at the Paris Mosque, 39 rue Geoffroy-Saint-Hilaire, with Jean Paulhan; see Heller, *Un Allemand à Paris, 1940–1944*, pp. 97–98.

123. Organisation Todt, Leitstelle Paris, 33 Champs-Élysées, v. d. L./Kr, Paris, note to Kommandant von Gross-Paris, Abt. Unterkunft, z. Hdn. Herrn Oblt. Reissner, Paris, 2 December 1941, AN, AJ/40/785, MBF 38 [folder 4].

124. See État Français, Secrétariat d'État aux Communications et au P.T.T. et au Tourisme, Comité d'Organisation Professionnelle de l'Industrie Hôtelière/ Hôtels—Restaurants—Débits de Boissons, note to Dr. Gehrhardt, Conseiller Supérieur de Guerre, Hôtel Majestic, Paris, 3 February 1942, Annexes 1 and 2, AN, AJ/40/784, folder 7, MBF 35, 22105E. For the restaurant rating system adopted 7 May 1941 by the French government, see Guy, *Histoire de la gastronomie en France*, p. 132.

125. Annexes 1 and 2 in État Français, Secrétariat d'État aux Communications et au P.T.T. et au Tourisme, Comité d'Organisation Professionnelle de l'Industrie Hôtelière/Hôtels—Restaurants—Débits de Boisson, Paris, 3 February 1942, to Monsieur le Dr. Gerhardt, Conseiller Supérieur de Guerre, Hôtel Majestic, Wi II L4/21/42, AN, AJ/40/784 [folder 7], MBF 35 22105 E.

126. Der General der Luftwaffe Hanesse, Generalleutnant, to the Chef der Ver-waltungsstabes des MBF, Herrn Kriegsverwaltungschef Ministerialdirektor Dr. Michel, Paris, 19 January 1943; and Michel (?), to Hanesse, Paris, 26 January 1943, AN, AJ/40/784 [folder 8], MBF 3822105 F.

127. Secrétariat d'État à l'Agriculture et au Ravitaillement, Contrôle des Restau-rants/Janvier, Février, Mars, Avril Année 1942, to Verwaltungsstab, Zu Hd. V. Herrn Dr. Gerhardt, Hotel Majestic, Paris, 4 May 1942, AN AJ/40/784 [folder 4].

128. Albert Belmas and Xavier de La Tour, report, 17 June 1942, AN, AJ/40/784 [folder 4], MBF 39 22105 B, "Straffenmassnahmungen gegen Gaststätten." For a detailed investigation of the restaurant at the Hotel Claridge, see Kommandanten von Gross-Paris, Verwaltungsstabes, Wi. II/L4/151/42, Paris, 25 September 1942, AN, AJ/40/784 [folder 6], MBF 39 22105 D. Infractions were found in the restaurant's operations serving French clientele; a German part of the restaurant was exempted.

129. Geheim, Wi VI (X) 106/4 geh., to Herrn OKVR Dr Gehrhardt, im Hause, Paris, 12 August 1942, AN, AJ/40/784 [folder 8], MBF 38 22105 F.

130. Kommandanten von Gross-Paris, Verwaltungsstab, OKVR Dr. Fischer, Wi II L4/22105 C, to the Befehlshaber der Sicherheitspolizei und des Sicherheits-dienst, Paris, 3 November 1942, AN, AJ/40/785, MBF 38 [folder 1]; and Komman-dant von Gross-Paris, Militärverwaltung, Wi/gew. 1/520; W. II/L3/250/63, Paris, 19 May 1943, AN, AJ/40/784 [folder 5], MBF 39 22105 C. See also Dr. Knochen, SS-Standartenführer u. Oberst d. Polizei, to MBF, Chef des Stabes Oberst i. G. Koss-mann, Paris, 28 January 1943, and OKVRat Lippert, report, Paris, 16 February 1943, AN, AJ/40/784 [folder 5], MBF 39 22105 C.

131. Jünger, *Journal de guerre et d'Occupation, 1939–1948*, entry of 4 July 1942, p. 147.

132. Dr. Grosse, "Aufzeichnung für Herrn Gesandten Schleier," 23 June 1943, in "Missstände im Gaststättengewerbe Allgemeines," AN, AJ/40/784 [folder 8], MBF

38 22105 F. For Schleier, see Michael L. Berkvam, "Germany, Embassy in Occupied Paris," in *Historical Dictionary of World War II France: The Occupation, Vichy, and the Resistance, 1938–1946,* ed. Bertram M. Gordon (Westport, Conn.: Greenwood Press, 1998), p. 158.

133. "Dr. Pazaureck, "Zweierlei, 'Ravitaillement' in Paris: Das Luxusrestaurant, das Supplement, der Schwarzhandel und die kleine Burger," *Die Zeit: Reichenberg/Sudetengau,* 3 August 1942, clipping sent by Reinhardt to OKVR Dr Gerhardt, AN AJ/40/784 [folder 8], MBF 38 22105 F.

134. "Die schönste Erinnerung an Paris und Frankreich," August 1941, library of the Mémorial–Cité de l'Histoire, Caen, Fonds Allemagne—Boîte 71 (2), kindly made available by Marie-Claude Berthelot, *documentaliste.*

135. Doré Ogrizek, *Paris, Frankreich Nord und West* (Paris: Odé, 1941). See also the advertisement for this book in the library of the Mémorial–Cité de l'Histoire, Caen, Fonds Allemagne—Boîte 71 (2), kindly made available by Marie-Claude Berthelot, *documentaliste.*

136. *Paris und Umgebung,* pp. 11–12.

137. Ibid., pp. 36–38.

138. For the Ogrizek tour books on France published in German during the Occupation, see WorldCat Identities, http://orlabs.oclc.org/identities/lccn-no96-53847 (accessed 20 January 2010). Ogrizek, an editor for Odé, coordinated the publication of tour guides covering much of the world during the 1940s and 1950s. The BNF's Opale digitized catalogue, accessed 2 July 2010, lists some sixty-five books under "Ogrizek, Doré" covering the period from 1943 through 1969.

139. "Saar-Verlag," http://de.wikipedia.org/wiki/Saar-Verlag (accessed 2 July 2010).

140. Dr. H.O.H., "Deutsch und Französisch," *Der deutsche Wegleiter,* no. 45 (26 May-6 June 1942): 4–5.

141. Quoted in von Kageneck, *La France occupée,* pp. 74–75. The text is from Heinz Lorenz, ed., *Frankreich, ein Erlebnis des deutschen Soldaten* (Paris: Ode, 1942).

142. Heinz Lorenz, *Soldaten fotografieren Frankreich: Ein Bilderbuch mit Erzählungen* (Paris: Wegleiter Verlag, 1943), esp. p. 7.

143. "Feldgraue Malen in Paris," Reischach Press Service, Paris, 4 November 1943, AN, AJ 40/1192, envelope 3.

144. Ian Buruma, "Occupied Paris: The Sweet and the Cruel," *New York Review of Books,* 17 December 2009, p. 26.

145. See Mary Louise Roberts, "Wartime Flânerie: The Zucca Controversy," in *French Politics, Culture and Society* 27, no. 1 (Spring 2009): 102–10. The war years continue to be the subject of exhibitions in Paris and elsewhere; see Celestin Bohlen, "Occupation of France during World War II Revisited in Words," *New York Times,* 8 June 2011, http://www.nytimes.com/2011/06/09/arts/09iht-nazifrance09.html?_r=1&emc=tnt&tntemail1=y (accessed 9 June 2011).

146. "Das Konzert der Berliner Philharmoniker im Trocadéro-Theater, Paris," *Der deutsche Wegleiter,* no. 5 (1 October 1940): 4–5.

147. Gordon, *Ist Gott Französisch?,* p. 291.

148. Guéhenno, *Journal des années noires,* entry of 24 March 1941, p. 138.

149. Paul Strecker, "Das Antlitz von Paris: Von Jahrhunderten geformt und gewandelt; Ein Spiegel der Entwicklung; Das Musée Carnavalet," *Pariser Zeitung* 3 (17 January 1941): 4.

150. For Rehbein, see "Merkblatt für die Truppenbetreuung des Kommandanten von Gross-Paris," undated, http://nsl-archiv.com/Buecher/Bis-1945/Merkblatt%20fuer%20die%20Truppenbetreuung%20des%20Komandanten%20von%20Gross-Paris%20(1940,%204%20S.,%20Scan).pdf (accessed 14 February 2010).

151. Private Dr. Rehbein, "Das Antlitz Frankreichs," *Der deutsche Wegleiter*, no. 54 (26 September–10 October 1942): 4–8.

152. Dr. H.O.H., "Deutsch und Französisch."

153. Abschrift an den Militärbefehlshaber in Frankreich, 1 November 1940, AN, AJ/40/451, folder M.B.F. C. 59. L. VII A.G. 102.

154. Nicholas Stargardt, "Losses at Kursk," *Times Literary Supplement*, 10 October 2008, pp. 7–9. This article reviews Richard J. Evans, *The Third Reich at War, 1939–1945* (London: Allen Lane, 2008). See also Walter Reich, "We Are All Guilty," *New York Times Book Review*, 17 May 2009, http://www.nytimes.com/2009/05/17/books/review/Reich-t.html (accessed 6 April 2018). The work of the journalist Ernst Klee documents this behavior.

155. Ian Buruma, "The Twisted Art of Documentary," *New York Review of Books*, 25 November 2010, p. 44. Buruma cites Barbara Engelking and Jacek Leociak, *The Warsaw Ghetto: A Guide to the Perished City* (New Haven: Yale University Press 2009), p. 247. The unfinished film *Das Ghetto*, made by the Nazis in Warsaw, was used in a film by the Israeli filmmaker Yael Hersonski, whose own film *"Quand les nazis filmaient le ghetto* (When the Nazis Filmed the Ghetto; in English, *A Film Unfinished*) juxtaposes the wartime Nazi film with survivors' accounts. Hersonski's film was shown in France in 2009. Nicole Mullier, "TV: Quand les nazis filmaient le ghetto de Varsovie," email to H-Français, H-FRANCAIS@H-NET.MSU.EDU (8 December 2010).

156. See, for example, Heller, *Un Allemand à Paris, 1940–1944*. For the *Wegleiter* tourist itineraries, see *Der deutsche Wegleiter*, no. 59 (5–19 December 1942).

157. See the extensive discussions of Sartre, especially in Susan Rubin Suleiman, *Crises of Memory and the Second World War* (2006; Cambridge: Harvard University Press, 2008); and Riding, *And the Show Went On*.

158. Heller, *Un Allemand à Paris, 1940–1944*, pp. 51–52.

159. Ibid., p. 123.

160. Michèle C. Cone, *Artists under Vichy: A Case of Prejudice and Persecution* (Princeton: Princeton University Press, 1992), p. 150; Heller, *Un Allemand à Paris, 1940–1944*, pp. 118–19; and Gilles and Jean-Robert Ragache, *La vie quotidienne des écrivains et des artistes sous l'Occupation* (Paris: Hachette, 1988), p. 127. Picasso was visited on at least one occasion by German agents who insulted him and damaged some of his painting but otherwise was left alone. See André-Louis Dubois, *À travers trois républiques: Sous le signe de l'amitié* (Paris: Plon, 1972), pp. 144–45.

161. Romy Golan, *Modernity and Nostalgia: Art and Politics in France between the Wars* (New Haven: Yale University Press, 1995), p. 158. See also Suzanne Perkins, "Matisse, Henri," in Gordon, *Historical Dictionary of World War II France*, p. 238.

162. Jünger, *Journal de guerre et d'Occupation, 1939–1948*, entry of 10 June 1940, p. 65.

163. Ibid., entry of 30 May 1941, p. 111.

164. Ibid., entry of 18 September 1942, p. 161.

165. Heller, *Un Allemand à Paris, 1940–1944*, p. 164.

166. Ibid., pp. 164–65.

167. Ahlrich Mayer, *L'occupation allemande en France*, trans. from German by Pascale Hervieux, Florence Lecanu, and Nicole Taubes (Paris: Privat, 2002), p. 29. For an example of a self-serving postwar apologia for living the good life in occupied Paris while Germany carried out its belligerent policies, see Heller, *Un Allemand à Paris, 1940–1944*, p. 168.

168. See Jünger, *Journal de guerre et d'Occupation, 1939–1948*, entry of 4 July 1942, p. 147.

169. Breker, *Paris, Hitler et moi*, p. 146.

170. Ibid., pp. 152–53.

171. Dr. von Tieschowitz, "Deutscher Kunstschutz in Frankreich," *Der deutsche Wegleiter*, no. 52 (29 August–12 September 1942): 7.

172. See AN, AJ/40/573 [folder 12], "Führungen, Reisen, Aufsätze." The term *Kunstschutz*, meaning "protection of art," used by the Germans in occupied Belgium and northeastern France during World War I, was known by the peoples of those countries as "pillage" and "spoliation." See Antoine Fleury, *Le rôle des guerres dans la mémoire des Européens: Leur effet sur la conscience d'être européen* (Bern: Peter Lang, 1997), pp. 17–18.

173. The spoliation is described extensively in Heller, *Un Allemand à Paris, 1940–1944*, p. 32; and Hector Feliciano, *The Lost Museum* (New York: HarperCollins, 1997).

174. Dr. von Tieschowitz, "Deutscher Kunstschutz in Frankreich," *Der deutsche Wegleiter*, no. 52 (29 August–12 September 1942): 4–5. See also Erhard Göpel, *Die Normandie* (Rouen/Paris: Armee-Oberkommando, 1942), p. 140. I am indebted to Rémy Desquennes of the Conseil régional de Basse-Normandie for the use of this book from his collection.

175. Göpel, *Die Normandie*, p. 94.

176. Dagobert Frey, "Errichtung eines kunsthistorischen Stützpunktes in Paris," Der Reichsminister für Wissenschaft, Erziehung und Volksbildung, W N 2218, WV, Berlin, 19 February 1941, Akten Nr. V kult 414 betr. Deutsche Institute in Frankreich, Band Nr. 1, AN, AJ/40/564 [folder 3].

177. Nikola Doll, "Politisierung des Geists: Der Kunsthistoriker Alfred Stange und die Bonner Kunstgeschichte im Kontext nationalsozialistischer Expansionspolitik," in *Griff nach dem Westen: Die "Westforschung" der völkisch-nationalen Wissenschaften zum nordwesteuropäischen Raum (1919–1960)*, ed. Burkhard Dietz, Helmut Gabel, and Ulrich Tiedau, Studien zur Geschichte und Kultur Nordwesteuropas, vol. 6 (Münster: Waxmann Verlag, 2003), pp. 979–80.

178. Krümmel, Der Reichsminister für Wissenschaft, Erziehung und Volksbildung, WN 768, "Zum Schreiben vom 5. April 1941—kult U 1662—betr. Einrichtung eines Kunsthistorischen Stützpunktes in Paris," an das Auswärtige Amt, Berlin, 19 Mai 1941; and idem, WN 1175/41, 19 Juli 1941, Akten Nr. V kult 414, betr: Deutsche Institut in Frankreich, Band Nr. 1, AN, AJ/40/564 [folder 3].

179. Joseph Buchkremer, Dombaumeister, "Reise nach Paris, 15.–25. Juni 1942," cover, AN, AJ/40/573 [folder 11].

180. Ibid., cover and p. 7. The earlier German tour mentioned was the "Studienfahrt deutscher Kunsthistoriker durch ausgewählte Gebiete Frankreichs vom 21.9–6.10.1941." The Italians also expressed interest in a possible recovery of artwork taken by the French in 1798; see Dr K. H. Bremer, Deutsches Institut, Paris,

note to Militärbefehlshaber in Frankreich, Paris, 23 December 1941, AN, AJ/40/564 [folder 5].

181. Göpel, *Die Normandie*, p. 94.

182. Dr. Hesse, Oberst, Der Feldkommandant, Feldkommandantur (R)758, Kommando-Stab, St-Cloud, 9 June 1943, "Fahrten an die Loire zur Besichtung einiger Schlösser," AN, AJ/40/573 [folder 11]. Two hundred fifty francs in 1943 would have equaled $54.25 in 2015 (see note 51 above). This figure is deceptive, however, because of the German-enforced undervaluing of the franc vis-à-vis the mark.

183. Magdeleine Hours, *Une vie au Louvre* (Paris: Robert Laffont, 1987), p. 60. Hours, who also managed to hide documents during the war, had a distinguished career at the Louvre; see Hervé Gauville, " Magdeleine Hours, une vie dédiée au Louvre: L'experte scientifique est morte à l'âge de 92 ans," *Libération*, 1 April 2005, http://www.liberation.fr/culture/0101524270-magdeleine-hours-une-vie-dediee-au-louvre (accessed 23 June 2011).

184. Franz Albrecht Medicus and Hans Hörmann, *Schlösser in Frankreich: Bilder und Beschreibungen* (Paris: Wegleiter Verlag, 1944), pp. 7, 63, 86, 17, 167, 109, and 119.

185. MVR Dr. Hans Hörmann, "Reisebericht über die Dienstreise im Bereich des Kommandanten des Heeresgebiets Südfrankreich vom 14.-17.9.43 einschl.," and "Tätigkeitsbericht über die Dienstleitung während des Heeresgebiets Südfrankreich in Lyon vom 9. Sept mit 22. Oktober 1943," Geheime Kunstschutz Frankreich, AN, AJ/40/573 [folder 2].

186. Bericht des OKVR Dr. [Hans] Möbius über seine Dienstreise nach Périgueux und in das Vézère-Tal vom 26.2.43, to Kommandant des Heeresgebietes Südfrankreich Qu/Kult St. Qu., 26 February 1943, AN, AJ/40/573 [folder 8]. Because of the German occupation, and the use of the Lascaux caves to hide weapons by the Resistance, the cave paintings, discovered in September 1940 by Marcel Ravidat and two friends, were not opened to public view until 1948. See "Marcel Ravidat, Discoverer of Lascaux Cave Paintings, Dies at 72," *New York Times*, 31 March 1995.

187. Jacques Jaujard, Director of Museums, Ministère de l'Education Nationale/Beaux-Arts/Direction des Musées Nationaux et de l'École du Louvre, 7 March 1944; and Oberbefehlshaber West (Oberkommando Heeresgruppe D), Inspekteur der Landesbefestigung. Az. 39 Geol. 16a, Br. B. Nr. 109/44 geh., to MBF Abt. Verw. ½, AN, AJ/40/573 Kunstschutz [folder 2].

188. Der Chef der Militärverwaltung, Für den Militärbefehlshaber, to the Direction des Beaux-Arts, Palais-Royal, Paris, 19 April 1943, Der MBF V 1/2 kult, AN, AJ/40/573 Kunstschutz [folder 2].

189. RD, "Die Kathedrale von Rouen zum zweiten Male durch deutsche Soldaten vor der Zerstörung gerettet," Reischach Press Service, Paris, 2 June 1944, AN, AJ 40/1193, envelope 1.

190. Bernhard von Tieschowitz, MVR, Bericht über die Verbringung des Mathildenteppichs aus Bayeux von Sourches nach Paris, 27 June 1944, to Oberbefelshaber durch die Hand des Herrn Leiters der Abteilung Verwaltung und des Chefs den Militärverwaltung mit der Bitte um Kenntnisnahme, Verw. 1/2 Kult (Kunstschutz) Nr. 212/44 geh., AN, AJ/40/573 [folder 8].

191. Philippe Dagen, "Les musées français face à l'Histoire, pendant l'Occupation," "Le Centre Pompidou présente 39 œuvres volées par les nazis," and "Sous l'Occupation, le marché de l'art se portait à merveille," *Le Monde*, 19 November 1996,

4 April 1997, and 12 April 1997, respectively. See also Alan Riding, "France to Display Art Looted by the Nazis," *New York Times,* 3 April 1997. The attempts to return stolen artworks were only minimally successful. Between 1999 and 2013 a government-sponsored commission distributed €33 million in compensation to the owners of art that could not be found, but returned only nine artworks. See Hélène Fouquet, "France Strives to Return Nazi-Stolen Art to Its Owners," Bloomberg Business, 21 February 2013, http://www.bloomberg.com/bw/articles/2013-02-21/france-strives-to-return-nazi-stolen-art-to-its-owners (accessed 15 January 2016).

192. Jünger, *Journal de guerre et d'Occupation, 1939–1948,* entry of 8 December 1941, p. 125.

193. "Deutsche Soldatengraben in Paris," *Der deutsche Wegleiter,* no. 40 (14–28 March 1942): 5–7 and 24. German soldiers killed during the Second World War in France have since been reburied in La Cambe and other military cemeteries in Normandy.

194. Schaumburg, Der Kommandant von Gross-Paris, Ia Nr. 170/42 geh., Paris, 28 March 1942, AN, AJ/40/451 [folder 3, no. 34].

195. JB [Josef Berdolt], "Die Amerika-Heimkehrer in Frankreich eingetroffen," Reischach Press Service, Paris, 19 May 1942, AN, AJ 40/1192, envelope 1.

196. Neuendorf, Nationalsozialistische Deutsche Arbeiterpartei, Auslands-Organisation, Landesgruppe Frankreich, Der Landesgruppenleiter. Ndf/Fk WI.II/L3/233/43, Paris, note to MBF, Chef der Verwaltungsstabes, Herrn Kriegsverwaltungsstabes Dr. Michel, Paris, 22 February 1943, AN, AJ/40/785, MBF 38 L3 [folder 1].

197. Robert Kanigel, *High Season in Nice,* quoted in French and English Riviera, Excelsior Hotel—Nice in WWII, https://nicebrighton.wordpress.com/2011/02/05/excelsior-hotel-nice-in-wwii/ (accessed 11 November 2015).

198. Ibid.

199. For their convenience, shortly after occupying much of France, the Germans moved France to their time zone, a change that was retained after the war and gave rise to the expression "France on German time." See Yvonne Poulle, "La France à l'heure allemande," Bibliothèque de l'École des chartes 157, no. 2 (1999): 493–502, www.persee.fr/doc/bec_0373-6237_1999_num_157_2_450989 (accessed 16 January 2016).

200. *Grieben Reiseführer,* vol. 212, *Paris Kleine Ausgabe mit Anhang: Ergänzungen 1943* (Berlin: Grieben-Verlag, 1938; Paris: Imprimerie Curial-Archereau, 1943), 1–2. The 1943 edition of the Grieben guidebook was a reissue and expanded edition of a 1938 publication.

201. Ibid., pp. 2–3.

202. Ibid., pp. 7–8.

203. Arendts [?], Der Chef der Generalstabes, Im Auftrag, Abschrift, MBF, Abt. IIa/IIb, Nr. 761/43 geh., "Mitnahme von Gepäck durch Urlauber in SF-Zügen," 9 November 1943, AN, AJ/40/451 [folder 4, no. 75], Akte Nr. 130 geh., betr: Allgemeine Vorschriften und Bestimmungen für Wehrmachtsangehörige und Wehrmachtsgefolge, Band Nr. IV (Jahrgang 1943).

204. Guéhenno, *Journal des années noires,* entry of 5 April 1943, p. 384.

205. F., "Ausstellung der Waffen-SS auf den Champs-Élysées 44," *Der deutsche Wegleiter,* no. 89 (29 January–12 February 1944): 22–24.

206. Guéhenno, *Journal des années noires*, entry of 12 June 1944, p. 481.

207. Audiat, *Paris pendant la guerre*, pp. 260–61.

208. Th. Dorza, "Im Calvados: Impressionen aus der Normandie," *Pariser Zeitung*, 8 August 1944.

209. Jünger, *Journal de guerre et d'Occupation, 1939–1948*, entry of 8 August 1944, p. 337.

210. Audiat, *Paris pendant la guerre*, p. 269.

211. Victoria Kent, *Quatre ans à Paris*, translated from Spanish by Pierre du Castillan (Paris: Le Livre du Jour, 1947), entry of 21 August 1944, p. 203.

212. Audiat, *Paris pendant la guerre*, p. 293.

213. Ibid., p. 296.

214. Ibid., p. 321.

215. Ian Buruma, "The Argument That Saved Paris," *New York Review of Books*, 15 October 2014, http://www.nybooks.com/blogs/nyrblog/2014/oct/15/argument-saved-paris/ (accessed 3 November 2015); and "Nazi General Didn't Save Paris," *The Local*, 25 August 2014, http://www.thelocal.fr/20140825/nazi-general-didnt-save-paris-expert (accessed 2 November 2015).

216. Choltitz's memoir was published as Dietrich von Choltitz, *Soldat unter Soldaten* (Konstanz: Europa-Verlag, 1951).

217. Collins and Lapierre, *Is Paris Burning?*, p. 53.

218. Ibid., pp. 89–90.

219. Geoffrey M. White, "Is Paris Burning? Touring America's 'Good War' in France," *History & Memory* 27, no. 2 (Fall–Winter 2015): 82.

220. A CD-ROM was produced by the historian Marc Ferro featuring this, among other moments of the war, in France. See Daniel Schneidermann, "La seconde guerre mondiale, pour mémoire," *Le Monde Télévision Radio Multimédia*, 20–21 October 1996, p. 35. Emblematic of the iconic status of Paris was the photo book published within months of the Liberation; see *La semaine héroïque, 19–25 août 1944* (Paris: S. E. P. E., 1944).

5. The Liberation, 1944

1. For the French economic exploitation of *tourisme de mémoire*, see Henning Meyer, "Der Wandel der französischen 'Erinnerungskultur' des Zweiten Weltkriegs am Beispiel dreier 'Erinnerungsorte': Bordeaux, Caen und Oradour-sur-Glane" (Ph.D. diss., Université Michel de Montaigne Bordeaux 3, 14 November 2006), p. 529.

2. "Réception des Missions militaires alliées chargées de la protection des Sites et Monuments," 4 December 1944, p. 200; and "Normandie," 8 January 1945, p. 215, Touring Club de France, AN-20000028–10.

3. Note from the Secrétaire-Général, Commissariat-Général du Tourisme, to the Commissaire Général, 9 October 1945, folder "Comité d'Organisation des Agences et Bureaux de Voyages, AN, F/14/13714.

4. L. R. Blanchard, *Les Journalistes Américains . . . See France* (Rochester, N.Y.: Gannett Newspapers, 1946), p. 7.

5. The argument that American awareness of the heavy damage and frequent resentment caused by Allied bombing in Normandy is largely a recent phenomenon is summarized in Robert Zaretsky, "How the French Saw D-Day: What World War II

Looked Like When It Was Your Village Being Overrun," *Boston Globe*, 1 June 2014, https://www.bostonglobe.com/ideas/2014/05/31/how-french-saw-day/U7JLZNta UxTw4s5qaNKueO/story.html (accessed 27 November 2015).

6. Blanchard, *Les Journalistes Américains*, pp. 16–17.

7. Ibid., pp. 18–19.

8. Ibid., p. 20.

9. Ibid., pp. 21–22.

10. Triboulet subsequently represented Calvados in the French parliament under various center-right political parties.

11. Elisabeth Raffray, "La protection du patrimoine militaire de la Seconde Guerre mondiale en Basse-Normandie: Le mur de l'Atlantique et le port artificiel d'Arromanches" (master's thesis, École du Louvre/Muséologie, 1998–99), pp. 6–7.

12. Author's interview with Philippe Chapron, director of the Musée mémorial de la Bataille de Normandie, Bayeux, 19 May 2009. The Michelin map was number 102.

13. Eddy Florentin, *Les 5 plages du 6 juin: Guides Historia/Tallandier* (Paris: Tallandier, 1988), pp. 142–45. An additional twelve with four more related sites are listed for Great Britain; see pp. 146–49.

14. Duncan Campbell-Smith, "Between Beaches," review of John Forfar, *From Gold to Omaha, Times Literary Supplement*, 29 January 2010, p. 28.

15. Olivier Wieviorka, *La mémoire désunie: Le souvenir politique des années sombres, de la Libération à nos jours* (Paris: Seuil, 2010), pp. 219–20.

16. "Itinéraire No. 1100: Le Circuit de la Libération," in *Horizons de France et d'Europe* (Paris: Compagnie Française de Tourisme, 1948), pp. 1–2 and 12. For an extended discussion of this tourist circuit in the context of the Gaullist narratives of the invasion, see my chapter "French Cultural Tourism and the Vichy Problem," in *Being Elsewhere: Tourism, Consumer Culture, and Identity in Modern Europe and North America*, ed. Shelley Baranowski and Ellen Furlough (Ann Arbor: University of Michigan Press, 2001), p. 250.

17. Gilbert Fernez, Secretary General, Comité du Souvenir de la Résistance du Havre et de la Région, letter to General Direction, Arts and Letters, 16 October 1961, AN, F21/7085D, folder "Seine-Maritime/Le Havre/Monument commémoratif de la Résistance."

18. Pierre Kœnig, "Préface," in Patrice Boussel, *Guide des plages du débarquement* (Paris: Librairie Polytechnique Béranger/Département Technique des Presses de la Cité, 1964), pp. 5–6.

19. Francis Ambrière, "Préface," in *Les guides bleus: Normandie* (Paris: Hachette, 1965), p. vi. Ambrière was director of the *Guides bleus*. Among several memorials introduced to the tourist was the American Military Cemetery at Colleville-sur-Mer; ibid., p. 443.

20. Eugene Fodor, ed., *Fodor's Modern Guides: France, 1967* (New York: David McKay Co., 1967), pp. 232–34.

21. Stephen H. Chicken, *Overlord Coastline: A History of D-Day with Special Emphasis on What Can Be Seen Today* (Staplehurst, Kent: Spellmount, 1993), p. xix.

22. Ibid., p. 42.

23. Toni and Valmai Holt, *The Visitor's Guide to Normandy Landing Beaches: Memorials and Museums*, (Ashbourne, Derbyshire: Moorland, 1994), pp. 263–66 and 36.

24. "D-Day Remembered, 1944–1994," *Travel + Leisure*, supplement (May 1994): 6 and 14, respectively.

25. "D-Day 50/Plymouth—Torbay—Slapton," brochure published by the Plymouth Marketing Bureau and the English Riviera Tourist Board (Exeter: A. B. Graphics, n.d.).

26. Mary Blume, "Normandy's 50th-Anniversary Invasion," *New York Times*, 22 January 1994, http://www.nytimes.com/1994/01/22/style/22iht-dday.html (accessed 3 January 2016).

27. Kate C. Lemay, "Gratitude, Trauma, and Repression: D-Day in French Memory," in *D-Day in History and Memory: The Normandy Landings in International Remembrance and Commemoration*, ed. Michael R. Dolski, Sam Edwards, and John Buckley (Denton: University of North Texas Press, 2014), pp. 173–74.

28. "Espace Historique de la Bataille de Normandie/Normandie Terre-Liberté," Comité départemental du Tourisme du Calvados, Caen, 1994.

29. Holt and Holt, *The Visitor's Guide to Normandy Landing Beaches*, p. 34.

30. Ibid., p. 6.

31. "Normandie Pass: Des reductions sur vos visites," issued by the tourist office, Basse-Normandie, no. SIRET Normandie Mémoire, 444 116 453 00036.

32. Author's interview with Philippe Chapron, 19 May 2009. Chapron indicated that statistics were kept on the number of visitors to the local area but not specifically to the museum. The museum employed eight people who staffed the equivalent of eleven positions, according to Chapron.

33. Don van den Bogert, "Musée-Mémorial de la Bataille de Normandie," ww2museums.com, STIWOT (Stichting Informatie Wereldoorlog Twee), http://www.ww2museums.com/article/62/Mus%E9e-M%E9morial-de-la-Bataille-de-Normandie.htm (accessed 17 July 2010).

34. *Arromanches: Histoire d'un Port* (Cully [Calvados]: OREP Éditions, 2009), p. 30. See also François-Guillaume Lorrain, "Obama à Omaha, un must," *Le Point*, no. 1916 (4 June 2009): 70. For the relationship between the museum and local tourism, see Meyer, "Der Wandel der französischen 'Erinnerungskultur' des Zweiten Weltkriegs am Beispiel dreier 'Erinnerungsorte,'" p. 210.

35. The figures were 210,500 in 1960 and 227,500 in 1961, according to the *Annuaire statistique de la France 1962* (Paris: Imprimerie Nationale and Presses Universitaires de France, 1962), p. 291, and 213,500 in 1962; 258,000 in 1963; and 284,000 in 1964, according to the *Annuaire statistique de la France 1965* (Paris: Imprimerie Nationale and Presses Universitaires de France, 1965), p. 396. The figures were gathered by the Institut national de la statistique et des études économiques (INSEE).

36. Author's interview with Frédéric Sommier, director of the Musée du débarquement, Arromanches les Bains, 18 May 2009. As of 2009, the museum employed seventeen with an additional six or seven seasonal workers for the summer. Some forty thousand students, half French and half English, visited annually. A third of these visited in groups, the remainder as individuals, Sommier indicated.

37. "Les Dix Sites Bas-Normands Payants les Plus Visités," *INSEE Basse-Normandie—Bilan 2011*, p. 29, http://www.insee.fr/fr/insee_regions/basse-normandie/themes/dossiers/bilan_2011/pdf/tourisme.pdf (accessed 24 December 2015).

38. Lemay, "Gratitude, Trauma, and Repression," pp. 173–74.

39. Daniel J. Sherman, "Objects of Memory: History and Narrative in French War Museums," *French Historical Studies* 19, no. 1 (Spring 1995): 50.

40. See in particular Olivier Wieviorka, *Normandy: The Landings to the Liberation of Paris,* trans. M. B. DeBevoise (Cambridge: Belknap Press of Harvard University Press, 2008), pp. 227–28; and Wieviorka, *La mémoire désunie,* pp. 222–24.

41. Michèle Perissière, "Le Mémorial de Caen: Un musée pour la paix," in *Des musées d'histoire pour l'avenir,* ed. Marie-Hélène Joly and Thomas Compère-Morel (Paris: Éditions Noêsis, 1998), p. 189. See also Sherman, "Objects of Memory," p. 50.

42. Shannon L. Fogg, *The Politics of Everyday Life in Vichy France: Foreigners, Undesirables, and Strangers* (Cambridge: Cambridge University Press, 2009), p. xiii.

43. Claude Origet du Cluzeau, *Le tourisme culturel: Que sais-je?* (1998; Paris: Presses Universitaires de France, 2007), pp. 64–65 and 66–67.

44. Author's interview with Marc Pottier, educational and research director of the Mémorial–Cité de l'histoire, Caen, 18 May 2009.

45. Foreign visitors, Pottier noted, tend to go more to the cemeteries than to the Mémorial, and they generally frequent sites closer to the sea, so Arromanches receives more foreign visitors than does the Mémorial. Author's interview with Marc Pottier, 18 May 2009. See also Jean-Michel Tobelem and Luc Benito, *Les musées dans la politique touristique urbaine* (Paris: L'Harmattan, 2002), p. 269.

46. Élizabeth Gautier-Desvaux, "Musées d'histoire et amenagement culturel du territoire: Le "cas" du Mémorial de Caen," in Joly and Compère-Morel, *Des musées d'histoire pour l'avenir,* p. 311.

47. Sabine Gignoux, "La nouvelle histoire du Mémorial de Caen," *La Croix,* 16 July 2010, http://www.la-croix.com/Culture/Actualite/La-nouvelle-histoire-du-Memorial-de-Caen-_NG_-2010-07-16-554378 (accessed 24 December 2015).

48. "2014: Fréquentation des sites et lieux de visite de Normandie," www.calvados-tourisme.com, http://www.calvados-tourisme.com/fr/pros/documents/OBS-2014-Bataille-de-Normandie.pdf (accessed 22 August 2016). By December 2017 the museum counted more than 375,000 paying visitors for that year. See Laurent Neveu, "Caen. Le Mémorial, ça coûte . . . et ça rapporte," *Ouest France,* 10 December 2017, https://www.ouest-france.fr/normandie/caen-14000/caen-le-memorial-ca-coute-et-ca-rapporte-5437641 (accessed 7 April 2018).

49. Thierry Beaurepère, "Célébrations du débarquement: Les attentes de 5 professionnels normands; Le 70e anniversaire du débarquement devrait doper la fréquentation de la région de 15% à 20%," *Tour Hebdo: Le portail des professionels du voyage,* 8 April 2014, http://www.tourhebdo.com/actualites/detail/74627/celebrations-du-debarquement-les-attentes-de-5-professionnels-normands.html (accessed 24 December 2015).

50. "Les 30 sites culturels les plus fréquentés (entrées totales)," in *Mémento du tourisme,* 2015 ed. (Ivry-sur-Seine: Direction Générale des Entreprises, 2015), p. 132.

51. Alphons Schauseil, *Normandie* (Cologne: Vista Point Verlag, 1997), p. 157.

52. Raffray, "La protection du patrimoine militaire de la Seconde Guerre mondiale en Basse-Normandie, p. 5.

53. Friedhelm Boll, "'Vous n'avez pas honte de venire ici?' Widerpsrüche in der Erinnerungskultur der Normandie," in *Médiation et conviction: Mélanges offerts*

à Michel Grunewald, ed. Pierre Béhar, Françoise Lartillot, and Uwe Puschner (Paris: L'Harmattan, 2007), pp. 139–40.

54. Ibid., p. 141.

55. Ibid., pp. 143–44. Computer war games with Nazi protagonists appeared as well during the early years of the twenty-first century. See Jonathan Kay, "Defying a Taboo: Nazi Protagonists Invade Video Games," *New York Times,* 3 January 2002.

56. On power and culture, see Theodor Adorno, *The Culture Industry: Selected Essays on Mass Culture,* ed. with intro. by J. M. Bernstein (1991; London: Routledge, 2001), p. 189.

57. Boll, "'Vous n'avez pas honte de venir ici?,'" pp. 147–49.

58. Jean-Michel Frodon, "La mémoire du siècle comme parc d'attractions," *Le Monde,* 1 October 1998. For *The Longest Day* as an evocation of America's moral crusade for freedom, see Michael R. Dolski, "'Portal of Liberation': D-Day Myth as American Self-Affirmation," in Dolski, Edwards, and Buckley, *D-Day in History and Memory,* pp. 57–58.

59. Henry Rousso, *Vichy: L'événement, la mémoire, l'histoire* (Paris: Gallimard Folio histoire, 2001), p. 345.

60. Serge Halimi, "Avoir pour soi l'histoire," *Le Monde Diplomatique,* 9 December 2010, http://www.monde-diplomatique.fr/publications/atlashistoire/edito (accessed 9 December 2010).

61. "Le mur du çon (de l'Atlantique)," *Le Canard Enchaîné,* 22 June 2011, cited in "La victoire du 8 juin 1945," Clioweb, 22 June 2011, http://clioweb.canalblog.com/ (accessed 23 June 2011).

62. Quoted in Beaurepère, "Célébrations du débarquement.

63. Geoffrey M. White, "Is Paris Burning? Touring America's 'Good War' in France," *History and Memory* 27, no. 2, ed. Geoffrey M. White and Eveline Buchheim (Fall–Winter 2015): 76.

64. Quoted in Beaurepère, "Célébrations du débarquement.

65. From my visit to the cemeteries at La Cambe and Colleville-sur-Mer and interview with Lucien Tisserand, conservator, Service pour l'Entretien des Sépultres Militaires Allemandes, Travail pour la Paix, Cimitière Militaire Allemand de La Cambe, 15 May 2009. I am indebted to Daniel Letouzey and Rémy Desquesnes, who arranged this visit and also accompanied me on several visits to war-related sites in Normandy in May 2009 and for arranging the interview with Tisserand.

66. Lindsey A. Freeman, "The Manhattan Project Time Machine: Atomic Tourism in Oak Ridge, Tennessee," in *Death Tourism: Disaster Sites as Recreational Landscape,* ed. Brigitte Sion (London: Seagull Books, 2014), p. 61. For a more recent iteration of the festival, including the Normandy battle reenactment, see "Festival News and Updates—June 9, 2016," Secret City Festival, Oak Ridge, Tenn., http://www.secret cityfestival.com/news/ (accessed 5 September 2016).

67. Gérard Le Marec, *Guide des maquis et hauts-lieux de la Résistance en Bretagne/ Ille-et-Vilaine/Loire-Atlantique* (Paris: Presses de la Cité, 1987), pp. 10–12.

68. For Parodi, see Odile Rudelle, "Parodi, Alexandre," in *Historical Dictionary of World War II France: The Occupation, Vichy, and the Resistance, 1938–1946,* ed. Bertram M. Gordon (Westport, Conn.: Greenwood Press, 1998), pp. 275–76.

69. Alexandre Parodi, introduction to *La Libération de Paris* (Paris: Comité de Tourisme de Paris, 1945), unpaginated (English-language edition); emphasis added.

70. Gérard Namer, *Batailles pour la mémoire: La commémoration en France, 1944–1982* (Paris: SPAG, 1983), pp. 7–8.

71. COFBA (Franco-Allied Goodwill Committee), *France* (Paris: Franco-Allied Goodwill Committee, 1947), p. 23.

72. Ossip Pernikoff, letter to the Minister of Education and Beaux-Arts, 11 October 1947, AN, F21/7075, folder "Seine Ossip Pernikoff." The story of the melting of the bronze statues with political implications during wartime and in postwar France is told in Kirrily Freeman, *Bronzes to Bullets: Vichy and the Destruction of French Public Statuary, 1941–1944* (Stanford: Stanford University Press, 2009). See also Jean Guéhenno, *Journal des années noires (1940–1944)* (Paris: Gallimard, 1947), entry of 7 January 1942, p. 266.

73. Pernikoff, letter to the Minister of Education and Beaux-Arts, 11 October 1947. On Pernikoff, see also Edmond Labbé, "Préface," in Ossip Pernikoff, *La France: Pays du Tourisme* (Paris: Plon, 1938), p. 15. See also Elizabeth Karlsgodt, *Defending National Treasures: French Art and Heritage under Vichy* (Stanford: Stanford University Press, 2011).

74. Dr. Camino, Deputy Mayor of Cambo, letter to Goutal, Ministry of Education, 28 March 1962, AN, F21/7074, folder "Basse-Pyrénnées."

75. Le Marec, *Guide des Maquis et hauts-lieux de la Résistance en Bretagne*, p. 10.

76. A. Cornu, Secretary of State for Beaux-Arts, letter to the Prefect of the Seine, 17 September 1953, AN, F21/7085C, folder "Paris/Monument Gambetta."

6. Sites of Memory and the Tourist Imaginary

1. Henry Rousso, *The Vichy Syndrome: History and Memory in France since 1944*, trans. Arthur Goldhammer (Cambridge: Harvard University Press, 1991), p. 22.

2. Extrait du B. O. (*Bulletin Officiel*) du 20.6.1945, p. 45, AN, F21/7075, folder "Seine."

3. "La bataille des Glières: Vivre libre ou mourir," website, last modified, 26 May 2011, http://alain.cerri.free.fr/index4.html (accessed 14 July 2011).

4. "Déplacement du Président sur le Plateau des Glières (Haute-Savoie)," Présidence de la République—L. Blevennec / P. Segrette, http://www.elysee.fr/president/mediatheque/photos/2011/mai/deplacement-du-president-sur-le-plateau-des.11487.html (accessed 1 June 2011).

5. "François Hollande dans son fief pour rendre hommage aux '99 pendus de Tulle,'" edited by SLY with AFP, TF1 News, 9 June 2014, http://lci.tf1.fr/france/societe/francois-hollande-dans-son-fief-pour-rendre-hommage-aux-99-pendus-8432093.html (accessed 5 January 2016).

6. "Au Mont-Mouchet, Hollande rend hommage aux résistants et à leur 'foi en l'avenir' de la France," edited with AFP, TF1 News, 6 July 2014, http://lci.tf1.fr/politique/au-mont-mouchet-hollande-rend-hommage-aux-resistants-et-a-leur-8447624.html (accessed 5 January 2016).

7. Laurent Borderie, "Devoir de mémoire: La visite du Chef de l'État, Emmanuel Macron est très attendue ce samedi à Oradour-sur-Glane," *La Montagne*, 10 June 2017, https://www.lamontagne.fr/oradour-sur-glane/politique/2017/06/10/la-visite-du-chef-de-letat-emmanuel-macron-est-tres-attendue-ce-samedi-a-oradour-sur-glane_12437286.html (accessed 7 April 2018).

8. "Accueil > Le tourisme dans nos régions > Faucigny Glières > Découvertes > Patrimoine bâti," "Le Tourisme dans nos régions: Visite des territoires du Mont Blanc, à la découverte des cépages," http://www.cepagesmontblanc.com/cms.php/patrimoine_bati (accessed 14 July 2011).

9. "Les Hébergements associatifs en Savoie—Haute-Savoie," FDTA—FDTS—2003–2006, http://www.tourismeassociatifdessavoie.com/home/Auberge-des-Glieres, 96.html (accessed 14 July 2011). By 2016, the listings on the site had changed and the reference to historic pathways was gone.

10. For a geography of Resistance sites in Paris, see Jean-Louis Goglin and Pierre Roux, *Souffrance et liberté: Une géographie parisienne des années noires (1940–1944)* (Paris: Paris Musées, 2004).

11. Olivier Wieviorka, *La mémoire désunie: Le souvenir politique des années sombres, de la Libération à nos jours* (Paris: Seuil, 2010).

12. Jean Leveque, "Dear Friends," *For You* (June 1945): 4.

13. Bertram M. Gordon, "Collaboration, Retribution, and Crimes against Humanity: The Touvier, Bousquet, and Papon Affairs," *Contemporary French Civilization* 19, no. 2 (Summer–Fall 1995): 250. See also Johann Michel, *Gouverner les mémoires: Les politiques mémorielles en France* (Paris: Presses Universitaires de France, 2010), pp. 69–70.

14. These trials, focusing on "crimes against humanity" and highlighting French complicity in the Holocaust, evoked formal apologies in France which included that of President Jacques Chirac in 1995.

15. Under construction beginning in 1964, the airport was opened officially on 13 March 1974. See Linternaute/Histoire, http://www.linternaute.com/histoire/annee/evenement/1974/1/a/50947/inauguration_de_l_aeroport_charles-de-gaulle.shtml (accessed 18 August 2012). As of 2011 it handled more traffic than any other European airport except for Britain's Heathrow. This remained the case through 2017. See Airports Council International's year-to-date figures as of April 2018, cited in "List of Busiest Airports by Passenger Traffic," Wikipedia, https://en.wikipedia.org/wiki/List_of_the_world%27s_busiest_airports_by_passenger_traffic#2015_statistics (accessed 8 April 2018).

16. Christopher Smart, "French Politicians—Even Socialists—Tug at de Gaulle's Mantle," *Christian Science Monitor*, June 18, 1985.

17. "Sous la botte et sous les bombes," in Pascal Ory, *Voyage dans la France occupée* (Mayenne: L'Express Bibliomnibus, 2014), p. 20.

18. Suzanne Daley, "Colombey-les-deux-Églises Journal: Still Holding Court, the Mythic Gaullist Who Was," *New York Times*, 30 November 1999.

19. Christian Cornevin, "Commémoration: Le trente et unième anniversaire de la mort du Général; Colombey aura bientôt son musée," *Le Monde*, 9 November 2001.

20. "Colombey-les-deux-églises," "forums-regions.com," www.forums-regions.com/forum/post2310.html (accessed 7 January 2010).

21. François Forestier, "Quand Faulkner inventait de Gaulle," *L'Express*, 11 October 1985. There are twenty-six books listed under "de Gaulle" in the 1985–86 edition of *Books in Print*; see *Books in Print: Subject Guide, 1985–86*, vol. 2 (New York: Bowker, 1985), p. 2566.

22. Noël-Jean Bergeroux, "Que reste-t-il du gaullisme?" *L'Express*, 21 June 1985. For a reference to the systematic study of contemporary history in France, see Stanley

Hoffmann, "De Gaulle et la nation face aux problèmes de défense, 1945–1946," book review, *American Historical Review* 90, no. 4 (October 1985): 949.

23. "La maison natale de Charles de Gaulle, d'un lieu de mémoire à un lieu d'histoire," Fondation Charles de Gaulle, http://www.charles-de-gaulle.org/pages/maison-natale.php (accessed 5 January 2016).

24. "La maison natale au fil des jours," Maison Natale Charles de Gaulle, http://www.maison-natale-de-gaulle.org/frameset-fil-jours.htm (accessed 16 July 2010).

25. "La fabrique d'histoire," Maison Natale Charles de Gaulle, http://www.maison-natale-de-gaulle.org/frameset-fabrique.htm (accessed 16 July 2010); and http://www.charles-de-gaulle.org/pages/maison-natale/presentation/fabrique-d-histoire.php (accessed 5 January 2016).

26. Historial Charles de Gaulle at Invalides, Paris, http://www.invalides.org/pages/Historial%20de%20Gaulle.html (accessed 20 January 2010); and http://www.charles-de-gaulle.org/pages/historial.php (accessed 8 January 2017).

27. "1944 La Bataille de Normandie: La memoire," http://www.normandie44lamemoire.com/musees/lesmusees2.htm (accessed 17 July 2010 and 5 January 2016).

28. Serge Barcellini and Annette Wieviorka, *Passant, souviens-toi: Les lieux du souvenir de la Seconde Guerre mondiale en France* (Paris: Plon, 1995), pp. 7–8.

29. Heinrich Hoffmann, *Mit Hitler im Westen* (Munich: Verlag Heinrich Hoffmann, 1940), pp. 113 and 115, respectively.

30. Peter Scholl-Latour, *Leben mit Frankreich: Stationen eines halben Jahrhunderts* (Stuttgart: Deutsche Verlags-Anstalt, 1988), p. 487. See also C. de Hauteclocque, "Leclerc, Philippe," in *Historical Dictionary of World War II France: The Occupation, Vichy, and the Resistance, 1938–1946*, ed. Bertram M. Gordon (Westport, Conn.: Greenwood Press, 1998), p. 218. See also Alfred Wahl, cited in Morgane Pellennec, "Strasbourg," in Ory, *Voyage dans la France occupée*, p. 46.

31. "Battle of Alsace/Bataille d'Alsace," map no. 104 (Clermont-Ferrand: Michelin, 1992).

32. "Office de tourisme de Strasbourg et sa région," brochure, Strasbourg, Office de Tourisme de Strasbourg et sa Région (1993), p. 25.

33. Council of Europe/Conseil de l'Europe, "Série de fiches d'informations: Activités et réalisations," Directorate of Information, September 1992, back cover.

34. H. Nonn, "Strasbourg, ville internationale: Forces, faiblesses, objectifs," *Revue géographique de l'Est* 2 (1992): 100. The Council of Europe adopted the European flag of twelve gold stars in a circle on a field of blue in 1955.

35. "Strasbourg: Site officiel de l'Office de tourisme de Strasbourg et sa région," Patrimoine, http://www.otstrasbourg.fr/article.php?id_article=30&url_ret=rubrique.php?id_rubrique=23 (accessed 8 July 2010).

36. Thierry Gandillot and Marcelle Padovani, "Europe: La guerre des capitales," *Le Nouvel Observateur*, 29 November–5 December 1990, p. 104. French political leaders defending the interests of Strasbourg in the fight over the seat of the European Parliament in the period from 1988 through 1990 included, in addition to Mitterrand, Jacques Delors, Édith Cresson, Roland Dumas, and Laurent Fabius. See issues of the *Dernières Nouvelles d'Alsace* from this period; also "Strasbourg défie Bruxelles," *Le Monde*, 8 March 1990.

37. See, for example, the brochure published by the Strasbourg Office of Tourism, "Office de tourisme de Strasbourg et sa région," p. 25, which, in addition to the European Parliament and the Council of Europe, lists six other international organizations based there.

38. "Strasbourg: Site officiel de l'Office de Tourisme de Strasbourg et sa Région," Patrimoine, http://www.otstrasbourg.fr/rubrique.php?id_rubrique=34&lang=en (accessed 8 July 2010); and under http://www.otstrasbourg.fr/en/discover/strasbourg-the-european-capital.html (5 November 2015).

39. Suzanne Daley and Stephen Castle, "A Parliament on the Move Grows Costly," *New York Times*, 28 June 2011, http://www.nytimes.com/2011/06/29/world/europe/29strasbourg.html?_r=1&ref=world (accessed 28 June 2011).

40. Gérard Namer, *Batailles pour la mémoire: La commémoration en France, 1944–1982* (Paris: SPAG, 1983), pp. 170–71.

41. M.-P. de Leonard, letter to Reverend Father Regamey, 22 September 1947, and René Perchet, Director of Architecture in the Education Ministry, letter to the General Director of Arts and Letters, AN, F21/7085D, folder "Paris/Monuments commémoratifs 'La voie douloureuse'"; also Barcellini and Wieviorka, *Passant, souviens-toi!*, pp. 170–75.

42. Serge Barcellini, "Les commémorations," in *Des musées d'histoire pour l'avenir,* ed. Marie-Hélène Joly and Thomas Compère-Morel (Paris: Éditions Noêsis, 1998), p. 53. See also M.-P. de Leonard, letter to Reverend Father Regamey, 22 September 1947; René Perchet, Director of Architecture in the Education Ministry, letter to the General Director of Arts and Letters, AN, F21/7085D, folder "Paris/Monuments commémoratifs 'La voie douloureuse'"; and Barcellini and Wieviorka, *Passant, souviens-toi*, pp. 170–75.

43. Philippe Dagen, "Une cloche de bronze à la mémoire des fusillés du Mont-Valérien," *Le Monde*, 12 April 2002.

44. Pierre Gastineau and Romain Rosso, "La mémoire de nos terres," *L'Express* 3084 (11 August 2010): 12–13. See also "Le Mont-Valérien: Haut-lieu de la mémoire nationale," http://www.mont-valerien.fr (accessed 6 January 2016).

45. "Mont-Valérien: La visite virtuelle," http://www.mont-valerien.fr/visiter/la-visite-virtuelle/ (accessed 6 January 2016).

46. Sarah Bennett Farmer, "Oradour-sur-Glane: Memory in a Preserved Landscape," *French Historical Studies* 19, no. 1 (Spring 1995): 35. See also her fuller study, *Martyred Village: Commemorating the 1944 Massacre at Oradour-sur-Glane* (Berkeley: University of California Press, 1999).

47. Farmer, "Oradour-sur-Glane," p. 40. For an extensive study of Oradour sur Glane, see Henning Meyer, "Der Wandel der französischen 'Erinnerungskultur' des Zweiten Weltkriegs am Beispiel dreier 'Erinnerungsorte': Bordeaux, Caen und Oradour-sur-Glane" (Ph.D. diss., Université Michel de Montaigne Bordeaux 3, 14 November 2006); also, on the problems of maintaining a site as nature gradually encroaches upon it, Chris Pearson, *Scarred Landscapes: War and Nature in Vichy France* (Basingstoke: Palgrave Macmillan, 2008), p. 174. See also Jean-Jacques Fouché and Gilbert Beaubatie, *Tulle: Nouveaux regards sur les pendaisons et les événements de juin 1944* (Saint-Paul: Lucien Souny, 2008).

48. L. R. Blanchard, *Les Journalistes Américains . . . See France* (Rochester, N.Y.: Gannett Newspapers, 1946), p. 37. The journalists also visited Châteaubriand, where twenty-seven communists had been killed by the Germans.

49. Elisabeth Raffray, "La Protection du Patrimoine Militaire de la seconde guerre mondiale en Basse-Normandie: Le mur de l'Atlantique et le port artificiel d'Arromanches" (master's thesis, École du Louvre/Muséologie, 1998–99), pp. 6–7.

50. Dean MacCannell, *The Tourist: A New Theory of the Leisure Class* (New York: Schocken Books, 1976), pp. 98–99.

51. Victor H. Belot, *La France des pèlerinages* (Verviers: Guides Marabout, 1976), pp. 219–20.

52. Centre de la mémoire—Oradour-sur-Glane village martyr, http://www.oradour.org/index.php?rubrique=7 (accessed 8 July 2010).

53. "TourismeLimousin-Corrèze◦Creuse◦Haut-Vienne, Offre et fréquentation des sites et manifestations touristiques en Limousin: Les sites touristiques en Limousin en 2008," Observatoire régional du tourisme, http://lei.crt-limousin.fr/ortl/basedocumentaire/documents/20090525123650SitesTouristiques2008.pdf (accessed 6 January 2016).

54. "Limousin: La fréquentation des sites touristiques réserve des surprises," Cercle Jean Moulin, http://www.francebleu.fr/loisirs/sortir/limousin-la-frequentation-des-sites-touristiques-reserve-des-surprises-1441296072 (accessed 6 January 2016).

55. Erich Grau and Margit Kilian, *DuMont Kunst-Reiseführer: Das Limousin* (Cologne: DuMont Buchverlag, 1992), p. 105; and Georges Chatain, "L'autocritique d'un guide touristique allemand," *Le Monde,* 11 October 1996.

56. Grau and Kilian, *DuMont Kunst-Reiseführer,* p. 276.

57. Chatain, "L'autocritique d'un guide touristique allemand," p. 34.

58. "Un guide touristique mis à l'index," *Le Monde,* 8 November 1996. See also my article "Warfare and Tourism: Paris in World War II," *Annals of Tourism Research 25,* no. 3 (July 1998): 632.

59. "Oradour-sur-Glane, France," TripAdvisor, http://www.tripadvisor.com/Tourism-g488286-Oradour_sur_Glane_Haute_Vienne_Limousin-Vacations.html; and http://www.tripadvisor.com/Attraction_Review-g488286-d304759-Reviews-Oradour_sur_Glane_old_town-Oradour_sur_Glane_Haute_Vienne_Limousin.html#REVIEWS (accessed 6 January 2016).

60. Ministère de la Défense, Mémoire et patrimoine, "Mémoire," http://www.defense.gouv.fr/site-memoire-et-patrimoine/memoire/hauts-lieux-de-memoire/le-memorial-des-martyrs-de-la-deportation (accessed 19 August 2012).

61. Jacques Baudot, "Rapport d'information no. 6 — Le Défi de la mémoire—Politique de la mémoire menée par le ministère des Anciens combattants et victimes de guerre," Commission des Finances, du contrôle budgétaire et des comptes économiques de la Nation—Rapport d'information no. 6–1997/1998, Sénat français, http://www.senat.fr/rap/r97-006/r97-006_mono.html (accessed 19 August 2012).

62. See Union des Engagés Volontaires Anciens Combattants Juifs 1939–1945, letter to Robert Rey, Director of Artistic Production, Ministry of Education, 26 November 1948, AN, F21/7085C, folder "Paris/Monument des Combattants Juifs."

63. Barcellini and Wieviorka, *Passant, souviens-toi,* pp. 461–462.

64. Rosemary Wakeman, *The Heroic City: Paris, 1945–1958* (Chicago: University of Chicago Press, 2009), p. 340.

65. I attended this ceremony in 1974. See also Venita F. Datta, "Vélodrome d'Hiver," in Gordon, *Historical Dictionary of World War II France,* p. 360; also Barcellini and Wieviorka, *Passant, souviens-toi,* pp. 461–62.

66. Thomas Wieder, "Vél d'Hiv: M. Hollande réaffirme le rôle de la France," *Le Monde*, 23 July 2012, http://www.lemonde.fr/politique/article/2012/07/23/vel-d-hiv-m-hollande-reaffirme-le-role-de-la-france_1736986_823448.html (accessed 6 January 2016).

67. "Drancy and Other Monuments in France by Artist Shlomo Selinger," Center for Holocaust and Genocide Studies, University of Minnesota, 2009, http://www.chgs.umn.edu/museum/memorials/drancy/index.html (accessed 19 July 2010).

68. Nivelle Pascale, "Drancy, la mémoire est dans l'escalier," *Libération*, 11 September 2001, http://www.liberation.fr/culture/0101386042-drancy-la-memoire-est-dans-l-escalier (accessed 19 July 2010).

69. "Des croix gammées tracées au Mémorial de la déportation à Drancy," *Le Monde*, 11 April 2009, http://www.lemonde.fr/societe/article/2009/04/11/des-croix-gammees-au-memorial-de-la-deportation-de-drancy_1179766_3224.html (accessed 19 July 2010).

70. "Hollande inaugure le mémorial de la Shoah de Drancy, Le lieu de mémoire a été bâti sur le site de l'ancien camp d'internement d'où furent déportées près de 70 000 personnes," *Le Point*, 22 September 2012, http://www.lepoint.fr/societe/hollande-inaugure-le-memorial-de-la-shoah-de-drancy-21-09-2012-1508566_23.php?xtor=EPR-6-[Newsletter-Quotidienne]-20120921 (accessed 21 September 2012). See also Scott Sayare, "At Holocaust Center, Hollande Confronts Past," *New York Times*, 21 September 2012, http://www.nytimes.com/2012/09/22/world/europe/at-drancy-holocaust-center-hollande-confronts-grim-chapter-for-france.html?ref=world (accessed 22 September 2012).

71. Email, Subject: Randonnee sur lieux de memoire, from H-Francais, La liste des Clionautes, Enseigner l'Histoire et la Geographie en France (H-FRANCAIS@H-NET.MSU.EDU) on behalf of Bruno Modica (bruno.mod34@orange.fr), sent 10 April 2010, 9:28 am, to H-FRANCAIS@H-NET.MSU.EDU, from cercil_wanadoo.fr.

72. Laurent Grailsamer, "Le 'Drancy de la zone libre,' selon Serge Klarsfeld," *Le Monde*, 10 May 1997. See also Jean-Claude Marre, "Des archives du camp d'internment des juifs à Rivesaltes sont retrouvées dans une décharge," and "L'employé ayant découvert les archives du camp de Rivesaltes s'explique," *Le Monde*, 10 and 11 May 1997, respectively.

73. Jacqueline Trescott, "France to Shine a Light on Its Notorious Camp: U.S. Holocaust Museum Will Help Create Memorial," *Washington Post*, 2 May 2006, http://www.washingtonpost.com/wp-dyn/content/article/2006/05/01/AR2006050101735.html (accessed 19 July 2010).

74. Gastineau and Rosso, "La mémoire de nos terres," pp. 13 and 15.

75. Sarah Wildman, "Heads Up, Rivesaltes, France: Paying Tribute to the Persecuted," *New York Times*, 14 October 2007, http://query.nytimes.com/gst/fullpage.html?res=9507E7D6133FF937A25753C1A9619C8B63&sec=travel&spon=&pagewanted=2 (accessed 19 July 2010).

76. "Faces Behind Barbed Wire: The Rivesaltes Internment Camp Memorial," Congregation Kol Am, Saint Louis, 2010, http://kolamstl.org/events/past-events/faces-behind-barbed-wire-the-rivesaltes-internment-camp-memorial/ (accessed 19 July 2010).

77. "Ouverture du site," Mémorial du camp de Rivesaltes, http://www.memorialcamprivesaltes.eu/actualite/2/5-ouverture-du-site.htm (accessed 4 December 2015); "L'histoire du Camp de Rivesaltes," http://www.memorialcamprivesaltes.

eu/2-l-histoire-du-camp-de-rivesaltes.htm, and "Inauguration du Mémorial de Rivesaltes," http://www.memorialcamprivesaltes.eu/69-inauguration-du-memorial-de-rivesaltes.htm (both accessed 21 January 2016).

78. Gastineau and Rosso, "La mémoire de nos terres," p. 14.

79. "Fondation du Camp des Milles," http://www.campdesmilles.org/fondation-30-ans-de-combat.html, and, for Hollande's speech, http://www.camp desmilles.org/site-memorial-objectifs.html (both accessed 22 January 2016 but no longer available as of 8 April 2018).

80. Alain Carteret, *Vichy charme* (Olliergues: Éditions de la Montmarie, 2006), p. 86.

81. See, for example, Georges Rougeron, *Quand Vichy était capitale, 1940–44* (Le Coteau: Éditions Horvath, 1983), p. 5.

82. It is likely that many in the crowd that gathered at the Paris Hôtel de Ville in April 1944 to see Pétain in what would be his only visit to Paris as head of state already recognized that Vichy was a lost cause and came out of curiosity to witness those who would soon become historic relics. See the account by Jean Tracou, who helped organize the trip, in "Visite du Maréchal Pétain à Paris, le 15 avril 1944," *Le Maréchal* 133 (1st trimester 1984): 1–2.

83. Marcel Déat, "Analogies historiques," *L'Œuvre*, 30 November 1940.

84. Michel Braudeau, "L'album de vacances (V) Vichy," *L'Express*, 6 September 1985.

85. *Oxford English Dictionary*, vol. 19 (Oxford: Clarendon Press, 1989), p. 603, s.v. "Vichy," "Vichyite," and "Vichyssoise."

86. Georges Mathiot, *Le tourisme réceptif français: Sa place dans l'économie nationale et internationale, sa position devant la nouvelle règlementation de 1942–1943* (Nancy: Société d'Impressions Typographiques, 1945), pp. 169–70.

87. Rousso, *The Vichy Syndrome*, p. 73. See also a reproduction of the ordinance, dated 20 November 1944, in Carteret, *Vichy charme*, p. 209.

88. *Guide du pneu Michelin 1945* (Paris: Services du Tourisme Michelin, 1945), pp. 975–77. See also my essay "French Cultural Tourism and the Vichy Problem," in *Being Elsewhere: Tourism, Consumer Culture, and Identity in Modern Europe and North America,* ed. Shelley Baranowski and Ellen Furlough (Ann Arbor: University of Michigan Press, 2001), p. 249.

89. Eric Conan, "Vichy malade de Vichy," *L'Express*, 26 June 1992.

90. Ibid., pp. 36–37.

91. Rousso, *The Vichy Syndrome*, p. 73. See also Carteret, *Vichy charme*, p. 190.

92. "Le Président de la République à Vichy," *Le Maréchal*, n.s., 3 (May 1959): 1.

93. Conan, "Vichy malade de Vichy," p. 37.

94. This citation may be found under "Vichyite" in the *Oxford English Dictionary*, 19:603. See also my article "The Morphology of the Collaborator: The French Case," *Journal of European Studies* 23 (pts. 1 and 2), nos. 89–90 (March–June 1993): 1–25.

95. Dominique Veillon, *La collaboration: Textes et débats* (Paris: Librairie Générale Française/Le Livre de Poche, 1984), p. 36.

96. Braudeau, "L'album de vacances (V): Vichy," p. 67.

97. Christian Jamot's figures for spa visitors to Vichy are 300,000 in 1939 and 32,000 in 1962; see Christian Jamot, "Vichy: Du tourisme à la ville, de la ville au tourisme," *Geocarrefour* 76 (February 2001): 134.

98. "Les chiffres de la fréquentation thermale de 2000 à 2012 (graphique)," AUVERGNE > ALLIER > VICHY 10/10/14, http://www.lamontagne.fr/

auvergne / actualite / departement / allier / vichy / 2014 / 10 / 10 / les-chiffres-de-la-frequentation-thermale-de-2000-a-2012-graphique_11177386.html; and, for the analysis, "La diversification des activités des stations thermales," session 2011 (Paris: Conseil Régional du Tourisme, Ministère de l'Économie des Finances et de l'Industrie, n.d.), http:// www.entreprises.gouv.fr / files / directions_services / tourisme / acteurs / cnt / rapport-stat-therm.pdf (both accessed 6 January 2016).

99. Braudeau, "L'album de vacances (V): Vichy," pp. 62–67. A more recent study of Vichy postcards mentions nothing about the Hôtel du Parc or any other sites related to the war years. See Hsiao-Yueh Yu, "Postcard narratives: A case of Vichy in France," *Tourism Management Perspectives* 26 (April 2018), 89–96.

100. Conan, "Vichy malade de Vichy," p. 38. For one iteration of this tour, see "Vichy, capitale de l'État français 1940–1944," http:// www.allier-tourisme.com / dolce-vita / fr / loisirs.php?VICHY,-CAPITALE-DE-L'ÉTAT-FRANÇAIS-1940-19 44&p=839001074 (accessed 10 October 2009). I took the tour, offered by the Office du tourisme, on 9 June 2010 and was one of nine guests in the group, excluding the guide. One was German; the others all spoke French. The German visitor had an audio device with which he recorded the guide's talk, with permission at the beginning. The others were two middle-aged French couples (in one the woman may have been in her thirties), two other middle-aged men, and a young woman, perhaps in her twenties, who appeared to be a student, as she took extensive notes. The relatively small number in the group was due in part to rainy weather. For another account of this tour, see John Campbell, "Vichy, Vichy, and a Plaque to Remember," *French Studies Bulletin* 60.1, no. 98 (Spring 2006): 3.

101. Conan, "Vichy malade de Vichy," p. 37.

102. *Michelin France (Guide vert)* (Clermont-Ferrand: Michelin and Co., 1989), p. 254.

103. Thierry Wirth, *Hier à Vichy (1940–1944)* (Lyon: Les Trois Roses, 2008), pp. 71–72. See also Carteret, *Vichy charme*, pp. 73–74.

104. Conan, "Vichy malade de Vichy," p. 37.

105. Ibid.

106. Campbell, "Vichy, Vichy, and a Plaque to Remember," p. 4.

107. Michel Di Paz, "Plaque Is Unveiled in Vichy 50 Years after Jews Deported," *Jewish Telegraphic Agency*, 27 August 1992, http:// www.encyclopedia.com / doc / 1P1-2238849.html (accessed 14 July 2010).

108. Recounted by tour guide, Office du tourisme, "Vichy, capitale de l'État français 40–44" tour, 9 June 2010. For Klarsfeld's role, see Campbell, "Vichy, Vichy, and a Plaque to Remember," p. 4. Kirrily Freeman suggests that the plaque was vandalized and removed soon after 2000 but I saw it and photographed it in 2010. See Kirrily Freeman, "A Capital Problem: The Town of Vichy, the Second World War and the Politics of Identity," in *The Long Aftermath: Cultural Legacies of Europe at War, 1936–2016*, ed. Manuel Bragança and Peter Tame (New York: Berghahn, 2016), 145. That the plaque was still standing was confirmed in an email to the author from Alain Carteret, 10 April 2018.

109. Jessica Burstein, "Vichy Yearns to Be French City, Not Just World War II Memory," *New York Times*, 27 December 2015, http:// www.nytimes.com / 2015 / 12 / 28 / world / europe / vichy-yearns-to-be-french-city-not-just-world-war-ii-memory. html?emc=eta1 (accessed 27 December 2015).

110. Jean Débordes, *À Vichy: La vie de toutes les jours sous Pétain* (Paris: Éditions du Signe, 1994), p. 290.

111. *France* (Watford, Herts.: Michelin, 1994), p. 272.

112. Danielle Rouard, "Les Toulonnais: 'Prenez garde que votre tour ne vienne . . . ,'" *Le Monde,* 1 April 1997.

113. Jamot, "Vichy: Du tourisme à la ville, de la ville au tourisme," p. 136.

114. "Issue number 9 of MODERGNAT (May 2005), with Marshal Pétain and Claude Malhuret on its cover, is titled 'Vichy Faces Its Past,' alluding to the older formulation of Henry Rousso, "'a past which does not pass.' This continuing theme, as much as it interests journalists, does little for the readers." See Carteret, *Vichy charme*, p. 68, cited in "Patrimoine Vichy," http://pagesperso-orange.fr/carteret/Patrimoine%20Vichy.htm (accessed 7 October 2009).

115. INSEE—Institut national de la statistique et des études économiques, "Pays de Vichy-Auvergne," http://stats-auvergne.nexenservices.com/territoire/zonage.php?id=830011 (accessed 19 September 2009).

116. Bertram M. Gordon, "The 'Vichy Syndrome' Problem in History," *French Historical Studies* 19, no. 2 (Fall 1995): 515–16.

117. Carteret, *Vichy charme*, pp. 28 and 177. See also Alain Carteret, *Vichy: Deux millénaires* (Vichy: Published by the author, 2001), cited in "Patrimoine Vichy," http://pagesperso-orange.fr/carteret/Patrimoine%20Vichy.htm (accessed 7 October 2009).

118. Carteret, *Vichy: Deux millénaires* (accessed 7 October 2009 and 4 November 2015).

119. Alain Carteret, *Napoléon III: Bienfaiteur de Vichy et de la France* (Olliergues: Éditions De La Montmarie, 2003), pp. 216–17, cited in "Patrimoine Vichy," http://pagesperso-orange.fr/carteret/Patrimoine%20Vichy.htm (accessed 7 October 2009 and 4 November 2015).

120. Ibid.

121. Campbell, "Vichy, Vichy, and a Plaque to Remember," pp. 4–5.

122. Carteret, *Vichy charme*, p. 75. Also, author's interview with Bertrand de Solliers, Vichy, 8 June 2010.

123. "Informations pratiques," "Vichy, capitale de l'État français 40–44" tour, Via France, Digital Content & Marketing Solutions, http://www.viafrance.com/fr/vichy/evenements/vichy-capitale-de-l-etat-francais-40-44-visite-e-281127 (accessed 23 August 2016). See also "Ville de Vichy," https://www.ville-vichy.fr/agenda/les-visites-guidees-de-l-office-de-tourisme (accessed 9 January 2017).

124. "Vichy, capitale de l'État français 40–44" tour, Office du tourisme, Vichy, 9 June 2010.

125. "Vichy, capitale de l'État français 40–44," Destination Vichy/Office de tourisme et de thermalisme de Vichy, http://www.vichy-tourisme.com/visite_detail.htm?id_visite=7 (accessed 25 January 2010).

126. "Vichy, capitale de l'État français 40–44" tour, 9 June 2010.

127. "L'œuvre du souvenir des défenseurs de Verdun, ossuaire de Douaumont," in *Les Batailles de Verdun (1914–1918)* (Clermont-Ferrand: Michelin and Co., 1921), p. 20. Another guidebook, the *Guide rouge de Verdun et de ses champs de bataille,* published during the interwar years, notes that the first stone for the Douaumont ossuary was laid on 22 August 1920 by Marshal Pétain. See *Le guide rouge de Verdun et de ses champs de bataille* (Verdun: H. Frémont et Fils, n.d.), p. 55. Writing in a pro-Pétain periodical in 1956, Jacques Benoist-Méchin, who had served in the Vichy government, described

the Verdun battlefield as "sacred ground." See Jacques Benoist-Mechin, "Le Maréchal Pétain," *Écrits de Paris: Revue des questions actuelles* (November 1956): 30.

128. For 52 percent of those surveyed, Pétain remained "the man of Vichy," but for 42 percent he was the "victor of Verdun." See "Sondage exclusif: Pétain; Les Français n'ont rien oublié"; and Henri Amouroux, "À la fois Verdun et Vichy," *Pèlerin Magazine*, 5761 (30 April 1993): 17. See also Henrik Prebensen, "Y a-t-il un revirement de l'opinion publique française en 1940? (Si vous pensez que non, passez à l'article suivant)," *La langue, les signes et les êtres: Actes du colloque de l'Institut d'études romanes de l'Université de Copenhague, le 3 octobre 1998; Études romanes* 44 (1999): 177.

129. See the bibliographic series *Catalogue général de la Librairie française* (Nendeln, Liechtenstein: Kraus Reprints, BNF, 1840–1933), followed by the series *Biblio*, which runs from 1934 to 1979. The *Bibliographie de la France* begins in 1980. Its name changes to the *Bibliographie nationale française* in 1990, and continues in this form to the present. In 2001, the *Bibliographie nationale française* notices begin appearing on CD-ROM. The Rameau index, a subject index, continues the series of volumes published through 1999. For the year 2001, see http://bibliographienationale.bnf.fr/Livres/CuM_01.h/IndexRameau-1.html.

130. For references to "Pétain," see the "matières" indexes by five-year periods in the *Bibliothèque annuelle de l'histoire de France* (Paris: CNRS).

131. "Pétain," Google Books Ngram Viewer, https://books.google.com/ngrams/graph?content=Pétain&year_start=1900&year_end=2014&corpus=19&smoothing=3&share=&direct_url=t1%3B%2CPétain%3B%2Cc0 (accessed 6 January 2016). Interestingly, the Google chart for "Pétain" shows an uptick in the early 2000s in the German-language series.

132. "Some people may find the film slow at times, but if you are at all interested in this important period of history then the film is highly recommended." Comment by Stephen Stratford (stephen@sp-stratford.demon.co.uk), IMDb, 16 January 1999, http://www.imdb.com/title/tt0107815/#comment (accessed 12 January 2009).

133. "La dernière 'rue Pétain' de France débaptisée dans les Ardennes," *Le Point*, 3 December 2010, http://www.lepoint.fr/societe/la-derniere-rue-petain-de-france-debaptisee-dans-les-ardennes-03-12-2010–1270462_23.php?xtor=EPR-6-[Newsletter-Quotidienne]-20101203 (accessed 3 December 2010). See also John Tagliabue, "Both Hero and Traitor, but No Longer on the Map," *New York Times*, 2 January 2011, http://www.nytimes.com/2011/01/03/world/europe/03petain.html (accessed 10 January 2017).

134. Rousso, *The Vichy Syndrome*, p. 42. Jérôme Cotillon also suggests that the perpetuation of Vichyite ideas revolves more around Pétain than, for example, Pierre Laval or Admiral Jean-François Darlan; see Jérôme Cotillon, *Ce qu'il reste de Vichy* (Paris: Armand Colin, 2003), pp. 235–36.

135. Jean Prateau, *Les îsles d'ouest* (Paris: Arthaud, 1954), pp. 129 and 133.

136. Ibid., p. 133.

137. "Transparence," *Le Maréchal* 154 (2nd trimester 1989): 7. For discussion of the steps toward sacralization of tourist sites, see MacCannell, *The Tourist*, p. 44.

138. "Pétain à Douaumont," *Le Maréchal* 1 (23 July 1957): 4.

139. "De l'Île d'Yeu à Douaumont," *Le Maréchal* 2 (11 November 1957): 2.

140. H. Dorgérès, "L'œuvre constructive du Maréchal pour la paysannerie," *Le Maréchal*, n.s., 2 (April 1959): 1.

141. "Une visite à faire," *Le Maréchal*, n.s., 3 (May 1959): 2.

142. Pierre Henry, "La célébration de la mort du Maréchal à l'Île d'Yeu," *Le Maréchal*, n.s, 4 (June–July 1959): 4.

143. "Pélerinage à Verdelais," *Le Maréchal*, n.s., 4 (June–July 1959): 4.

144. Jacques Isorni, "La querelle de Douaumont," *Écrits de Paris* (May 1966): 45.

145. Flora Lewis, "Petain's Coffin Reburied on Prison Isle in Atlantic," *New York Times*, 23 February 1973, http://www.nytimes.com/1973/02/23/archives/petains-coffin-reburried-on-prison-isle-in-atlantic-daughterinlaw.html?_r=0 (accessed 5 March 2017). Herbert R. Lottman, *Pétain, Hero or Traitor: The Untold Story* (New York: William Morrow and Co., 1985), p. 383, suggested that the kidnappers wanted the body reburied in the church at Les Invalides in Paris, where the remains of both Napoleon I and his son repose.

146. The poll was conducted by the Bordeaux newspaper *Sud-Ouest;* see "The Body Snatchers," HP-Time.com, 5 March 1973, http://www.time.com/time/magazine/article/0,9171,903881,00.html?iid=chix-sphere (accessed 22 September 2008).

147. Ibid. For extensive documentation of the theft and recapture of the Marshal's remains, see "Vol du cercueil de Philippe Pétain," *Wikipédia, L'Encyclopédie libre*, note 4, https://criminocorpus.org/media/filer_public/a0/4b/a04baec3-9370-4a74-898f-34ffd104351c/at_petain_03_0002.pdf, (accessed 8 April 2018).

148. By 1984 the ANPV had split in two, making at least three organizations competing for the loyalties of Pétain adherents. See *Le Maréchal* 133 (1st trimester 1984): 7.

149. "Association Nationale 'Pétain-Verdun,'" *La Voix de l'Île d'Yeu* 3 (1st trimester 1990): 9. See also "Assemblée générale annuelle" and "Cérémonie du 11 novembre 1989," ibid., pp. 7–8.

150. "3 février 1990: Sur la tombe de Robert Brasillach," ibid., p. 7.

151. "La captivité du maréchal au Fort de la Pierre Levée à l'Île d'Yeu," *Le Maréchal* 109 (1st trimester 1978), front cover. See also Jacques Isorni, "Extraits du Livre d'or du centenaire," ibid., p. 2.

152. "Pélerinage [*sic*] au Portalet," *Le Maréchal* 112 (4th [*sic*] trimester 1978): 14. For the visits to the Île d'Yeu and Douaumont, see pp. 1–2. A 1980 issue of *Le Maréchal* reported on a pilgrimage to Verdun organized by the war veterans of the RATP (the Paris transit system) in which both French and Germans participated, along with representatives of the German (presumably Federal Republic) and American embassies; see "47ème Pèlerinage des 'Combattants de la R.A.T.P.," *Le Maréchal* 118 (2nd trimester 1980): 16.

153. Cotillon, *Ce qu'il reste de Vichy*, p. 208.

154. "Un patrimoine à sauver," *Le Maréchal* 152 (4th [*sic*] trimester 1988): 16. By 1992 the ADMP had succeeded in the restoration of the Cauchy-à-la-Tour house. See "A.D.M.P. Association to Defend the Memory of the Pétain Marshal [*sic*]," http://www.marechal-petain.com/versionanglaise/admp.htm (accessed 27 September 2008). For a discussion of issues involved in the conservation of a site of *patrimoine*, see Claude Orijet du Cluzeau, *Le tourisme culturel: Que sais-je?* (1998; Paris: Presses Universitaires de France, 2007), p. 61.

155. Cited in Ferro, "Pétain est-il toujours là?," *Le Nouvel Observateur*, 21–27 September 1989, p. 12.

156. "Musée Pétain de l'Île d'Yeu: Le maréchal bien caché," *La Voix de l'Île d'Yeu* (Autumn 1989): 2. Another of the ANPV's publications, *L'Appel de Douaumont*,

organized a group to lay a wreath at the Île d'Yeu gravesite. See "Pèlerinage à l'Île de Yeu, 11 novembre 1989," insert, *L'Appel de Douaumont* 29 (September 1989).

157. Claire Andrieu, "Managing Memory: National and Personal Identity at Stake in the Mitterrand Affair," *French Politics and Society* 14, no. 2 (Spring 1996): 28.

158. See, respectively, "Verdun: 21 février 1916–21 février 2006: Pour le 90ème anniversaire de la bataille de Verdun, l'Association pour Défendre la Mémoire du Maréchal Pétain (A.D.M.P.) honorera la mémoire du 'Vainqueur de Verdun' par le dépôt d'une gerbe sur sa tombe à l'Ile d'Yeu," and "Communiqué de l'A.D.M.P.: 150ème anniversaire de la naissance du Maréchal à Cauchy-à-la-Tour. Comme chaque année l'A.D.M.P. célèbrera cette naissance dans sa ferme natale le samedi 22 avril 2006," http://www.marechal-petain.com/actualites/petainactualites.htm (accessed 22 September 200)8.

159. "Pèlerinage à l'Île d'Yeu, pour ne pas oublier," http://www.marechal-petain.com/actualites/petainactualites.htm (accessed 22 September 2008).

160. "Rendez-vous lundi 12 novembre 2007: Voyage à Verdun," ADMP website, http://www.admp.org/ (accessed 23 September 2008).

161. These pilgrimages included a solemn mass in honor of Pétain's 163rd birthday at his birthplace and ancestral home in Cauchy-à-la-Tour, Pas-de-Calais, one of which I observed on 25 April 2009. As of 6 January 2016, the ADMP website, http://www.marechal-petain.com/admp.htm, referred the reader to another site, http://www.admp.org, which was no longer operative.

162. Rachid Amirou, *Imaginaire du tourisme culturel* (Paris: Presses Universitaires de France, 2000), p. 7.

163. Mike Robinson and Marina Novelli, "Niche Tourism: An Introduction," in *Niche Tourism: Contemporary Issues, Trends and Cases,* ed. Marina Novelli (Amsterdam: Elsevier, 2005), pp. 8–9.

164. Andrea Loselle, "Revisiting Sigmaringen," "Travel and Travelers: Special Issue," Georges van den Abbeele, guest editor, *Sites* 5, no. 1 (Spring 2001): 200–202.

165. Jean Mabire, *Drieu parmi nous* (Paris: La Table Ronde, 1963), p. 251.

166. Jean-Didier Wolfromm, "Chaban, le libérateur pressé," *L'Express,* 31 August 1984.

167. Francis Bergeron and Philippe Vilgier, *Guide de l'homme de droite à Paris: Paris by Right* (Paris: Éditions du Trident, 1987), pp. 192 and 195, respectively.

168. Ibid., p. 64.

169. Ibid., pp. 58–59.

170. Ibid., pp. 105–6.

171. Ibid., pp. 109, 136, and 185, respectively.

7. Tourism, War, and Memory in Postwar France

1. See the discussion by Jean Viard, *Court traité sur les vacances, les voyages at l'hospitalité des lieux* (La Tour d'Aigues, France: Éditions de l'Aube, 2000), p. 121.

2. Rosemary Wakeman, *The Heroic City: Paris 1945–1958* (Chicago: University of Chicago Press, 2009), p. 25. For the continued interest in the liberation of Paris, see Marion Cocquet, "Paris (re)libéré: Pour les commémorations du 25 août 1944, la capitale appelle ses habitants à partager leurs archives personnelles," *Le Point* 2023

(25 June 2011), http://www.lepoint.fr/culture/paris-re-libere-25-06-2011-1345892_3. php?xtor=EPR-6-[Newsletter-Quotidienne]-20110625 (accessed 26 June 2011).

3. Cédric Gruat, *Hitler à Paris, juin 1940* (Paris: Éditions Tirésias, 2010), pp. 149–50.

4. For tourist spectacles, see Dean MacCannell, "Sights and Spectacles," in *Iconicity: Essays on the Nature of Culture; Festschrift for Thomas A. Sebeok on his 65th Birthday,* ed. Paul Bouissac, Michael Herzfeld, and Roland Posner (Tübingen: Stauffenberg Verlag, 1986), p. 421.

5. For more on the difficulties of measuring tourism in France statistically, see my article "The Evolving Popularity of Tourist Sites in France: What Can Be Learned from French Statistical Publications?," *Journal of Tourism History* 3, no. 2 (August 2011): 94–95 and 102–3.

6. Alexandre Panosso Netto, "What Is Tourism? Definitions, Theoretical Phases and Principles," in *Philosophical Issues in Tourism,* ed. John Tribe (Bristol: Channel View Publications, 2009), p. 59.

7. For the continuations of Sieburg's imagery, see Ernst von Salomon, *Boche in Frankreich* (Hamburg: Rowohlt, 1950), pp. 144–45.

8. For her list of sites, see Inge von Wangenheim, *Der Goldene Turm: Eine Woche Paris* (Rudolstadt: Greifenverlag, 1988), p. 6.

9. Daniel Schneidermann, "Images: 14 Juillet, gross symbole!," *Le Monde,* 15 July 1994.

10. See, for example, the brochure published by the Strasbourg Office of Tourism, "Office de tourisme de Strasbourg et sa région" (Strasbourg: Office de Tourisme de Strasbourg et sa Région, 1993), p. 25, which, in addition to the European Parliament and the Council of Europe, lists six international organizations based there.

11. See Tony Judt, "Europe: The Grand Illusion," *New York Review of Books* 43, no. 12 (11 July 1996): 6.

12. See Arthur Frommer, *Europe on 5 Dollars a Day* (New York: Simon and Schuster, 1969), p. 17.

13. Jennifer Schuessler, "The Dark Side of Liberation: Documenting Abuse by G.I.'s in France during World War II," *New York Times,* 21 May 2013, http://www.nytimes.com/2013/05/21/books/rape-by-american-soldiers-in-world-war-ii-france.html (accessed 11 January 2017). This article reviews Mary Louise Roberts, *What Soldiers Do: Sex and the American G.I. in World War II France* (Chicago: University of Chicago Press, 2013). Roberts was not the first to treat this question. See also J. Robert Lilly, *Taken by Force: Rape and American GIs in Europe during World War Two* (New York: Palgrave Macmillan, 2007); and Anne Sebba, *Les Parisiennes: How the French Women of Paris Lived, Loved, and Died under Nazi Occupation* (New York: St. Martin's Press, 2016), pp. 311–14.

14. L. R. Blanchard, *Les Journalistes Américains . . . See France* (Rochester, N.Y.: Gannett Newspapers, 1946), p. 25.

15. Schuessler, "The Dark Side of Liberation." See also Blanchard, *Les Journalistes Américains,* p. 25.

16. Charles Simic, " Oh, What a Lovely War!," review of Ian Buruma, *Year Zero: A History of 1945, New York Review of Books* (10 October 2013), http://www.nybooks.com/articles/archives/2013/oct/10/year-zero-1945-oh-what-lovely-war/?insrc=toc (accessed 5 January 2014).

17. I have acquired a few such items at the Marché aux puces as well as the occasional *salon des livres* in Paris. See also Gérard Le Marec and Pierre Philippe Lambert, *Partis et mouvements de la collaboration: Paris, 1940–1944* (Paris: J. Grancher, 1993).

18. "Origins and Aims of the French American Welcome Committee," *For You* 1 (March 1945): 5.

19. "Paris Fashion," *For You* 1 (1 March 1945): 20. The unfolding season was covered in subsequent issues.

20. *For You* 1 (1 March 1945): 43.

21. "Paris. . . . This Fortnight," *For You* 3 (12 April 1945): 6–7.

22. *Paris Leave Booklet* (Paris: Canadian Forces Hospitality and Information Bureau "Canada Corner," n.d.), pp. 95, 2, 3, and 80.

23. Ibid., p. 95.

24. See, for example, Doré Ogrizek, ed., *France, Paris and the Provinces: Text by Roger Roumagnac. Gastronomy by Pierre Andrieu*, trans. Marguerite Bigot and Madeleine Blaess, illustrated by G. Beuville, L. Firsca, E. Grau-Sala, V. Pilon, and G. de Sainte-Croix (Paris: Odé [Impr. de Croutzer-Depost], 1944); and Doré Ogrizek, Roger Roumagnac, Pierre Andrieu, Marguerite Bigot, Madeleine Blaess, et al., *France, Paris and the Provinces* (New York: Whittlesey House, 1948).

25. Lysiane Bernhardt, "Paris. . . . This Fortnight: The Champs-Elysées Completely Changes Its Aspect with the Time of Day," *For You* 6 (July 1945): 7.

26. See "Paris*Spectacles: What's On in Paris; Free Guide," 25 April–1 May 1945 (Paris: Dubois and Bauer, 1945).

27. L. R. Blanchard, *Les Journalistes Américains*, p. 7.

28. Ibid., p. 62.

29. André Rauch, *Vacances en France de 1830 à nos jours* (Paris: Hachette, 1996), p. 110.

30. Ibid., p. 111. For Uriage, see John Hellman, "Uriage, École des cadres," in *Historical Dictionary of World War II France: The Occupation, Vichy, and the Resistance, 1938–1946*, ed. Bertram M. Gordon (Westport, Conn.: Greenwood Press, 1998), pp. 357–58.

31. Le Ministre des Travaux Publics et des Transports à Monsieur le Minstre des Finances (Direction du Budget), n.d., folder "Tourisme 1946–1947," AN, F/14/13714.

32. Note from the Secrétaire-Général, Commissariat-Général du Tourisme, to the Commissaire Général, 9 October 1945, folder "Comité d'Organisation des Agences et Bureaux de Voyages, AN, F/14/13714.

33. Commissariat Général au Tourisme, et Office Français du Tourisme, Budget Général de l'Exercise 1945, n.d., Office Français du Tourisme and Section V—Matériel de Propagande à l'Étranger, folder "Tourisme 1946–1947," AN, F/14/13714.

34. Caisse des Monuments Historiques, Ministère des Travaux Publics & des Transports, "Exposé des Motifs," n.d., folder "Tourisme 1946–1947," AN, F/14/13714. The "Exposé des Motifs" was included in a draft for a law in support of state financing for historic monuments.

35. L. Richerot, Président, Département de l'Isère, Chambre départementale professionnelle de l'industrie Hôtelière, letter to Monsieur Reymond, Chef du cabinet du Ministre des Travaux Publics, 1 February 1946, folder "Tourisme 1946–1947," AN, F/14/13714.

36. Ministère des Travaux Publics et des Transports, Commissariat au Tourisme, "Budget de l'Exercise 1946, Chapitre 73, Article 4, Dépenses à l'Étranger," folder "Tourisme 1946–1947," AN, F/14/13714.

37. Ministère des Travaux et des Transports, Cabinet du Ministre, "Le Système Coopératif appliqué au Tourisme: Conditions de la reprise du Tourisme," p. 2, n.d., folder "Tourisme 1946–1947," AN, F/14/13714.

38. Major and Mrs. Holt's Battlefield Guide Books & Maps—travel advice on visiting the battlefields of WW1 and WW2, http://www.guide-books.co.uk/hints.html. See also Major and Mrs. Holt's Battlefield Guide Books and Maps—Unique, http://www.guide-books.co.uk/authors.html (both accessed 31 December 2015).

39. "2010 Updated schedules," War Research Society, "BATTLEFIELD TOURS" (Operated by Alex Bulloch MBE), http://www.battlefieldtours.org.uk/ (accessed 6 January 2010). As of 2018, the Battlefield Tours website still existed in name but its contents were devoted exclusively to women's clothing (accessed 8 April 2018).

40. "Lorient, une base sous-marine surdimensionée," Le Monde, 11 February 1997.

41. "Votre séjour: Visites guidées, Base de sous-marins de Keroman," Lorient Bretagne-Sud Tourisme, http://www.lorientbretagnesudtourisme.fr/votre-sejour/base-de-sous-marins-de-keroman-lorient.html (accessed 31 December 2015). See also Pays de Lorient, Office du tourisme, "Base de sous-marins Keroman: Visites guidées," http://www.lorient-tourisme.fr/quelles-activites/fiche.cfm?id=50a9ea28-b646-452a-98f2-07205fe6f389 (accessed 14 July 2010).

42. Marc Francon, Le guide vert Michelin: L'invention du tourisme culturel populaire (Paris: Economica, 2001), p. 54. See also Marc Francon, "Le guide VERT—Toute Michelin se collectionne!" ACGCM Association des Collectionneurs de Guides et Cartes Michelin, http://www.acgcm.com/guide_vert.html (accessed 23 May 2010).

43. Rauch, Vacances en France de 1830 à nos jours, p. 91.

44. Barbara Esteve, Consumer Care Department, Michelin North America, Inc., michelin.webtire@us.michelin.com email to author, 28 June 2010.

45. Michelin France (Guide vert) (Clermont-Ferrand: Michelin and Co., 1989), p. 29.

46. The Green Guide France (Clermont-Ferrand: Michelin, 1994), p. 30.

47. Ibid., pp. 57, 143, 151, 187, and 174.

48. For Bayeux, see ibid., p. 75.

49. Ibid., p. 112.

50. Ibid., p. 54.

51. France: Le guide vert (Clermont-Ferrand: Michelin, 2011), pp. 132 and 140.

52. Ibid., p. 197.

53. Ibid., pp. 324–27 and, for Bayeux, p. 337.

54. Ibid., pp. 321 and 439, respectively.

55. Ibid., pp. 380 and 648, respectively.

56. Ibid., pp. 423 and 488–489, respectively.

57. Pierre Py, Le tourisme: Un phénomène économique (Paris: La documentation française, 2007), pp. 11–13. On the problematic nature of tourism statistics, see also Saskia Cousin and Bertrand Réau, Sociologie du tourisme (Paris: La Découverte, 2009), p. 4.

58. ORT-CRT Normandie, 2003, http://sig.cr-basse-normandie.fr/atlas/cartes/dday.jpg 25 May 2009, Courtesy of Daniel Letouzey. The French figures are for

2006 and are taken from "Vacances—Tourisme en France," Observatoire national du tourisme, 2006, http://tourisme-reservations.com/index2.php?option=com_content&do_pdf=1&id=67 (accessed 26 June 2009), which does not list the Normandy landing sites at all.

59. Author's interview with Marc Pottier, Directeur du pôle Educatif et Recherche (Director of the Educational and Research Unit) Mémorial–Cité de l'histoire, Caen, 18 May 2009.

60. *Plages du ébarquement et bataille de Normandie* (Boulogne Billancourt: Michelin, 2014), pp. 23–24.

61. Alain Monferrand, "Le tourisme culturel," in *Des musées d'histoire pour l'avenir*, ed. Marie-Hélène Joly and Thomas Compère-Morel (Paris: Éditions Noêsis, 1998), p. 335. For the top tourist destinations in France, see "Vacances—Tourisme en France."

62. Culture and history were fundamental to this growth, and many regions still had the potential, Monferrand wrote, to exploit their *patrimoine* for tourist expansion. See Monferrand, "Le tourisme culturel," pp. 335–36 and 340–41. Monferrand warned that local historical museums had to avoid duplicating their exhibits (p. 337), an issue also raised by Frédéric Sommier, director of the Musée du débarquement, Arromanches les Bains, who noted that in Normandy each museum had its own specialization; author's interview, 18 May 2009.

63. See Gordon, "The Evolving Popularity of Tourist Sites in France," pp. 91–107.

64. See Mike Robinson and Melanie Smith, "Politics, Power and Play: The Shifting Context of Cultural Tourism," in *Cultural Tourism in a Changing World: Politics, Participation and (Re)presentation*, ed. Mike Robinson and Melanie Smith (2006; Clevedon: Channel View Publications, 2009), pp. 4–6.

65. Marc Boyer, *Le tourisme en France: Vade mecum* (Colombelles, France: Éditions EMS Management & Société, 2003), p. 176.

66. "Les sites touristiques en France: Les 30 sites culturels les plus fréquentés (entrées totales)," Ministère de l'Économie de l'Industrie et du Numérique, *Memento du tourisme 2015* (Ivry-sur-Seine, France: Direction Générale des Entreprises, 2015), p. 132.

67. Cousin and Réau, *Sociologie du tourisme*, p. 23. There are no destination listings, for example, in either the *Annuaire statistique de la France 1985* (Paris: Ministère de l'Économie, des Finances et du Budget/INSEE, 1985) or the *Annuaire statistique de la France 1993* (Paris: Ministère de l'Économie, 1993).

68. "Les 30 sites culturels les plus fréquentés (entrées totales)," *Mémento du tourisme*, 2015 ed. (Ivry-sur-Seine: Direction Générale des Entreprises, 2015), p. 132.

69. Author's interviews with Frédéric Sommier, director of the Musée du débarquement, Arromanches les Bains, and Marc Pottier, Mémorial–Cité de l'histoire, Caen, respectively, both 18 May 2009. Neither comment addressed the ages of the students, whether pre- or post-puberty, nor whether that would have been significant.

70. The *Biblio* series shifts in 1979 to the *Bibliographie de la France*, which appears to show a higher count for Second World War themes, as reflected in its 1979 count, as compared to the *Biblio* count for the same year. Figure A2 has been adjusted to make the ratios in the two publications series equivalent. For an earlier discussion of book publication sequences as a measure of "rétro" interest in Vichy France, see

Bertram M. Gordon, "The 'Vichy Syndrome' Problem in History," *French Historical Studies* 19, no. 2 (Fall 1995): 506–7.

71. See, for example, the discussion of the relationship of film with other aspects of culture in Theodor Adorno, *The Culture Industry: Selected Essays on Mass Culture,* ed. with intro. by J. M. Bernstein (1991; London: Routledge, 2001), p. 9.

72. Internet Movie Database, IMDb Statistics, http://www.imdb.com/stats (accessed 29 July 2016).

73. Bertram M. Gordon, "La grande France": The Rise and Decline of a Filmic Icon," presented to the Western Society for French History, Los Angeles, 11 November 2000, p. 6.

74. See Sylvie Lindeperg, *Les écrans de l'ombre: La Seconde guerre mondiale dans le cinéma français (1944–1969)* (Paris: CNRS Editions, 1997), pp. 29–32.

75. "Un cinéaste sur la piste de Klaus Barbie," *Le Point,* 26 September 1986, p. 77.

76. Rousso lists the films annually from 1944 through 1968, then shifts to an annual tabulation starting with August of each year for 1969–70 through 1989; see Henry Rousso, *The Vichy Syndrome: History and Memory in France since 1944,* trans. Arthur Goldhammer (Cambridge: Harvard University Press, 1991), pp. 318–23.

77. Author's interview with Bertrand de Solliers, Vichy, 7 June 2010. See also Thierry Wirth, *Hier à Vichy (1940–1944)* (Lyon: Les Trois Roses, 2008), pp. 71–72; and Alain Carteret, *Vichy charme* (Olliergues: Éditions de la Montmarie, 2006), pp. 73–75. Not all the films were equally successful. Jean Marbeuf's film *Pétain,* for example, which opened in Paris in May 1993 (see Jean-Michel Frodon, "Un 'Pétain' chagrinant et pitoyable," *Le Monde,* 7 May 1993), had closed by July.

78. See "Index chronologique," in Jean-Marcel Humbert and Lionel Dumarche, *Guides des musées d'histoire militaire* (Paris: Lavauzelle, 1982). pp. 463–70.

79. Ibid.

80. "Fortified Military Architectures in Europe: Conflicts and Reconciliations," European Institute of Cultural Routes, http://www.culture-routes.lu/php/fo_index.php?lng=en&dest=bd_pa_det&rub=57 (accessed 24 June 2009, since removed).

81. For a discussion of the need to address more fully the role of gender in tourism studies, see Kevin Meethan, *Tourism in Global Society: Place, Culture, Consumption* (Houndmills: Palgrave, 2001), p. 171. See also my chapter "Destinations and the Woman as a Motif in Film and Tourism," in *Construction d'une industrie touristique aux 19e et 20e Siècles: Perspectives internationales/Development of a Tourist Industry in the 19th and 20th Centuries, International Perspectives,* ed. Laurent Tissot (Neuchâtel: Alphil, 2003), p. 370.

82. On age and its relationship to gender in tourism, see Chris Ryan and Birgit Trauer, "Aging Populations: Trends and the Emergence of the Nomad Tourist," in *Global Tourism,* 3rd ed., ed. William F. Theobald (Amsterdam: Elsevier, 2005), pp. 516–17.

83. Jean-Denis Souyris and Bernard Delage, *Voyage et troisième âge* (Talence, France: Maison des Sciences de l'Homme d'Aquitaine, 1979), pp. 34–35. The French term *troisième âge,* or "third age," refers to the retirement years. See also my chapter "Leisure," in *French Popular Culture: An Introduction,* ed. Hugh Dauncey (London: Arnold Publishers, 2003), p. 155.

84. "French retirement age change to 62 becomes law," *The Guardian*, 10 November 2010, https://www.theguardian.com/world/2010/nov/10/french-retirement-age-reform-62 (accessed 8 April 2018).

85. Fred Kupferman, *Laval* (Paris: Balland, 1987), p. 515.

86. The rubric under which de Gaulle's work was listed is "Domaine: Littérature et débats d'idées—Littérature et histoire." See "Enseignements primaire et secondaire: Programme de littérature de la classe terminale de la série littéraire pour l'année scolaire 2010–2011," NOR : MENE0931164N, RLR : 524–7, note de service no. 2009–200 du 21–12–2009, MEN—DGESCO A1–4, Ministère Éducation Nationale, http://www.education.gouv.fr/cid50190/mene0931164n.html (accessed 24 January 2010). This directive was brought to the author's attention by Laurent Gayme, laurent.gayme@laposte.net, "De Gaulle en TL," H-Francais, La liste des Clionautes, Enseigner l'Histoire et la Geographie en France [H-FRANCAIS@H-NET.MSU.EDU], 21 January 2010.

Conclusion

1. Michel Goubet, cited in Amandine Hirou, "Toulouse," in *Voyage dans la France occupée*, ed. Pascal Ory (Mayenne: L'Express Bibliomnibus, 2014), p. 142. For Carrière, see also "Musée de la Résistance et de la déportation Toulouse: Robert Carrière, passeur de mémoire," *La Dépêche du Midi*, 27 May 2014, http://www.ladepeche.fr/article/2014/05/27/1888877-robert-carriere-passeur-de-memoire.html (accessed 22 January 2016).

2. Alexander Urquhart, review of Lee Marshall, ed., *The Time Out Guide to the South of France*, *Times Literary Supplement*, 28 July 2000, p. 29.

3. "Le tourisme urbain dans l'hôtellerie française: Un poids de plus en plus important," Direction du Tourisme, Département de la stratégie, de la prospective, de l'évaluation et des statistiques, Tourisme infos stat no. 6 2008, p. 5, http://www.tourisme.gouv.fr/stat_etudes/tis/2008/tis2008_6.pdf (accessed 8 July 2010).

4. Pierre Gastineau and Romain Rosso, "La mémoire de nos terres," *L'Express* 3084 (11 August 2010): 12–13.

5. Quoted ibid., p. 14.

6. Jean-Pierre Bady, *Que sais-je? Les monuments historiques en France* (Paris: Presses Universitaires de France, 1985), p. 78.

7. Jennifer Craik, "The Culture of Tourism," in *Touring Cultures: Transformations of Travel and Theory*, ed. Chris Rojek and John Urry (London: Routledge, 1997), p. 122. For a brief history of the fortifications, see Richard F. Crane, "Maginot Line," in *Historical Dictionary of World War II France: The Occupation, Vichy, and the Resistance, 1938–1946*, ed. Bertram M. Gordon (Westport, Conn.: Greenwood Press, 1998), p. 230.

8. Bertram M. Gordon, "The Morphology of the Collaborator: The French Case," *Journal of European Studies*, 23:89 and 90 (March–June 1993), p. 2.

9. Chris Rojek, "Indexing, Dragging and the Social Construction of Tourist Sites," in Rojek and Urry, *Touring Cultures*, pp. 54–55.

10. David Lowenthal, *The Heritage Crusade and the Spoils of History* (Cambridge: Cambridge University Press, 1998), p. xiii. See also Dean MacCannell, *The Tourist:*

A New Theory of the Leisure Class (New York: Schocken Books, 1976), p. 41. In the United States, sites of memory correspond to "cultural tourism" and "heritage tourism," which to the California Council for the Humanities means "a destination with a story." See James Quay, "Cultural Tourism and the Humanities," *Humanities Network* 19, no. 2 (Spring 1997): 1 and 6.

11. Chris Rojek and John Urry, "Transformations of Travel and Theory," in Rojek and Urry, *Touring Cultures*, p. 12. For the distinction between "tours" and "pilgrimages," see David W. Lloyd, *Battlefield Tourism: Pilgrimage and Commemoration of the Great War in Britain, Australia and Canada, 1919–1939* (Oxford: Berg, 1998), pp. 19 and 40–44.

12. See Simon Milne, Jacqueline Grekin, and Susan Woodley, "Tourism and the Construction of Place in Canada's Eastern Arctic," in *Destinations: Cultural Landscapes and Tourism*, ed. Greg Ringer (London: Routledge, 1998), p. 102.

13. Lloyd, *Battlefield Tourism*, p. 29.

14. Emmanuel de Roux, "Jacques Le Goff, historien, 'L'amour du patrimoine peut s'accomplir en respectant l'autre,'" *Le Monde*, 7 January 1997.

15. Harry G. Matthews and Linda K. Richter, "Political Science and Tourism," in *Annals of Tourism Research* 18 (1991): 120–35.

16. A. V. Seaton and J. J. Lennon, "Thanatourism in the Early 21st Century: Moral Panics, Ulterior Motives and Alterior Desires," in *New Horizons in Tourism: Strange Experiences and Stranger Practices*, ed. Tejvir Singh (London: CAB [Commonwealth Agricultural Bureaux] International, 2004), pp. 63–64.

17. Peter E. Tarlow, "Dark Tourism: The Appealing 'Dark' Side of Tourism and More," in *Niche Tourism: Contemporary Issues, Trends and Cases*, ed. Marina Novelli (Amsterdam: Elsevier, 2005), p. 50.

18. Gary Krist, "Tragedyland," *New York Times*, 27 November 1993.

19. Ibid.

20. See Wiebke Kolbe, "Reisen zu den Schlachtfeldern des Zweiten Weltkriegs," *Nachrichten aus der Forschungsstelle für Zeitgeschichte in Hamburg (FZH) 2008* (Hamburg: FZH, 2009), p. 47.

21. Gastineau and Rosso, "La mémoire de nos terres," p. 13. "Les dix sites Bas-Normands payants les plus visités," *INSEE Basse-Normandie—Bilan 2011*, p. 29, gives the figure as 371,000 for 2011.

22. "Le tourisme de mémoire," Direction de la mémoire, du patrimoine et des archives du Ministère de la défense, Ministère de la défense et des anciens combattants (April 2011). This brochure is available on the website Tourisme de mémoire, updated 1 July 2012, Ministère de la défense: Mémoire et patrimoine, http://www.defense.gouv.fr/site-memoire-et-patrimoine/memoire/tourisme-de-memoire-et-memoire-partagee/tourisme-de-memoire (accessed 19 August 2012).

23. Ibid.

24. Ibid.

25. "Tourisme de mémoire," updated 22 November 2015, "Ministère de la défense: Mémoire et patrimoine," http://www.defense.gouv.fr/memoire/memoire/tourisme-de-memoire-et-memoire-partagee/tourisme-de-memoire (accessed 7 December 2015).

26. Many of the papers presented at a conference on history museums, held at the Historial de la Grande Guerre in Peronne, addressed these questions in 1996.

See Jean Davallon, "Conclusion du colloque," in *Des musées d'histoire pour l'avenir,* ed. Marie-Hélène Joly and Thomas Compère-Morel (Paris: Éditions Noêsis, 1998), pp. 351–56.

27. Professor Willa Z. Silverman taught the course and led the group. See "Dispatch: France and the Holocaust_ (eight-part series), Penn State Live, 18 July 2007, http://live.psu.edu/story/25109 (accessed 21 July 2008 and no longer available). The class trip to France was offered again in 2010. See "Willa Z. Silverman," http://www.willazsilverman.com/teaching-related (accessed 9 April 2018).

28. G. J. Ashworth, "Holocaust Tourism: The Experience of Kraków-Kazimierz," *International Research in Geographical and Environmental Education* 2 (2002): 365. For a discussion of attempts to avoid the creation of a "Bergen-Belsen-Land" at the site of the former concentration camp there, see Rainer Schulze, "Resisting Holocaust Tourism: The New Gedenkestätte Bergen-Belsen, Germany," in *Death Tourism: Disaster Sites as Recreational Landscape,* ed. Brigitte Sion (London: Seagull Books, 2014), pp. 24 and 129–30. For parallels between "Auschwitzland" kitsch and Ground Zero, commemorating the 11 September 2001 attacks in New York, see Debbie Lisle, "Gazing at Ground Zero: Tourism, Voyeurism and Spectacle," *Journal for Cultural Research* 8, no. 1 (January 2004): 9–10 and 16.

29. The French version of the film is *Et puis les touristes* (And Then the Tourists). I am indebted to Frédérique Guyader of IRSEA (Institut de recherche sur le Sud-Est asiatique) in France for information about this film.

30. Bruno Modica, review of Jean-François Forges and Pierre Jérôme Biscarat, *Guide historique d'Auschwitz* (Paris: Éditions Autrement, 2011), Les Clionautes: Service de presse Histoire contemporaine, 10 January 2011, http://www.clio-cr.clionautes.org/spip.php?article3306 (accessed 13 February 2011).

31. Ibid. Additional reading recommended for French teachers taking their students to see Auschwitz is Essabaa Samia, *Le voyage des lycéens: Des jeunes de cité découvrent la Shoah* (Paris: Stock, 2009); see Nicole Mullier, "voyage a Auschwitz," email from H-Francais, La liste des Clionautes, Enseigner l'Histoire et la Geographie en France, h-francais@h-net.msu.edu, (22 March 2009).

32. Modica, review of Forges and Biscarat, *Guide historique d'Auschwitz.*

33. Mary Blume, "Normandy's 50th-Anniversary Invasion," *New York Times,* 22 January 1994, http://www.nytimes.com/1994/01/22/style/22iht-dday.html (accessed 3 January 2016).

34. "First World War, High Wood," Philip Johnstone, *The Guardian,* 13 November 2008, http://www.theguardian.com/world/2008/nov/14/high-wood-philip-johnstone (accessed 3 January 2016).

35. For the role of murder trials as a tourist attraction in the United States, see Lizette Alvarez, "A Murder Trial as Tourist Draw in Central Florida," *New York Times,* 25 June 2011, http://www.nytimes.com/2011/06/26/us/26casey.html?_r=1&scp=1&sq=alvarez&st=nyt (accessed 27 June 2011).

36. "Lyon: Uneasy at First, France's 2nd City Survives Barbie's Trial Spotlight," *Los Angeles Times,* 5 July 1987.

37. See "Un cinéaste sur la piste de Klaus Barbie," *Le Point,* 26 September 1986, p. 77, note 83.

38. Musée, "L'histoire, essentiel au présent," Centre de l'histoire de le Résistance et de la déportation, http://www.chrd.lyon.fr/chrd/sections/fr/musee/

histoire_du_centre_d (accessed 9 April 2018). See also Laurent Douzou cited in Olivier Le Naire and Sami Tarek, "Lyon," in Ory, *Voyage dans la France occupée*, p. 142.

39. Philippe-Jean Catinchi, "Un centre pour mémoire," *Le Monde Télévision Radio Multimédia*, 19–20 January 1997, p. 5.

40. Laurent Douzou, cited in Le Naire and Tarek, "Lyon," p. 143.

41. Laurent Guigon, "Le mémorial d'Izieu sans sa 'Dame,'" *Le Monde*, 19 October 1996. See also Bertrand Poirot-Delpech, "Procès Barbie, dix ans déjà," *Le Monde*, 7 May 1997.

42. Direction de l'Architecture, Sites, Ministry of Education, letter to M. Jaujard, Director General of Arts and Letters, 14 October 1948, AN, F21/7079, folder "Monuments Commémoratifs/Protection des Sites Classés."

43. See Duncan Campbell-Smith, "Between Beaches," review of John Forfar, *From Gold to Omaha*, *Times Literary Supplement*, 29 January 2010, p. 28; and Friedhelm Boll, "'Vous n'avez pas honte de venir ici?' Widerpsrüche in der Erinnerungskultur der Normandie," in *Médiation et conviction: Mélanges offerts à Michel Grunewald*, ed. Pierre Béhar, Françoise Lartillot, and Uwe Puschner (Paris: L'Harmattan, 2007), pp. 139–40, respectively; see my discussion in chapter 6.

44. Gastineau and Rosso, "La mémoire de nos terres," p. 15.

45. See, for example, the "Join the Army and See the World" interwar British poster with images of the Rock of Gibraltar, a Burmese temple, a harbor in Malta, two pyramids and the Sphinx in Egypt, a nighttime scene in Hong Kong, and a village along the seacoast of Jamaica, catalogue number Art.IWM PST 13502, Imperial War Museums, http://www.iwm.org.uk/collections/item/object/8847 (accessed 24 August 2012).

46. Eric Conan, "Vichy malade de Vichy," *L'Express*, 26 June 1992. For the current iteration of this tour, see "Vichy, Capitale de l'État français 1940–1944," http://www.auvergne-tourisme.info/patrimoine-culturel/vichy/vichy-capitale-de-l-etat-francais-1940-1944/tourisme-PCUAUV000FS001RS-1.html (accessed 22 January 2016).

47. Sarah Bennett Farmer, "Oradour-sur-Glane: Memory in a Preserved Landscape," *French Historical Studies* 19, no. 1 (Spring 1995): 43.

48. Annette Lévy-Willard, Maréchal, nous y revoilà (interview with historian Cécile Desprairies), *Libération*, 12 October 2012, http://www.liberation.fr/societe/2012/10/19/marechal-nous-y-revoila_854540 (accessed 23 January 2016). For the development of the Villages vacances familiales, see André Rauch, *Que sais-je? Les vacances* (Paris: Presses Universitaires de France, 1993), pp. 111–13.

49. Isabelle Richefort, "Les sources de l'histoire des voyages dans les archives du Ministère des affaires étrangères" in *Voyages et voyageurs: Sources pour l'histoire des voyages*, ed. Thérèse Charmasson (Paris: CTHS [Comité des travaux historiques et scientifiques], 2010), pp. 327–28.

50. Peter Tame notes that the "other side" of this picture, the behavior of the French in occupied Germany, is evoked in Roger Nimier's novel *Le Hussard bleu*, "in which some very cynical young French soldiers accompany the invading forces of the Allies, pushing deep into Germany to conquer the Wehrmacht, but are only really interested in German women." Tame, note to the author, 16 June 2015.

Index

Page numbers in *italics* indicate illustrations. French and German names with a *von, de,* and *du* are alphabetized under the family name.

Aachen Cathedral, 136, *137*
Abetz, Otto, 101, 117, 132–33
Adams, Henry, 31
Adorno, Theodor, 10, 209
After the Battle (periodical), 8, 17
Agincourt museum, 22
alcohol consumption, 87, 124
Algeria, 79; French conquest of, 25–26; independence of, 55, 175–76, 180
Alsace, 3, 4, 65, 79; Battle of, 167–68; Maginot Line tourism in, 24, 58, 246n28; Struthof concentration camp in, 171
American Express, 30, 82
Amirou, Rachid, 11, 51
Amouroux, Henri, 112
Andrieu, Pierre, 71, 99
appellation contrôlée, 27, 39
Aragon, Louis, 174
Arc de Triomphe, 25, 48, 50, 170; Hitler's visit to, 105, 106; liberation parade through, 194; postwar tourism at, 161, 207, 208
Arendt, Hannah, 7
Arromanches, 2, 19, 149–54, *150*, 208
art "protection" by Germans, 135–40, 144–45, 269n172
art tourism, 129–30, 132–35
Artois, Comte d', 186
Ashworth, G. J., 222
Association for the Defense of the Memory of Marshal Pétain (ADMP), 16, 179, 182, 184, 186–89
Association nationale Pétain-Verdun (ANPV), 188–89
Atlantic Wall, 159, 211; Hitler and, 260n38; postwar memorials at, 155–56; Rommel and, 108, 261n44
"atomic tourism," 159

auberges de jeunesse. See youth hostel movement
Aubrac, Lucie, 96
Audiat, Pierre, 90, 109, 143
Augier, Marc, 2, 93–95
Auriol, Vincent, 62
Auschwitz, 18, 175, 222, 223
"authenticity," 59, 63, 151, 171
Autobahnen, 37, 261n44
automobiles, 20; *Autobahnen* for, 37, 261n44; during Occupation, 72–74, *73*; restaurant guides and, 39; tour guides for, 32. See also *Guides bleus*
Auvergne region, 64, 68, 75, *76*

Badinter, Robert, 177
Bady, Jean-Pierre, 217
Baedeker guidebooks, 101, 109, 122
Baker, Josephine, 36, 40, 41, 199
Balestre, Jean-Marie, 95
Baranowski, Shelley, 100
Barbie, Klaus, 14, 165, 171, 210, 223–24
Barcellini, Serge, 14, 63, 218
Barrés, Maurice, 50
Barrot, Olivier, 97
Bauer, Alain, 55
Baumgarten, Alexander Gottlieb, 11
Bayeux museum, 166–67
Bayeux Tapestry, 139, 151–52
Beach, Sylvia, 41
Beauvoir, Simone de, 133
Belle Époque tourism, 20–21, 26–33, 39, 183, 214
Benjamin, Walter, 11–12, 20, 99, 193, 214
Benstock, Shari, 41
Bergeron, Francis, 58, 191–92
Bernhardt, Lysiane, 199
Berthelot, Jean, 65, 72, 77, 109

Beuchot, Pierre, 181, 210
Biarritz, 47, 140
Bizet, Georges, 107, 118
Blanchard, L. R., 147–48, 154, 159, 171, 196, 199
Blitzmädchen (women's auxiliaries), 109–10, 197
Bloch, Marc, 4
Blom, Philipp, 62
Blower, Brooke Lindy, 41
Blum, Léon, 87
Blume, Mary, 152, 222–23
Boegner, Philippe, 68–69, 70, 107
Boll, Friedhelm, 34, 156–57, 225
Bordeaux, 23, 27, 67
Bouffard, Agnès, 153
Bougrab, Jeannette, 158
Bourquin, Christian, 176, 177
Bousquet, René, 208
Boyer, Marc, 10, 23, 39, 77, 207
Brasillach, Robert, 96, 188, 191
Brauchitsch, Walter von, 110, 123
Breker, Arno, 103, 117, 119, 132–35, 259n18
Brinon, Fernand de, 101
Britain, Battle of (1940), 54–55
Brittany, 67, 159–61, 203
Brosset, Diego Charles, 211
Browning, Christopher, 7
Bruge, Roger, 56
Buchkremer, Joseph, 136, 137
Buddenbrock, Cecilia von, 42
Burgundy, 21–22, 34, 135
burlesque shows, 16, 23, 32–33, 194, 197
Burrin, Philippe, 69
Burstein, Jessica, 182
Buruma, Ian, 130, 132, 144, 196
Butler, Richard, 9, 15

cabarets, 33, 71, 119, 199, 263n82
Caen, 149, 151; Mémorial de la Paix in, 16, 154–55, 206, 208, 216, 220
Caisse nationale des monuments historiques et des sites (CNMHS), 13, 189
Calais, 23, 186
Campbell, John, 181–82, 184
Cannes, 26, 41, 77, 84
Cardinne-Petit, Robert, 67, 249n15
Carné, Marcel, 40
Carnegie, Andrew, 31
Carrière, Robert, 214
Carteret, Alain, 177, 182–84, 233n59
Cartier, Jacques, 159
Cassatt, Mary, 31
Casson, Lionel, 18

Chaban-Delmas, Jacques, 191
Chalons-sur-Marne, 22
Chamonix, 36–37, 74
Chantiers de la jeunesse (organization), 78, 80, 94
Chaprong, Philippe, 274n32
Chartres, 21, 28, 31, 40
Chateaubriand, François-Auguste-René de, 159
Châteaubriant, Alphonse de, 94
Chaucer, Geoffrey, 91–92, 217
Chenot, Bernard, 84
Cherbourg, Battle of, 151
Chesnel, Marc, 97
Chevalier, Maurice, 40, 199
Chiappe, Jean, 121
Chicken, Stephen H., 151
Chirac, Jacques, 14, 174
Chirat, Raymond, 97
Choltitz, Dietrich von, 100, 144–45
cinema. See film
Civil War (U.S.), 202–3, 219
Clemen, Paul, 135
Cluzeau, Claude Origet du, 155
Cocteau, Jean, 134, 199
Cointet, Michèle, 68, 124
Colleville-sur-Mer cemetery, 147, 155–56, 159, 208
Collins, Larry, 103, 144–45
Colombey-les-Deux-Églises, 165, 205
colonies de vacances. See vacation colonies
communists, 93, 97, 161; in Resistance, 5, 163, 169, 170, 219
Compiègne railway car, 142; postwar tourism at, 62–63, 171, 195; World War I armistice at, 4, 34, 47, 128, 247n40; World War II armistice at, 59–62, 128, 247n37
Conan, Eric, 13, 180, 181, 225–26
Cote, Sebastien, 87
Côte d'Azur, 5, 26, 39, 41, 216; during Occupation, 77, 141
Coty, René, 154
Coulet, Noël, 21
Coulon, Pierre, 183
Craik, Jennifer, 217
Crécy, battle site of, 22
cruise lines, 20, 29, 30

Daladier, Édouard, 87
Dardenne, Lionel, 144
Darnand, Joseph, 185
Dautry, Aroul, 146
de Botton, Alain, 12, 108, 193
de Gaulle, Charles, 4, 16, 204–6, 210, 225; centenary celebration of, 166; death of,

56, 165; Faulkner's film script about, 166;
Martyrs of the Deportation memorial and,
174; memoirs of, 212; memorials to, 16,
165–67, 225; Mont-Valérien monument
and, 169–70; during Paris Liberation, 9,
145, 160–61, 194; provisional government
of, 149–50, 167; on Vichy, 178, 179
Déat, Marcel, 119, 178
Deauville, 30, 39, 84
Debord, Guy, 9, 221
Dejonghe, Étienne, 110
Delannoy, Jean, 39
Demais, Jean-Claude, 152
Deryckère, Gérard Sébastien, 92, 256n134
Desnos, Robert, 174
Deutsche Arbeitsfront (DAF), 102,
120–21, 128
Der deutsche Wegleiter (periodical), 2, 16, 71,
215; on benefits of wartime tourism, 100;
on Paris, 102, 113–15, 114, 120, 122, 142
Disney Company, 35, 208, 212, 219
Distelbarth, Paul, 44
Dorgelès, Roland, 66, 67
Doriot, Jacques, 191
Dos Passos, John, 41
Douaumont ossuary, 34, 156, 216
Douzou, Laurent, 224
Drancy, 16, 162, 174–75
Drieu la Rochelle, Pierre, 190, 191
drôle de guerre ("phony war"), 3, 65–66
Dubois, André-Louis, 259n18

Eichmann, Adolf, 7
Eiffel Tower, 30, 142, 207; construction of,
29; films about, 32, 40; German soldiers
at, 111, 112; Guide bleu on, 46, 47; Hitler
at, 103–6, 104
Éluard, Paul, 174
Ente nazionale italiano per il turismo, 37
Escoffier, Auguste, 27
espionage, 101
Esser, Hermann, 81, 100–101
Estienne, Charles, 21–24, 43, 214
Euro Disney, 35, 208, 212
European Institute of Cultural Routes
(EICR), 55
European Union, 168
Évian spa, 28
exchange rate, during Occupation, 109, 122,
138, 262n51, 264n105

Fabre-Luce, Alfred, 110
Fairbanks, Douglas, Sr., 41
Farmer, Sarah Bennett, 170, 226

fashion industry, 26, 49, 100, 197
Faulkner, William, 166
Faure, Christian, 75
Fermont fort, 58
Ferro, Marc, 181, 272n220
film(s), 38–40, 209–10; during Belle
Époque, 31–33, 38; Benjamin on, 99; of
Folies-Bergère, 32, 40; about Holocaust,
217, 222; during Occupation, 70, 89,
249n22, 256n121, 259n13; "revisionist,"
217; for tourism promotion, 209–10;
about Vichy, 181, 184, 186, 210; about
Warsaw Ghetto, 268n155. See also specific
film titles
Fisher, M. F. K., 39
Fitzgerald, F. Scott, 41
Fitzgerald, Zelda, 41
flâneurs, 12, 20, 26, 193
Flaubert, Gustave, 28
Foch, Ferdinand, 4, 62, 248n56
Fodor guides, 151
Fogg, Shannon L., 4–5, 154
Folies-Bergère, 197, 199; films about, 32, 40;
German view of, 41; during Occupation,
78, 115, 119; transvestites in, 124
folklore groups, 75, 78, 79, 85, 91
Fontainebleau, 110, 116, 118, 121, 139, 142
For You (periodical), 198, 198
Franco, Francisco, 61, 176, 247n51
Franco-Allied Goodwill Committee, 161
Franco-German youth congresses, 101
Franco-Prussian War (1870–1871), 33,
71, 128
Freeman, Lindsey, 159
Freemasonry, 5, 96–97, 192
Frenay, Henri, 96
French Colonial Exhibition (1931), 41
French Revolution, 24–25, 121, 136, 220;
centennial of, 29, 30, 46
Frick, Henry, 31
Fritzsche, Hans, 59
Frommer, Arthur, 196

Gabler, Fritz, 81
Gambetta, Léon, 161–62
gambling establishments, 26, 84, 142,
197, 199
Gamelin, Paul, 57
Gastineau, Pierre, 176, 216, 220, 225
Gastronomic Tourism Committee, 91
gastronomy, 199; during Belle Époque,
27–28; during Occupation, 71, 112–13,
125–27, 141–42; origins of, 237n38;
restaurant ratings and, 38–39, 241n100

Gaulle, Charles de. *See* de Gaulle, Charles
Gay, Philippe, 155, 158–59
Geiger, Wolfgang, 42
Gershwin, George, 196–97
Gigli, Beniamino, 107
Gildea, Robert, 92, 107
Gilliot, Christophe, 22
Giono, Jean, 78, 93
Goebbels, Joseph, 101, 112; Compiègne railway car and, 59–60, 106; Paris visit by, 44, 102, 106, 117; on Versailles, 106, 128
Goering, Hermann, 31, 140
Goethe, Johann Wolfgang von, 48, 138
Goldhagen, Daniel Jonah, 7
Gontaut-Biron, Count de, 187
Göpel, Erhard, 135, 136
Gould, Frank Jay, 41
Graburn, Nelson, 11, 18
Gramsci, Antonio, 191
Grand Tour, 23–24, 236n22
Great Depression, 41
Green Guides. See Guides verts
Gromaire, Marcel, 2
Grosse, Felix, 127
Gruat, Cédric, 31–32, 105–6
Guéhenno, Jean, 81, 96, 124, 131, 142
Guggenheim, Peggy, 31
guidebooks, 197–201, *198, 200*, 214; Baedeker, 101, 109, 122; DuMont, 172; Fodor, 151; Frommer, 196; Grieben, 141; historical revisionism in, 172–73; of Maginot Line, 58; of Normandy, 150–53; of Occupied Paris, 113–17, *114, 116*; Odé, 71, 128–29, 267n138; of railways, 21–24, 43; of World War I battlesites, 33–35
Guides bleus, 36, 44–47, 214; *Der Deutsche Wegleiter* and, 115, 203–4; of Normandy, 151; of Paris, 29, 49–51
Guides verts, 16, 181–82, 203–6. *See also* Michelin guides
Gutenberg, Johannes, 22

Hahn, H. Hazel, 26
Halbwachs, Maurice, 13
Halder, Franz, 61
Halimi, André, 70, 259n13
Halimi, Serge, 158
Hälker, Maria-Anna, 172
Halles, Les, 50
Hanesse, Friedrich-Carl, 126
Hatch, Alden, 30
Haussmann, Georges-Eugène, 20, 26
Hearst, William Randolph, 31
Heimat ("homeland"), 130–31

Heller, Gerhard, 15, *133,* 134, 261n49, 269n167
Hemingway, Ernest, 36, 38, 41
Henry, Pierre, 187
Henry IV, king of France, 23, 48
heritage ("*patrimoine*"), 84, 175, 217–20, 224–25; liberation of France and, 97–98; memory tourism and, 1–2, 7, 14–15; military, 15, 21, 55; Normandy and, 146, 156; Occupation and, 78, 83; Touring Club and, 37; UNESCO sites of, 13, 24, 168, 232n52. *See also tourisme de mémoire*
Hersonski, Yael, 268n155
Heymel, Charlotte, 44
High Wood, Battle of, 222–23
Himmler, Heinrich, 135
Hitler, Adolf, 42–43, 109, 117; Franco and, 61, 247n51; on French armistice, 60–62, 100; Maginot Line visit by, 53–54; Paris visit by, 30–31, 102–6, *104,* 109, 117, 259n17; World War I battle site visits by, 103
Hobsbawm, Eric, 27
Hoffmann, Heinrich: *Mit Hitler im Polen* by, 132; *Mit Hitler im Westen* by, 30, *54,* 60, 62, 103–5, *104,* 167
Hollande, François, 164, 174, 175, 177
Holocaust, 157, 182, 296n28; French complicity in, 7, 13–14, 174; *lieux de mémoire* of, 162–65, 173–77, 221–22; Martyrs of the Deportation memorial and, 164, *173,* 173–74; Mémorial de la Shoah and, 15, 174, 215; Rivesaltes concentration camp and, 16, 175–77, 215, 220, 225; Vélodrôme d'Hiver and, 5, 13–14, 16, 162, 174. *See also* Jews
Holt, Toni, 153
Holt, Valmai, 153
homosexuality, 124, 174
Hope, Bob, 152
Horcher, Otto, 119
Hörmann, Hans, 138, 139
Hours, Magdeleine, 270n183
Humboldt, Alexander von, 48
Hure, René, 88

Invalides, Hôtel des, 50, 105, 106, 117
Is Paris Burning? (film), 17, 103, 133
Is Paris Burning? (book), 103, 144–45
Isorni, Jacques, 187–88

Jackson, Julian, 4, 37–38
Jamot, Christian, 180, 182
Jeanblanc, Anne, 31

Jeunesses de l'Europe nouvelle (JEN), 2, 92–94

Jews, 163; French restrictions on, 125; during Occupation, 5, 13–16, 80, 82, 164; Vichy exhibitions against, 96–97; of Warsaw Ghetto, 132, 174, 268n155. *See also* Holocaust

Joan of Arc tourism, 34, 43, 187, 212; memorials to, 22, 226; Resistance fighters' view of, 65, 72, 78

Jodl, Alfred, 247n37

Johnstone, Philip, 222–23

Jonas, Raymond, 46

Joyce, James, 41

Jünger, Ernst, 15, 102, 108, 133–34, 143; on Parisian restaurants, 127; on Paris's curfew, 140

Kageneck, August von, 111–13, 129

Kemp, Anthony, 55

Kent, Victoria, 143

kitsch, 18, 102, 129, 221–25, 234n68, 296n28

Klarsfeld, Serge, 177, 182

Kleiner Führer durch Paris (guidebook), 115, *116*

Klug, Günther Hans von, 135

Knochen, Helmut, 127

Kœnig, Pierre, 62, 150–51

Kolbe, Wiebke, 219

Kraft durch Freude (KdF), 35, 37, 85, 101, 110; Baranowski on, 100; Deutsche Arbeiterfront and, 102, 120–21; Polish tours of, 132

Krell, Rudolf, 123

Krist, Gary, 219

Kulturvolk, Germans as, 130, 215

La Ferté fort (Ardennes), 56, 57, 59, 246n22

Lane, George, 153

Langeron, Roger, 105

Lanzmann, Claude, 210, 224

Lapierre, Dominique, 103, 144–45

Lascaux caves, 21, 139, 214, 270n186

Lasierra, Raymond, 2

Lassels, Richard, 236n22

Lattre de Jassigny, Jean, 210

Laval, Pierre, 68, 77, 117, 190, 212

Le Havre, 196, 206

Le Marec, Gérard, 160, 161

Leclerc, Philippe, 143, 160, 167, 194

Lefèvre, Delphine, 158

Légion des volontaires français contre le Bolchévisme, 93, 94

Lemay, Kate C., 152–53

Lenglet, François, 242n116

Lenôtre, G., 48–49

Les Milles concentration camp, 177, 220

Levisse-Touzé, Christine, 112–13

L'Herminier, Jean, 205

"Liberation Circuit" tour, 148–50, *149*, 167

lieux de mémoire ("sites of memory"), 17, 146, 214, 219, 226; of Holocaust, 162–65, 173–77, 221–22; in Italy, 233n53; in the Loiret, 175; of Maginot Line, 58, 63; Mont-Valérien and, 170; of Normandy, 18; during Occupation, 91; of Oradour-sur-Glane, 171; statistics on, 206, *228*. See also *tourisme de mémoire*

Linder, Max, 32

The Longest Day (book), 209

The Longest Day (film), 17, 133, 157, 209

Lorraine, 3, 79, 220; Cross of, 71, 72, 92, *149*, 165, 170, 205; Maginot Line tourism in, 58, 246n28

Loselle, Andrea, 190

"Lost Generation," 41

Louis XIV, king of France, 23, 210

Louis-Philippe, king of the French, 25, 50

Lourdes, 28, 47, 92, 256n135

Louvre, 25, 30, 115–17, 138–40, 192; Buchkremer on, 136; in *Guides bleus,* 25, 49, 115; Taitinger on, 144–45

Lowenthal, David, 217

Lynn, Vera, 152

Lyon, 23, 39, 199–211, 224; during Occupation, 58, 78, 79; Roman ruins near, 96

Lyon-Touriste (periodical), 16, 78, 85, 91

Mabire, Jean, 190

MacCannell, Dean, 9, 30, 45, 194; on "heritage," 217; on "staged authenticity," 63, 171

Macron, Emmanuel, 164

Maczak, Antoni, 23

Maginot Line, 12, 53–54, *54,* *59;* Atlantic Wall and, 108; German tourists of, 53–54; television programs on, 56; as tourist sites, 53–59, 63, 210, 211, 217

"Maginot mentality," 54

Maillol, Aristide, 133

Maistre, Xavier de, 12

Malhuret, Claude, 181, 182

Malte-Brun, Conrad, 25

Mandel, Georges, 121, 163

Marathon, Battle of, 18

Marbœuf, Jean, 181, 186

Marie-Antoinette, queen of France, 24–25, 50

Marseille, 23, 72, 199, 206
Massol, Hubert, 188
Masson, Claude-Armand, 58
Mathiot, Geroges, 84, 86–87
Matisse, Henri, 133
Maugham, W. Somerset, 53
Maximilian I, Holy Roman emperor, 43, 243n127
Mayer, Ahlrich, 134
Mazière, Christian de la, 188, 190
McCabe, Scott, 108
Meaux Musée de la Grande Guerre, 35
Medicus, Franz Albrecht, 138
Meinen, Insa, 124
Méliès, Geroges, 32
Mellon, Andrew, 31
memory tourism. See tourisme de mémoire
Mercier, Sandrine, 83
Merkel, Angela, 166
Merleau-Ponty, Maurice, 11
Mesplier-Pinet, Josette, 14–15
Metternich, Franz-Wolff, 135
Michel, Elmar, 81
Michelin guides, 16, 181–82, 203–6, 214; for Auvergne region, 64, 75, 76; precursors of, 23; restaurant ratings in, 38–39, 241n100; of Vichy, 181–83; of World War I battle sites, 33–34; after World War II, 72, 148, 178, 203–6
Mieszkowski, Jan, 25
Millet, François, 121
Mitterrand, François, 14, 55, 186, 224; on Compiègne monument, 62; during Vichy, 208
Möbius, Hans, 135, 139
Modica, Bruno, 222
Monferrand, Alain, 206–7
Mont Blanc, 30, 37, 40
Mont Saint-Michel, 31, 40, 155, 200, 206
Montaigne, Michel de, 23
Montarron, Marcel, 95–96
Mont-Dore, 36–37, 47
Montmartre, 71; films about, 40; German tourists in, 110, 113, 120, 121; Goebbels on, 44; Guide bleu on, 45–46, 50–51; Hitler on, 106
Mont-Valérien, 164, 169, 169–70, 215
Mortier, Gaston, 86
Moulin, Jean, 13, 14, 163, 167, 210
Moulin Rouge, 32, 40, 102, 117, 219
movies. See film(s)
Mozart, Wolfgang Amadeus, 131
Muslims, 125, 198
Muxel, Paule, 184

Namer, Gérard, 169–70
Napoleon I, 65, 210, 212; German tourists and, 117–18, 121; tomb of, 50, 106, 117; Waterloo and, 18–19, 25
Napoleon II, 92–93, 103, 117–18
Napoleon III, 20, 28, 33, 46, 183
Napoleonic wars, 18–19, 25
Nice, 26, 28, 47, 102; during Occupation, 77, 78, 81, 84, 141
Nimier, Roger, 297n50
Nora, Pierre, 13, 14
Nordling, Raoul, 144
Normandy, 30, 136–38, 143, 146, 171, 211; fiftieth anniversary of, 152, 154–55, 159; guidebooks of, 150–53, 203, 206; museums of, 148, 151–54, 166–67, 206; sixtieth anniversary of, 154; touristic promotion of, 152–54, 214; twentieth anniversary of, 150–51

Obama, Barack, 158
Observatoire régional du tourisme (ORT), 171–72
Odé guidebooks, 71, 128–29, 267n138
Ogrizek, Doré, 128–29, 267n138
Ollier de Marichard, Pierre, 201
Olympic Games, 29
Ophuls, Marcel: Hôtel Terminus by, 210, 224; The Sorrow and the Pity by, 56, 188, 190, 210
Oradour-sur-Glane, 16, 57, 164, 165, 205; memorial at, 170–73, 226
Organisation Todt (OT), 108, 125, 261n44
Ory, Pascal, 165

Panicacci, Jean-Louis, 17
Panossi Netto, Alexandre, 194–95
Papon, Maurice, 14, 165, 171, 208
Paray-le-Monial, 28
Parély, Mila, 178
Paris: as "Babylon," 46, 48, 105, 122; Belle Époque tourism of, 20–21, 26–33, 38; catacombs of, 74, 142; as "city of light," 26; Deutsches Institut in, 136; as fashion capital, 49; French Revolution and, 24–25; German imaginary of, 102, 107; German tourists in, 107–23; Guides bleues of, 29, 49–51; Hitler's visit to, 30–31, 102–6, 104, 109, 259n17; during interwar years, 38–52; liberation of, 97–98, 143–45, 160–62, 167, 194, 219; liberation parade in, 194; Mozart on, 131; during Occupation, 68–75, 69, 70, 73, 78; Resistance monument in, 164; terror attacks of 2015 in, 55

Paris Commune (1871), 25, 29
Paris Programmes (periodical), 16, 71, 197, 215
Parodi, Alexandre, 160–62
Pascal, Blaise, 43
patrimoine. *See* heritage
Paulhan, Jean, 133
Paxton, Robert O., 67
Pechanski, Denis, 176–77
Père Lachaise cemetery, 25, 51
Pernikoff, Ossip, 52, 161, 162
Péronne, 34–35, 156
Pétain, Philippe, 3–6, 216–17; anti-alcohol policy of, 87–88; grave of, 179, 186–89; museums about, 210; tourist sites associated with, 16, 177–91, 216–17; Verdun and, 34, 185; Vichy government of, 61, 64, 68, 117
Petrarch, Francesco, 11
Peyronnet, Jean Claude, 171
Piaf, Édith, 263n82
Picasso, Pablo, 133, 268n160
pilgrimage(s), 91–93, 149, 217; to Compiègne, 62; *Guide bleu* on, 47; to Lourdes, 28, 47, 92, 256n135; medieval, 21, 23; to Oradour-sur-Glane, 170; Pétainist, 177–79, 186, 187, 189; to Saint-Martin-de-Vercors, 171
Pingusson, Georges Henri, 174
Plumyène, Jean, 2
Poland, 132, 268n155
Pompidou, Georges, 186–88
Popular Front, 35, 66, 201, 214
postal system, development of, 22, 24, 30
Pottier, Marc, 155, 206, 208, 275n45
prehistoric cave paintings, 21, 139, 214, 270n186
Preston, Thomas B., 28
prostitution, 109, 111–12, 123–25, 196
Proudhon, Pierre-Joseph, 46
Py, Pierre, 206

Rabelais, François, 23
Raeder, Erich, 61
Raffray, Elisabeth, 156
railroads, 20–21, 26–30; during Occupation, 72, 81, 86, 90–91; during World War II, 65–67
Rassemblement national populaire (RNP), 85, 119
Rauch, André, 37, 39, 44, 204
Ravidat, Marcel, 270n186
Rencourel, Benoîte, 47
Renoir, Jean, 178

Resistance, 65, 71–72, 140–42; casualties among, 204; communists in, 5, 163; films of, 194, 249n22; Joan of Arc and, 78; Le Havre monument to, 150; memorials to, 163–73, *169*, 214–15, 219; narratives of, 163–65, 169, 194, 214–15, 219; tourist sites of, 16, 57, 160, 162, 201, 224
"resistancialist" memory, 163
"return to the soil" program, 4, 75–78, 122, 215
Reynaud, Paul, 3
Ribbentrop, Joachim von, 117
Richelieu, Cardinal, 23
Richerot, Louis, 202
Riding, Alan, 124
Rioux, Jean-Pierre, 89
Ritz, César, 27
Rivesaltes concentration camp, 16, 175–77, 215, 220, 225
Riviera, 17, 26, 38, 41, 65, 199
Roberts, Mary Louise, 196
Robinson, Mike, 11
Rojek, Chris, 217
Roman sites, 21, 55, 96, 123, 212, 226
Rombise, Antoine de, 48
Rommel, Erwin, 18, 108, 153, 261n44
Roosevelt, Franklin D., 166
Rosso, Romain, 176, 216, 220, 225
Rouen, 22, 103, 135, 139, 147
Rouff, Marcel, 39
Rousseaux, André, 44
Rousso, Henry, 13, 157, 163, 179, 183, 210
Rundstedt, Gerd von, 107–8, 135

Sacré-Cœur basilica, 13, 45–46, 50, 105–6
Sailland, Maurice-Edmond (Curnonsky), 39
Saint-Denis basilica, 48, 51
Saint-Exupéry, Antoine de, 84
Saint-Germain-en-Laye château, 139, 142
Saint-Malo, 159, 200
Saint-Tropez, 26, 39
Salazar, Noel B., 6, 11, 51, 195
Salomon, Ernst von, 195
Sangnier, Marc, 93
Santiago de Compostela, 21, 23, 91–92, 217
Sarkozy, Nicolas, 164, 166
Sartre, Jean-Paul, 38, 133
Sauvan, Suzanne, 75
Saving Private Ryan (film), 17, 153, 157
Schaumburg, Ernst von, 129
Schindler's List (film), 217, 222
Schleier, Rudolf, 127
Schweizer, Jacques, 92–94
Ségogne, Henry de, 84

Selinger, Shlomo, 175

Senones, Marion, 89

Seramour, Michaël, 55–56, 58

Sévigné, Madame de, 24, 185

Sèvres Museum, 48, 139

Shirer, William L., 60; on German tourists, 1, 19, 31, 102, 109, 226

Sieburg, Friedrich, 99, 105, 195, 196; *Gott in Frankreich?* by, 36, 41–44, 98, 107, 214

Sigmaringen Castle, 188, 190, 210

Simic, Charles, 196

sites de mémoire. See *lieux de mémoire*

ski resorts, 37, 74

Solliers, Bertrand de, 184

Somme, Battles of, 34, 156, 205

Sommier, Frédéric, 154, 208

The Sorrow and the Pity (film), 56, 188, 190, 210

Soubiroux, Bernadette, 28

Soukhomline, Vassili, 66, 96–97, 109–10

Soyer, Alexis, 27

spa resorts, 41, 47, 101; at Vichy, 24, 27, 81–84, 179–80

Spang, Rebecca L., 237n38

Spanish Civil War, 61, 176, 247n51

Speer, Albert, 103, 135, 259n17

Spielberg, Steven: *Saving Private Ryan* by, 17, 153, 157; *Schindler's List* by, 217, 222

Spode, Hasso, 101

Stalingrad, Battle of, 5, 101, 112, 140

Stange, Alfred, 136

Stein, Gertrude, 36, 41

Stendhal (Marie-Henri Beyle), 25

"Stendhal syndrome," 31, 107, 238n66

Strasbourg, 72, 105, 167–68, 195

Strength through Joy. See Kraft durch Freude

Stülpnagel, Otto von, 74

Sturm, Gustav Braun von, 101

submarine warfare, 112, 203

Taine, Hippolyte, 6

Taittinger, Pierre, 144–45, 162

Tame, Peter, 297n50

Tanguy, Rol, 162

Tarlow, Peter, 218

Taureck, Margot, 43

terroir ("region"), 27, 75

terrorism, 140; Paris attacks of 2015, 55; World Trade Center and, 296n28

thanatourism ("dark tourism"), 16, 184, 218–19, 225, 234n68

Todt, Fritz, 125

Toesca, Maurice, 67

Torrie, Julia S., 42, 107

Toulouse-Lautrec, Henri de, 32

Tour de France (bicycle race), 29

Touring club de France, 27, 36–39, 92, 214; during Occupation, 65, 78–79

tourism, 1–12; adventure, 95–96; art, 129–30, 132–40; "atomic," 159; "dark," 16, 184, 218–19, 225, 234n68; definitions of, 10, 194–95; espionage and, 101; future of, 225–26; "intellectual," 86; movies about, 31–33, 38–40; niche, 189, 218; sexual, 109, 111–12, 123–25, 196; virtual, 89

tourism imaginaries, 11, 51, 195; academic working groups on, 232n42; cultural memory and, 163–64; German, 100, 102, 105, 107–9, 124; of occupied France, 64, 98; power relationships and, 99

tourisme de mémoire, 1–2, 7, 9–10, 148; brochure on, 220–21; de Gaulle and, 165–66; growth of, 153, 194, 202–8, 213–14; website of, 295n22. *See also* heritage; *lieux de mémoire*

tourist gaze, 9, 11, 12, 109

Touvier, Paul, 14, 165, 171, 208

travel agencies, 33–34, 82–85, 202–3

Triboulet, Raymond, 148

Truillé, Jean, 86

Tulle, 164, 172

Tunisia, 79

UN World Tourism Organization (UNWTO), 6, 9, 16, 216; "tourism" defined by, 10

UNESCO World Heritage Sites, 13, 24, 168, 232n52

Urbain-Dubois, Félix, 27–28

Urry, John, 9, 11, 12, 217

vacation colonies (*colonies de vacances*), 36–38, 80, 214, 226

Vainopoulos, Richard, 83

Val d'Isère, 37, 82

Valls, Manuel, 177

Vauban, Sébastien Le Prestre de, 24

Vélodrôme d'Hiver, 5, 13–14, 16, 162, 174. *See also* Holocaust

Verdun, 34, 156, 185, 221

Versailles, 24, 121, 139; during Occupation, 106, 113, 118, 128; during Paris Commune, 29; Rehbein on, 131

Vichy, 4–6, 163, 201, 206, 217; anti-homosexual policies of, 87, 124; anti-Jewish exhibitions of, 96–97; films about, 181, 184, 186, 210; as provisional capital, 67–68; rationing by,

4–5; reorganization of tourism industry of, 83–86; "return to the soil" program of, 4, 75–78, 122, 215; spa at, 24, 27, 81–84, 179–80; struggles with wartime image of, 12–15, 162, 177–85, 215; temperance policies of, 87, 124; tourism of, 16, 58, 77–91, 162, 177–92, 204
Vilgier, Philippe, 58, 191–92
Les visiteurs du soir (film), 17
Volkswagen, 37

Waffen-SS française, 93–96, 142, 171, 188, 257n139
Wagner, Richard, 118, 121
Wakeman, Rosemary, 5
Wall, Geoffrey, 9, 15
Warlimont, Walter, 61, 144
Warsaw Ghetto, 132, 174, 268n155
Waterloo, Battle of, 18–19, 25
Weber, Eugen, 29
Wegleiter. See *Der deutsche Wegleiter*

Weiss, Robert, 122, 123
Weygand, Maxime, 186, 211
Wharton, Steve, 256n121
White, Geoffrey M., 145, 158
Wieviorka, Annette, 14, 63, 218
Wieviorka, Olivier, 14, 148, 164–65
Wildman, Sarah, 176
Williams, Alan, 26
Wohin in Paris. See *Der deutsche Wegleiter*
Wolfromm, Jean-Didier, 191
World's Fair of 1855 (Paris), 27

youth hostel movement, 36–38, 80, 93–94
Ypres, Battle of, 62

Zanuck, Darryl, 157. *See also The Longest Day* (film)
Zaretsky, Robert, 273n5
Zimet, Joseph, 216
Zola, Émile, 50
Zucca, André, 130

CPSIA information can be obtained
at www.ICGtesting.com
Printed in the USA
BVHW03*0525091018
528826BV00001B/3/P

9 781501 715877